The Rise and Fall of Television Journalism

The Rise and Fall of Television Journalism:

Just Wires and Lights in a Box?

Steven Barnett

BLOOMSBURY ACADEMIC

First published in 2011 by:

Bloomsbury Academic
An imprint of Bloomsbury Publishing Plc
50 Bedford Square, London WC1B 3DP, UK
and
175 Fifth Avenue, New York, NY 10010, USA

CIP records for this book are available from the British Library and the Library of Congress.

ISBN 978-1-84966-611-4 (paperback)
ISBN 978-1-84966-646-6 (ebook)

This book is produced using paper that is made from wood grown in managed,
sustainable forests. It is natural, renewable and recyclable. The logging and manufacturing
processes conform to the environmental regulations of the country of origin.

Printed and bound in Great Britain by the MPG Books Group, Bodmin, Cornwall.

Cover design: Paul Burgess
Cover image: Getty

www.bloomsburyacademic.com

For the three girls in my life
who keep me sane.

Contents

Preface

July 4 2011 was a momentous date for British journalism. Within three weeks of a single story being published, the 158-year-old weekly *News of the World* had closed down, two of its former editors had been arrested along with other senior journalists, the head of London's Metropolitan Police force and one of his deputies had resigned, the newspaper's owner Rupert Murdoch and his son James had been summoned to give evidence to a parliamentary committee, the chairman of the Press Complaints Commission had announced her intention to step down, and the Prime Minister David Cameron had set up a judicial inquiry into media ownership and standards of journalism under Lord Justice Leveson. It was a story that left the press, political and police establishments reeling. It was, potentially, a transformative moment not only in British journalism but in British public life.

That was the day on which the *Guardian* published its front-page exclusive that the mobile phone of Milly Dowler, a Surrey schoolgirl who had been abducted and murdered in 2002, had been hacked by a private detective employed by the *News of the World*. He had even deleted some of her messages, thereby giving false hope to parents and police that she might still be alive. Although the *Guardian* had been pursuing the story of illegal phone hacking for two years – and several senior politicians and celebrities had launched civil proceedings in respect of their own experience of phone hacking – this was the moment that the slightly rarefied complaints of a few members of the political and entertainment elite were transformed into an all-encompassing national scandal. As each new revelation emerged and each new arrest was announced, the sheer scale of amorality and corporate corruption astonished even the most sceptical observers.

It was not just the British public that was scandalized. Along with many other commentators of the media scene, in the three weeks that followed that *Guardian* story I was inundated with interview requests from astonished foreign reporters. From Brazil and Chile, the United States and Canada through Germany, France, Denmark, Norway and Spain to Russia, South Korea and China came the same line of questioning: how on earth could the British political establishment become so ensnared in the Murdoch embrace? What sort of journalism culture facilitated – even encouraged – the bribing of police officers and eavesdropping on the phone messages of bereaved relatives of terrorism victims and murdered children? What did it say about Britain's tabloid culture that a newspaper editor could parade on its front page heart-rending details of the Prime Minister's infant son being diagnosed with cystic fibrosis, knowing that this front-page splash would leave the Prime Minister and his family devastated?

While international observers looked on in disbelief, some British practitioners tried to rationalize. Let's not condemn, they said, the great British tradition of a raucous, rowdy, brash and irreverent tabloid press – an honourable legacy which went back over 100 years. Yes, of course, a few rough diamonds had overstepped the mark and no one could condone criminal activity in pursuit of a story. But the Murdochs had acted swiftly, the *News of the World* had closed and the problem could be swiftly resolved without recourse to draconian regulation. An unfettered press allowed to regulate itself, they said, was the only guarantor of a healthy democracy. They issued grave warnings of Soviet-style State censorship that would inevitably follow any attempt to invoke a regulatory system that might properly monitor and implement a code of ethical journalistic conduct. Any system which involved statutory sanctions would threaten democracy itself. Free speech would be chilled.

The sentiment was echoed by Rupert Murdoch himself in his evidence to the House of Commons select committee, when he spoke of how Britain benefits 'from having a competitive press and therefore having a very transparent society. That is sometimes very inconvenient to people. But I think we are better and stronger for it.' Implicit in this statement were two erroneous assumptions that need to be challenged. First, that the journalism which might be threatened by a stricter regime of regulatory oversight was that vital watchdog function which held power to account and which helped to root out dishonesty, incompetence or wrong-doing in high places. Second, that there was a direct connection between this vital democratic function of journalism and unfettered competition.

Either deliberately, or through blind faith in the free market, Murdoch missed the point. Much (though by no means all) of the reporting practised by the *News of the World* was light years away from the kinds of corruption-busting authority-defying journalism that all good democrats wish to see not only preserved but vigorously promoted. Increasingly it had come to rely on a diet of sex, sensationalism and scandal derived primarily from ruthless, unprincipled intrusions into the private lives of individuals, with a brutal disregard either for the factual accuracy of the stories or the potentially devastating impact on the characters involved. It was the journalism of the Colosseum rather the journalism of accountability.

This problem is not unique to the *News of the World* nor to Rupert Murdoch (though his various biographers agree that he is far more interested in scandalmongering and gossip than hard-nosed investigative journalism). But this vindictive style of journalism does appear to have become an integral element of the British newspaper culture, driven by the cut-throat nature of national competition and Wild West-style absence of any rules of engagement. It is neither pleasant nor edifying, and it is far removed from the kind of impertinent, anti-elitist, populist reporting that once characterized the best of British tabloid journalism – and which was indeed an essential ingredient of a healthy democracy.

For the purposes of this book, however, perhaps the crucial point is that this amoral, celebrity-baiting form of journalism is also far removed from the customs and practices of British television journalism. At its height – abetted by a regulatory framework laid down in law, codes of conduct that were invariably followed, genuine sanctions for transgression and limited competition – television in Britain produced at least as much genuinely informational and accountability journalism as the national press. In its heyday, it would fearlessly tackle difficult social, economic and political issues, and would routinely challenge corporate and public authority. It would, in other words, regularly provide huge national audiences with exactly the kind of democracy-enhancing journalism that newspaper editors profess to worry about today. And here's the irony: it was because of, not in spite of, a protective regulatory framework that the health and survival of its journalism could be guaranteed.

As that protective regulatory framework diminishes, and as competition intensifies, great television journalism is under threat. It has already virtually disappeared in the United States, where the legacy of Edward R. Murrow and other revered journalistic voices from the past were long ago overwhelmed by an unregulated market that cared little for the democratic role of journalism. And now it is under threat not just in the United Kingdom but in many other developed and developing countries whose politicians are being seduced into believing that the marketplace is the universal panacea. History warns us – screams at us – that this is entirely wrong. And therein lies the theme of this book, which I hope will have resonance well beyond the borders of the United Kingdom: that thoughtfully constructed, responsibly implemented and genuinely independent regulation can promote the best journalism, not restrain it; regulation can liberate it rather than censor it. And that message from history has been heavily underlined, I would argue, by those dramatic phone-hacking revelations which rocked Britain in the middle of 2011.

The first half of the book is essentially historical, tracing the institutional and professional roots of television journalism in the United Kingdom, making comparisons in particular with its evolution in the United States and drawing parallels where possible with Europe and other developed nations. The Introduction presents the main thesis and arguments around the role and importance of television journalism, where it diverges from other forms, and the theoretical context.

Chapter 1 looks at the roots of television journalism in public broadcasting and in the emerging philosophy and independence of the BBC. It also identifies some of the early warnings about the limitations of the medium as a vehicle for trustworthy journalism. Chapter 2 examines the origins of commercial competition, the different news culture on commercial television, the regulatory framework and its impact on journalism, and the contrast with the different approach to television journalism that was slowly emerging in the United States.

Chapter 3 covers the 1960s to the 1980s, a period that might be characterized as a golden age of television journalism in the United Kingdom, with a range of news programmes, challenging current affairs, the birth of a new channel pioneering innovative ideas about television journalism, and mass audiences which would never be achieved again. The United States, meanwhile, was beginning its deregulatory journey, leaving increasingly little room for serious journalism on television. Chapter 4 is a case study of two specific programmes in the 1980s, one on the BBC and one on commercial television, which were and remain iconic examples of robust accountability journalism in the toughest possible conditions – each in its different way illustrative of how independent institutional and regulatory frameworks facilitate rather than constrain difficult investigative reporting in the face of enormous opposition from the State.

Chapter 5 looks at a seminal moment in the politics of British broadcasting – the 1990 Broadcasting Act – and its impact on television journalism, specifically in the context of one of the most influential theoretical frameworks of the time: Herman and Chomsky's propaganda model. Chapter 6 charts the demise of long-standing, well-resourced current affairs programmes on commercial television, a direct consequence of deregulatory policies, and the growing tensions around news scheduling. It also examines some of the emerging debates around the nature and style of journalism on the BBC.

Chapter 7 is both a theoretical and empirical analysis of tabloidization, specifically applied to the television medium, looking at evidence for and against the 'dumbing-down' thesis in Britain and the United States. It includes some of the first results from our longitudinal research project on the output of UK news bulletins. Chapters 8 and 9 bring us up-to-date and look ahead at the future for, respectively, publicly funded and commercially funded television journalism. Chapter 8 analyses, in particular, the impact of the Hutton report on BBC journalism, and at the longer term consequences of government cutbacks and the squeeze on public funding. Chapter 9 analyses what remains of the regulatory structure for journalism on commercial television, and its prospects in a digital world of multiple channels, fragmented audiences and disappearing revenues. It asks whether existing frameworks are sustainable and looks at what happens – as in the United States – when they are abolished altogether.

Chapter 10 examines both the phenomenon and the history of 24-hour news channels, their peculiar characteristics and narrative styles, and their respective contributions to a more globalized concept of television journalism. Chapter 11 looks at one specific element of television journalism that in most developed countries, for the time being at least, sets it apart from print and online: a continuing requirement for impartiality. It argues that, despite growing political and technological pressure, it is a necessary if not sufficient condition for sustaining quality and integrity in television journalism. The Conclusions, apart from providing an overview of the argument, also demonstrate why the 'new' journalism of the blogosphere and 'user generated content' is no substitute for the mass audience reach, professional values and continuing trust invested in television. In other words television journalism, despite its declining efficacy, still has a vital part to play in an informed democracy. Television still matters – but for the medium to sustain a meaningful journalism requires a political and regulatory will that is slowly evaporating.

As ever, I am indebted to a number of people who have been generous with their time and support during the book's long gestation period. My colleagues Anthony McNicholas, Maria Michalis, Gordon Ramsay, Naomi Sakr, Jean Seaton, Colin Sparks, Jeanette Steemers and Daya Thussu have all provided invaluable help and wise counsel as have, at different times, Patrick Barwise, Roger Bolton, Benedetta Brevini, David Elstein, Matthew Engel, Ray Fitzwalter, Suzanne Franks, Peter Humphreys, Tim Luckhurst, Julian Petley, Stewart Purvis, Howard Tumber and John Tusa. Thanks also to my colleagues on the editorial board of the *British Journalism Review* for some endlessly fascinating debates around the themes raised here (occasionally facilitated by a glass or two of something stronger than coffee). At Bloomsbury Academic, I am very grateful to Lee Ann Tutton and Howard Watson for their sound advice and for eliminating some of my more egregious errors, and to Jennifer Dodd and Chloë Shuttlewood; and especially to Emily Salz for taking the book on, steering me away from some of the less interesting blind alleys, and introducing me to the wonderful cakes of the London Review Bookshop. Finally, to Alexandra, Joanna and Zoë, who have tolerated the occasional tantrum and have given a very convincing impression of believing that, one day, it would be finished – a very big thank you. And no, there isn't any money in it.

I would be happy to respond to any matters arising, objections to my arguments, or any factual errors that may need correcting. For these, I take full responsibility and apologize in advance. It is a fascinating time for journalists and for those who care about journalism. I hope this book represents a reasoned and worthwhile contribution to what is certain to be a very long-running debate.

Steven Barnett (s.barnett@wmin.ac.uk)

Professor of Communications,
University of Westminster

September 2011

Introduction: The Argument

If one or two or three corporations would undertake to devote just a small fraction of their advertising appropriation along the lines that I have suggested ... the economic burden would be bearable, and there might ensue a most exciting adventure – exposure to ideas and the bringing of reality into the homes of the nation.

To those who say people wouldn't look; they wouldn't be interested; they're too complacent, indifferent and insulated, I can only reply: There is, in one reporter's opinion, considerable evidence against that contention. But even if they are right, what have they got to lose? Because if they are right, and this instrument is good for nothing but to entertain, amuse and insulate, then the tube is flickering now and we will soon see that the whole struggle is lost.

This instrument can teach, it can illuminate; yes, and it can even inspire. But it can do so only to the extent that humans are determined to use it to those ends. Otherwise it is merely wires and lights in a box. There is a great and perhaps decisive battle to be fought against ignorance, intolerance and indifference. This weapon of television could be useful.

Edward R. Murrow[1]

I n 1958, the uncrowned king of American broadcast journalism, Edward R. Murrow, ended a speech to fellow broadcasters with these heartfelt words about the potential of television journalism. Even before it became immortalized by George Clooney in the Hollywood film *Good Night, and Good Luck*, Murrow's speech was known throughout the industry as a legendary call to arms – an almost despairing statement about what the medium was capable of achieving if its personnel were given the encouragement and the resources.

Scroll forward nearly 40 years – during which time American television news, in the view of most local and international observers, gradually and irrevocably became mired in precisely those entertainment values against which Murrow had warned. By the early 1990s, the veteran American foreign correspondent Mort

Rosenblum was attacking what he called the 'news thieves' of network television, and illustrating his pessimism with some depressing examples of foreign news coverage in the United States, such as Roone Arledge, President of ABC News, telling his news anchors to describe Sarajevo as 'site of the 1984 Olympics' to help viewers understand the besieged city's importance, or a CBS bulletin which one evening described its foreign news datelines as 'Chicago, Northern Maine and Outer Space'.[2] A few years later, his fear about the emasculation of foreign news was quantified: a forum at the Columbia University School of Journalism was told that that there had been a 42 per cent reduction in foreign news coverage on the three major networks between 1988 and 1996.

Another 15 years later and, despite continuing crises in Iraq, Afghanistan, and the Middle East, American network news in the twenty-first century is still notoriously dependent on crime, show business, tragedy and trivia to keep audiences up and advertisers happy. In a world which is less secure and more fissile, and where, arguably, it is more vital than ever that every nation's public is kept informed of what is going on in the international arena, there has been a wholesale flight in the United States from foreign coverage. The 'soft news' project at Harvard University's Joan Shorenstein Center found an inexorable shift across all news sources between 1980 and 1999 away from public policy issues and towards stories featuring more sensationalism, more human interest and more crime and disaster.[3] The Director General of the BBC, Mark Thompson, revealed in 2007 that one senior American TV executive had explained to him that foreign news was complex, dispiriting, expensive, dangerous to make and not liked by audiences. Another told him that 'Soon, international reporting is going to be the wire agencies and you.'[4]

Every now and then, there is a minor protest or even rebellion from journalists who still harbour serious intent. On 26 June 2007, Mika Brzezinski was one of three anchors presenting the news programme, 'Morning Joe', on the 24-hour news channel MSNBC. According to her producer, there was an obvious lead story: the release from prison of Paris Hilton, the hotel heiress and star of celebrity gossip magazines, after serving her sentence for drink-driving. But Brzezinski – along with many other serious journalists on both sides of the Atlantic – thought it was a non-story. She wanted to lead on an important development centred on the United States' operation in Iraq in which a senior Republican senator was calling for a change of policy – the first sign of a U-turn amongst George W. Bush's own supporters. But her producer had ignored her and the script led with Hilton. Live, on air, Brzezinski voiced her frustration: 'No, I hate this story and I don't think it should be the lead.' She put the script down and moved on to Iraq. An hour later, faced with the same running order, she became even more determined. 'My producer is not listening to me,' she said, and then tried to set fire to the script with a cigarette lighter. When that failed, she tore it up. And when the same script turned up an hour later, she walked over to the paper shredder and shredded it. In less than a month, the YouTube clip of this television journalist standing up for journalism live on air had received over 3 million hits.[5]

The problem with television

But Brzezinski's stand took the United States by storm precisely because it demonstrated how deeply ingrained the celebrity culture had become. If Murrow was convinced that television might have been useful in the battle against 'ignorance, intolerance and indifference', that particular fight has – in the view of most American commentators – long been lost. In fact, with the benefit of hindsight it is probably fair to argue, along with Neil Postman, that the battle was never winnable and that 'television's conversations promote incoherence and triviality [and] the phrase "serious television" is a contradiction in terms'.[6] Postman was not the first to argue that the inherent qualities of television as a communications medium made it incompatible with intelligent journalism, that the medium could speak only with 'the voice of entertainment', and that typography was a much more natural and effective way of knowing and seeing the world. As we shall see, there were warnings from within the BBC at least 40 years earlier. And Postman is certainly not the last. Around the world, scholars and journalists frequently seem to condemn the inexorable slide of television journalism into meaningless triviality. In France, Pierre Bourdieu was arguing in the late 1990s that television in an age of intense ratings competition inevitably seeks out the sensational and the spectacular; and in doing so, 'it exaggerates the importance of that event, its seriousness, and its dramatic, even tragic character'.[7]

The very idea of television as a reliable, authoritative source of news – let alone one in which the public places an inordinate amount of trust – is faintly ludicrous. Over the 60 years in which it has evolved and come to dominate the collection, interpretation and transmission of 'news', television has demonstrated frequently its manifest weaknesses as a reliable medium. Many of its most distinguished practitioners and recognizable faces have, while doing their utmost to mitigate the problems, been aware that they have often been fighting a losing battle: that the very qualities which make television so appealing to viewers are those which render their own job as purveyors of accurate journalism so difficult.

One of the earliest books written to acknowledge precisely these issues was by John Whale, who worked for nine years for ITN. Following Alexander Pope, who had pretended that the politician can 'see through all things with his half-shut eyes', he wrote that 'the round, unwinking gaze of the television camera is not as all-vigilant as it may seem', and called his book about television news *The Half-Shut Eye*.[8] Whale's book is instructive for two reasons. First, written in 1969 in the wake of some of the most tumultuous upheavals in the western world, he cited some graphic examples of television's inadequacies in communicating the subtleties of the political and cultural transformations that were occurring. Second, despite the fact that technology was, by twenty-first-century standards, primitive and unwieldy, it is telling how many of the intrinsic technological problems of the medium outlined by Whale have survived even the massive advances in sophisticated delivery mechanisms.

Many of the vital stories of the time remained untold because television did not possess the right narrative structures. In the United Kingdom the 1960s, like the decade which followed, featured a number of abstract economic and political stories which almost defied a pictorial approach: crises in the balance of payments, the rise of inflation, two separate attempts by Britain to break into the Common Market (both defeated by the French President's defiant '*non*'), the beginnings of a political stand-off on nuclear weapons, the futile attempts at talks to avoid Ian Smith's unilateral declaration of independence for Rhodesia. None of these events are beaten into the nation's consciousness in the same way as, for example, war scenes from Vietnam, riot scenes from Paris, the shooting of Lee Harvey Oswald in Dallas by Jack Ruby, the landing of a man on the moon or even England winning the football World Cup. Perhaps the most dramatic, chilling and potentially apocalyptic fortnight of the post-war world is also missing from this pantheon of collective memories: the 13 days of frantic diplomacy during 1962 in which the United States' President Kennedy went to the brink of nuclear war with President Khrushchev of the USSR, but finally persuaded his Russian counterpart to retreat from sending nuclear warheads to Cuba. Diplomacy does not make enthralling television.

Given the criticisms so frequently levelled at television by theorists and practitioners, it is perhaps surprising that the practice of journalism on television is almost unthinkingly equated with its practice in other forms, whether the older media of print and radio or the emerging online and mobile forms. Conceptually, it is possible to identify eight separate characteristics which separate journalism on television from its practice elsewhere and which appear to render it intrinsically unsuited to a serious and rigorous approach.

1 **Pictures**. Perhaps the most obvious and, as alluded to by John Whale above, the most debilitating characteristic is television's inalienable dependence on pictures to illustrate news items. It is not simply that vision

is required because a blank screen is unthinkable: it is the distorting effect which such a dependency has on a news agenda – and particularly a relatively serious news agenda. It is not possible to find exciting, dramatic or moving pictures to illustrate a looming recession, a deadlock in Middle East negotiations, a sudden rise in hospital waiting lists or a decision by train drivers to take strike action. It is, however, much easier to illustrate a hold-up in a supermarket with CCTV footage made available by the police, or the flaming wreckage of a plane crash, or paparazzi photos of an A-list celebrity cavorting with someone they shouldn't be. For serious television journalism, this is a daily problem. In the words of Andrew Marr, a former newspaper journalist turned BBC Political Editor: 'Every night of the week, today, BBC News programme editors wrestle with the problem of what to do when an important story of the day has no pictures to go with it, while a rather lesser story has vivid, unforgettable images ... Television is an impure medium, as much cabaret as lecture hall'.[9] For a TV news provider with different values, or driven by the need simply to maximize audiences, this is less of a problem: dramatic pictures will dominate the news agenda because they are more likely to captivate audiences.

2 **Entertainment.** Marr's comment about cabaret, echoing the earlier concerns of Murrow, Postman and many other communications theorists, conflate two different issues about the nature of television. One is to do with its role in people's everyday lives, an essentially anthropological point; the other is to do with the nature of the medium, an essentially technological point. Somewhat perversely, given that television news is still most people's primary source of information, it is predominantly a means of living-room and bedroom entertainment for the vast majority of people. In the interactive age, consultants like to talk about the difference between 'lean-back' technology (TV, DVD, VCR, etc.) and 'lean-forward' technology (computers and, increasingly, mobile phones, gaming, etc.). While the latter involve concentration, interactivity and generally harder work, the former are primarily vehicles of relaxation: the phrase 'slumped in front of the telly' still has a resonance despite the advent of red-button technology. Those seeking to maximize their revenue from commercial television also seek to maximize its entertainment potential and minimize any obligations towards the less serious and demanding. In his 2008 MacTaggart Lecture at the Edinburgh Television Festival, ITV's Chief Executive Peter Fincham used precisely this argument to make the case for less regulation of ITV.[10] Taking this to its logical extreme, news and current affairs become nothing but

alien interlopers trying to inveigle themselves into a hostile environment. The consequences for television journalism are twofold: inexorably reducing the spaces for serious material; and infecting the agendas and values of television news in order to sustain the entertainment momentum of the medium.

3 **Brevity**. It is the technological limitations of the medium that bring us back to Postman and others who dismiss the innate ability of television to 'do' serious journalism (just as, in Postman's analogy, communicating by smoke signals is a wholly ineffectual means of 'doing' philosophy). As the average length of the political soundbite has declined rapidly over the years to little more than ten seconds today, so the length of items, the time given to interviews and the space allotted to explanation and contextualization have inevitably diminished. Even within a determinedly serious news environment which does not assume a fickle, restless audience with its finger on the remote control – such as BBC2's 'Newsnight' or 'Channel 4 News' – there are simply the time pressures imposed by the number of words that can be spoken within a given time. A five-minute news item – twice the average length of an item for most bulletins on mainstream channels – will run to no more than 700 words, the length of a relatively short article on a single page of a broadsheet newspaper. Leonard Downie Jr, former editor of the *Washington Post*, quotes the renowned American newscaster Dan Rather telling his audience after one news item he had presented: 'If you're interested, read one of the better papers tomorrow!' He also reports Howard Stringer, former editor of CBS News, commenting on how television news leaves no room for writing: 'That's the dark secret of news, and it's why great news on TV isn't as satisfying as great news in print'.[11] Many correspondents who make the transition from print to screen are quickly struck by the need to be simple and concise, and by the volume of material that needs to be omitted.

4 **Cost**. Good journalism of any kind is not cheap, especially when it requires foreign travel, in-depth research or proper training. But good journalism for television requires more than just the salaries and expenses of trained, committed journalists. Even with modern-day digital technology, where lighting and sound can be combined with one-touch controls on a single lightweight camera, the machines themselves are expensive and require maintenance, and most locations require additional technological help to produce high-quality results. And every television package – let alone a complete bulletin or current affairs programme – requires a cast of support

staff to turn it into a transmittable item. While print journalists today will write, research, edit, input and sign off their own copy (with a little input from subeditors and headline writers), television journalists require producers, studio technicians, videotape editors, camera staff and researchers as well as programme editors to take responsibility for the finished product. Moreover, some stories are clearly cheaper than others: where footage is provided, for example, by the police or a PR company; or where no travel is required; or where there is natural daylight which doesn't require artificial lighting; or where a B-list celebrity is offering unprecedented access to some high-profile event in a desperate attempt to earn promotion to the A-list. As pressure rises to cut costs, whether to maximize profits on a commercial channel or conform to budget cuts on publicly funded channels, there are perennial cost pressures which impact on television news agendas.

5 **Complexity**. As with cost, the problem is less acute than it used to be. The arrival of satellite communications, portable dishes and 'sat-phones' allows today's television journalists to be considerably more flexible than their predecessors. But the technology of television transmission is still more complex than the laptop (and possibly a thesaurus) required by a print or online journalist. Guests must be brought to studios, lines must be prepared for live transmission, lighting must be satisfactory for outside broadcasts, and everything must be cut together to produce a highly streamlined, professional and glitch-free bulletin. Marr estimates that, even with a highly professional picture editor, cutting and reshaping one minute's worth of broadcast news takes about an hour. Even for current affairs journalism, where there is more time for finding ways round difficult technological issues, the story itself can be dictated by the complex requirements of television.

6 **Liveness**. There is nothing quite as dramatic as a breaking story, preferably with sensational pictures and even better if accompanied by a live, breathless commentary from a journalist on location to offer their own vivid description and interpretation of events. Even without the pictures and the drama, a live on-the-spot report will inject an aura of drama into drab or slow-moving stories. 24-hour news channels in particular, featuring journalists waiting expectantly outside anonymous-looking buildings, speculating on what may or not happen when the trial/board meeting/ operation/vote/conference has finished, is now a recurrent theme. And news bulletins, too, make greater use of the interpretative 'two-way' where the news anchor invites the channel's political editor or economics editor or transport editor to give their angle on the day's main story. Liveness can

give an illusion of something dramatic where none exists, an issue I revisit in Chapter 10. It can also, as we shall see with the furore surrounding the BBC report on the Iraq intelligence dossiers and the subsequent Hutton Inquiry, make for less reliable broadcasting if a journalist being interviewed has insufficient time for preparation.

7 **Personality**. Almost from the beginning, television's on-screen presenters and journalists became household names whose fashion choices, hairstyles, accents and appearance were matters of daily conversation. Some print journalists became personalities too, but that was secondary to their ability to find stories and write. Just as prime ministers and presidents today must have white teeth, look healthy and smile, so a successful television journalist will find it difficult to survive without an on-screen persona whatever their journalistic talents. As Andrew Marr puts it, 'television reporting is an exhibitionist's game. Right from the start it has attracted big characters, with strong views and few inhibitions; it may be related to newspapers, but it is half-brother to the theatre too.'[12] In other words, the natural inclination of the medium towards entertainment is reflected in the people who practise its journalism. There have been a few examples of modest, unassuming television practitioners – Charles Wheeler in the United Kingdom was certainly one, perhaps Murrow himself in the United States – but they are the exception. And as TV news bulletins strive to differentiate themselves from their competitors, the individuals who can combine authority with brand identity command increasingly absurd amounts of money which are commensurate with their status as celebrities rather than their abilities as journalists.

8 **Audiences**. Finally, the nature of the television audience is very different from anything found in print. It is – even for the niche 24-hour news channels – still essentially heterogeneous, with an older profile than the national population but in most other ways reflecting the gender, ethnic, class and regional demographics of the population as a whole. This makes it more difficult for editors and reporters to 'target' their reports more effectively. This is in stark contrast to national newspaper reporters: in the United Kingdom, the *Daily Mail* journalist understands both the nature of its target readership (female bias, middle-class, conservative, essentially Home Counties) and the nature of the *Mail*'s newspaper culture (family values, right of centre). Similarly *Daily Mirror* journalists know that they are writing for a predominantly working-class, more northern audience with a left-of-centre bias. Broadsheet newspapers in the United Kingdom, as around

the world, know that they can presuppose a basic level of knowledge and understanding about national and international events. Journalists at the BBC, ITN and Sky, whether writing for individual bulletins or for current affairs programmes, can have no such preconditioned ideas about their audiences. They are essentially writing and presenting for undifferentiated audiences, inevitably making it that much more challenging to compile a package which is equally comprehensible, engaging, informational and inoffensive to the impoverished granny in Eastbourne, the wealthy businessman in Yorkshire or a rocket scientist with a PhD in Cambridge.

These are the key reasons why television is not only different but, absent other compensating forces, militates against proper investment in high-quality, serious and well-trained journalism.

The importance of regulation

This raises some fascinating questions. Why, in the UK and most other developed countries, is television still seen in the twenty-first century as a vital conduit of serious, accurate journalism? Why, as audiences for mainstream news bulletins decline, have France, Russia and Qatar, as well as Rupert Murdoch's BSkyB in Britain, all been prepared to fund non-profitable, serious 24-hour TV news stations? Why do the vast majority of British and American citizens still view television as their main source of information for international, national and local news? Why is television news implicitly believed while most newspapers – especially the tabloids – are despised? How is it that, when asked to rate different kinds of journalists for trustworthiness, over half of the UK population feel they can trust TV journalists (nearly two-thirds for the BBC) compared to 43 per cent for broadsheet newspaper journalists, and a shocking 15 per cent for tabloid journalists?[13] Why would a Brzezinski-style on-air mutiny have little resonance in Britain? Why, in short, does Murrow's vision still endure in the UK, albeit for some scholars in a more diluted, less effective and more dramatized form than 20 years ago? And how vulnerable are those journalistic practices to the kinds of pressures that seem to have emasculated American television journalism?

The answer to these questions – and the thesis that runs through much of this book – is not one that appeals to most mainstream American political theorists, for it lies in external regulation and, ultimately, statutory interference. The unequivocal lesson from the UK – in the history, structure, contemporary practices of and recent changes in television journalism – is that the ability of the medium to fulfil Murrow's vision lies in the determination of legislators and regulators to foster and sustain television's potential. If governments are prepared to provide the statutory framework and regulators are prepared to implement the rules of that framework with toughness and consistency, television journalism can indeed educate, illuminate and stimulate. It is not a comfortable lesson for those who distrust the principle of political interference, and in particular the motives of those who seek to impose rules on a free media. And there is no question that, in the hands of the unscrupulous, the incompetent, the autocratic or the power-hungry, political constraints on the media can be potentially disastrous. If, however, the motives are essentially benign, if there are sufficient mechanisms of transparency and accountability, if the personnel appointed to implement the will of legislators are well-disposed public servants rather than political placemen, and if there is a prevailing culture of journalistic integrity which requires protection rather than invention, then political interference not only works – it becomes an essential prerequisite for the kind of journalism that Murrow envisaged.

That is a lot of ifs, but the principle has been recognized in the United States, too. In his review of the Clooney film which resurrected the notion of Murrow as a classic American hero of journalism, Nicholas Lemann argued in the *New Yorker* that the answer was not to 'Bring back Murrow'. Rather than sentimentally mourning the passing of great men we should, he said, endeavour instead to understand the structure that produced and encouraged them. He went on:

> The structure that encouraged Murrow, uncomfortable as it may be to admit, was federal regulation of broadcasting. CBS, in Murrow's heyday, felt that its prosperity, even its survival, depended on demonstrating to Washington its deep commitment to public affairs. The price of not doing so could be regulation, breakup, the loss of a part of the spectrum, or license revocation. Those dire possibilities would cause a corporation to err on the side of too much 'See It Now' and 'CBS Reports.'[14]

The reason, in other words, why Murrow could stand up to Senator McCarthy's one-man witch-hunt against his imagined 'Reds under the bed' was not just because he was a good journalist. It was primarily because the Federal Communications Commission had made it clear that this was the kind of programme they expected from responsible broadcasters in return for their licence to broadcast. And the reason why challenging journalism has all but disappeared from American television is because the government has deregulated broadcasting. What is left is a television culture that promotes profitable news divisions delivering programmes designed to maximize ratings presented by attractive people – in other words, news that surrenders to the entertainment model inherent in the medium itself. It is difficult, says Lemann, for journalists to comprehend the idea that outside pressure – from government officials – might have been responsible for creating the memorable, high-quality journalism whose passing we mourn. But, he concludes, 'look what has happened since it went away'.

The notion that political or regulatory intervention may be essential for securing the public good is not particularly alien to Western European political philosophy, rooted in social democracy, which prevailed for much of the second half of the twentieth century. It is still prevalent in most health, education and transport systems. In the field of communications, however, the arguments are more difficult to sustain when there is such an abundance of information sources, and where global conglomerates complain furiously that public subsidy and regulatory constraints are hampering their expansion and endangering a free press. Only a truly unfettered communications system, they argue, can vigorously uphold the watchdog functions of democracy. In fact, this is precisely the argument that free-market liberals pursued even before the age of 500-channel TV and the internet. In 1989, delivering the prestigious MacTaggart Lecture at the start of the Edinburgh Television Festival, Rupert Murdoch treated his British listeners to a 40-minute harangue about the inadequacies of British television and the evils of government influence. He concluded:

> Public service broadcasters in this country have paid a price for their state-sponsored privileges. That price has been their freedom. British broadcasters depend on government for protection; when you depend on government for protection, there will come a time when that government, no matter its political complexion, will exact a price. The pressure can be overt or, more likely, covert. The result is the same either way: less than independent, neutered journalism.[15]

He then made an extraordinary claim which turned the real-life evidence of British television journalism on its head: 'I cannot imagine a British Watergate, or a British Irangate, being pursued by the BBC or ITV with the vigour that the US networks did.' In fact, precisely the opposite was true. As we shall see, it was the highly regulated ITV that had been instrumental in exposing two miscarriages of justice following IRA bombings: the cases of the so-called 'Guildford Four' and 'Birmingham Six' pub bombings had been reopened as a direct result of evidence of police malpractice gathered by television journalists working for ITV current affairs programmes. And Murdoch could hardly have been unaware of the massive investigative operation mounted by another ITV programme into the killings of three alleged IRA operatives in Gibraltar three years earlier (described in more detail in Chapter 4). Not only had his own *Sunday Times* been hounding the TV company ever since but its editor, Andrew Neil, was sitting right next to Murdoch throughout his speech. Meanwhile, as we shall see, BBC journalists were hardly reticent in their own critical assessment of the then Conservative government.

By contrast, the American television networks had played no part in the explosive revelations about the Republican break-in at Watergate in the 1970s or about the scandal of the 'arms for hostages' trade-off with Iran in the 1980s. As every American journalist knows (and as Hollywood later acknowledged in *All the President's Men*) the Watergate exposé was directly attributable to two determined journalists from the *Washington Post*, backed by their editor and proprietor. The Iran revelations were down to the *New York Times*. It was newspapers, not television, which were investing in serious investigative journalism in the United States at the very time that television was leading the charge in the UK. Murdoch's speech heralded a period of intense deregulation in British television which was responsible for much of the gradual decline in investment in television journalism outside news. It may be an uncomfortable lesson for the evangelists of free-market populism, but the lesson from British and American television history is that state intervention can work for the public good.

That is precisely the lesson that shows every sign of not being learned in the UK in the twenty-first century. It is a huge irony because, on the face it, we should be embracing with open arms the liberating potential of new developments in television journalism. Less than 50 years after the Telstar satellite enabled the first, barely visible live transatlantic link on television, today's technology allows correspondents to broadcast live, in quality, from virtually anywhere on earth. Digital mobile-phone and camera technology means that anyone can send pictures of unfolding events, while the rise of UGC (user generated content) or 'citizen journalism' is beginning to redefine the contours of journalism itself. The explosion in new channels – facilitated by the switch in most developed countries from analogue to digital TV – has seen a rapid growth in 24-hour news channels based in different countries, with different agendas, different funding regimes and different news cultures.

These are all positive developments: more information from more places being delivered to more people through a powerful and trusted visual medium in virtually every living room in the developed world – and, increasingly, in the developing world too. But hand-in-hand with that technological progress has gone precisely the kind of deregulation and withdrawal from statutory intervention that Lemann identified as the essential prerequisite of quality, serious television journalism. Regulation in the positive sense – that is, regulation for quality – is in retreat. If the retreat continues, we will be left with nothing more than Murrow's wires and lights, Postman's incoherent conversations, and Bourdieu's phantasms, fears, and phobias. New technology may simply provide the means of conveying all that empty, trivial, sensationalized entertainment with more immediacy from more people.

Television, knowledge and democracy

Does it matter? There are plenty of supporters for the essentially liberal thesis that the market will deliver what people want. This is not just a simplistic application of Adam Smith's economic mantra to television journalism, but a rather more complex set of arguments about the nature of news and what people are interested in knowing about. From the Bible onwards, most people's primary concern has been the equivalent of the net-curtain syndrome: who's been doing what to whom, how often, where and (latterly) how much it cost. News, for many of us, is the equivalent of playground gossip: being in the know about the people and things that matter in our everyday lives. And while it may be a caricature to say that the celebrity magazine diet of sex and shopping comes closest to satisfying most people's appetite for news, it is probably true that international affairs and public policy issues tend not to be top of the 'must know' list. In the words of one theorist: 'We must not fool ourselves about the importance of news in the lives of citizens/audiences. The reality is that the average person is not now – and never has been – deeply interested in news. For most readers, viewers, and listeners, news consumption is brief and consists primarily of scanning major developments. Most people have only a superficial awareness of major occurrences and other things about which they should be concerned.'[16] Walter Lippman was making much the same point nearly 100 years ago.

That is, however, an overly depressing and ultimately damaging view of the limits of the human appetite for knowledge and understanding. It is also potentially self-fulfilling, as the diet of tragedy and sensation paints a picture of a gloomy world on our screens which we are more likely to switch off – probably to seek refuge in sex and shopping. This is damaging for democracy. Having charted the downward spiral in 'serious' news in the Harvard study mentioned above, Thomas Patterson concludes:

> The relentless quest for riveting stories ... works against the news media's intention to provide citizens a clear understanding of their stake in public affairs. The irony is that, in the long run, these distortions also make that world a less attractive and inviting one. Interest in public affairs declines and so, too, does interest in news. Democracy cannot operate effectively without a free press that performs well as watchdog and information source. In other words, the press must do its job well if democracy is to succeed.[17]

This connection between television news and democracy has been analysed by many eminent scholars over the years and extends, of course, beyond television to all forms of journalism. Without it, we would be more likely to face autocratic governments, not to mention corruption, negligence, incompetence and laziness in both public and private sectors. But what part does television play in fostering a healthier public culture? Where is the evidence that television is sufficiently important as a serious communicative tool to make it worth supporting – or restoring – regulatory mechanisms of protection?

Although effects research in this area is notoriously difficult, such evidence has been forthcoming from the United States and the United Kingdom. One 1994 study compared political knowledge in the United States to that in six other advanced industrial democracies, concluding that Americans are the least knowledgeable about foreign affairs. Given five factual questions about international political events and actors, the study found that 'the US public scored far lower on the international information scale than the public of any European G7 country and barely better than Spain, even though the US public is better educated'. After detailed statistical analysis, it concluded that this knowledge gap was at least in part directly attributable to the impoverished nature of foreign news reporting on American television.[18] More recently, a cross-national study in 2007 came to very similar conclusions. Analysing responses to 'hard' and 'soft' information questions in four countries with very different media systems (United States, United Kingdom, Finland and Denmark), the authors concluded that Americans were 'especially uninformed about international public affairs' and 'did much worse than Europeans in response to seven out of the eight common international hard news questions (the sole exception being a question about the identity of the Iraqi Prime Minister)'. Their statistical analysis demonstrates a clear connection between the low level of foreign coverage and hard news on American television and the 'high level of public ignorance that exists in America about the wider world and about public life in general'.[19] The authors end with a slightly wistful note of surprise that an entertainment-centred model of television that seems to yield an impoverished public life is increasingly being adopted around the world.

If television has the power to inform, it also has the power to misinform. An American study in 2003 found an astonishing level of ignorance about the background to the Iraq War: a series of public opinion surveys conducted between June and September of that year found that 48 per cent incorrectly believed that evidence of links between Iraq and al-Qaeda had been found; 22 per cent that weapons of mass destruction had been found in Iraq; and 25 per cent that world public opinion favoured the United States going to war with Iraq. Overall 60 per cent of the public believed at least one of these three misperceptions. Crucially, those misperceptions were highly related to support for the war. Among those who believed none of the above statements, only 23 per cent supported the war. This support rose to 53 per cent amongst those who believed one of the misperceptions, 78 per cent who believed two out of the three and 86 per cent who believed all three. In other words, it is highly likely that support for the war in Iraq would have been substantially lower – and vocal opposition commensurately higher – if American citizens had been properly informed.[20]

For the purposes of this book, however, the most critical finding of the study was how misperceptions were highly correlated with the source of information. Of those who had none of the three misconceptions – that is, were properly informed about the background to the war – 77 per cent obtained 'most of their news' from the public broadcasting television service PBS; 47 per cent derived their news from print sources; 45 per cent from either CNN or NBC; 39 per cent from ABC; 30 per cent from CBS; and just 20 per cent from Fox News. The corollary to these results were, not surprisingly, that those who relied primarily on Fox News were far more likely to hold one or more of the misconceptions: an astonishing 80 per cent compared to 47 per cent for those who relied on print sources and 23 per cent who relied on public broadcasting. The authors were clear that these variations were not explicable in terms of demographic variations, such as education or geographical location, because the differences remained even within these subgroups. In other words, exposure to a particular television channel – in this case, a channel with an avowedly pro-war and pro-government stance – was responsible for a fundamental knowledge gap amongst its viewers about the circumstances surrounding a decision to go to war.

Television and trust

This raises a further question about the uniqueness of the television medium: that it derives its power not just from its visual images and its ubiquity but from the implicit sense of trust which it commands. That, too, emanates from an elaborately created regulatory structure of impartiality which in some countries – as in the United States – has already been dismantled and in others – like the United Kingdom – is under threat. In the UK during 2007, a series of incidents in television raised serious questions about the integrity of those who worked within it. These were primarily about the use and misuse of premium-rate telephone lines to raise money in programme-related competitions (which, for the commercial stations, were making substantial contributions to the bottom line), but also impugned the methods of some producers who had 'invented' competition winners when none had emerged through the usual process. There ensued much furious breast-beating by an enraged press (partly relieved that for once allegations of sensationalism and pretence were being directed at a rival medium) and much fevered navel-gazing by the television industry itself. There was real concern that this 'crisis of trust' would spill over from entertainment television to the more profound areas of news and factual programmes where issues of trust and integrity were paramount.

This theme was pursued in 2007 by one of Britain's most senior television journalists in terms which were uncannily reminiscent of Murrow. Eighteen years after Rupert Murdoch delivered his Edinburgh tirade against the British television establishment, Jeremy Paxman – long-time presenter of the BBC's news analysis programme 'Newsnight' – used the same lecture in the same forum to offer an equally withering attack on those who did not understand the power of television journalism, the mechanisms which enabled it to flourish and the commitment of those who worked in it:

> We know what the dangers are. Left to its itself, the medium will achieve its potential to be no more than a giant electronic circus or freakshow. We know how bad it can get, whether it's the Russian station which has its newsreaders read the news while performing a striptease, or the Brazilian audience show with its Deformity of the Week feature. In Britain, for the first several decades of its life, television has been something better than that. The presence of the BBC was obviously a big factor. Regulation had something to do with it. But most of all, I think, television has maintained high standards of creative excellence and honesty because the people who worked in it believed they were doing a job which mattered.[21]

Paxman addressed other themes which will be explored in this book, in particular the irresistible pressure on all television news to seek out more drama and sensationalism in order to stand out in an overcrowded channel market, inevitably at the expense of depth and understanding. But, most of all, this was a call – just like that of Murrow – for vision and leadership to protect 'a trade which has the potential to do amazing things, to show people things they didn't know existed, to give them the power to make informed decisions about how they see the world and how they want to be governed'.

In other words, television does matter. It has the power to inform and to educate on the most pressing global issues of the day; it has the power to influence and to change people's minds; it is ubiquitous, heavily used and commands a sense of credibility that applies to no other medium of communication. Those are the positive qualities of the medium, the ones to be nurtured and exploited – but which have only survived courtesy of the protective framework that has existed since television's inception.

Comparative and theoretical context

While the core of this book is essentially an historical and institutional case study of the United Kingdom, using the United States as a benchmark for comparative analysis, many of the conclusions about the impact of competition, deregulation, marketization, changing audiences and cultural approaches to the practice of journalism can be generalized to other advanced democracies; in particular, the institutional and political influence of Public Service Broadcasting has been at the forefront of European developments in television over the last 60 years. As Peter Dahlgren wrote at the beginning of the century: 'In almost all Western European countries, the principles of public service shaped the emergence of television in the post-war years … Indeed, European television was typified by public service monopolies until relatively recently.'[22] Many of these public service broadcasters – and indeed those in Commonwealth countries such as Australia, Canada, New Zealand and South Africa – were modelled on the BBC, with funding and constitutional arrangements adapted to suit national political cultures.

Over the last 25 years, however, the principles, practices and structures of Public Service Broadcasting (PSB) have come under mounting pressure from political and technological changes as well as a more globalized media environment. Virtually every advanced democracy – and increasingly the emerging democracies of Eastern Europe – have witnessed a rapid growth in commercial broadcasting outlets, fuelled both by new cable and satellite technologies and the global ambitions of multinational media corporations. This in turn has increased the political pressure on governments throughout the world to scale back the activities and funding of public broadcasters, and to relax regulatory frameworks which may constrain commercial expansion. In terms of television journalism, the introduction of commercial competition – as the UK history illustrates and as the democratization of Eastern Europe also proved – has made a vital contribution to pluralism, independence and accountability to audiences beyond the elite. As Karol Jakubowicz, one of the most articulate supporters of PSB principles, has said: 'General democratization and rising affluence in European societies have levelled social divisions and stratification. The old paternalism of PSB as the voice of authority (or, even worse, of the authorities), or of the social elite, is thus no longer acceptable'.[23]

Nevertheless, as Jakubowicz and many others have pointed out over the years, by embracing uncritically the neoliberal principles of privatization, deregulation, commercialization and contraction of the public sector, we have also endangered the many positive principles of PSB that emerged in the first phase of monopoly provision. In terms of journalistic practice, this has been characterized by an attachment to principles of accuracy, fairness, impartiality, quality and adequate resourcing, as well as an increasing recognition of television's potential contribution to democratic life. This PSB legacy for television journalism – and particularly the contrast with a historically market-led system in the United States – has been rather ignored in comparative analyses of media systems. In particular, the most influential of these studies in recent years, by Hallin and Mancini, bracketed the United Kingdom with the United States in what they termed a 'North Atlantic or liberal model'.[24] Their exclusion of the distinctiveness of PSB philosophy and practice is one of many criticisms levelled at the Hallin and Mancini typology by Peter Humphreys, whose comprehensive critique recommends that a more informed approach could draw on the political-science theory of historic institutionalism (HI) which sees institutions 'as crucially important in explaining political outcomes'.[25]

This book allies an historical institutional approach with a more traditional political economy analysis. It examines the hugely significant – and still evolving – role of the BBC as well as the tradition of strong regulatory institutions which have historically imposed positive public service requirements on commercial broadcasters. It also analyses the impact of exogenous pressures such as shifts in the political environment, economic imperatives, and broader demographic, social and cultural change amongst audiences. It traces the beginnings of a statutory and regulatory framework which – despite all the innate obstacles of the medium itself – first created and then sustained a culture of serious, responsible, accurate and challenging journalism in British television. It looks at how government inquiries and commissions, successive Acts of Parliament, the BBC constitution, the BBC's internal culture, the regulatory bodies for commercial television and the various codes of practice have worked to create a brand of journalism that is very different from that practised in the newspaper industry. It examines the impact of the deregulatory policies of the 1980s on television news and current affairs. It looks at contemporary practices and arguments for and against the 'tabloidization' thesis, and whether there is real evidence for the degradation of news on television. It explores the growth and significance of 24-hour news channels, the role and continuing relevance of impartiality requirements, and whether the statutory and regulatory provisions which have sustained television can withstand the emergence of online and new media technologies.

In July 2011, Britain's national press was engulfed in an extraordinary crisis about criminal and immoral activities within the country's highest selling newspaper, the *News of the World*, which reverberated around the world, threatened the whole of Rupert Murdoch's global media empire, and raised fundamental questions about standards and ethics in print journalism. It was widely recognized that practices such as phone hacking would never be contemplated, let alone tolerated, within

UK television journalism. But the contrast between print and television philosophies should alert us, even in a 'converged' world, to the importance of sustaining television's contribution to journalism. Much good television journalism has survived in Britain but, as this book shows, it is in decline for reasons related more to changes in the political and regulatory environment than to new technology or the rise of the internet. As Murrow predicted and as Paxman has warned, we have either side of the Atlantic two very different models of how television news is constructed and the contribution to public life that it makes. The very real danger is that Britain and the rest of Europe may be heading inexorably down the American road.

1   Laying the Foundations: Policies, Practices and a Public Monopoly

The early political context for broadcast journalism

The arrival of television in Britain, formally inaugurated by the BBC on 2 November 1936 and covering only the London area, was barely noticed. Sir John Reith, the BBC's 'founding father' himself, regarded it as an unnecessary distraction from the real business of radio, and was anyway becoming engulfed – as was the rest of the country – in the rumours of impending constitutional crisis surrounding the King's relationship with Mrs Wallace, which culminated in his abdication the following month. Those who had been raised on the disciplines and practice of radio broadcasting were both unschooled in the practice of translating entertainment or information into vision and, more importantly, highly distrustful of the medium. For those who ran the BBC, radio was conducive to the thoughtful and the serious; television was only good for pantomime. In the words of Grace Wyndham Goldie, who was to become one of the great pioneers of early BBC television journalism, 'they associated vision with the movies and the music hall and were afraid that the high purposes of the Corporation would be trivialised by the influence of those concerned with what could be transmitted in visual terms'.[1] The thesis which Neil Postman came to personify in the 1980s was pre-empted by a good 50 years, even before television had entered most people's consciousness.

As Wyndham Goldie also pointed out, however, BBC television's journalistic legacy from radio was fundamentally important because it inherited 'two essential freedoms, achieved by few other television services as they developed around the world':[2] freedom from government intervention (although only the most ardent purist would say there was no government influence); and freedom from influence by commercial interests. Both these freedoms were not just the cornerstone for television journalism on the BBC but for the commercial television service that followed.

This legacy, while partly down to the tenacity of Reith and his determination to keep the meddlesome hands of politicians away from any direct interference, was also attributable to the committees which had been set up during the 1920s and 1930s to make recommendations for the future of broadcasting. This was no accident: these committees reflected the mood of the moment and the psyche of a nation that was not naturally inclined to hand over institutional control of a major organ of public influence to the State but was also somewhat distrustful of the wholly commercialized, commodified approach that personified American radio. The Sykes Committee was set up by the Post Office in 1923 to solve the funding problem of the British Broadcasting Company in the wake of widespread evasion of the tax on wireless sets, but understood clearly that 'broadcasting holds social and political possibilities as great as any technical attainment of our generation'. It therefore concluded – in words which would have resonated throughout Western Europe – that 'the control of such a potential power over the public opinion and the life of the nation ought to remain within the State and the operation of so important a national service ought not to be allowed to become an unrestricted commercial monopoly'.[3]

However, Sykes was also quick to point out the distinction of control remaining 'within the State' rather than broadcasting being managed *by* the State, which it firmly opposed. The reasons were twofold, and not only confined to fear of government censorship; there was a secondary concern simply about making news too boring: 'If a Government Department had to select the news, speeches, lectures, etc. to be broadcast, it would be constantly open to suspicion that it was using its unique opportunities to advance the interests of the political party in power; and, in the endeavour to avoid anything in the slightest degree controversial, it would probably succeed in making its service intolerably dull.'[4]

Ironically, concern about the impact of State intervention on news was superfluous given that discretion for news broadcasting on radio had been entirely circumscribed by the newspaper owners' terror of losing newspaper sales. The BBC was only allowed to broadcast news from 'certain approved News Agencies' and even then not until 7 p.m. so as not to interfere with the sale of evening newspapers – a restriction justified by Sykes on the grounds that newspapers spend heavily on news collection and distribution, and 'urge with justice that it would not be in the public interest that the broadcasting system ... should be allowed to publish news otherwise than from authoritative and responsible sources of information'.[5] In 1923, then, the nascent radio service was not trusted to treat news with the same respect for journalistic values as those virtuously embodied by an authoritative press.

Less than three years later, the Crawford Committee reported its conclusions on what should happen when the British Broadcasting Company's licence to broadcast expired at the end of 1926. Crawford, like Sykes, rejected a State-run institution in favour of a new corporation whose 'status and duties should correspond with those of a public service'. Crawford, however, seemed to move towards a greater flexibility about the BBC and news. The new organization should not be providing material 'as it pleases', said the committee, but then added – with what might be interpreted as astonishing foresight – that newspapers will adapt 'perhaps depending more upon narrative and criticism than upon the mere schedule of facts'. Moreover, it said, broadcasting could even have a promotional impact, heightening interest in news and therefore improving circulation figures.[6] And while it was tentative on the subject of whether 'controversial matter' could be safely entrusted to the new Corporation, on balance it was prepared to accept that 'if the material be of high quality, not too lengthy or insistent, and distributed with scrupulous fairness, licensees will desire a moderate amount of controversy'.[7]

The first test of independent journalism – the general strike

In fact, even before its inauguration as a public body, the BBC had an opportunity both to engage in unfettered news dissemination and to test political commitment to the principle of independence. On 3 May 1926, the unions called a general strike in support of the coal miners. Not only did this pitch workers against the government in a major political confrontation, it also took newspapers off the street because of the involvement of the print unions. Apart from the government-sponsored *British Gazette* – printed in Paris, flown to Britain daily and known to be essentially a government propaganda tool – the only source of news for a nation on the brink of industrial paralysis was the wireless and the BBC. Reith asked for and was given authority from the postmaster general to broadcast news at any time, and instituted bulletins every three hours from ten in the morning using material from Reuters. It was a difficult balancing act, given that influential cabinet voices – including the Chancellor of the Exchequer Winston Churchill – were arguing vociferously that the government should use its emergency powers to commandeer the BBC. Asa Briggs draws a distinction between the 'constitutional' position of the BBC – the government had legal authority to take it over – and the 'diplomatic' position held by a majority in the cabinet that 'it would be wiser to leave the BBC a measure of independence or at least of "semi-independence"'.[8]

In order to dissuade the Prime Minister from a wholesale takeover, Reith decided to commit his argument to paper. Two days into the strike, on 5 May, Reith penned what his biographer overenthusiastically called 'a classic statement of the case for broadcasting to be independent of government':

The BBC has secured and holds the goodwill and affection of the people. It has been trusted to do the right thing at all times. Its influence is widespread. It is a national institution and a national asset … This is not a time for dope, even if the people could be doped. The hostile would be made more hostile from resentment. As to suppression, from the panic of ignorance comes far greater danger than from the knowledge of facts.[9]

It was, in fact, a rationale which owed more to political survival than any grand vision of democratic intent: a source of information which was neither run by the government nor identified with it – but which behind the scenes had close links to it – was just what Prime Minister Baldwin and the like-minded members of his cabinet wanted. Thus, BBC coverage of the general strike was the first example of engagement in the delicate realpolitik of an independence that has always been conscious of – and sometimes constrained by – the BBC's relationship with the State. This has not, as we shall see, prejudiced its ability to conduct vigorous and independent journalism that can deeply antagonize governments, but it has – at some times more than others – involved an awareness of the political environment that can spill over into undue caution and voluntary self-censorship. As the BBC evolved into a self-sufficient journalistic institution – and as its values and constitution increasingly served as a model for other countries searching for a viable compromise between market and State in the evolution of broadcasting – this notion of 'constrained independence' is perhaps a more useful concept than Briggs' description of 'semi-independence'.

Since it had no journalistic resources of its own, the BBC took its news of the strike from two sources: the Admiralty office of the Deputy Chief Civil Commissioner, who acted as the link between government and Reith during the strike, and Reuters. According to Briggs, 'One or two BBC employees actually went out collecting news,' but bulletins were essentially rewritten second-hand affairs which tried to encapsulate the essence of what was happening around the country. Reith was keen to impress on listeners the BBC's sense of its own responsibility, himself telling listeners in the 10 o'clock bulletin of 4 May: 'The BBC fully realizes the gravity of its responsibility to all sections of the public, and will do its best to discharge it in the most impartial spirit that circumstances permit … We would ask the public to take as serious a view as we do ourselves of the necessity of plain objective news being audible to everybody.' The limits to that impartiality were manifested in examples of inaccurate reporting that have an uncanny echo of complaints made against television broadcasters in Britain during the bitter miners' strike of 1986: accounts of engine drivers and firemen returning to work in Oxford, for example, or the strike breaking down in Salisbury.[10]

It is therefore fair to conclude with Briggs that 'BBC news assisted the government against the strikers' not through blatant propaganda but, first, through selective presentation of news reporting and, second, through its ability to dispel any ugly rumours which might have fanned the flames of revolution (e.g. stories about the murder of police officers or riots at Hyde Park Corner). Some accused the BBC of producing news bulletins which were 'doped' and called it the BFC – the British Falsehood Corporation. It was not the last time the acronym was to be parodied in accusations of deliberate bias. In response to these general observations of partiality, Reith acknowledged openly in the *Radio Times* that the BBC had lacked 'complete liberty of action' during the strike but did not believe that any government 'would have allowed the broadcasting authority under its control greater freedom than was enjoyed by the BBC during the crisis'.[11] Given the nascent condition of broadcasting, he was certainly right. This was an organization searching for a new journalistic culture within the constraints of what was deemed acceptable by an establishment used to controlling information in a crisis. The BBC, in Briggs's words, 'reinforced authority' in a way which it found very hard to shake off – arguably even until the arrival of a new era and an iconoclastic director general in the 1960s.

But Reith had achieved two things for the future of broadcast journalism, with repercussions that arguably extended well beyond the confines of the United Kingdom as the BBC's influence began to be felt internationally. First, he had ensured that the then very vulnerable concept of 'impartiality' – however compromised it had been in practice – had at least not been uprooted and cast aside; it remained a legitimate aspiration for the broadcast medium (albeit currently limited to radio) and for broadcasting institutions. Second, he had ensured that broadcasting was now recognized as a potent force in national life. When it came to the BBC's next test of journalistic integrity, in the run-up to the Second World War, the second of those was rather more visible than the first.

'Constrained independence' consolidated

In the meantime, BBC progress towards a self-sufficient independent journalism moved slowly against the joint suspicions of government and press. With the beginning of the new corporation in 1927, the BBC was given permission not only to subscribe to news agencies but to undertake its own reporting. A year later, in March 1928, the ban on reporting matters of controversy was withdrawn on an experimental basis in the light of the 'loyal and punctilious manner' in which the BBC had conformed to its obligations.[12] This gradual loosening of the apron strings was assisted by the new constitutional system that established a ten-year

Royal Charter and independent 'governors', thus ensuring that the new British Broadcasting Corporation was dominated neither by the commercial marketplace nor by the State. As Reith wrote in the first *BBC Handbook*: 'The Royal Academy and the Bank of England function under Royal Charter. So does the BBC. It is no Department of State'.[13] Reith's cautious approach to controversy had not only paid dividends in terms of a secure future for the corporation; it had also established important ground-rules for a journalistic independence which made overt government interference quite awkward. The 'experiment' on covering controversy continued over the next 12 years, during which time it was understood (and explicitly stated in Parliament) that it was up to the independent BBC Governors to monitor and interpret the relevant material.[14]

Lack of direct intervention did not, however, mean lack of accommodation at sensitive times. The time limit on its Royal Charter meant that, as each ten-year expiry date neared, the BBC was subject to government review. An early example of the potential impact on BBC journalism of these delicate negotiations came in 1935, when the BBC Governors approved a proposal to broadcast talks from a renowned communist, Harry Pollitt, and a renowned fascist, Sir Oswald Mosley. The government disapproved and, while not prepared to intervene directly, did indicate that the strategy was unwise given the Charter's imminent expiry at the end of 1936. In the event, Pollitt and Mosley were discreetly dropped without any public suggestion of interference, and the BBC retained its reputation for independence. This sensitivity to negotiations around Charter renewal presaged similar examples of journalistic caution in the decades to come. As Seaton says: 'This cautious self-protection was shrewd, and may have been the only strategy available. However, it made the BBC vulnerable to bullying ... the most important constraint came to be the Corporation's anxiety to pre-empt the threats.'[15] This sensitivity of a publicly funded broadcaster to government thinking – which later became more memorably known as the 'pre-emptive cringe' – again resonated in other countries seeking to emulate the BBC model.

In the event, the 1936 Ullswater Report into the BBC's future was an almost unconditional endorsement of the BBC's achievements. No doubt aware of the propaganda techniques already being employed in Italy and Germany, it reiterated the need to safeguard a powerful medium of political expression. But it went further than its predecessors by arguing for more freedom in the broadcasting of news and for a 'strong and impartial editorial staff'. There was specific recognition of the importance of broadcasting in tackling controversial matters in ways that were relevant and covered different perspectives: 'If broadcasting is to present a reflection of its time, it must include matters which are in dispute. If it is to hold public interest, it must express living thought. If it is to educate public opinion, it must look upon the questions of the hour from many angles'.[16] This recognition was automatically extended to the television service, which had been entrusted to the BBC on the recommendation of another government report headed by Lord Selsdon a year earlier. At the same time, the balance of power between press and broadcasting had shifted significantly, and in November 1937 the BBC told the press agencies that it was terminating their agreement. Thus, from its modest beginnings on 2 November 1936, the BBC's television service started with both a clear mandate for reporting and with its institutional independence now cemented – albeit with qualifications – by the trust earned by Reith.

Early BBC news culture and the Dimbleby effect

By 1931, roughly half the UK population were reckoned to be listeners to radio but the 1931 *BBC Year Book* was still saying that 'the supply of news is mainly the task of the Press'.[17] Despite the cataclysmic political changes unfolding throughout Europe during the 1930s, therefore, the BBC's approach to news was sparing, with a concentration on quality and presentation; when there was insufficient news deemed to be worth broadcasting, the announcer said simply that 'there is no news tonight'. Although the definition of 'quality news' was never made explicit, the BBC's news values were very distinct from the popular press: the dress sense of 1930s film stars or footballers' wives did not feature in bulletin running lists.

Two other factors beyond the self-defined 'broadsheet' nature of the institution dictated how broadcast journalism developed within the BBC and applied equally to the culture of television journalism as it evolved – somewhat later – in other countries: an acute sense that audiences were more heterogeneous and variegated than the self-selected readerships of newspapers; and an awareness that the immediacy of the broadcast medium might demand a greater sensibility to the impact of stories on listeners. Scannell and Cardiff record a letter sent as early as 1923 from the BBC to the Broadcasting Editor of Reuters reminding him of the subtle differences between reading news from a newspaper and hearing it through a wireless, which might make the impact of crimes or disasters more shocking: 'we think it is a good policy as far as possible to eliminate from bulletins all crimes and tragedies that have no national or international importance. The hanging of a criminal, the burning of a child, or the assaulting of a woman are not news items suitable to a broadcast service.'[18]

When a tiny news section was created in 1927, its head described the object of the BBC news service as being specifically 'to avoid the errors into which journalists, as such, seem inevitably to fall', defining those errors in terms that became very familiar to critics of early twenty-first century journalism: sensationalism, inaccuracy, partiality and overstatement. The BBC was there, he said, to 'present news of all that is happening in the world in a clear, impartial and succinct language'.[19] Anticipating the day that the BBC would be able to ditch the agencies and take full editorial responsibility, the news section commissioned a report on how the news service might be established. The 11-page document noted in particular that the radio audience was drawn from all sections of the population, and that a news service designed to appeal to the mass population could not ignore human interest stories. Thus, at the very beginning, was introduced a conundrum with which latter-day broadcasters are still grappling: how do you reconcile authority, impartiality and lack of sensationalism with journalism that engages the audience?

The first radio bulletin emanating entirely from the news section went out on 10 February 1930. It became an independent department in 1934 and recruited its first two professional journalists – a home news editor and a foreign news editor – from the broadsheet press, along with two subeditors. President Roosevelt's inaugural speech was broadcast live in 1933 and there were the beginnings of independent reporting both at home and abroad – with the emphasis on accuracy and impartiality, and, of course, with appropriate deference to authority. The BBC was not there to probe but to relay. On the other hand, its journalism was also evolving in reaction to the needs of unfolding diplomatic dramas in Europe and in recognition of the liveness and immediacy of the broadcast experience. It was a delicate balance to maintain the authority of the institution and avoid the popular vulgarity of sensationalism while at the same time attempting to convey real-time vividness. The most important exponent of this new brand of live journalism that fused these conflicting editorial values was a 23-year-old journalist called Richard Dimbleby.

Having first been refused a job in the BBC News Department in 1936, Dimbleby wrote again outlining his vision for broadcast journalism. BBC news, he said, could be enlivened without compromising authority. BBC reporters could be available to cover unexpected (today we would say 'breaking') stories: fires, strikes, civil commotion, railway or pit accidents, or any other major catastrophes could be covered by a reporter sent from Broadcasting House who could broadcast an eyewitness account and secure interviews from people on the spot. 'News could be presented in a gripping manner, and, at the same time, remain authentic.'[20] The idea of exploiting the broadcast medium to combine immediacy and authenticity may seem ludicrously self-evident today, but at the time it was revolutionary. It was also expensive and cumbersome in terms of equipment, and therefore difficult to implement. Dimbleby got his job, and first marked the arrival of dramatic on-the-spot reporting when on 30 November 1936 he rushed to the scene of the huge fire that destroyed the Crystal Palace in south London and described the scenes of conflagration to radio listeners from a public phone box.

Nevertheless, developing an independent news culture was a slow process. While tension was building towards a crisis in the European capitals of Prague, Munich, Berlin and Vienna – and while Americans were being treated to the brilliant on-the-spot reportage of journalists like William Shirer and Ed Murrow from the heart of Europe – the BBC's News Department was still fledgling and overly dependent on the agencies. The years of delicate negotiation to avoid upsetting the press barons, and the diversion of resources into plays, talks, arts and music rather than journalism, were taking its toll. Moreover, the agencies were not delivering: Reuters' main clients were the popular press, which cared more about the domestic and the sensational than such foreign niceties as the annexation of the Sudetenland or the fall of the French cabinet. And even when the problem was recognized, the bureaucratic wheels of the BBC moved slowly. When eventually the decision was taken to hire more journalists, Dimbleby famously found himself on the Franco-Spanish border to witness the last stages of the Spanish Civil War and produce the kind of broadcast journalism to which the United States had become accustomed. In the words of Scannell and Cardiff, Dimbleby 'returned to London, deeply shaken by the experience, to the congratulations of his colleagues and – unprecedented tribute – a commendation for his work from the Board of Governors'.[21]

Pre-war self-censorship

Those months of pre-war diplomacy saw another, more blatant example of BBC self-censorship. In a country that still collectively remembered the terrible horrors of the Great War which had ended barely 20 years earlier, almost anything was preferable to another conflict. Moreover, there was considerable unease over the harsh restrictions on Germany imposed by the Treaty of Versailles and the dire economic consequences. So as Hitler inexorably continued his rearmament and annexation policies during the course of 1938, the British government sought ever more ingenious ways of avoiding a confrontation. The National government, under Prime Minister Neville Chamberlain, vigorously pursued this policy of appeasement with the support of most of the country, most Members of Parliament and most of the establishment including newspaper editors, senior civil servants, academics and members of the royal family.

There were, however, some vocal and influential dissenters. Anthony Eden resigned from the government as Foreign Secretary in protest in February 1938, but the most vociferous opponent was Winston Churchill. The crisis over Czechoslovakia came to a head in September 1938 when the leaders of Germany,

Italy, France and Britain met in Munich in an attempt to avoid war. Chamberlain's return to Britain, having conceded the Sudetenland to Hitler in return for very little except the avoidance of war, was recorded by cinema newsreels as being unremittingly triumphant. Very few expressions of doubt or foreboding were heard, let alone any outright opposition. This is scarcely surprising since, as former ITN Editor Stewart Purvis discovered from the newsreel archives, contrary voices had effectively been silenced: the American-owned British Paramount News received instructions from its head office to delete interviews with two prominent critics of appeasement.[22] A newsreel interview with anti-appeasement MP Harold Nicholson, on the day Chamberlain set off to Munich, was never screened. The public and journalistic reactions to Chamberlain's Munich enterprise was, Purvis argues, the result of deliberate news management: 'With a persistence which Tony Blair and Alastair Campbell would admire, Chamberlain and the Home Secretary Sir Samuel Hoare worked their contacts amongst proprietors, editors and even correspondents.'

Within such a triumphalist atmosphere of cheering crowds on Chamberlain's return from Munich, the BBC would always have found it difficult to air contrary views. This was a time of genuine public celebration, even if the voices of caution had been airbrushed from the media. As with the Falklands War in 1982 and the Iraq War in 2003, the absence of any concerted oppositional voices within Parliament made it more difficult for the BBC to provide critical voices with the airtime that a neutral and impartial journalistic approach might have demanded. According to Purvis, Richard Dimbleby's commentary on Chamberlain's return just about stayed within acceptable boundaries of objective journalism, but BBC bulletins that evening contained just one counterpoint to the national rejoicing (from Liberal leader Sir Archibald Sinclair). Beyond that, while not adding its own voice to the hyperbole of other media, the BBC made no attempt to temper the jubilation with a more sober or analytical perspective.

An internal report written some time later shed some interesting light on the thinking process within the BBC: 'There was no censorship by the Government of the BBC news bulletins or broadcast material, though the Corporation naturally kept in close touch with the appropriate departments and the bulletins fell in line with Government policy'.[23] In other words, this was compliant journalism by osmosis rather than direct intervention – the BBC as national institution with its roots in the heart of the establishment, rather than an organization in the vanguard of critical journalism. Intriguingly, however, this closeness to government did prompt some serious disquiet within the corporation that it had not properly executed its responsibility to the general public. John Coatman, having moved from head of the News Department to Director of BBC North, wrote a long memorandum on

5 October in which he bemoaned the BBC's inability to give British people the essential information it needed to understand the crisis. In the past, he said:

> We have not played the part which our duty to the people of this country called upon us to play. We have, in fact, taken part in a conspiracy of silence ... The position of this country is infinitely more dangerous than it has ever been in modern times, and the past few weeks have invested the BBC with a new importance, given it a more vital role in the national life, and have, therefore, laid a new responsibility on us who are its servants. This responsibility is to let the people of this country know, as far as the sources available to us allow, just what is happening.[24]

Coatman was at great pains to point out that no one was to blame, that the BBC did not conspire willingly or knowingly, and that in view of the short history of the corporation and its 'peculiar relationship to the Government', this was not surprising. It was not an unfair analysis, and his recognition that the BBC now had to acknowledge its duty to the people – to its licence payers – perhaps marked a turning point in BBC journalism.

Its problem was how to change recognition into implementation, given that it had become so absorbed into the machinery of State. In the words of Scannell and Cardiff, 'The continuous routine contact that had built up over the years between senior personnel in Broadcasting House, Whitehall and Westminster meant that they all abided by the same rules and code of conduct.'[25] But it was clear that, by the outbreak of the Second World War, there was at least sufficient self-reflection within the BBC for it to recognize its own potential as well its own failings. It would be some time before it could throw off the institutional mantle of deference – it would take a new director general, a new competitor and new social mores – but the groundwork had been laid for a culture which not only dictated the nature of television journalism in the UK but was hugely influential in its development around the world: a public institution that was operationally independent from government and not funded directly by it; that had developed an institutional ethic of impartiality and authority; that had begun to form a relationship with its audience; and that had begun to understand its obligation not only to provide full, independent and impartial information to that audience, but to use responsibly the unprecedented power of the broadcast medium. Unfortunately, there was no time before war was declared to start applying those principles to the nascent technology of television before the first TV service in the world was abruptly terminated – in the middle of a Mickey Mouse film – on 1 September 1939. But when the first post-war broadcast was transmitted on 7 June 1946 – with, fittingly, Richard Dimbleby commentating –

television inherited a journalistic modus operandi which still informs many national practices today.

The legacy of war: journalism, trust and BBC independence

The wartime relationship between State and broadcaster was a complex one in which independence was safeguarded but only on the basis that both shared a common aim – the swift dissemination of news, with authority and without compromising the war effort. The BBC Chairman of the time, Sir Allan Powell, used the telling phrase that the BBC was bound by 'silken cords' (though he added that these sometimes felt like 'chains of iron').[26] Briggs describes 'intimate if sometimes chequered relations' with almost every government department although the absence of a Goebbels-type figure with an obsessional interest in pursuing a single propagandist line was also instrumental in allowing the BBC to pursue a responsibly independent line.

Apart from consolidating the BBC's institutional and operational independence, the war years inevitably elevated the importance of news and journalism as a vital area of BBC activity. Culture, as we have seen, had been the BBC's driving force, not Information or even Democracy. News had been cautious, brief and uninspiring. But the news imperatives of the war not only galvanized broadcast journalism but started to change the habits of the nation. It was H.G. Wells who announced portentously in 1943 that 'the day of the newspaper was done' – a cry which has echoed down the years, as first radio, then television, then the internet have been predicted to bring the newspaper to its knees.[27] And George Orwell, while bitterly critical of the BBC's upper-class accents and lack of appeal to ordinary working people, nevertheless paid tribute to its news service and in 1944 wrote in the Labour Party newspaper *Tribune* that '"I heard it on the wireless" is now almost equivalent to "I know it must be true"'.[28]

This elevation of news and journalism, combined with the emergence of television as a medium of news transmission, placed additional pressure on the BBC's reputation for authority and accuracy. Television was not an obvious medium for 'doing' news, and drama was television's main preoccupation at the beginning. Plays could draw on a raft of experienced producers from the theatre and cinema, and a single production in a single studio could fill an hour's TV with a minimum of fuss and expense. The transfer of journalism from print required different skills, and indeed a different concept of journalism from the partisan and opinionated approach of most newspapers. Most importantly of all, the need for pictures might compromise the authority of the institution. When the BBC's newly appointed

Controller of Television Maurice Gorham suggested that radio bulletins might be supplemented by pictures with very little alteration to the material, the Director General's response was withering: 'The fact that the text of the bulletin would have to be received some hours in advance of transmission ... shows the necessity that would arise to subordinate the primary functions of news to the needs of visual presentation. Any such subordination would prejudice all sorts of values on which the BBC's great reputation for news has been founded'.[29]

His caution not only reflected a prescient awareness of the different demands of vision-led news, but also a jealous determination to protect the BBC's reputation for authority. Grace Wyndham Goldie told the story of how, as a radio producer, she had persuaded someone of importance to record an interview, but he insisted that it should be broadcast as if it was live so as not to spoil the sense of immediacy. She was told by her superiors that, even if just two people knew the truth, this was an unacceptable deceit: 'Once you undermined faith in this way there was no telling where it would end. Trust was integral. Any breach of faith with the public, I was told in what was practically a hushed whisper, might mean that people would not believe the BBC news'.[30] This was then, and remains, one of the cornerstones of BBC journalistic practice. It partly explains the furore following its reporting of the government's Iraq intelligence dossiers in 2002, explored in more detail later in this book, and other smaller incidents in which the BBC has been found not to be completely accurate or open with its licence-payers. In the first decade of the twenty-first century, this ingrained sense of truth-telling remains a fascinating counterpoint to some of the journalism practised by the popular press and in the blogosphere, where principles of honesty and integrity have arguably been under more intense pressure than ever before.

Thus, the television pioneers of Alexandra Palace – where the nascent service was based – had some difficulty in persuading the old radio hands at Broadcasting House that television was a) worth taking seriously as a medium, b) worth the diversion of valuable BBC resources and c) involved different demands and techniques from radio. Their cause was not helped by the cumbersome and expensive nature of cameras required for outside broadcasts, and the gradual realization that the medium involved all sorts of issues about accurate representation of 'the truth'.

Discovering television's limitations

Even at this early stage, it was clear to the beleaguered television forces that the use of visual material would have to be handled with care, rigour and integrity in order to preserve BBC standards of trust and impartiality. Vision could increase understanding, could avoid the unintentional bias of a radio reporter painting an inaccurate picture and could convey a different quality of truth. It was first-hand experience rather than second-hand impression. And it gave viewers the impression that they, too, were witnesses to televised events. But cameras could also be used carelessly or deliberately or even maliciously to convey an erroneous impression of the truth, a risk which Wyndham Goldie and her colleagues recognized early on:

> If, for example, a cameraman, in giving a teleview of an election meeting, deliberately picked out for close-ups of the audience the faces of the disgruntled and the objecting and the bored, he might ... give a bias to the teleview. And this would be more dangerous in television than in, say, pictures in a newspaper since television feels like seeing for ourselves and therefore more like the truth than anything seen in a newspaper or a cinema film.[31]

This was precisely the argument employed 35 years later when TV images of the 1984–5 miners' strike were condemned for portraying a one-sided picture of violent strikers because cameras were positioned behind police lines. Moreover, as the Glasgow Media Group subsequently demonstrated, partial images of picture-dominated television journalism can have a long-lasting impact on those exposed to it. The abiding memory for those not immersed in that conflict was of daily and violent confrontations involving running battles, baton-wielding police and stone-throwing miners'.[32] In fact, the vast majority of pickets were peaceful and uneventful, some even friendly and cooperative, but the cameras were not there and quiet conversations were not newsworthy. The partial reality conveyed by the television cameras created a popular and long-lasting misunderstanding of events, precisely the problem identified in the earliest days of television journalism.

It also became apparent that the presence of cameras would materially affect behaviour in the political sphere. While television ostensibly could serve democracy through coverage of party conferences and political activism, it soon became clear that electorates did not look kindly on live images of party dissent even if they were an honest representation of political reality or, indeed, evidence of a vibrant political culture. Rather, such images were interpreted as evidence of poor discipline and weak leadership, which created an electorally damaging impression. And so in Britain – as in the United States and democracies around the world – political managers began to manipulate and orchestrate the images available for broadcasters.

Gradually, the presence of cameras created a new political reality: one of acclamation, self-confidence, consensus and glorification of political leaders. The back-stabbing, ferocious argument and internal conflict was gradually replaced by televised theatre – events specifically created or meticulously stage-managed for the television cameras. Thus, Daniel Boorstin wrote in 1961 of the 'pseudo-event' which was being 'planted primarily ... for the immediate purpose of being reported or reproduced. Therefore, its occurrence is arranged for the convenience of the reporting or reproducing media. Its success is measured by how widely it is reported'.[33] Although Boorstin cited Roosevelt as 'the first modern master' of the pseudo-event, even before the arrival of television cameras, it was for him the famous Nixon-Kennedy televised presidential debates of 1960 that epitomized the televisual artefact. In the glare of the television cameras, the substantive political issues of the day were subsumed beneath the youthful elegance of Kennedy and the contrast with Nixon's visible perspiration and 'five o'clock shadow'. Famously, post-debate polls showed that radio listeners believed Nixon had won the debate, while television viewers gave it to Kennedy.

While television journalists over the next 20 years began to learn techniques for overcoming this manufactured 'production' of politics for the television screen, the battlefields of Suez, Korea and Vietnam during the 1950s and 1960s were to pose precisely the opposite conundrum: how to convey scenes which were uncontrived, raw and entirely representative but were so gruesome or graphic that no responsible broadcaster could beam them directly into people's living rooms. The problem of what might constitute acceptable boundaries in televised coverage of war, tragedy or disaster has been debated at great length since the arrival of television cameras potentially allowed the public screening of real death or injury, which the vast majority would never before have witnessed (and would certainly not wish their children to see). While institutional and regulatory expectations militated against conveying explicit images to television screens, some argued that such self-censorship on grounds of taste and sensitivity failed to convey the harsh reality that might in turn have had an immediate and adverse impact on public opinion. These omissions are not only relevant to war coverage: whether it be destitution in South America, famine in Africa, brutal murder in Indonesia or people throwing themselves off the burning towers of the World Trade Center, the reluctance to show reality in all its gory awfulness has been as important an influence on television journalism as its antithesis – creating a cleansed, antiseptic reality.

The BBC's institutional response

All these issues were being recognized, in different ways, as problems that moving pictures posed for the conduct of journalism, and the BBC worried about the impact on its sacrosanct news values. Led by Sir William Haley, a conservative Director General steeped in radio values, it rejected any accommodation to the new medium in favour of a radio news summary relayed from Broadcasting House and accompanied in vision by a clock. Haley's approach was endorsed by the man who took over control of a unified News Division in 1948, a dour New Zealander called Tahu Hole who 'believed strongly not only in "objectivity" but in consistency: the BBC's news services must not speak with different voices'.[34] The result was an institutional straitjacket which squeezed the life out of any sense of journalistic enterprise and compounded the delays in launching a Television News service.

One of the issues which concentrated the minds of these committed traditionalists was the idea of an on-screen presenter. The very notion of having a newsreader in vision was anathema because it would by definition entail a personalization that might undermine the strict canon of impartiality: a disembodied voice cannot impart meaning, but a visible newsreader will have expressions and body language that would detract from the purely anonymous delivery of a statement of facts. From the perspective of the twenty-first century, this may seem bizarre and endearingly quaint, but it is not completely stupid. It is impossible to see a face on television without thinking about the individual and the personality – let alone the colour of the tie or the state of visible inebriation. Television newsreaders quickly established themselves as 'personalities' whose marital status, family lives and private endeavours were – and still are – treated as legitimate material for tabloid gossip columns. And however much they may seek to distance their public persona from any personal or political opinion, it is at least a legitimate argument that an on-screen personality is incompatible with strict adherence to an impartiality doctrine.

While the news purists therefore maintained the cloak of anonymity for presenters of news bulletins, more adventurous spirits at the BBC found other outlets for developing more covert forms of television journalism. In particular Norman Collins, appointed Controller of Television in June 1947, was determined to make television more topical. He introduced 'Foreign Correspondent' in April 1949, featuring regular reporting on foreign affairs, as well as televised reporting of the general election results in February 1950. Given that there were no trained television reporters, 'Foreign Correspondent' relied on a combination of newsreel techniques (silent film with voiced-over commentary) and reporters reading their commentaries live in the studio. The first series were 'picture portraits' of post-war life in some European capitals, the second more overtly political and looking at the prospects for European integration. It was basic and crude, but it was the forerunner of the BBC's stable of current affairs programmes: 'Tonight'; '24 Hours'; and 'Panorama'.

This was followed, under the aegis of Wyndham Goldie, by 'International Commentary' in November 1950. Both programmes, in the words of Paddy Scannell, 'avowedly experimental and both seminal for the development of the

BBC-style current affairs programme'.[35] Foreign affairs was a 'safe' area for a public broadcaster that still shied away from tackling anything contentious. Britain was still one of the great powers, its foreign policy did not divide the political parties and the world beyond Britain was still something of an unknown quantity to the great majority of British people. To offer a 'window on the world' – as 'Panorama' was subtitled – was an important element of public service journalism in the days before package holidays, cheap flights, satellite television and instant email to the other side of the world. Meanwhile, coverage of domestic politics was left to television appearances by politicians and print journalists. A programme called 'In the News' started in August 1950, featuring four politicians meticulously chosen to represent the main political parties. And in 'Press Conference', introduced in 1952, politicians were interrogated by a panel of print journalists who had no professional equivalents in broadcasting. In other words, the formal conduct of political news on television was conducted by the politicians with the BBC acting as referee and gatekeeper.

Another route to covering contemporary issues was, as Scannell has shown, through television documentary. This was partly achieved through drama-documentaries that covered social issues such as delinquency, marriage, old age, prostitution, strikes, women at work or legal aid. More significantly, it was achieved through a programme, which began in September 1952 called 'Special Enquiry', that attempted to cover issues of great national importance through local stories. According to the Radio Times, 'Special Enquiry', 'was aiming to forge a new style of television journalism, something peculiar to the medium of television, but as honest and incisive as British journalism at its best'.[36] The inspiration for this very new genre of television was a combination of the populist photojournalism of Picture Post and the studio presenter/commentator format of 'See It Now', which had proved so popular and influential for CBS in the United States.[37] This format allowed the BBC to develop a form of almost covert journalism that carefully avoided explicit politicization but actually dealt with issues that lie at the heart of politics. It was a form of journalism that could avoid controversy partly because – unlike, say, in the 1980s – there was a broad political consensus about the problems of post-war Britain, and partly because politicians were being given their own overtly balanced platform from which to canvass political solutions.

These somewhat more populist approaches to television journalism were assisted by the gradual development of newsreel techniques emanating from the BBC's Film (rather than News) Department. Encouraged by a new Director General, Sir Ian Jacob, and more importantly the imminent arrival of a competitive television service in 1955, a new series entitled 'News and Newsreel' started on 5 July 1954. It was an uncomfortable compromise between the Film and News divisions and their respective – and very different – takes on virtually every aspect of content and presentation. Wyndham Goldie's view was that 'neither Tahu Hole nor any of his staff had the faintest idea of how to present news in visual terms' and that they actually despised the television medium. She famously described the long and ongoing battle between the two departments as 'like a battle between a school of whales and a herd of elephants,' which nevertheless contained within it a war of principles about the nature of television, the nature of news and the nature of the BBC.[38] The BBC surely had to maintain its reputation for authoritative 'hard' news, but should the values of the television variant be subordinated to the entertainment needs of the medium, or should it maintain the highest journalistic standards even at the expense of the programme's intrinsic attraction?

BBC journalism after the 14-day rule

To some extent, proper coverage of 'hard' politics was severely constrained anyway by a rule that forbade the BBC from making reference to any issue that was to be discussed in Parliament over the following fortnight. With hindsight, this '14-day' ruling seems bizarre but it speaks volumes about the suspicion with which politicians throughout the developed world viewed this developing medium and the jealousy with which they guarded their own power. A more common political response within Europe was to chain the public broadcaster more closely to the government of the day. In the United Kingdom, the response was more subtle: respect the BBC's carefully nurtured independence, but circumscribe the scope of its political reporting. In the immediate aftermath of the war, senior politicians were strongly opposed to allowing the BBC to engage in any political broadcasting, however impartially, beyond official broadcasts by government and opposition. Arguably, this was a prescient – if essentially anti-democratic – anxiety about the ultimate power of the legislature seeping away under the scrutiny of unelected commentators. Aware that the press barons were already exploiting their command of the printed word to mount a challenge to the legislators, MPs were extremely reluctant to surrender in addition their control of the broadcast medium. Because there was a real possibility of a complete ban on coverage of any domestic politics, the BBC accepted terms written into an aide-memoire in 1947, which stated that there were to be no BBC broadcasts 'on any question while it is the subject in either House' beyond the straight reporting of Parliamentary proceedings.[39] This was later clarified to cover discussion 'on any issues for a period of a fortnight before they are debated in either house'.

The BBC consistently argued that the restriction should be abolished, but in the immediate post-war period was in no position to stand up to the united front of Parliament. As late as 1953, Winston Churchill was arguing in a parliamentary debate that, 'it would be shocking to have debates in this House forestalled, time after time, by expressions of opinion by persons who had not the status or responsibility of MPs'.[40] Churchill's case was complicated by the prior existence of an unrestrained press; indeed, nearly 25 years earlier Churchill's predecessor, Stanley Baldwin, had famously borrowed the words of his cousin Rudyard Kipling to rail against the newspaper proprietors' 'power without responsibility – the prerogative of the harlot throughout the ages'. Even so, there was a legitimate case that television was different. Baldwin's fury with Northcliffe, proprietor of the *Daily Mail*, and Beaverbrook, proprietor of the *Daily Express*, was aimed at the 'direct falsehood, misrepresentation, half-truths' that he believed characterized their newspapers' campaign to promote Empire Free Trade, but there had been other newspapers that expressed equally strong opinions in the opposite direction. Television was becoming more widespread; it was already enjoined to be impartial and likely to be more trusted; and it was in people's living rooms. Moreover, it was immediate and by necessity selective: there would only be room to cover a given number of issues, which would be chosen by the broadcaster. MPs, said the party leaders, would become pressurized by the weight of publicity being given to issues being prioritized by an unelected, unaccountable body. It was neither surprising nor illogical that government and opposition leaders remained firmly opposed to what – as it turned out – was very accurately perceived as a threat to their own power and influence.

By the mid 1950s, however, the balance of power was shifting. It was becoming increasingly anomalous that a publicly funded media organization was prevented from disseminating any information about issues of immediate political relevance.[41] Most important of all, preparations were already in train for a rival commercial (or 'independent') broadcaster with its own news provision: any informal arrangement for restricting political news would have to apply equally to the new channel, and would therefore surely have to be formalized. So, by 1955, the BBC felt sufficiently emboldened to make it clear that it was no longer prepared to follow a voluntary behind-the-scenes vow of silence. The government flexed its muscles by making the 14-day rule both official and public but was roundly condemned by the press as imposing an unnecessary restraint on free speech. The rule was ultimately doomed by a combustible combination of domestic politics and a wholesale transformation of the television industry. The Suez crisis of 1956 – in which television news was forced for the most part to stay eerily silent – and the initiation of the BBC's long-awaited competitor ensured that the 14-day directive lasted little more than a year.

Suez and BBC independence

In the folklore of British political television, it was the BBC's battle with the government over Suez in 1956 that is regarded as the watershed. It certainly represented a turning point in cementing the BBC's ability to resist government pressure, at least at times when Parliament did actually represent the differences of opinion that existed throughout the country. With the country deeply divided over the government's decision to invade Egypt after President Nasser had taken control of the Suez Canal, there had been mounting tension between the government and the BBC in the run-up to the invasion. The BBC Chairman, Lord Cadogan, was an old friend and former colleague of the Prime Minister, Anthony Eden, and not unsympathetic to his foreign policy aims. The Governors agreed at a meeting in September 1956 that 'the BBC should do nothing to underline the existence of party division and disunity at a time of crisis,' which sounded suspiciously like an injunction to senior editors not to cover faithfully the division of parliamentary opinion.[42]

By this time, however, the ethos of independent journalism had become more internalized amongst the BBC hierarchy, and it continued to report both sides of the increasingly bitter debate. Even a threat from Eden's Press Officer that the Prime Minister's patience was running out, and that he 'had instructed the Lord Chancellor … to prepare an instrument which would take over the BBC altogether and subject it wholly to the will of the Government,' was to no avail.[43] When Eden insisted on speaking to the nation on the eve of the invasion on 3 November to present himself as a Churchillian leader in the nation's hour of need, opposition leader Hugh Gaitskell demanded and was granted the right of reply – which he exploited to great effect the following night. The BBC Governors did not intervene.

In the event, the political and diplomatic fallout from Suez cost Eden his health and his job, and just two months later he resigned, leaving the BBC intact and its journalistic reputation enhanced. The threat to its journalistic integrity was certainly real, but so was the sense of editorial resistance from within. Writing about the events 12 years later, Harman Grisewood, who had been the Director General's chief assistant, was in no doubt about the importance of that moment: 'If Eden had had his way, it would, in my view, have been the end of the Corporation as it had been known up till then. I believe most of the senior people would have resigned rather than try to carry out orders of suppression.'[44] As we shall see, this row presaged a similar outcry in 1986 when BBC Governors did attempt to suppress a programme that the government had condemned.

Conclusion

This was the end of an austere decade for television journalism characterized, in the words of Jonathan Dimbleby, by 'a doctrine of broadcasting which [terrorized] a young, enthusiastic and energetic News Room into petrified immobility [and] which was to be remembered with great bitterness by nearly all those who lived through it'.[45] Nevertheless, in those first 30 years of the BBC and first ten years of soulless television journalism, it is extraordinary how many of the potential problems and crises of modern-day television journalism around the world were anticipated. The overbearing restrictions imposed internally by senior managers and externally by parliamentary diktat may now seem harsh and difficult to comprehend, but they were rooted in legitimate anxieties about how journalism might evolve within the television medium. The selective nature of camera images; the importance of decisions made by newsroom editors; the ability of television to set political agendas; the problem of trying to sustain a journalistic culture of impartiality; the slide towards entertainment-led bulletins; the dominance of picture-led stories; the need for sensitivity when covering tragedy or violence in such an immediate and powerful medium; the drive, within the BBC, to avoid the sensationalism and inaccuracy associated with tabloid journalism; the vulnerability of a publicly funded broadcaster to covert political pressure; and the danger of television undermining the sovereignty of Parliament – all have been criticisms levelled at contemporary practices of television journalism, and all continue to represent major challenges for the future.

Suez was a turning point for securing a BBC that had learned how to withstand government attempts at intimidation even if, at times, there were more subtle accommodations. In terms of hard-nosed political journalism and a reputation for accuracy and trust, the events of late 1956 were profound. But in terms of the more far-reaching impact on approaches to and definitions of television journalism over the next 40 years, there had been a much more significant development the year before Suez. On 22 September 1955, the BBC faced competition for the first time, when commercial television began transmitting in the London area and included the very first television news not transmitted by the BBC. Independent Television News (ITN) was created as a separate but integral part of the new commercial channel, Independent Television (ITV), and changed the face of British television journalism forever.

2 Competition and Commercialism: The Early Days

Ending the BBC monopoly on news

The battle to create a commercial television channel had been prolonged, tortuous and bruising. It resulted in a classically British compromise that attempted to combine the entrepreneurial dynamism being promoted by free-market liberals with the paternalism of those concerned about the impact of commercialism on standards. With hindsight, the subsequent story of television journalism suggests that both were right: without a modernizing kick up the rear of Broadcasting House by an eager competitor, the BBC might have taken a great deal longer to discard the dinner jackets, allow newsreaders in vision and inject a little more life into its reporting. Equally, the stark reality of outright commercialism has, as we shall see, led to a noticeable decline in the more expensive forms of television journalism as well as the marginalization of current affairs from commercial television schedules. But the highly regulated structure of commercial television which emerged in the United Kingdom in the 1950s provided a platform for an independent, well-funded television news service that achieved a worldwide reputation for quality and rigour, and which was – well into the twenty-first century – a highly effective competitor to the BBC as well as a stark reminder to the rest of the world of what effective television regulation could achieve. For British television journalism, as for British television, regulated commercial television offered the perfect combination of resources, stability and protection of professional standards. But only after a fight.

It started with the Beveridge Report, published in January 1951, which contained some interesting reflections on what it described as 'Controversial Broadcasting'. While anxious that long-standing impartiality requirements should be extended from the BBC to any other broadcasters, Beveridge was clear about the advantages of broadcasting news in sound and vision: 'Generally, we should like to see broadcasting used more and more as a means of assisting the democracy to understand the issues upon which it is required to decide at elections.'[1] A short section outlined the similarities between TV and sound, quoting the rather colourful words of BBC Director General Sir William Haley, who looked forward to a time:

> When it is possible every evening for every citizen in this country not only to hear but to see what has been happening in the world that day; when the great events of nations and in the international field can be remotely 'attended' by the inhabitants of almost every town and village; when the colour, the excitement, the variety, and the worth-whileness of everyday life can be communicated to the richest, the poorest, the loneliest and the most gregarious; when harmony, design and grace can be visually as well as audibly taken into every home …[2]

All of this would 'have the capacity to make for a broader vision and a fuller life'.

This wonderfully idealized vision of the potential of television news – with barely a nod in the direction of its inherent weaknesses or capacity for distortion – was in stark contrast to the conclusions of four committee members after their reconnaissance visit to the United States. One member, Lord Elgin, reported that 'the breakneck speed of the American service is most evident. Both in the ordinary news bulletins … and in the set pieces of news commentary, such as that delivered by Mr Utley over the Television service, there is running through the whole delivery the sense of extreme urgency'. A recognizable trait of American news in the twenty-first century – and the contrast in cultural norms between the United States and Europe – was clearly well advanced from the very beginning.

Although Beveridge recommended preserving the BBC monopoly, it was a minority report from the committee dissident Selwyn Lloyd that proved decisive after a change of government in October the same year. As the new Conservative government initiated a debate over the precise mechanisms for running a new commercial channel, a number of conflicting demands and anxieties determined the eventual outcome of the new proposals. One driving force for change was a conviction amongst many members of the new government and its MPs that the BBC was a hotbed of leftist revolution – a belief strengthened by successive defeats to Labour in the 1945 and 1950 general elections which Churchill, as leader of the Conservative Party, could scarcely believe. According to Grace Wyndham Goldie, 'Many Conservatives were convinced that the BBC had fomented a radical attitude in political matters and that, as an organisation, it was biased against Conservatism. Winston Churchill himself believed that the BBC was infiltrated by communists.'[3] Such accusations of bias became an almost obsessional preoccupation (as it has been for successive governments in the UK and in other countries in respect of their own public broadcasters) and the prospect of an alternative source of broadcast news was warmly welcomed.

This was tempered by severe reservations that traditional British standards of good taste would plummet once advertising was allowed. These fears were not allayed when news came back from the United States that one American network's coverage of the Coronation had been interrupted by a commercial featuring a chimpanzee called J. Fred Muggs. Here was proof, argued the critics, that a commercially funded channel would need a firm regulator with real power to control the inevitable excesses of commercialization. At the same time, many Labour MPs were distrustful of the right-wing bias that private enterprise might bring to coverage of politics. They, too, needed reassurance that there would be a firm hand on the non-partisan tiller. Their fears were exacerbated when two of the first three consortia to be awarded contracts featured newspaper groups with long-standing Conservative affiliations.

The new regulatory philosophy – birth of ITN and the ITA

In order to resolve all these tensions and political anxieties, the Television Bill published in March 1954 advanced the idea of an Independent Television Authority (ITA), a name with sufficient gravitas to match that of the BBC's 'Corporation' and with sufficient powers to maintain appropriate standards of quality: that programmes were predominantly British, that they did not offend against good taste and that news observed the same rules of accuracy and 'due impartiality' that had been religiously followed by the BBC. In the parliamentary debate that followed, the suggestion that the ITA might be given responsibility for news was rejected by the government, but one Conservative backbencher suggested a formula which turned out to be uncannily prescient: 'I was thinking that some of the programme contractors might have that obligation put upon them that they should get together and form a joint agency for the presentation of news.'[4]

Implicit in the furious debates around the beginnings of commercial television in Britain was a consensus shared by the great majority, whether fervent supporters or bitter opponents, that the unfettered free market would not deliver either the quality or range of output which Parliament required, and that only a rigorous and properly functioning system of regulatory oversight would ensure the maintenance of high standards as well as diversity of programming. It is a regulatory philosophy that has been passed down from the ITA to its three successors, the Independent Broadcasting Authority (IBA), the Independent Television Commission (ITC) and the Office of Communications (Ofcom). In each case, the provision of high quality, accessible and well-resourced television news has been at the forefront of some of the major regulatory battles. But it was the first of those battles, within the first

12 months of its coming into being, that most fiercely tested the resolve of the first television regulator and established an important precedent.

Within three months of the Television Act receiving Royal Assent in July 1954, the ITA had offered contracts to four programme contractors for the first three regions (London, Midlands and Northern). Included in the contracts was a proviso that the ITA was reserving 'the news and newsreel period' for a separate company. The four successful companies charged with launching commercial television in the United Kingdom were Associated-Rediffusion; Associated Television (ATV); Associated British Corporation (ABC), replacing a contractor which withdrew; and Granada Television. They made it clear that they wanted to maintain responsibility for a news company, while accepting some kind of oversight from the ITA. In January 1955, the ITA Chairman was asked to approve an agreed plan in which the four programme companies would create a specialist subsidiary whose governing board would have eight members, two from each company. The memo went on:

> The working head of the organisation – that is to say, the editor-in-chief – will be appointed only after consultation with the Authority and with its prior approval. If this approval is withdrawn, the appointment will lapse, and a new editor be found. The Authority will have the right to appoint a senior adviser to the company. I am given to understand that his advice would be welcome over the whole range of the news problem, but of course his real function will be to watch the operation of the news through the eyes of the Act.[5]

In practice, that advisory role was deemed to be so important that it was the Director General of the ITA himself who attended those meetings.[6] So it was that Independent Television News Ltd (ITN) became incorporated on 4 May 1955, not just with an editor who had to be approved by the regulator, but with a constant regulatory presence at all meetings of its board. This may not have been the kind of laissez-faire free-market approach to commercially funded television that most libertarian Conservatives had been demanding, but it provided some solace to those on the left who were deeply fearful that a business-run news channel would inevitably become the author of a right-wing, advertiser-dominated television journalism.

It also meant that the structures were in place to ensure that the journalism of impartiality which had become a hallmark of the BBC since its inception was transferred seamlessly to its competitor, and therefore established a journalistic tradition which was no longer applicable to an institution (the BBC) but to a medium (television). With the Television Act and the birth of the ITA, television journalism became entrenched as a very different beast from its committed, partisan, opinionated newspaper equivalent. That it survived at all as an integral and vibrant part of British television at the heart of peak-time commercial schedules was in no small measure due to a battle fought and won by the ITA in the first 12 months. Like many of the regulatory rows to follow, this was not about the nature of the journalistic culture, nor about allegations of bias or impropriety. It was purely and simply about money.

The ITA goes into battle

It was a difficult start-up time for the new ITV companies as advertisers bided their time and the wider post-war economy struggled. The companies were looking for every conceivable way of saving money, and news was a double bind: not only did it involve an estimated expenditure of £400,000 for the first year, but there was the opportunity cost of news replacing a potentially high-rating programme that would maximize advertising revenue. The problem was exacerbated by the late arrival of ABC, which had not been involved in earlier discussions and went decidedly cold on the financial commitment to news that was being demanded. In Autumn 1955, its Chairman wrote to the ITA expressing the company's dismay at the 'heavy, indeed reckless capital expenditure which is contemplated', and arguing that 'the weekly running costs are of an unwarrantably high order'. Having argued that the structure should be overhauled to reduce expenditure and improve quality (a contradiction that has run through virtually every plea to regulators since), it concluded that the company was: 'disinclined to participate in the News Company, as at present constituted. We believe we could prepare our own news items at much smaller cost and with much greater efficiency.'[7]

Here was a challenge, from the very outset, to one of the underlying principles of the new regulatory regime. Not only would such a declaration of independence breach one of the contractual covenants on which commercial television was being established, but such a fragmented approach to news would inevitably leave it both impoverished and much more difficult to police in terms of the obligations of the Television Act. In response, the ITA's Director General Sir Robert Fraser first reminded ABC of its explicit agreement to join the news company and the assurances it had given both about financial commitment and duration of bulletins: two per day, each of eight-and-a-half minutes with the second followed by a five-minute newsreel.[8] He followed this up with a statement of regulatory intent which offers a fascinating insight to the philosophy of television journalism being promoted by the ITA. On 24 November 1955, Fraser wrote:

I have always felt that television must accept, and happily, a great responsibility in the field of public affairs, and particularly the responsibility of giving people each day a lively account of the significant events of the world in which they live. It should, in brief, give the news. More than this, it should present the news in such a way that it possesses what my chairman once called 'democratic value'. That is to say, the news should not consist of a featureless recitation, but be told or shown to the viewers in such a way as to be enlightening. If that is to happen, not only must the news programmes rest upon these principles, but they must be allowed whatever length and position in the programmes are necessary to let them do this democratic job.[9]

In fact, decisions had already been taken by the ITN Board to reduce the early bulletin from 15 to 7 minutes and put back the later bulletin from 10 p.m. to 10.45. Whatever the grand democratic ideals of the regulator, hard-headed business decisions dictated a more urgent and pragmatic response. This provided the first test of regulatory mettle, to which the ITA responded with what became a standard regulatory tactic: compromise. Fraser laid down three propositions to the ITV companies: that all contractors would include adequate national news, supplied by ITN; that it interpreted 'adequate' to be at least 20 minutes per day; and that such news must include 'some element of film', which would necessarily be more expensive. While swallowing the bitter pill of time and film, the companies exploited the budgetary discretion that was left to them, and early in the New Year proposed slashing their annual expenditure on news from £350,000 to £200,000.

At this point the first editor-in-chief of ITN, Aidan Crawley, frustrated by what he saw as the supine position of the ITA in the face of the contractors' manifest lack of commitment, tendered his resignation. The ITN Board was, he said, 'determined not only to limit the scope of the News Company's operations to the narrowest conception of news, but to reduce the cost of such news to the barest minimum'.[10] According to his successor, Crawley's resignation provoked 'uproar in the press, questions in Parliament and demands that the ITA should take over ITN and produce the news itself'.[11] Dramatically, the ITA Chairman agreed to be interviewed on that evening's ITN news bulletin by one of the news company's new and ambitious newscasters, Robin Day. Day records that he asked Clark whether light entertainment companies were the right kind of people to provide news and how he reacted to press criticism that the ITA was being 'weak-kneed' in exercising its control over ITV. Clark replied that the ITA's policy from the start had been that news should be one of the principal features of the programme schedule and that, 'We intend to uphold that.'[12]

The ITA's problem, prefiguring identical dilemmas for succeeding regulators both in the United Kingdom and where similar resource-intensive obligations were imposed on commercial operations elsewhere, was the sense of impending financial crisis which was afflicting ITV. Although it created an important precedent for upholding commercial television's mandatory news operation, the compromise on investment still left some wondering whether the regulator had already become 'captive'. It did, however, solve the immediate crisis of commitment. ABC finally committed itself to ITN in March 1956, and ITV began the uphill struggle for profitability and recognition as a serious purveyor of news. As Sendall wrote in summing up this seminal episode: 'If the Authority's effort at self-assertion was not spectacularly successful, it could at least feel that it had shielded ITN from a real risk of child suffocation'.[13] The new news entity had survived to challenge the status quo.

A different news culture

That survival proved fundamental to initiating change in the practice of television journalism at the very moment that national and international events were to establish the dominance of television as a news medium. Day's robust style of interviewing, which he brought to his interview with Clark and which became his established trademark over a broadcasting career spanning four decades, was revolutionary for a medium that had inherited the BBC's deferential approach to public affairs. Ministers had not been interrogated, they were simply invited to bestow their views on a waiting audience. ITN was determined to change this stuffy, establishment approach to television news, and its arrival helped to shake BBC journalism out of its dusty complacency.

Another ITN innovation was to replace the anonymous (and unseen) newsreader with a 'newscaster' who was not only in full view but had a name and a personality. Despite becoming familiar household names, BBC wartime newsreaders had retreated to their pre-war anonymity as soon as the war ended. Geoffrey Cox, who became the new and highly successful editor-in-chief of ITN, wrote later that this dispassionate method of conveying the news was ideally suited to radio, especially on the high-minded Reithian BBC:

> The technique conveyed a subtle sense that the bulletins were the work of the high priests of a sacred order devoted to assessing, analysing and then finally determining The News, which was then brought forth from the inner recesses of the temple to be proclaimed in its purest form, unsullied on the way by contact with vulgar minds. Even if one were to regard it as a gimmick, it was a highly effective gimmick.[14]

But it was not appropriate for a more populist broadcaster in the modern era, and ITN were happy to follow the established American tradition of recognizable newsreaders who would actively participate in the process of gathering and editing as well as presenting the news. The effect on the BBC was immediate: 18 days before ITN made its television debut on 22 September 1955, the BBC decided to place their newsreaders in front of the cameras.

Day himself was one of a new breed of journalists that first Crawley and then Cox sought out to bring a different style and more vitality into television news. A framework had now been laid down – in terms of impartiality, structure, transmission times and commitment – which still allowed plenty of flexibility in interpreting precisely how this new journalism would operate. And it was not to be a carbon copy of the BBC, but somewhere equivalent to the midmarket newspapers. Day described Crawley's requirements as a style which combined 'the responsibility of the *Manchester Guardian* and the vigour of the *Daily Express*'.[15] Cox also described ITN's news values as being pitched between the quality and the popular press, with the goal of 'carrying the main stories which made the front page of the *Daily Telegraph* and the back page of the *Daily Mirror*'. In other words, he wanted the hard news of the front pages, but also all the other ingredients of a successful newspaper: sport, show business, fashion, feature pages, crime and human interest stories. Film stars were treated as news, in an era when cinema going was still the primary form of entertainment. And in describing the drama and excitement of watching the finished product being aired, Cox himself was well aware of the fundamentally different approach he was nurturing: 'For the moment we were no longer just in journalism. We were in show business, as dependent for the success of our production as is any playwright or any theatrical producer.'[16]

Along with Day came Christopher Chataway, familiar to viewers as the current 5,000 metre world-record holder, who took pole newscaster position and introduced the very first bulletin on 22 September 1955. Chataway resigned within a year, telling Cox that he feared viewers would quickly tire of seeing the same face on their screens every day. It was not long before channels on both side of the Atlantic came to realize that the 'cult of the newscaster' was to become a significant feature of television journalism and eventually to distort its financing. Another early recruit was Lynne Reid Banks, later to acquire fame as a novelist but then a repertory actress and magazine journalist. She described how, 'Aidan [Crawley] wanted us to be more populist than the BBC, to be noticed, to be more flexible, more public-friendly, so we pioneered vox-pops. People had never seen the like of it before.'[17]

The arrival of the on-screen personality did present a dilemma of which Cox was very aware, given the strict requirement for impartiality. On the one hand, as an experienced newspaperman, he was delighted with what he saw as a safeguard against potential pressure from government and against the 'views and whims' of the programme contractors who owned ITN. He saw the impartiality requirements as liberation for television news editors from the kinds of proprietorial influences that were widespread in Fleet Street, giving them the freedom to create something new in popular journalism. On the other hand, how could you ensure that the separation of news and comment – whose lines were never completely separated in print – were not blurred? This had not been a problem for the BBC where the news culture had been almost religiously impersonal, but within a style which was deliberately designed to humanize and personalize the news, it was a potential issue. It meant, in Cox's words, 'building up our own case law in the new visual journalism'.[18] The importance of the live presenter was exaggerated by what was still a very crude technology of delivery. The vast majority of film being shot was still silent, voiced-over after the event in the style of cinema newsreels. The trick was to avoid the sensationalist, entertainment-based approach of the newsreels and to combine authenticity with a proper sense of journalistic perspective.

This new style, faithful to core journalistic standards of accuracy while attempting to involve audiences rather than bestow news upon them, served ITN well as it started to find its feet through the big news stories of 1956 and 1957: first the Suez crisis, then the Soviet crushing of dissident unrest in Hungary, then the resignation of Anthony Eden as Prime Minister and his succession by Harold Macmillan. On TV coverage of this domestic political drama, the *Observer* wrote that 'ITN with deft flashbacks and live interviews with bystanders, established their usual lead over the BBC's News Department'. The *Sunday Times* agreed, adding caustically that 'News treatment, in fact, is almost the only aspect of ITV worth watching. Geoffrey Cox's team beat the BBC on the big story'.[19] Despite its shoestring budget, out of which it had to finance its own studio, equipment, premises, reporters and management, and despite owners who were profoundly anxious about survival and would rather fill the news time with more lucrative light entertainment, ITN had not only pioneered a new brand of television journalism but had become the one area of the new commercial service to receive critical as well as popular acclaim. Wyndham Goldie described it as 'the most effective of all the challenges which the competitive system offered the BBC'.[20] Late in 1956, the BBC responded again by naming their newsreaders, with Robert Dougall and Richard Baker spearheading a specialist television team.

This critical success was reinforced six years later by the next committee set up to examine the state of broadcasting, led by Sir Harry Pilkington. Established in response to widespread concerns about commercial television's 'retreat from culture', and to make recommendations about the next stage of television expansion, Pilkington pilloried much of ITV's output and shared the conclusion of the ITA's Chairman that, 'more control will be needed to prevent a Gadarene descent'.[21] In keeping with the high-minded tone of much of the report, it warned against 'the obvious temptation to select an item for showing simply because it is visually exciting or even because film of it is available,' and drew attention to the need to 'guard against the risk that the art of television presentation may distort the significance of news items'. Having issued its warnings, the Pilkington Report was happy to conclude that television news was an area where competition had worked well and now offered two services of high quality but different in style and approach. It also endorsed Geoffrey Cox's proposals for an extended role for ITN in current affairs, arguing that it would be 'regrettable if a service widely regarded as one of independent television's best achievements did not continue to develop and improve'.[22]

Current affairs on commercial television – ITV stakes its claim

Apart from the perceived success story of ITN, there was another reason why Pilkington wanted to encourage the news company to move into current affairs: it was as dismissive of the ITV companies' approach to 'information' or factual programming as the rest of its schedule. But the ITV companies had started to experiment with their own forms of television journalism and were certainly not disposed to give up any more of their airtime to ITN. Moreover, they were supported by Sir Robert Fraser at the ITA who regarded news feature and documentary programmes as 'the conscience of the programme companies' and told Geoffrey Cox: 'If these were taken away from the companies and given to ITN, the companies would be only entertainment makers, entirely given over to the showbiz mind.'[23] Thus, on both ITV and BBC, there developed parallel systems: one department or organization responsible for collecting and reporting the news (ITN versus BBC News) and another department or organization devoted to analysing, interpreting, exploring or investigating it (ITV contractors versus BBC Current Affairs and Documentary Departments, based in different studios at Lime Grove). Fraser's clear-sighted approach was vindicated within a few years: a number of ITV contractors started to invest in current affairs, and two programmes, in particular, carved out for themselves not just distinctive approaches to television journalism but a journalistic legacy for ITV which lasted for decades.

In January 1956, the London weekday contractor Associated-Rediffusion launched 'This Week', which tried from the outset to bridge the gap between the serious and the entertaining. Its entertainment roots were contained in the fairly desperate urgency of ITV contractors in the first year to avoid financial ruin, and probably owed something to Associated-Rediffusion's first Controller of Programmes Roland Gillett's blunt analysis of the problem: 'Let's face it once and for all. The public likes girls, wrestling, bright musicals, quiz shows and real-life drama. We gave them the Halle Orchestra, Foreign Press Club, floodlit football and visits to the local fire station. Well, we've learned. From now on, what the public wants, it's going to get.'[24]

He recruited Caryl Doncaster as the first producer of 'This Week', who described her brief as creating 'a programme of stories behind the news world-wide … It won't be all political. There will be a bit of everything in it, including humour and glamour. It won't be highbrow because we want a wide audience'.[25] In the event, and driven in particular by the parlous state of the new contractors' finances, there was more glamour than serious reflection within a magazine format that ran four to six items in each weekly programme and covered 300 items in its first 50 weeks. One history of the programme described its early days as '"tabloid television" before the label became a pejorative one', though it did find room for interviews with President Nasser of Egypt and with Prime Minister Harold Macmillan. It also offered an early training ground for young reporters, and its editor Peter Hunt left his mark by choosing the powerful and evocative Karelia march as the title music which survived every change of format.[26]

It suffered, however, from a surfeit of triviality and from the growing concern pre-Pilkington – especially as ITV company profits started to mount – that the emphasis on light entertainment had gone too far. The mood shifted, and so did the programme. In 1961, it was handed over to journalist Cyril Bennett and film director Peter Morley, who had already established a reputation for producing substantial documentaries. They abandoned the magazine format, started to cover one or at most two stories in each programme, and abandoned the light-hearted: 'Flippancy, humour and glamour were on the way out, together with celebrity interviews, film reviews and April Fool jokes.'[27] While in the United States, as we shall see, the forces of commercialism continued unabated, and while most of the rest of Europe had not ventured down the commercial route at all, the United Kingdom was reining in unbridled populism.

Meanwhile, a second programme had been started by the northern contractor, Granada, with a more serious purpose. It lasted only two years from 1958 to 1960, but was born of a different approach to factual programming and spawned the other long-standing current affairs series which helped to define ITV journalism in the twentieth century. Introduced as a regular half-hour news documentary series, 'Searchlight' specialized in investigating social issues such as homosexuality, sexual disease and the new contraceptive pill. Its more serious agenda was partly down to its producer, Tim Hewat, and partly to the corporate philosophy of its originating company.

Led by the Bernstein brothers, Sidney and Cecil, Granada's vision of commercial television was grander than just a frivolous entertainment medium that could turn a tidy profit. They were certainly motivated by money; but they also understood the cultural potential of a medium that had already demonstrated in the United States that it could be a powerful force for courageous journalism. According to Ray Fitzwalter, who spent most of his working life making current affairs programmes at Granada, 'Under the Bernsteins, Granada treated broadcasting as a moral and cultural imperative, not to be subordinated to the number of viewers, the dash for quick profits or the desire for a quiet life'.[28] While perhaps a slightly idealized view, there is no question that the journalism espoused by Granada owed as much to its institutional nonconformist culture as to any public interest responsibilities laid down by a paternalistic regulator.

After a break of two years, 'Searchlight' was succeeded in 1962 by 'World in Action', still under the direction of Hewat. The new programme introduced an investigative tradition to commercial journalism, which was to provoke, first, some serious clashes with po-faced regulators and, later, some very uncomfortable moments for the government. From the very beginning, it was prepared to challenge the ITA's carefully crafted and meticulously policed interpretation of impartiality by making programmes that clearly imparted a point of view. The disapproval that this engendered – and the inevitable clashes it eventually provoked – can still be seen in the somewhat jaundiced analysis of Bernard Sendall who, writing his history of ITV some 20 years later but Deputy Director General of the ITA at the time, could barely disguise his disdain:

> Neither in *Searchlight* nor in its more famous successor did Hewat make any bones about the fact that he was editorialising. He did not try to suppress evidence which disagreed with his own conclusions provided the latter emerged with unmistakeable clarity. He had no time for properly balanced discussions or debates and he took the view that it was a sufficient defence against the charge of partiality to say that all the partial statements made were perfectly accurate quotations.[29]

Somewhat grudgingly, Sendall goes on to acknowledge that, 'Whether or not they saw their objective clearly, Granada undoubtedly contrived to extend the frontiers of broadcasting about public affairs'. But the company also derived its journalistic imperative from a desire to counteract – from a distinctly northern perspective – a perceived Oxbridge and establishment condescension that still characterized much of Britain's emerging current affairs journalism. Sir Denis Foreman, appointed by the Bernsteins as managing director of Granada, said later of 'World in Action': 'The approach was anti-Dimbleby. What we were fed up with was the complacent, well-meaning, middle-class programmes, like *Panorama* and *This Week*, always following, on the whole, the middle of the road, comfortable, decent line.'[30] Apart from an attack on middle-class complacency, it was also an attack on the metropolitan bias of an essentially London-centric approach to news at the heart of much mainstream reporting. It demonstrated from the outset one of the intrinsic advantages of a regionally based ITV system that – despite its inherent inefficiency and recipe for constant infighting amongst the contractors – offered the nation different local and regional perspectives. As ITV gradually moved into a single conglomerate in the twenty-first century and consolidated its regional reporting, one of the great cultural and journalistic advantages of that early structure was squandered.

Between them, Associated-Rediffusion and Granada demonstrated from the outset that television was capable of different interpretations and different approaches to serious journalism outside straight news reporting. They drew their inspiration partly from their own organizational cultures, partly from their geographical and regional roots, partly from the established television traditions of impartiality and seriousness, partly from a regulatory environment that was attempting to reassert itself, and partly from the journalistic values of Fleet Street, both broadsheet and tabloid. While steeped to some extent in traditions established by the BBC, they also ensured that the BBC itself started to develop a current affairs tradition that mixed serious analysis with light-hearted banter.

Current affairs on the BBC

The first 'Panorama' aired in November 1953 but bore no resemblance to the current affairs programme which followed (and still continues). It started as a fortnightly arts and reviews programme along with interviews with 'People in the News' but was not a success and Grace Wyndham Goldie decided to relaunch it as a new programme that would be 'harder, more concerned with the world outside Britain and outside the confines of the studio'.[31] Now subtitled 'A Window on the World', Richard Dimbleby was brought in as anchor to reinforce the harder edge. As we have seen, this was also an opportunity for the more adventurous elements of BBC Television to counter the strangulating effect of Tahu Hole and his news department's inability to understand or exploit a visual news medium.

In fact, Dimbleby himself had already outlined his vision of a new kind of television journalism to the Head of the Film Department, Philip Dorte. Five years earlier, Dimbleby had written that he had in mind, 'the coverage of a field which

I submit television has not yet tackled. It is the big and vital field of topical but non-immediate news,' which he distinguished from 'immediate' news and 'permanent' news.[32] Though crude, it is possible to discern in this categorization a distinction that survives in approaches to television journalism to the present day: the immediate news of the bulletins and the 24-hour channels; the analysis of some of the longer news and current affairs programmes; and the investigative or documentary strands that are less visible now in most television services but were particularly strong on UK television during the 1970s and 1980s. The relaunch of 'Panorama' with a serious and established journalist at the helm announced the arrival of the BBC into the real world of difficult social and political issues for the mass audiences that television was now building. It was a world which the BBC had largely ignored in which, as Dimbleby's son and biographer wrote:

> People endured hardship and poverty; where there was ignorance and prejudice; where the powerful in one country would overrun the weak in another ... *Panorama* became the first BBC programme to tread in the political minefields that competent reporters always have to cross. For the first time the BBC allowed the people to be heard, on topics which mattered, in ways which were memorable.[33]

There is no question that the arrival of commercial television had acted as a catalyst for the kind of journalism that both Wyndham Goldie and Dimbleby had separately been promoting within the BBC and that finally found an outlet in 'Panorama' – albeit, as Denis Foreman observed, within a distinctly middle-class and non-controversial framework. But it also facilitated a different kind of journalism: a topical, less analytical and more populist approach that would have had Reith recoiling in horror and that was the forerunner of the highly successful 'Nationwide'.

'Tonight' emerged out of the end of the so-called 'Toddlers Truce', the agreement that television should be off-air between 6 and 7 p.m. so that parents could haul their offspring off to bed. Beginning in February 1957, 'Tonight' had a more casual (though highly disciplined) approach to everyday issues involving research, interviews, film reports and information which was in keeping with the gradual relaxation of formality and post-war austerity of 1950s Britain. It started to catch the mood, initiated by the BBC's upstart commercial rival, of an irreverence towards figures of authority and a respect for the lives and stories of 'ordinary' people. It embraced the new approach to political interviewing, which placed journalism before deference and – while not yet imitating the particularly robust approach of Robin Day on ITN – was prepared to challenge ministers rather than doff an institutional hat. It was still meticulously balanced and impartial but, in Wyndham Goldie's words, 'its fundamental approach was egalitarian. Gardeners and housewives and eel-catchers were treated as seriously as Members of Parliament. Power ... did not confer wisdom, and those who wielded it could be questioned'.[34]

Wyndham Goldie attributed the enormous popularity of 'Tonight' to a 'kind of national explosion of relief' that authority was not always right or necessarily deserving of respect; and she wondered whether a television programme was now capable of contributing to, rather than simply reflecting, a national mood. In this case, there was no question that the slightly impertinent, slightly sceptical approach was well calibrated to the nation's growing impatience with paternalism and the growing belief that ordinary people – and not just the elite – had a right to be heard. The democratization and popularization of television journalism both followed and helped to accelerate the democratization of post-war Britain. And any sense of lingering deference to authority was finally disposed of by a programme that emerged out of the journalistic tradition of 'Tonight', and became the first television example of journalism as political satire: 'That Was the Week that Was'.

'TW3' and the birth of television satire

Since Eden's clash with the BBC over Suez (comprehensively lost) and the arrival and gradual acceptance in British television of the 'new journalism' of interrogation and accountability, it was 'TW3', as 'That Was the Week that Was' soon became known, that generated the earliest debates about how far satirical disrespect could go – particularly for a publicly funded broadcaster. Its emergence was certainly facilitated by the arrival of a new Director General, Hugh Carleton Greene, a journalist by profession and a much more adventurous and open-minded individual than his more inhibited predecessors. Not for the last time, the personality of its leader was to have a major impact on the journalistic approach of the BBC, and Greene was a man with a sense of humour who was committed to good journalism. The programme was a combustible combination of factors, right for its time: a host of talented writers emerging from the lighter journalistic tradition of 'Today'; an institutional shift in values within the BBC; a competitor that had rapidly instilled in the BBC an awareness of its audience and its ratings; a medium which was now in most people's homes and had quickly become rooted in people's everyday lives; and a shifting social and political milieu in which deference was being abandoned and lampooning the establishment was becoming acceptable.

The programme itself was a fascinating combination of wit, satire, sketches, music, audience participation and topicality, broadcast live and dealing with the events and controversies of the week. Though essentially an entertainment programme, it was the first of its kind to have its roots in serious journalistic endeavour and it launched some of the most famous names of the next 20 years in journalism, politics and comedy: David Frost, Ned Sherrin, future Director General Alasdair Milne as producer, future Labour cabinet minister Gerald Kaufman as a writer, and Bernard Levin, the future *Times* columnist, as star interviewer. It started in November 1962, going out late on a Saturday evening, and grew to an astonishing audience of 8–10 million as politicians, religious leaders and other icons of establishment respectability were parodied in a mixture of sketches and jokes well beyond the limits of anything seen on television before.

It was an indication of the robustness and confidence of the BBC that the programme was left to continue without interference despite the inevitable complaints from leading political and establishment figures – primarily the incumbent Conservative government. Not only was a general election due within 18 months, but negotiations around renewal of the BBC Charter were in progress during 1963 in anticipation of its expiry at the end of 1964. Moreover, the summer of 1963 saw the Conservative government in turmoil as the Profumo scandal broke and the British electorate lapped up the ensuing Denning Report, with its lurid tales of drunken orgies and swimming pool parties amongst the rich and famous. This was meat and drink to television satirists (as it was to journalists in general) and the programme returned for its second series at the end of September, due to run into the following year. In the event, it ran until the end of 1963 when the Director General bowed to mounting anxieties about personal attacks and unacceptably crude jokes.

While interpreted at the time as surrendering to political pressure, the decision to axe the programme was related more to the team's excesses of bad taste and vituperation, as well as legitimate concerns about impartiality. In that sense 'TW3' prefigured two abiding trends in television journalism: first, that as an instrument of journalistic analysis and interpretation, satire can be a powerful and popular tool; the legacy of 'TW3' continued through 'Spitting Image' and 'Bremner, Bird and Fortune' to 'Have I Got News For You' and 'Mock the Week' in the United Kingdom, and Jon Stewart's 'Daily Show' in the United States. Second, that while political satire in the print media can exist outside any constraining framework (subject to the laws of libel and obscenity), television is more constrained by the boundaries of taste and decency and, in those countries where they exist, by statutory codes on impartiality. Political satire on television was and is partly about holding leaders to account, but it is also about maintaining a sensibility to the very intimate nature of the medium and its ability to offend.

The programme lasted just long enough to cover (in an astonishingly moving, respectful and highly polished programme prepared in less than 48 hours) what was then the most momentous event of the television news era: the assassination of President Kennedy. It was the culmination of a news year in the United Kingdom which had been a gift to a burgeoning visual medium. Starting with six foot snowdrifts as Britain faced the worst snowstorms for years, it was followed by the death of Labour leader Hugh Gaitskell (widely believed to be the prime minister in waiting) and Britain's humiliating exclusion from the Common Market at the hands of the French President Charles de Gaulle. The unfolding Profumo scandal kept the nation glued to their newspapers as well as their screens and culminated in the resignation of Prime Minister Harold Macmillan and his succession by Alec Douglas-Home. August saw the biggest heist of the century so far when a London-bound train was ambushed and the Great Train Robbery was christened. And the celebrity status of pop stars was confirmed as the first signs of Beatlemania were recorded for the nation's news bulletins. As Geoffrey Cox wrote, the swinging sixties were 'under way on our doorstep, encouraged, enlarged, and no doubt to a degree created by this new medium which reflected these trends immediately into a multitude of homes'.[35]

Impact of new technology

None of that year's news events could have made quite such an impact through the nation's – or increasingly the world's – television sets were it not for some crucial technological advances that transformed the power of television journalism forever. When their television bulletins first started, both the BBC and ITN were shooting in silent film. Sound crews were sometimes assigned to record interviews, which would be voiced over, but the simultaneous recording of vision and sound evolved only slowly and with cumbersome, heavy apparatus that involved a sound recordist holding a microphone plugged into the camera with trailing cables and special lighting systems. The ground-breaking television reports of both the Hungary uprising and the Suez crisis in 1956 were shot silently. Then the lighter, portable and more flexible 16 mm cameras arrived, having made their debut in the United States, and transformed the immediacy of television news. It meant that the staple diet of competitive journalism, the breaking story, could now be covered properly by the medium which had begun to establish itself as the primary source of daily information. It was the beginning of the end of print and radio as the first places to find breaking news.

The one remaining piece of television journalism's technological jigsaw fell into place, albeit in fairly primitive form, on 10 July 1962. The Telstar satellite was launched from Cape Canaveral, allowing sound and pictures to be relayed from different parts of the world for around 20 minutes per day. Satellite time had to be booked in advance and was very expensive, but it was the beginnings of a more globalized journalism in which other countries' people, problems, politics, culture, wars and everyday lives were transported into the rapidly growing number of living rooms around the world that had television sets. While perhaps the most dangerous political moments of the century, the 13 days in which the United States and the USSR came to the brink of nuclear war during the Cuban missile crisis, was unavailable for the instant reaction and analysis of 24-hour news channels (a theme to which I return in Chapter 10), Telstar did bring memorable pictures to the United Kingdom of Soviet leaders doing battle with the Americans in the United Nations security council, and images of rockets on the Soviet cargo ships bound for Cuba. It allowed the crisis to come alive in a way that would not have been possible even a year earlier.

From July 1962 the world was, quite suddenly, a smaller place and much more accessible to television journalism; the more sophisticated gadgetry of today's global practitioners has simply extended that early trend. In the words of Andrew Marr: 'Though satellite technology has advanced hugely since 1962 – we now carry 'sat-phones' and small plastic dishes that allow us to communicate from almost anywhere in broadcast quality – the essential breakthrough is more than forty years old. The quality has risen and the price has fallen, but that's about it'.[36]

The legacy of regulation

By the mid 1960s, television journalism in the United Kingdom had come of age. It was new, dynamic, not very technologically sophisticated and rough around the edges, but it had by then already been subjected to – and framed by – the financial, structural, institutional, regulatory, professional, social, political and technological forces that would continue to shape its essential character for the next 40 years. It had inherited and then adapted the professional journalistic practices and ethics of the press, both tabloid and broadsheet. At the same time, it had adopted the established BBC framework, institutionalized through statute, of impartiality in its treatment of political issues – although definitions of impartiality were even then subject to different interpretations. It had also adapted itself to – and been influenced by – the changing social and cultural environment in which it operated, in particular a recognition that establishment figures could and should be held accountable for their actions. It had demonstrated a robust ability to stand up to and confront government.

It had also by this time manifested itself in a number of different forms which set the pattern for the future: straight news reporting of major events; background analysis and contextualization; investigative reporting into social problems or injustices; serious current affairs series; lighter magazine-type programmes; and satirical approaches to issues and personalities. It had also begun to encounter some of the problems that would become more acute in the following decades: the risk of a news agenda being dictated by pictures; the personality cult of the newscaster; the difficulties of 'doing' serious news on television; and the growing conviction in political circles that television was a medium that would have to be 'managed' in order to maximize electoral appeal.

Most of all, television journalism in the United Kingdom had, despite the medium emerging as primarily suited to and dominated by entertainment, become established as a serious presence. This owed much to the legacy of the BBC and Reith, and the skilful internal diplomacy of Grace Wyndham Goldie in overcoming the stultifying effect of those who sought to impose the straitjacket of radio journalism practices on BBC television. But it owed even more to the regulatory structures and values that ensured that the arrival of a commercial television service seeking to maximize its ratings and minimize its early losses did not result in the wholesale rejection of serious journalism. It was regulatory intervention which, until they had established a comfortable level of revenues and profits, coerced reluctant commercial contractors into providing what British legislators – and British viewers, too – regarded as an essential ingredient of a balanced television service. That regulatory intervention was almost entirely responsible for giving the UK the best of both worlds: a high-quality news service that combined the democratizing, popularizing and accessible vitality of a new commercial service with the trustworthy, informational, analytical reliability of the BBC legacy – both decently resourced and accessible in peak time. The success of this system, which, as we shall see, was extended as the broadcasting system expanded over the next 40 years, was in stark contrast to the United States where television journalism, which showed such early promise (and put the BBC's pedestrian efforts to shame), gradually withered in the face of commercial pragmatism and regulatory spinelessness.

Over the Atlantic – a very different regulatory model ...

While the British tradition of television journalism started in a straitjacket of unadventurous and uncontroversial reporting before being propelled into action through the force of regulated competition, the American tradition started with enormous ambition but soon became mired in the straitjacket of untrammelled commercialism. Faced with the growing chaos of unregulated airwaves where different stations were attempting to broadcast on the same wavelength, Congress introduced the 1927 Radio Act which established the principle of public ownership of the airwaves. The legislation called on the President to appoint a five-member

Federal Radio Commission to allocate licences according to the 'public interest, convenience and necessity' and subject to renewal every three years.[37] Whether deliberately or not, these were ambiguous words which might have proved a powerful tool in the hands of a determined regulator, but from the very beginning were neither clarified nor used as a means of compelling recalcitrant stations to treat journalism seriously.

American radio therefore took a directly commercial route, with little in the way of serious news. During the 1920s, radio stations were regarded as a medium for entertainment and sport, rather than journalism, and were therefore allowed to use the agencies, parent company newspapers (many were owned by newspaper magnates) and other printed material without encumbrance. By the early 1930s, however, a combination of the slump and rapid expansion of the radio network forced a rethink by the big newspaper groups who 'managed over long negotiations in the Biltimore Hotel in New York, to force on the networks ... conditions very similar to those clamped on the BBC 11 years earlier'.[38] Under this 'Biltimore Treaty' the broadcasters agreed not to gather news themselves and not to put out news before 9.30 a.m. to protect the morning papers, or before 9 p.m. to protect the evening papers. Unlike Britain, however, this self-imposed purdah did not survive. The sheer number of stations, along with the rapid unfolding of events in Europe and the willingness of sponsors like Esso to put their money into news bulletins, soon ensured that the agreement collapsed.

At the same time, the new Communications Act of 1934 created a Federal Communications Commission (FCC) comprising seven presidentially appointed commissioners of whom no more than four could be members of the same political party. Though the FCC was supposed to be the guardian of the public interest (the words of the 1927 Act still applied), it was rarely exercised by issues of broadcast standards except those involving taste and decency. The regulatory framework changed little until the 1990s (except for the reduction of the number of commissioners from seven to five in 1983), and nor did the willingness of the FCC to intervene to promote a different conception of the public interest in broadcasting. The notion of *positive* regulation – that is, imposing programme obligations on commercial contractors which may be less lucrative but of greater public benefit – was alien to the American broadcasting culture, which distrusted any government intervention in the media beyond maintaining acceptable standards of taste. This First Amendment philosophy is a distinction that remains to the present day and marks a clear dividing line between American and European approaches to television. That contrast has had a tangible impact on the respective nations' culture of television news.

American radio journalism, and from there television journalism, was therefore left to the vagaries of commercial sponsors and the broadcasters' own sense of public responsibility. Columbia Broadcasting Service (CBS), in particular, established an early reputation for serious news when William L. Shirer and Edward R. Murrow, sent to Europe in 1937 as Talks producers rather than journalists, found themselves broadcasting at the centre of a Europe in turmoil. Murrow's reports from London to the United States during the blitz – simple, authoritative, powerful and immediate – turned him into a legendary figure and, by providing graphic reports of a nation under siege, helped to turn the tide of American isolationism. The war transformed American news and news consumption: 'despite the incongruity of having messages from sponsors interwoven with messages from the battlefield, radio news in the United States developed at such a pace that by the war's end it had ousted the newspapers as the main source of news for the American people'.[39] Television was not far behind: on 7 December 1941, an experimental CBS television station in New York brought live news of the Japanese air attack on Pearl Harbor, using maps and diagrams to compensate for the lack of live pictures. The reach and attractiveness of television was boosted by the United States' love of sports, by coverage of the 1948 political conventions, and by coverage of the Korean War in 1950 and accompanying United Nations debates. CBS introduced a regular 15-minute weekday bulletin, closely followed by the National Broadcasting Company (NBC).

... and a different news culture

In presentational terms, these nightly bulletins owed more to the newsreel tradition of the cinema than the straight-laced approach of William Haley and Tahu Hole at the BBC. Started by Charles Pathe in the United States in 1907, cinema newsreels had by the 1930s become an integral part of its movie-going experience. They were entertainment-led, highly patriotic and uncritical portraits of American life. The most influential of them, a series started in 1935 called 'The March of Time', mixed dramatic re-enactment with real-life footage. Whether this was good journalism embellished with a little added drama or fakery masquerading as fact was hotly contested at the time, but it was certainly miles from the BBC tradition of a staid transmission of facts.

Angered by American brashness and distortion, J. Arthur Rank funded a British version, 'This Modern Age', which ran for five years from 1946 and won successive documentary film awards. Unlike its American precursor, the British version opted from the beginning for an impartial approach which kept its reporters out of vision – a technique that was adopted and continued by ITV's 'World in

Action'. Each country's newsreels, therefore, were shaped by their own news cultures and inevitably influenced the television news cultures which followed. In the United States' case, 'The newscasts of the early 1950s contained the weaker qualities of the newsreel and remained less important than documentaries for many years. The evening newscasts of CBS and NBC were hardly the flagships of their news divisions. Perhaps they were the tugboats.'[40] News stories were barely distinguishable from commercials, and did little to conceal their institutional values: a 1950 NBC news bulletin contained several references to 'Commies' and 'Reds'.

The documentary tradition, however, was flourishing. Murrow had returned to broadcasting in 1947 and eventually teamed up with two powerful figures in CBS to initiate an era of television journalism – outside the insipid news bulletins – that established him as the 'great inspiration for broadcast journalists for decades to come'.[41] The first was producer Fred Friendly, with whom he worked on a series of radio documentaries called 'Hear It Now', which in 1951 transferred to television under the title 'See It Now'. The second was CBS founder and Chairman William S. Paley, who passionately believed in the role and importance of broadcast journalism. According to Harry Reasoner, long-time correspondent with both CBS and American Broadcasting Company (ABC), there was an assumption in early American television that 'network news would be free-spending, in spite of the fact that at that time no one foresaw that news could ever turn a profit'.[42] Paley himself was quoted as telling any of his correspondents who expressed anxiety about costs, 'You worry about the news, I've got Jack Benny to bring in the profits'.[43] It was precisely this philosophy that Sidney Bernstein was to advocate for Granada several years later, explicitly holding up Murrow as a model for broadcast journalism. 'See It Now' commanded a $23,000 weekly production budget, more than the CBS main evening bulletin, and did not once return a profit on income from its sponsor the Aluminum Company of America (Alcoa).

It was soon established as the flagship programme of CBS News, covering a range of stories from mental health to Christmas in Korea. It established both Murrow's reputation as a journalist and television as a hugely powerful medium of accountability. During the course of 1953, the activities of Joseph McCarthy, Chairman of the Senate committee tasked with investigating Communist infiltration, was being broadcast on a daily basis. McCarthy's brutal hounding of anyone with the most tenuous links to left-wing politics ensured that dozens of innocent citizens from humble government employees to Hollywood stars were victimized and often ostracized simply through being asked to appear before the committee. The relentless interrogations of this committee were being 'conveyed pitilessly by television into the homes of the friends and neighbours and acquaintances of those being interrogated'.[44]

The first 'See It Now' programme to tackle the issue, in October 1953, featured a young Air Force reservist who had been asked to resign his commission because his father and sister had read 'subversive newspapers'.[45] But in March the following year, the programme launched a direct and powerful attack on McCarthy himself, the fear he was propagating and the freedom that was being compromised through his televised witch-hunts. It was not the first public challenge to McCarthy – Eric Sevareid had already been exposing the lies and half-truths on radio – but it was more effective for being transmitted on network television in prime-time. Oblivious to the impact, McCarthy initiated allegations of communist infiltration in the US Army, at which point his electrifying hold on politicians and the public fell away. He was eventually, and belatedly, censured by the Senate and died in 1957.

As an example of watchdog journalism at its most potent, the programme was hard to beat. But it also illustrated a serious deficiency in relying on the free market to fund controversial broadcast journalism. 'See It Now', its producers and its presenter had been vilified by those in thrall to the communist-conspiracy theorists, and sponsors did not want to be associated with material that created such political upheaval. The network insisted on granting equal time to any politician claiming unfair treatment, a condition that Murrow believed severely compromised the programme. Paley agreed and CBS cancelled the programme in the middle of 1958. Much to his employers' consternation, he used the Radio and Television News Directors Association (RTNDA) convention in October of that year to argue – in the words that opened this book – that the commercial imperatives of television were emasculating its journalistic potential. In the absence of any political or corporate will to intervene, it was difficult to see how serious journalism would be compatible with American network television. According to one commentator: 'No single journalist would operate so independently again. Perhaps despite his own wishes, Murrow's career showed as well the inextricable tie between television news and celebrity. "Show business" values were rooted in the American culture of television news.'[46]

Kennedy's assassination and the events that followed – the swearing in of Lyndon B. Johnson as the new President, the arrest and subsequent murder of suspect Lee Harvey Oswald live in front of television cameras, the State funeral in Washington, DC, with the heartbreaking images of a grieving Jackie Kennedy and the two small Kennedy children – generated huge audiences and consolidated the importance of television news. CBS and NBC expanded their evening bulletins from 15 to 30 minutes, despite their lack of profitability. Murrow's legacy may have proved short-lived but the networks, for the moment, still recognized their place in public life.

3   Competition, Commercialism and the 'Golden Age'

Pilkington and current affairs journalism

Two crucial political decisions which flowed directly from the Pilkington Report profoundly influenced the nature of British broadcasting – and its journalism – until the end of the twentieth century. The first was to hand the third television channel, which had now become technologically possible, to the BBC. This gave the BBC a number of competitive advantages, allowing it to schedule complementary programming across two channels, to innovate while still attracting mass audiences, to schedule major sports events without compromising the non-sports audience and to provide extended in-depth coverage of major breaking stories while maintaining a normal schedule for non-news junkies. As a result, the BBC could pioneer ground-breaking comedy like 'Monty Python's Flying Circus', create in-depth news programmes like 'Newsnight', schedule time-hungry major sporting events like Wimbledon and test match cricket, and provide extensive, detailed coverage of budgets or political crises without alienating large sections of the audience. This flexibility cemented the BBC's place at the centre of Britain's cultural life, thereby helping to give it the stability and self-assurance to withstand government pressure when necessary. The culture of journalistic independence, slowly nurtured by Reith and advanced by the battles over Suez and 'TW3', became sufficiently entrenched over the next 25 years to provoke a number of serious confrontations with incumbent governments.

The second political decision was to increase the powers of the ITA through the 1963 Television Act. This was a direct response to the views of the Pilkington committee that the commercial excesses of ITV needed to be curbed and a greater emphasis placed on fulfilling the medium's cultural and democratic potential. This reinvigoration of public service principles was not so much a return to the elitist paternalism of Lord Reith's early BBC as a consumerist vision of broadcasting designed to safeguard programmes which – though not the highest rating – still attracted sizeable and appreciative audiences. The emerging philosophy of the British regulatory system, which became more marked during the 1970s and

1980s, was to act as an enabling framework that protected 'minority' audiences and programme diversity. The ensuing choice for audiences went hand-in-hand with conventional definitions of Public Service Broadcasting, and the fulfilment of television's civic and public responsibilities.

Television journalism was probably the most important beneficiary of this institutionalized philosophy, in particular through the two ITV current affairs programmes that had made their debuts early in ITV's history. In the 1960s both 'World in Action' and 'This Week' brought to the living rooms of millions insights and analysis of some of the complex social issues of the era, and arguably contributed to the social revolution of that decade. Issues such as birth control, abortion, race, housing, homosexuality and employment were featured through films that examined the hardships and dilemmas of real people. One particularly contentious episode of 'This Week', for example, examined the growing campaign for the legalization of abortion not through a detached studio argument between adherents of competing positions but through comparing the real-life experiences of two women from contrasting backgrounds. It uncovered some of the horror and pain encountered through illegal 'back-street' abortions: 'practices which were absolutely common but whose existence was scarcely whispered, were openly discussed on the television screen'.[1] This was the journalism of social injustice, revealing to the nation the kinds of lifestyles, practices, beliefs and outrages that existed 'out there' but received little exposure. It was the first manifestation of what the playwright Alan Bennett later called 'introducing the nation to itself'.

The nation was also being introduced to other nations as crises, tragedies, humanitarian disasters and civil wars in faraway places – some linked to Britain through empire or culture, others not – found their way on to peak-time television. Mandela's imprisonment in South Africa in 1964, Ian Smith's unilateral declaration of independence in Rhodesia, the Vietnam War, the Six-Day War in the Middle East, unstable regimes in South America and China's cultural revolution were all part of the repertoire of 'This Week'. Each one of these programmes would certainly have won their companies higher audiences and more money had their slots been filled with light entertainment or movies, but the companies by now were content with the regulatory trade-off. With no competition for advertising and steadily rising profits, programming requirements imposed by the newly invigorated ITA no longer faced resistance: 'The commercial owners of the companies had not abandoned their aim of maximizing profits, but were very satisfied with their monopoly over advertising. It was a secure settlement which gave confidence to those who wanted to develop social and informational programming.'[2] Current affairs on commercial television was now benefiting from cash and commitment almost to the point of indulgence. It was a sound principle of Public Service Broadcasting, but not a sound principle of free-market economics and it would not survive the onslaught of Thatcherite liberalism in the 1980s.

Pilkington and ITV news – the birth of 'News at Ten'

An expanding role for journalism on British commercial television went beyond current affairs. Pilkington's praise for ITN's news operation had been echoed in the government's White Paper preceding the 1963 Act and in the parliamentary debates that followed, resulting in a new power for the ITA to ensure that ITV companies provided adequate time and finance for news. In May 1965 the new Early Bird satellite, which was available 18 hours a day, was launched. The hourly cost of £3,000 prohibited regular use, but it meant that a breaking international story could now be covered at virtually any time. ITN now had access to more money, more facilities and more pictures; what it really needed to exploit all three was more time.

By 1967 all ITV franchises were due for renewal with new contracts to be awarded to those who, as before, could better convince the regulatory authority of their commitment to delivering a well-funded, mixed schedule. The ITA took this opportunity to ask ITV companies to re-examine their peak-time schedule, in particular with a view to increasing the existing 15 minutes of news at 8.55 p.m. to half an hour. Faced with no improvement, the ITA used its own powers to devise a major shake-up of the weekday schedules featuring a half-hour news bulletin at 10 o'clock. The ITV companies feared a slump in their late-night audiences and loss of advertising revenue, and offered a counter-proposal of 20 minutes. But in the end, faced with a persistent regulator and with franchises up for renewal, they capitulated. On 8 March 1967, the ITN board was informed that the ITA would require a 26½-minute bulletin – a half-hour slot, allowing for commercial breaks. Cox described it as 'the biggest opportunity any organisation in British television has had to show that news can be made into full programmes, rather than bulletins'.[3] And according to the board minutes, it was the Director General of the ITA who described in detail the content and style which was expected:

> Sir Robert Fraser said that … The programme must have a recognizable character, just as the more popular newspapers had. He hoped that the Editor would see it as a 'people's news programme' and that the change of time and length would not mean that it would set out to appeal to a different audience to that of the present main bulletin. The programme should be heavily illustrated with still pictures and film.[4]

From the perspective of the twenty-first century, it may seem extraordinary that the head of a regulatory agency should be dictating the length, timing and editorial style of evening news on commercial television. But this regulatory imposition was a huge success in terms of programming, revenue, audiences, prestige and above all authoritative television journalism. It proved to be one of the network's biggest revenue earners as advertisers realized the commercial worth of the disproportionately male ABC1 audience. It also provided, along with the soap opera 'Coronation Street', two key fixed points in the ITV schedule with which audiences could identify. 'News at Ten' started as a three-month experiment on 3 July 1967, aiming to offer 'something new, different, clearly distinct from the prevailing pattern of news bulletins'.[5] As well as a two-person presentation team, there were more reporter-led film packages, which in turn demanded more news-gathering resources from the ITV companies and diminished dependence on news agencies.

After a shaky start that earned mixed reviews in the press, ITN was to build a reputation every bit as authoritative as the BBC in every area of news reporting. From the beginning, it established itself with the audience: the first five programmes were all in the top 20 most-watched programmes, and two were in the top 10. Politicians loved it, both as another outlet for themselves and as a counterpoint to the BBC stranglehold on news. And the ITV companies themselves were soon won over. By 1971, Lew Grade of ABC was telling a parliamentary select committee: 'I resisted *News at Ten* – and I was wrong.'[6] Thirty years later, the ITA's regulatory successor – in a very different broadcasting environment – was to prove less robust in the face of equally determined resistance from ITV companies, and 'News at Ten' would disappear. In the intervening years, the programme built a loyal audience for news, a reputation for rigorous and well-resourced reporting, and a sense of authority for ITV itself. It was Britain's regulatory framework which had brought about the birth of ITN and then mandated 'News at Ten'; as a direct result, the BBC became a better, more responsive television news provider and the British public was better informed.

In asserting its authority, the ITA went beyond 'News at Ten'. Concerned that this increase in informational programming in peak-time might tempt ITV companies to move factual programmes out of peak, it decreed that certain current affairs programmes were to be given fixed time slots for transmission across the network: in particular, 'This Week' was to be broadcast at 8.30 or 9.00 p.m. on Thursdays, and 'World in Action' at mid-evening on Mondays. This again was a crucial decision in providing a foundation for confident and well-resourced television journalism: 'The move effectively underpinned the two series, protecting them against the more commercial impulses of their producing companies.'[7] That confidence, inspired by the regulator, was ironically to promote some of the bitterest confrontations with the self-same regulator in the 1970s over issues of impartiality. By contrast, the 1980s were to see television journalists and the regulator pitted against the government.

It was a journalistic confidence born not only of mandated programmes and scheduling, but also of protection from owners deemed to be overly obsessed with ratings. A new contractor for the London region emerged in 1967, Thames Television, which enhanced the serious agenda of 'This Week'.[8] Jeremy Isaacs, one of the most accomplished television journalists of his generation and later to become the first Chief Executive of Channel 4, had been the producer of 'This Week' in the mid 1960s and in 1974 became Thames Director of Programmes. According to the programme's historian, Patricia Holland, he told one of the programme's journalists: 'the ratings are not your problem. They're my problem. You must do what you feel you ought to be doing and do it the way you feel you ought to do it.'[9] It was this kind of philosophy that produced some of the most ground-breaking journalism of the 1970s, but was also to provoke some of the biggest rows as one of the most sensitive areas in twentieth-century British politics came to the boil: Northern Ireland.

Northern Ireland, regulation and commercial television's challenge

From the time of Ireland's partition in 1922, the mostly Protestant Northern Ireland remained part of the United Kingdom with elected MPs in Westminster. A growing sense of victimization and discrimination amongst the Catholic minority was given voice in a series of civil rights marches in 1968 and placed Northern Ireland firmly on the news agenda. In August 1969, Catholics attacked one of the annual Protestant marches, leading to retaliation and violence, which resulted in a frightened and embattled Catholic community having to erect barricades and appeal for protection from the British Army. The Army arrived and stayed. In August 1971, following the shooting of a British soldier earlier in the year, the British government introduced internment without trial and over 300 Catholics were detained. The sense of grievance within the province increased on both sides and the Irish Republican Army (IRA) began to attract an increasing number of willing volunteers. Then on 30 January 1972 came 'Bloody Sunday' when a British Army unit, claiming that it had come under fire while policing a Catholic anti-internment march, killed 13 people.[10]

The consequence of those events was a profound mood shift in the province and in Britain: more recruits for the extremist wings on both sides, the escalation of violence and the beginnings of a terrorist campaign by the Provisional IRA, which would extend to the British mainland and impact on the lives of millions.

As politicians and governments sought to control what they perceived as a campaign of intimidation and indiscriminate violence – and were determined, at least in public, to cede no ground whatever to armed resistance – some terrible dilemmas were created for television journalists, their institutions and their regulators as television sought to move beyond the everyday storytelling of explosions, confrontations and political machinations to shed some light on this complex and apparently insoluble conflict.

For British governments of both political colour – as for much of the popular press – it was a simple matter of black versus white, good versus bad, the defence of freedom versus an enemy intent on destruction. But for many television journalists of that generation, the issues were more sophisticated and required proper interrogation of some of the simplistic political positions being offered – as well as some investigation into allegations of human rights abuses and police collaboration with Protestant extremists. Perhaps the most illuminating and detached approach to the journalistic dilemma was contained in an outstanding academic study of how terrorism was covered in the 1970s by Philip Schlesinger and his colleagues.[11] They concluded that media coverage of terrorism could be analysed through four perspectives: the 'official' perspective that emanated from the government, police and Army; this is supported by the 'populist' perspective often applied by large sections of the popular press, which regarded as legitimate any actions (even extrajudicial) to combat the terrorist threat; the 'oppositional' perspective, which justified the violence of terrorism as a legitimate means to an end; and the 'alternative' perspective, which sought to interpret and understand – but not to legitimize – the context for acts of terrorist violence. It was this alternative perspective, which was generally pursued by British television current affairs programmes of the 1970s and 1980s, that placed them in almost inevitable conflict with establishment-based official versions.[12]

The clashes that began here, and were pursued even more relentlessly under Margaret Thatcher's premiership, lasted until the early 1990s. They were prompted by a whole generation of new, bright, dynamic, idealistic and determined journalists, working in an exciting and still relatively new medium, who by now were accustomed to exploiting the opportunities of television to explain, analyse, contextualize, investigate and inform. They had access to airtime, to millions of viewers and to resources. But they found their journalistic ambitions frustrated by an establishment intent on, as they saw it, censoring any oppositional or non-official views. At the end of 1971 a young BBC radio journalist, who was about to move to 'This Week' to follow the illustrious career of his father, wrote an unsigned article in the *New Statesman* outlining the restrictions placed on BBC reporters. The author was Jonathan Dimbleby and he explained why the constraints were anathema to a philosophy of journalism that sought simply to explain:

> The censorship and restrictions placed on reporters and editors make it practically impossible for them to ask the question 'why'? Why do the Catholics now laugh openly when a British soldier is shot down and killed, when a year ago they would offer the army cups of tea? Why do the Catholics refuse to condemn the bombings and the shootings? Why do they still succour the IRA?[13]

Ten years later, the approach at the top of both the BBC and the regulatory body had changed to a more flexible view of the responsibilities of current affairs journalism, provoking much bigger confrontations with politicians who were then unable to rely on regulators to act as State censor at one remove. For the moment, however, the ITA ensured that regulatory protection from undue commercialism was a double-edged sword when it came to practising uncomfortable journalism, and there were frequent complaints during the early 1970s of interference on subjects outside Northern Ireland. In the words of Ray Fitzwalter, a 'World in Action' producer who saw three of his programmes banned, 'The problem principally arose from an Authority made up of establishment figures, politicians, former military men, diplomats, businessmen, a trade unionist, a former civil servant and a clergyman, and the fact that they took on the role of publisher for which they were spectacularly ill suited. It was the natural instinct of such figures to want to suppress information that might be upsetting to others in authority'.[14]

In 1972, the ITA was rechristened the Independent Broadcasting Authority (IBA) as it prepared to take commercial radio under its wing, with some suggestion that its regulatory philosophy may have relaxed a little.[15] Following a 1973 'Weekend World' interview of David O'Connell, which the IBA had allowed despite his status as a self-confessed IRA spokesman, the regulator wrote to all ITV contractors explaining its position in terms that still stand as an enlightened expression of how good television journalism can help audiences to understand the history and complexity of issues involving terrorism. It recognized that certain groups and individuals acted 'outside the properly constituted democratic machinery' (i.e. engaged in terrorist activity) but continued that: 'An understanding of why they act in this way is essential to any attempt to report and explain the Northern Ireland crisis. It is for this reason that there are occasions when interviews with illegal organisations are justified. The main problem is how to report accurately without giving the platform which most politically motivated groups seek.'[16]

The regulator's resolve – and television's ability to cover Northern Ireland in a relatively dispassionate way – was severely weakened by an IRA bomb in a

Birmingham pub in November 1974 which killed 21 people. That it came only a few days after another 'Weekend World' interview of O'Connell only strengthened government determination to limit the IRA's exposure, and the result was the Prevention of Terrorism Act that outlawed the IRA and made it virtually impossible for broadcasters to justify its members' appearances. It also made the regulator more wary. A 1975 'This Week' programme looking at IRA fundraising links with the United States was prevented from transmission. A 1977 programme which exposed the use of inhuman and degrading treatment being used on terrorist suspects in Northern Ireland went ahead, but was bitterly condemned by the Northern Ireland office and the Shadow Northern Ireland Secretary Airey Neave. The *Daily Telegraph* fumed: 'This is the third go the producers and reporters of *This Week* have had against the forces of law and order in Ulster ... If the IBA will not stop this homicidal irresponsibility, the government must step in.'[17]

This concerted opposition may have been responsible for a less robust approach by the IBA when 'This Week' attempted a further programme on the mistreatment of suspects in June the following year, in anticipation of an Amnesty International visit which had confirmed allegations of brutality. This time the IBA stepped in and prevented the programme from being broadcast but the Association of Cinematograph and Television Technicians (ACTT), the main broadcasting union, ensured that no other programme was allowed to replace it. The result was a blank screen saying simply that the programme had been cancelled. The film, however, did appear the following night – on the BBC's 'Nationwide' over the caption 'the film the IBA bosses will not let you see'. It was an interesting rebuttal of the oft-heard argument that publicly funded broadcasters are more susceptible to censorship by pro-government forces and established again the independent journalistic credentials of the BBC. It demonstrated, moreover, the importance of having a plurality of outlets for serious television journalism.

Beyond Northern Ireland, there were other examples of a conservative regulatory approach thwarting the journalistic ambitions of commercial television. In 1973, the IBA ignored ITV's own legal advice and banned a 'World in Action' programme revealing the corrupt practices of Yorkshire architect John Poulson, who had employed two prominent Labour Party figures. There was no detailed explanation, though sceptics pointed to several personal connections between members of the IBA and those named in the programme. It eventually went out three months later with some superficial changes, and the whole report was vindicated when Poulson and others were later convicted. This censorious approach of the regulator was in stark contrast to the uncompromising support offered by ITV senior managers when commercial interests were at risk. Another 'World in Action' investigation, examining some of the unpleasant side effects of aspirin, met huge opposition from the pharmaceutical companies who were then ITV's largest advertiser. The programme was referred up to Granada's Sidney Bernstein whose reaction to the programme-makers was: 'Do what you have to do.'[18] Such calculated alienation of sponsors was, of course, much easier in a television advertising monopoly, and a similar referral in today's highly competitive climate might not attract such a cavalier response. But it illustrated again how the risk to campaigning television journalism in the 1970s came from the rule book rather than the cheque book.

As well as difficult investigative journalism, current affairs programmes were taking advantage of their generous budgets and improving technology to bring some of the most dramatic international stories to British screens. In the United States, the Vietnam War and its political fallout, the assassinations of Martin Luther King and Bobby Kennedy, and the first moon landing were followed by the Watergate scandals and President Nixon's resignation. There was the Six-day War in 1967 as Israel invaded and occupied parts of Egypt, Syria and Jordan, followed by the Yom Kippur War six years later. In Eastern Europe, the Soviet invasion of Prague in 1968 was followed by consolidation of the Cold War during the 1970s. Despite more concerns from the ITA/IBA about impartiality, most journalists felt a repugnance about the apartheid regime in South Africa and found ways of circumventing its embassy's attempts to suppress or conceal the living conditions of blacks. There were programmes on the African National Congress, on Mandela's imprisonment, on life in the black townships, on the Bantustans set up ostensibly to provide black urban South Africans with independent homelands, on the Soweto riots and on the death of the black activist Steve Biko in police custody. Jonathan Dimbleby made half-a-dozen programmes about Ethiopia as well as covering Tanzania, Peru, Brazil and Bolivia, the floods in Bangladesh and the earthquake in Guatemala. Even in a three-channel system, such programmes were not guaranteed good ratings, but 'This Week' was 'regularly in the top 20 with 10 million viewers'.[19] The range of peak-time current affairs meant that British viewers in the 1970s and into the 1980s had access to a range of views, perspectives and stories about their own nation and the world outside at accessible times. These programmes attracted good ratings even when there was popular entertainment available on other channels.

A shift in emphasis on commercial TV

While resources and standards were not a problem, two very different concerns had been growing as current affairs journalism blossomed on British commercial television. Both were to be resolved in the 1980s, in very different ways, as a new brand of political conservatism fractured the post-war consensus that had dominated for 35 years. The first was a series of unreasonable and increasingly outrageous demands by the ACTT and other unions as they saw revenues flowing into the ITV companies and exploited the company managements' unwillingness to interrupt services. There were generous overtime agreements, which meant soaring programme costs every time a programme stretched into the evening or – as was sometimes necessary – overnight. There were minimum crewing agreements (nothing less than seven was acceptable except by special permission), first-class travel and pay claims which – even given company profits – were disproportionate to the work undertaken. In the unpredictable world of current affairs television, the unions' inflated demands constrained the flexibility of producers and artificially raised the cost of programmes. Fitzwalter wrote about 'World in Action': 'My producers would constantly need to film at unusual times or in unusual places. This would forever give the unions openings for new demands or a claim that programme makers had not obeyed the arcane rules they sought to enforce.'[20] An 11-week strike during the summer of 1979, when ITV went off the air, was only settled after huge pay rises, vastly increased costs and a cost to the network of £100 million in revenue. Margaret Thatcher had just won the election in May of that year, and would make the ending of union militancy one of the hallmarks of her administration during the 1980s. Her government's radical shake-up of the structures of British broadcasting were to have damaging and lasting consequences for the quality of television journalism, but anyone surveying the commercial television landscape in the late 1970s would have sympathized with any initiative to curb such blatant abuses of union power.

The second concern was the nature of television journalism itself, and a growing unease within commercial television that the journalistic agenda was becoming self-indulgent and insufficiently sensitive to audience needs – that it was being issue-led rather than story-led, and in doing so was becoming removed from long-standing journalistic values of accessibility, drama and storytelling. This anxiety was reinforced by straightforward commercial arguments that a more populist approach would generate better ratings, and that constant battles with the regulator were perhaps not the best guarantor of a continuing franchise. One result was the suspension in 1978 of 'This Week' to give way – albeit temporarily – to a new programme in the same slot, 'TV Eye', with a more populist brief in both subject matter and journalistic approach: more human interest and greater emphasis on visual drama and stories, fewer long-haul investigations or issues requiring extensive research and explanation. While the shift in emphasis was heralded by some as an early example of 'dumbing down', the programme continued to produce some exceptional foreign reporting on, for example, unrest in Iran, brutality in Cambodia, uprising in the Polish shipyards of Gdansk and civil war in Rhodesia.

It was ironic that, while commercial television's current affairs was under attack on one wing for an overly political and elitist agenda, it was being criticized elsewhere for being insufficiently analytical and surrendering to some of the baser visual evils of the television medium. A major debate about the nature and direction of television journalism on another ITV programme was taking root, which was ultimately to have much deeper and long-lasting ramifications for British television journalism in general and the BBC in particular.

Birt and the 'bias against understanding'

In 1972, the London weekend contractor London Weekend Television (LWT) started its own contribution to serious television journalism with a Sunday lunchtime programme called 'Weekend World'. It was to last until 1988 and was the first in what became an abiding lunchtime television tradition of a 'heavy' political interview, usually involving a senior politician keen to make a splash in the following day's newspapers (when political news was traditionally at a premium). As politicians gradually came to understand the exposure value of television, and as television itself became more competitive, the Sunday lunchtime programme became a convenient staging post for both programme controllers and cabinet ministers: the former seeking publicity for their channel in a burgeoning media environment, the latter seeking publicity for their new policy initiative or barely concealed leadership bid.

'Weekend World' soon established a particular identity and philosophy of its own, led by its cerebral presenter Brian Walden (the former Labour MP but moving steadily rightwards) and a production team that worked prodigiously to ensure that Walden had a thoroughly researched brief that enabled him to interrogate – intensely, logically and intellectually – heavyweight political figures. The creator of 'Weekend World' was John Birt, who turned it into one of the most admired ITV current affairs programmes of the 1970s and helped to ensure his promotion in 1981 to Director of Programmes.[21] It was based on a very precise and systematic interpretation of journalism, which started with a process of meticulous research to establish the 'story' and was followed by a series of draft scripts before filming. There were two benefits to this approach. First, it was a more economical way of using what could be a very expensive medium, even at the height of network extravagance. Second, it offered a rigorous and stimulating intellectual environment in which scripts were constantly being challenged and revised. Though a somewhat ascetic vision of television journalism, it attracted a loyal following.[22] Its critics, however, pointed to some obvious flaws, in particular the reduction of interviewees to little more than walk-on parts in a predetermined script, and rejection of the kinds of investigative journalism that could be messy and inconclusive. Such concepts of journalism did not fit easily within the Birtian analytical tradition.

Some three years into the run of 'Weekend World', Birt wrote a lengthy feature for *The Times* that attempted to sketch out his theory. He wrote: 'There is a bias in television journalism, but it is not a bias against any particular party or point of view – it is a bias against *understanding*.'[23] He argued that television news stories had to be confined to a maximum of two minutes in order to squeeze as many items as possible into the traditional bulletin. In doing so, news stories inevitably became divorced from their wider context, thereby depriving viewers of the opportunity to understand economic, social and political debates in any true depth. Traditional studio discussions were a poor journalistic tool which 'scarcely ever promote understanding of complicated problems and are little more than an entertaining way of feeding the viewer's already existing prejudices'.

Seven months later, Birt teamed up with *The Times*'s Economics Editor Peter Jay to write two articles pursuing the same theme. The first was diagnosis: what was the reason for this bias against understanding? The answer lay in television journalism's schizophrenic roots, half-newspaper newsroom and half-Hollywood movie – 'the misbegotten child of two ill-assorted parents'. The authors painted a fairly unflattering portrait of unmanaged journalists randomly pursuing their stories with little sense of how they fit together: 'Journalism is organized to collect innumerable nuggets of self-contained fact, to report an atomised world of a million tiny tales.' The resultant news values, they said, produce stories of attention-grabbing immediacy without context: foreign stories about Vietnamese orphans rather than an explanation of the Indo-China conflict; budget stories about the price of beer going up rather than an analysis of the underlying economic strategy. Meanwhile, current affairs programmes were deemed to be rooted in the movie tradition, dominated by the need for 'exciting locations and lively situations with animated talkers in between'. Every reporter is under pressure to become something of a 'personality' through tough or confrontational interviews, with a finished product which inevitably detracts from a properly informed and contextualised understanding of the issues.

The second article proposed a solution: a reformed television service which would provide viewers with 'the maximum feasible understanding of the important (and diverting) events which happen in the world about them'.[24] They prescribed the programmes, the staffing arrangements and even the appropriate channel. They argued for brief daily bulletins, which 'would simply carry the bald news-breaks' without analysis, followed by an hour-long 'flagship' bulletin scheduled at around 10 or 11 p.m. covering in depth no more than five or six stories. This would be complemented by a weekly hour-long programme covering up to three stories and a monthly 90-minute programme devoted to 'continuing themes of our times', as well as a range of feature programmes. And this should all be implemented on BBC1, under the auspices of a unified and centrally directed news and current affairs department, with journalists organized into subject teams under a single editor (politics, foreign, financial and so on). In the short term, neither the argument nor its authors received much support amongst the journalistic cadre either at the BBC or outside the confines of LWT's current affairs studios.[25] Some 12 years later, however, Birt would be in a position to implement his theory and fundamentally influence the BBC's conception of journalism.

Channel 4 and a new approach

While John Birt was expounding his theory for the reconstitution of journalism practice, a much more profound revolution was under way in British television: the gradual evolution of a fourth channel, which was conceived in part by independent producers convinced that television's institutions were dominated by a social and political elite and were throttling diversity. The result was a unique arrangement of public service obligations and commercial funding, providing the springboard for a different approach to television journalism that survives to the present day.

One of the ironies of the incoming Conservative government in 1979 was that its first substantial contribution to British broadcasting was to implement a framework for the fourth channel, which had been designed under the previous Labour administration as part of a centre-left ideological framework in opposition to a perceived establishment, male, metropolitan, middle-class culture. The intellectual background for the creation of Channel 4 was the report of the Annan Committee, delivered in 1977, which essentially favoured a structural solution to fostering diversity rather than the liberal market approach that was to prevail in the 1980s. Its recommended approach was a new organization with a mandate for cultural diversity, operating as a publisher rather than a fully integrated broadcaster. It would thus be able to take advantage of the growing number of journalists and programme-makers operating outside the existing duopoly who felt that their voices and their stories were not being heard.

The end result was the 1981 Broadcasting Act and a fourth channel with a statutory obligation to provide 'innovation and experiment in the form and content' of programmes and to ensure 'generally that Channel 4 is given a distinctive character of its own'.[26] It was to be funded by advertising, as was ITV. But rather than having to compete for advertising revenue, and therefore risk having to prejudice or sacrifice its remit to be different, its airtime was to be sold by ITV, which would therefore maintain its monopoly over commercial revenue. As a means of creating competition for airtime to benefit advertisers, it was useless. But as a means of ensuring a stable income for a fledgling channel with a very specific remit that explicitly rejected audience maximization as its primary aim, it was ingenious. Because it was released from having to compete for commercial funding it was able to concentrate on defining and building its unique public service identity to be innovative and experimental, and to offer programming that wasn't available elsewhere. This remit provided a firm statutory foundation for diversity, which was to spawn a new breed of current affairs and determine the nature of Channel 4's news output for the next 30 years.

Although Parliament established the general framework, it was still down to Channel 4's founders and leaders to interpret 'distinctiveness' for each genre of programming. In both news and, separately, current affairs, explicit ambitions were set from the very beginning by its first Chief Executive, Jeremy Isaacs, who himself had already established a distinguished record in factual programming. His blueprint for news involved a one-hour bulletin at 7 p.m. Although he accepted that an hour of television might contain fewer words than the front page of a national newspaper and that television was essentially a visual medium, he did not believe that this made it 'inevitably a trivializing medium'. Why not, he asked, 'provide a framework in which different choices were possible, and promulgate a brief for a programme instructing that different choices would be made'?[27] In other words, the editorial agenda for the channel's news would follow the spirit of the channel's statutory remit, and would take an explicitly 'broadsheet' approach that emphasized analysis and eschewed violence and sensationalism:

> We did not want stories of individual crime, or of minor natural disaster. We did not want coverage of the daily diaries of the Royal Family. *Channel 4 News* would deal with politics and with the economy. It would bring coverage of the City, and of industry. It was to report on developments in science and technology, and in the arts. It was to cover the politics of other countries and to supplement that reporting with the output and insights of foreign television news programmes.[28]

Given its track record and expertise, ITN was the obvious choice as news supplier for Channel 4.[29] Isaacs, however, was concerned about the implications for diversity and the organizational culture of ITN: could the journalistic practices established over 25 years of supplying news for a populist, mainstream commercial channel be adapted to a wholly different journalistic philosophy? The omens were not good: when Channel 4's first commissioner of news and current affairs, Liz Forgan, outlined her vision for the news agenda of 'no sport, no royal stories, no plane crashes and lashings of foreign news', the response from an ITN director was: 'Well, my dear, there's just one thing you have to understand: the news is the news is the news'.[30]

In practice, however, there was little choice given the huge capital costs of setting up a brand new organization. Reluctantly, the contract went to ITN whose first 'Channel 4 News' bulletin went out on the channel's opening day in November 1982. Audiences disappointed, falling to below 250,000 (against aspirations for 1.5 million) and within a year Isaacs was complaining that depth was being sacrificed for longer news stories. In a purely market-led system, the solution would have been simple: a reversion to classic news values, and the kinds of crime, royalty and celebrity stories that features in any peak-time bulletin. But the Isaacs–Forgan vision was protected by parliamentary fiat, by regulatory oversight and by the absence of commercial pressure. Audiences mattered as a means of evaluating whether the content and timing of bulletins was sufficiently relevant to sufficient numbers of people, but not in terms of whether their size and demographic profile was attractive to advertisers.

The redemption of 'Channel 4 News' came in two forms: a new editor from within ITN, Stewart Purvis, who had the technical, managerial and journalistic abilities to turn the programme round. And the beginnings of a miners' strike in 1984, which became the bitterest, most emotional and most violent industrial dispute of the Thatcher years. Not only pit villages but individual families were deeply divided, and beyond the headline confrontation lay extremely complex issues about trade union power, industrial modernization, political chicanery and energy policy as well as huge personality issues involving Prime Minister Margaret Thatcher, the leader of the miners Arthur Scargill and the Coal Board Chairman Ian MacGregor. In one inspired programme, Purvis brought them together for a debate and secured 2 million viewers. In another, the graphic account of Channel 4 reporter Jane Corbin from one of those divided mining villages, Shirebrook, ran for 24 minutes and, according to internal ITN papers, 'It made a deep impression on viewers; the prime minister remarked in a newspaper interview how much it had moved her'.[31] Audiences climbed slowly to a million, and entrenched a serious, dedicated one-hour bulletin which successfully challenged the old shibboleths of how to 'do' television news. Within ten years, despite burdening the channel's schedulers with a difficult launch-pad for the evening ratings, the 7 p.m. news bulletin had become part of the channel's DNA. Astonishingly, as we shall see, it has continued to maintain both its audience and its distinctive, serious character well into the competitive multichannel age.

This rethinking of approaches to television journalism, rooted in Channel 4's statutory remit, was also applied to its current affairs output. A number of different production companies were commissioned to make topical programmes on issues of interest to non-mainstream audiences who were habitually ignored by the established current affairs programmes. The inevitable hit in low ratings was simply part of the public service compact, and Isaacs' stated aim was to 'make programmes of special appeal to particular audiences … to provide platforms for the widest range of opinion in utterance, discussion and debate'.[31] Within five years one programme, 'Dispatches', had established itself in the peak-time schedule as Channel 4's answer to 'Panorama' on BBC and 'World in Action' and 'This Week' on ITV, not only adding another serious voice to the coverage of contemporary issues, but guaranteeing a new outlet for aspiring journalists who were unable or unwilling to join the established broadcasters. And while the channel's early years were not short of controversy over taste and decency issues, as the 1980s progressed and Margaret Thatcher's ideological revolution took hold, there were few objections to its iconoclastic approach to news and current affairs. This may have been partly because its audiences were still small compared to its three rivals, and partly because the controversies raging elsewhere left no room for energy to be expended on such a relative minnow. For at the time that Isaacs was steering Channel 4 through its difficult early stages, the mainstream broadcasters were facing their toughest journalistic challenges yet. This was particularly true of the BBC.

BBC journalism and the Thatcherite onslaught

As we have seen, the BBC was, from the very beginning, a prime target for politicians and prime ministers who passionately believed they were not getting a fair hearing from the national broadcaster. By contrast, there have been virtually no similar confrontations between ITN and incumbent governments: the main ITN histories, in particular those by Geoffrey Cox and Richard Lindley, as well as the ITV histories by Sendall and Potter, contain very few instances of overt expressions of government discontent. There are a number of reasons: by virtue of being privately funded, ITN is less vulnerable; for the same reason, there is probably less of a sense of 'expected duty', particularly in times of crisis; there are fewer outlets for provoking prime ministerial wrath; and unlike the BBC, ITN plays very little part in the kinds of analytical or investigative reporting that are more likely to antagonize incumbent governments than straightforward news reporting.

Conversely, the BBC operates not just across a number of television channels but a dedicated news channel, several national radio stations, a network of local radio stations and a host of current affairs programmes that are not easily subjected to the kind of centralized editorial control that is possible within a single commercially funded news gatherer. Indeed, those who worry about the BBC's vulnerability to government pressure tend, as we shall see in Chapter 8 in respect of the Hutton report and its fallout, to underestimate both the strength of journalistic independence that flows through individual programmes (and their respective editors) and the sheer logistical problems of controlling such an enormous variety of programmes, styles, platforms, journalists, producers and journalistic traditions. It was precisely this problem of trying to keep tabs on such sprawling interpretations of journalism across a burgeoning institution that began to create major problems in the 1980s. Faced with a prime minister with the most powerful mandate since the war and an ideological commitment which fractured the post-war political consensus, a major confrontation about BBC journalism was almost inevitable.

An integral element of that sprawling journalism in the 1980s was the dichotomy between news and current affairs. While 'Panorama' was developing into a more serious incarnation of current affairs journalism, a different tradition with its roots in the 'Tonight' programme continued with the highly successful and popular 'Nationwide', mixing relatively light news items with the more politically significant and analytical.[33] These different interpretations of current affairs evolved within a series of converted houses in Lime Grove with its own club-like atmosphere, both managerially and journalistically separate from News – a legacy of the straitjacket imposed on the early days of news by Tahu Hole. One of the most talented and cerebral journalists to rise up the ranks of Lime Grove was Alasdair Milne, who succeeded Ian Trethowan as the BBC's Director General in July 1982.

Politically, the timing was unfortunate. Among the political problems inherited by Margaret Thatcher and her Conservative government in 1979 was the conflict in Northern Ireland, an issue which had created particular personal reasons for her to harbour a very strong antipathy towards the BBC. Shortly before her triumphant 1979 election day, an Irish terrorist splinter group, the Irish National Liberation Army (INLA), had murdered Thatcher's close political ally and architect of her election campaign, Airey Neave, with a car bomb as he emerged from the House of Commons car park. Within a few weeks, an INLA spokesman was interviewed (anonymously) on BBC television, with the explicit knowledge and permission of the Director General Ian Trethowan. The audience was only one million, but one of them was Airey Neave's widow who then wrote to the press recounting how she had suddenly been confronted on television by a man representing her husband's murderers. Thatcher denounced the broadcast in the House of Commons, and her furious outburst was then echoed by a fortnight of hostile press coverage and hundreds of protest letters. Although Trethowan later regretted his decision, it had been reached according to a well-established journalistic tradition of attempting to illuminate and reveal to the public gaze some of the darker aspects of national politics. Post 9/11, debates about allowing airtime to terrorists became almost de rigueur as Osama bin Laden and al-Qaeda acolytes exploited 24-hour news operations to seek publicity and convey their particular vision of the world. In the early 1980s, the UK debate was only just starting and the journalists of the BBC were faced with a very different culture from their own commitment to explanation and investigation, rooted in their professional journalistic values and the BBC's institutional ethos.

Another clash was therefore inevitable when, in April 1982, Thatcher ordered British military action to retake the Falkland Islands from Argentina – a policy which was reluctantly supported in Parliament by the opposition Labour Party and therefore, unlike Suez, lacked any mainstream political opposition beyond some Labour left-wingers. Thus, any traditional journalistic response of detached analysis was bound to be met with outright hostility from the government, particularly when troop lives were being lost and the government itself was at risk of electoral defeat if the military action failed. Both 'Newsnight' and 'Panorama' attempted to run objective programmes examining the origins of the conflict and the views of Britain's opponents, which provoked a furore in the jingoistic right-wing press and a predictably vitriolic response from the Prime Minister in the House of Commons. In the wake of those programmes Milne himself, as Director General designate, faced a nasty and acrimonious meeting of Conservative backbenchers, which left him in no doubt about the highly politicized atmosphere in which BBC journalism was now operating.

At the same time as attacking specific programmes, Thatcher took two further steps to impose her political mark on the BBC that would have longer term consequences for television journalism in Britain. First, she ensured that both the Chairman and the Vice-Chairman were Conservative sympathizers: the land-owning aristocrat George Howard, appointed as Chairman in 1980, was followed in 1984 by Stuart Young, a successful businessman and brother of one of her staunchest cabinet allies; and Vice-Chairman William Rees-Mogg, appointed in 1981, had been editor of *The Times* for 14 years and was a keen Thatcher cheerleader who shared her views about the BBC's innate bias.[34] Second, determined to replace the licence fee with some form of commercial funding, she appointed a committee, chaired by the committed free-marketer Professor Alan Peacock, to examine the case for advertising. In the event, the Peacock Committee rejected advertising on the BBC, but instead produced a deregulatory blueprint for the wholesale restructuring of commercial broadcasting, which was to play a defining part in the rapid decline of news and current affairs on commercial television. In the meantime, there were to be two major tests of the resilience of television journalism in the face of a prime minister at the height of her powers and resolutely opposed to any coverage of Northern Ireland that portrayed the IRA and its struggle as anything other than a despicable and murderous campaign.

The two programmes in question are covered in more detail in the next chapter. In retrospect, they might have represented the peak of a current affairs presence in British broadcasting that has never recovered its depth, dynamism and resourcefulness – not because television journalists were cowed by prime ministerial threats then or since, nor because there are insufficient protections for difficult journalism even if it threatens the political or corporate establishment; but because the structural and technological changes that were being set in motion – the ideological move to deregulation, the shift to a more globalized and liberalized economy and the competitive pressures from an abundance of new electronic sources – would soon make the production of original, hard-hitting television journalism an altogether less attractive option for broadcasters. Golden ageism is a dangerous obsession, and there has been some first-class broadcast journalism in the United Kingdom over the last 25 years. However, it is difficult to escape the conclusion that the mid to late 1980s was indeed a golden age of opportunity for television journalists in Britain, which combined the positive impact of healthy competition and a thriving commercial sector with strong regulatory oversight to enhance the public interest rather than private profit.

As a result, in a relatively small economy compared to the United States, two confident and well-funded news gatherers competed for audiences, old-fashioned scoops, speed and professionalism – but not for revenue; and established current affairs programmes thrived in peak-time on four different channels, each with its own branding, tradition, professional pride, research teams, resources and opportunities for young trainees wanting to be indentured into the craft. Not only did these programmes provide stability, funding and diversity but between them they covered the journalistic waterfront from difficult investigative journalism designed to hold government and other powerful agencies to account, to observational documentaries about the changing social and cultural lives of Britain, to in-depth analysis of the key national and international stories being covered in news bulletins. This is not a provable hypothesis, but it is at least possible to argue that British audiences in the late 1980s had more opportunities to understand and learn about the world around them through television than at any time before or since – and that, as the ratings showed, those opportunities were regularly grasped. It is therefore hugely ironic that at that very moment, the political and legislative climate was moving fast to remove the structures that were fostering this investment in high-class journalism and a more informed public. In that respect Britain, not for the first time, was about ten years behind the United States where the cold winds of the free market had already demonstrated how it can change forever the quality and quantity of television journalism.

Over the Atlantic

In 1961, the newly elected US President John F. Kennedy had appointed Newton Minow as Chairman of the Federal Communications Commission. In his first public speech, addressing the National Association of Broadcasters in May 1961, Minow was blunt both about the importance of television in promoting the public interest and the failure of commercial television to deliver. In words of which Murrow would have been proud, Minow told the broadcasting panjandrums that their industry possessed, 'the most powerful voice in America. It has an inescapable duty to make that voice ring with intelligence and with leadership'. He then contrasted the potential of the medium with what it actually produced:

> When television is good, nothing – not the theater, not the magazines or newspapers – nothing is better. But when television is bad, nothing is worse. I invite each of you to sit down in front of your television set when your station goes on the air and stay there, for a day, without a book, without a magazine, without a newspaper, without a profit and loss sheet or a rating book to distract you. Keep your eyes glued to that set until the station signs off. I can assure you that what you will observe is a vast wasteland.[35]

He contrasted this 'vast wasteland' – a graphic description of mediocrity that is still quoted today – with the broadcasters' own Television Code, which stated that, 'Program materials should enlarge the horizons of the viewer,' and urged them to respect and implement their own house guidelines. And he left them an explicit threat that there would be no automatic renewal of broadcast licenses, and that the FCC would be monitoring performance against promises.

The networks took note. In 1963, both CBS and NBC expanded their news bulletins from 15 minutes to 30 minutes, followed by ABC in 1967. This was not yet campaigning, investigative or challenging journalism, and political reporting in particular consisted of, according to Daniel Hallin, 'little more than unedited film of official speeches and press conferences, introduced by the anchor and followed by his commentary'.[36] It was primitive compared to the printed press and in particular the reputations for independent journalism forged by long-standing prestige papers like the *Washington Post* and *New York Times*. It was, however, a beginning and the potential value of high-quality current affairs was recognized by the CBS launch in 1968 of '60 Minutes'.

Created by Don Hewitt, who had directed Murrow's 'See It Now', the vision of '60 Minutes' was to combine the serious analytical and investigative approach of 'See It Now' with Murrow's less high-minded series, 'Person to Person', which had involved in-home interviews with celebrities. The programme was to be a combination of what one TV critic had called 'high Murrow and low Murrow', a fusion of journalistic approaches that, as we have seen, was also being adopted by current affairs on commercial TV in Britain. It was a spectacular success not only in raising the standard of television journalism, but – crucially – in terms of ratings and profitability. It demonstrated to the networks that news was not simply a trade-off for hanging on to a broadcast license but could be good for business. The 1960s and 1970s have been described as 'the golden age for news on television' in the United States, with substantial coverage of elections, serious documentaries, a coterie of highly paid and well-informed foreign correspondents and a commitment to the highest journalistic standards – personified by CBS News President Richard Salant who insisted on a hard-news approach that eschewed showbiz and journalistic gimmicks in a no-frills style of which Tahu Hole would have been proud.[37]

There were, however, the seeds of change to come: extravagant expenses and lifestyles; on-screen presenters whose celebrity status began to command huge salaries; the gradual loosening of regulatory oversight; the phenomenal profits that saw '60 Minutes' turned from journalistic innovation to corporate cash cow; and a gradual fading of the networks' founding fathers, such as William Paley at CBS and Leonard Goldenson at ABC, who had been committed to serious journalism.

Two major shifts of emphasis signalled fundamental changes in the 1980s. The first was the regulatory environment. Leonard Downey, in his analysis of the early years of American network news, suggests that networks were conscious of their public and democratic role, and that regulatory oversight – as with the fledgling ITV system in the United Kingdom – was critical: 'Feeling the gaze of government regulators, they wanted to demonstrate qualities of good citizenship and public service'.[38] From the beginning of Ronald Reagan's presidency in 1980, however, the FCC and its new Reagan appointee Mark Fowler pursued an avowedly pro-business line which was in stark contrast to the continuing regulatory obligations in the UK. Fowler announced his explicitly market-led approach in a jointly authored article in 1982: 'Our thesis is that the perception of broadcasters as community trustees should be replaced by a view of broadcasters as marketplace participants. Communications policy should be directed toward maximizing the services the public desires … The public's interest, then, defines the public interest.'[39]

There could not have been a starker contrast with Minow's approach to the public interest and the commercial broadcasters' obligations 20 years earlier. It effectively let the networks off the leash and reassured them that they would not be held accountable for a decline in standards or investment in serious broadcast journalism. The FCC was off their backs.

This explicitly deregulatory approach was quickly followed by a series of takeovers that saw the broadcasters swallowed up by corporations with a mindset dictated by the bottom line – and therefore intent on turning news divisions into profit centres. CBS was taken over by the New York investor Laurence Tisch who proceeded to cut costs and numbers with little regard for journalistic integrity. ABC fell to an ambitious media company one-tenth of its own size, Capital Cities, whose takeover was predicated on savage cost-cutting. And NBC was swallowed up by General Electric whose Chairman Jack Welch was renowned (and admired) in Wall Street for his ruthlessness in the pursuit of profit and business efficiency. His subordination of news to business imperatives was illustrated in October 1987 when the stock market plunged and NBC news anchor Tom Brokaw, along with every other commentator, reported grimly about 'Black Monday'. The following day, NBC President Lawrence Grossman received a call from Welch, accusing him of ruining the company's stock price through their news programmes' negative reporting.[40]

Perhaps the best example of how the ratings and profit potential of television journalism transformed professional practice in the United States in the 1980s was the emergence of a new form of current affairs within Rupert Murdoch's fledgling Fox network. It started in 1986 with 'A Current Affair', which revelled in its lack of fairness and for which, according to Murdoch's biographer, 'good taste was never a problem'.[41] By the end of 1989, it was making $25 million a year. This was followed by 'America's Most Wanted', which offered 're-enactments of gruesome crimes, and encouraged TV viewers to question their neighbours, and phone in to report suspicious activity ... It thrived on America's obsession with violent crime and with voyeuristic crime-solving.'[42] In 1989 it became the second most-watched programme on Fox and helped to turn the new network into profit.

This was certainly not television journalism as visualized by Murrow, Dimbleby, Pilkington or Minow. Its purpose was predicated almost entirely on voyeurism, fear and sensationalism, pushing out the boundaries of what was acceptable in order to generate the best financial return for the smallest outlay, and its emergence was certainly facilitated by the relaxed regulatory approach of the FCC. Supporters would argue that such programmes simply reflected an appetite for a kind of 'reality' television that the high-minded and stuffier networks had been unwilling to pioneer, and therefore was testament to the power of the marketplace. But such programmes replaced, rather than complemented, other more serious and ambitious forms of television journalism. They meant that commercial television in the United States rarely again provided contextual analysis, informative documentary or challenging investigations that held power to account. Meanwhile, at that very moment, both commercial and public television in Britain were demonstrating how analytical and watchdog forms of television journalism could challenge the State while still generating significant audiences.

4 'Real Lives' v 'Death on the Rock': Journalism, Terrorism and Accountability

Two particular programmes in the 1980s represented key moments in the evolution of broadcast journalism in the United Kingdom and demonstrated the vigorous and robust nature of the institutions that originated them. In their different ways, they also illustrate the profoundly important role of regulatory structures, institutional legacies, professional practices and individual personalities in defending journalistic independence in a democracy when there are powerful political and ideological forces at work trying to constrain independent accountability journalism. The case studies of the BBC's 'Real Lives' and ITV's 'Death on the Rock' help us to understand not only the basis on which illuminating independent television journalism can be constructed, but also how protective structures and strong editorial cultures can face down the threats posed by a strong-willed government. They also demonstrate eloquently why television journalism is less able to fulfil the same democratic function today either in the United Kingdom or in many other countries with a highly developed broadcasting system.

The story of 'Real Lives'
The programme
'Real Lives' was the generic name of a series made in the BBC's Documentary Features department during the summer of 1985 that sought to get behind the public image of well-known figures. Although not formally part of the BBC's news or current affairs operation, its making demonstrated at the same time both a strength and a weakness of the BBC. Its strength was that the serious journalistic tradition extended beyond those departments formally associated with journalism, and therefore enabled real editorial diversity to thrive even within the walls of a single organization. Its weakness was that this very diversity made it more difficult to keep an eye on provocative or contentious programmes that, while an essential ingredient of independent journalism, might need sensitive handling. In a publicly funded and therefore publicly accountable organization such as the BBC, it was (and remains) important that internal early warning systems exist for controversial

programmes about difficult political issues. This is crucial in understanding some of the furore which enveloped the BBC in subsequent controversies: internal organizational changes that have been prompted by a need for institutional clarity in the editorial decision-making process are sometimes confused for initiatives designed to promote a more censorious approach to political journalism. In recent BBC history, accountability rather than censorship has generally been the objective of internal change.

One programme within the Real Lives documentary series was called 'At the Edge of the Union'. Made by the experienced producer Paul Hamann, it sought to illuminate the Northern Ireland conflict by looking at it through the eyes of two opposing political figures on Derry city council: Gregory Campbell, leader of the Democratic Unionist Party, and Martin McGuinness of Provisional Sinn Fein, rumoured to be the IRA's chief of staff (which he then denied) and openly supportive of violence in the struggle for a united Ireland. Both were elected members of the Northern Ireland Assembly who drew salaries from the British government and had been routinely interviewed on Northern Ireland radio and television. The programme was designed to allow the subjects to speak for themselves, in documentary-style, rather than to subject them to interrogation, in hard current affairs style. This contrast in styles was, itself, to become a core part of the ensuing controversy given that the two protagonists were not being challenged for their views on promoting terrorism or violence. But the guiding objective was to cast light on what, for most observers, was an almost unfathomable level of hatred and fanaticism, and allow the participants to demonstrate their extremism through their own words. It was an important and courageous example of illuminating journalism rather than interrogative journalism. In the words of Hamann himself, interviewed just three months later: 'This Department has had a long tradition of making documentaries without a reporter and, we would like to think, [of] getting through to the truth of a situation more than perhaps … our colleagues in Current Affairs.'[1]

Precisely because of the sensitivities involved, very clear BBC guidelines for interviewing terrorists had been drawn up and the relevant section was unambiguous: 'Interviews with individuals who are deemed by ADG [the Assistant Director General, responsible for news and current affairs] to be closely associated with a terrorist organisation may not be sought or transmitted – two separate stages – without the prior permission of DG [Director General].' However, this particular case was less clear: Martin McGuinness was an elected representative who denied involvement with terrorism and – whatever the unconfirmed rumours – had not been convicted of any violent act. The series producer was told that, because McGuinness was an elected politician, the guidelines did not apply and the programme was scheduled for transmission on 7 August 1985. Neither the

Director General Alasdair Milne nor his Chairman Stuart Young were aware of its existence.

The politics

Margaret Thatcher's uncompromising attitude to the IRA, forged by the murder of Airey Neave in 1979, had been further reinforced in October 1984 when she and members of her cabinet had been the target of an IRA bomb at the Conservative Party conference in Brighton. And the temperature was further heightened on 14 June 1985 when a TWA aircraft from Athens to Rome was hijacked by Lebanese Shia extremists who shot dead an American Navy pilot amongst the passengers, forced the plane to fly between Beirut and Algiers, and did not release the final hostages until 30 June. During the course of this 16-day hostage crisis American television networks had given extensive coverage to the Arab instigators, publicity which had infuriated Margaret Thatcher. Two weeks later, in a speech to the American Bar Association's London convention on 15 July, she made her frustration with media exposure abundantly clear: 'we must try to find ways to starve the terrorists of the oxygen of publicity on which they depend'. Under the circumstances, it was perhaps surprising that the timing of 'Real Lives' went unquestioned and moreover that the programme was featured prominently in the preceding week's Radio Times listings magazine. It even included some of McGuinness's deliberately provocative statements to be aired in the programme, such as: 'We believe that the only way the Irish people can bring about the freedom of their country is through the use of arms' and 'It will be the cutting edge of the IRA that will bring freedom.'[2] Advance copies of the magazine were available from 26 July, just 11 days after Margaret Thatcher's speech.

A Sunday Times reporter, Barrie Penrose, saw the programme billed and immediately made connections.[3] His newspaper, under its editor Andrew Neil and proprietor Rupert Murdoch, had been devoutly supportive of Thatcher and was a long-standing critic of the BBC. Here was a story which would fit ideally with the newspaper's narrative, and Penrose worked hard to stoke the flames of controversy. Having confirmed that McGuinness was a participant in the film, he asked the Prime Minister at a press briefing how she would feel if a British broadcaster was to interview the IRA Chief of Staff, and received the predictable response that: 'I would condemn them utterly.' Two days later, the Sunday Times article was published, particularly unfortunate timing because the Director General Alasdair Milne was on a fishing holiday in Finland and his deputy, Michael Checkland, had only just been appointed. Checkland summoned the Board of Management to see the programme first thing on Monday morning at Broadcasting House and all thought it transmittable, with a few minor amendments. Alan Protheroe, Assistant Director General and the most senior journalist in the BBC's hierarchy, was clear that it was an unexceptional and solid piece of journalism that demonstrated with terrible clarity the polarized views of two Northern Ireland leaders:

> Very similar people, working class background, charismatic, clear-speaking, family men, teetotal, churchgoers, ostensibly practising Christians, but both of them actually advocating the most horrendous views ... And it struck me that this was a programme that would add immeasurably to the public understanding of the difficulties of governing Northern Ireland, and indeed the difficulties that the government would have in trying to reconcile these two views.[4]

It was, in other words, precisely the kind of challenging and enlightening journalism that an independent broadcaster should be doing. Constitutionally, that was where matters traditionally rested: editorial decisions were vested in the Board of Management, and it was a long-standing principle that the BBC governing board did not preview programmes. When the Board of Governors was abolished and replaced by the BBC Trust in 2007 – with a much more defined constitutional relationship to the BBC executive – the same principle was extended to the new body. Behind this long-standing convention lies a crucial question of editorial control: Governors – or Trustees – do not preview programmes because they are then free to praise, criticize or if necessary condemn after transmission. By previewing, they become complicit in the editorial and creative process and are compromised when it comes to dealing with post-transmission complaints.[5] The BBC's Board of Management therefore informed the Chairman of their decision that the programme was satisfactory, did not breach editorial guidelines, and would be broadcast as planned. Under normal circumstances, the Board of Governors would have let the matter rest there until the programme had gone out as scheduled.

At this point, however, the Home Secretary Leon Brittan intervened. The Home Office had responsibility for both broadcasting policy – including matters involving the BBC – and national security, and on the Monday morning he delivered a message to the BBC Chairman through his officials saying that the programme gave 'spurious legitimacy to the use of violence for political ends'. The message continued: 'The Home Secretary thought that it was contrary to the public interest that a programme of this kind apparently envisaged should be broadcast. He very much hopes that the BBC will not do so.'[6] He also indicated that he would ask to see the programme pre-transmission if the BBC decided to go ahead, thus placing the Chairman Stuart Young in an invidious position. How could he support his management against the government if he had not himself seen the programme?

At Young's insistence, Brittan then wrote formally to the BBC Chairman, and underlined the profoundly political nature of his intervention by rejecting outright the advice of his Home Office officials who understood clearly the bitter confrontation that would follow.[7] In his letter, he acknowledged the BBC's constitutional independence and insisted that he was in no way attempting to impose censorship. But, he said, he also had ministerial responsibility for 'the fight against the ever present threat of terrorism' and deliberately echoed the Prime Minister's evocative phrase to warn against providing a platform for murderers: 'Recent events elsewhere in the world have confirmed only too clearly what has long been understood in this country; that terrorism thrives on the oxygen of publicity ... Even if the programme and any surrounding material were, as a whole, to present terrorist organisations in a wholly unfavourable light, I would still ask you not to permit it to be broadcast.'[8]

How to strike the right balance between restricting public access to sensitive information and legitimate public enlightenment has been at the forefront of journalistic debate from the censored reports of the First World War to the twenty-first-century debate on Wikileaks. It is a particularly difficult area for public broadcasters, which are, arguably, more vulnerable to political interference and more accountable for their decisions. As we have seen, political attempts to exert editorial pressure on the BBC were confined essentially to demands for self-censorship rather than imposing an outright programme ban, and that is precisely the route which Brittan took on 'Real Lives'. It was not subtle but nor was it outright government censorship, and Brittan himself was unrepentant about his duty to represent the potential risk as the minister responsible for law and order. For him the question was 'whether it is consistent with the responsibilities of the BBC as a Public Service Broadcasting organisation to give a platform for people that advocate violence', and he drew parallels (often cited in arguments around freedom of speech and terrorism) with whether the BBC would have given currency to the advocacy of genocide by 1930s Nazi leaders.[9] The analogy may have been dubious, but it was not an entirely unreasonable position for a government minister to take, and it became a test of the BBC's resilience in the face of intense but legitimate pressure from a democratically elected minister.

The BBC response

Given the intervention of a senior government minister citing national security concerns, Young had no choice but to call a joint emergency meeting the next day of the Board of Governors and Board of Management. Milne by this time was out of contact on a boat to Sweden, but Young devised what he later called 'a very clear gameplan' to deal with Brittan's letter. With the *Sunday Times* and other pro-Thatcher newspapers ready to leap on the bandwagon, there was clearly a risk that the BBC Governors would be accused of recklessly putting the country in danger by allowing a programme to be aired of which they had deliberately remained ignorant despite the Home Secretary's warnings about national security issues. He subsequently explained his strategy thus:

> What I wanted to do was to view the programme, to be able to stand behind the editorial integrity of that programme and then to write to the Home Secretary to say that the Board of Governors have taken the exceptional step of viewing the programme, that they have every confidence in management, that the programme editorially is sound, that it will be transmitted as scheduled. However, if there are matters relating to the security of the state that the Governors know nothing about, then the Home Secretary in his capacity as being Minister responsible for Law and Order should ban the programme under Section 13.4 of the Licence Agreement.

Viewing the programme would therefore allow Governors to fulfil their duty as trustees of the public interest, would deflect the political attack and would enable them to stand foursquare behind management's editorial integrity. It was a coherent strategy with three flaws: it assumed that the Governors would approve the programme; it failed to appreciate that, if they did approve it, such previewing would make the Governors complicit in any subsequent editorial storm; and most grievously of all, it failed to appreciate the perception of abject surrender to blatant political pressure if the Governors chose not to approve it.

At the meeting itself, there were therefore two decisions to take: first, whether Governors should view the programme and then, depending on that decision, whether they should approve it for transmission. Accounts of those involved suggest that BBC managers, while opposed to previewing on principle, recognized the difficult position created by the Home Secretary and did not advance their arguments with particular vigour. While absolutely clear and unanimous that the programme was fit for transmission after one or two small amendments, their case was weakened on two fronts: the absence of the Director General who had ultimate editorial responsibility; and the technical breach of reference-up rules which meant that Milne himself had neither approved the interviews nor seen the programme.

The Governors, meanwhile, were ambivalent: they felt let down by inadequate internal reference procedures, but they also felt under intolerable political pressure. Perhaps the most crucial problem was a deep-seated lack of faith in the very journalism they were supposed to be protecting. The Secretary, David Holmes, described the Governors as having 'a view that all the journalists in the BBC are without principle, that they are by and large incompetent, are a group of people in whom they cannot be proud'. This unsophisticated approach to journalism was compounded by what the Director of Television Brian Wenham called a 'fairly severe collapse of trust' between the two Boards which prevented the Governors from simply accepting the unanimous editorial decision of BBC executives.[10] It remains an important lesson for any public broadcaster attempting to balance accountability with journalistic independence that those acting as institutional guardians should understand and respect the nature of the journalism being undertaken. The consequence in this case of the Governors' distrust was that they watched the programme with little respect for the collective editorial view of their management and with a jaundiced view of the journalism they practised.

It was, therefore, not surprising that the tone during and after viewing changed to one of almost unanimous hostility, fuelled in particular by the view of Vice-Chairman William Rees-Mogg that the documentary form of journalism was unsuitable for tackling terrorism in Northern Ireland. In his subsequent interview, he described the programme as a fly-on-the-wall technique that 'has a tendency to ... present both people as being perhaps misguided people, but nevertheless as having their own point of view, and if you happen to like blowing up innocent people, well that's your privilege.'[11] Despite warnings from the Chairman about the consequences, most of Rees-Mogg's fellow Governors followed his lead. All except one voted in favour of non-transmission.[12] There was some confusion as to whether the decision was an outright or temporary ban but, as far as the management group were concerned, this was a straightforward veto that overturned the professional journalistic judgement of those who had made and approved the programme. In his assessment of the decision the BBC's Northern Ireland Controller James Hawthorne, who had been intimately involved in the decision-making process, expressed the shock and anger of his colleagues: 'However they put it, the Governors had made a decision under pressure from the Home Secretary and against the considered advice of the most experienced and senior editors of the BBC. They had banned the programme because they disliked it. They had made liars of us all.'[13]

The aftermath

The decision created predictable outrage, making the front pages of all the next day's papers. Milne, having returned home on 3 August 1985, was certain that the Governors' decision had to be reversed if the BBC were not to suffer permanent damage. While the Governors endorsed the ban at another board meeting on 6 August, they had been taken aback by the furore which their decision had provoked and confirmed that their decision was not necessarily permanent. Amongst broadcast journalists, in particular, there was fury at what was perceived as unacceptable government interference on a massive scale, which required a determined show of resistance. Members of the National Union of Journalists at the BBC decided to strike for 24 hours on 7 August, the day originally billed for the transmission of 'Real Lives'. Such was the universal sense of outrage that they were joined by journalists at ITN, in radio and, unprecedentedly, by colleagues at the BBC World Service, which on the day was reduced to playing music. This caused some amusement in the Soviet Union which had always insisted that the BBC's External Services were no more than Western government propaganda, but dismay to Britain's allies in the United States and the West. The solidity of the strike and the unanimity of those involved took the Governors by surprise. Alan Protheroe believed that the Governors were 'amazed at the way that journalists in television and radio throughout the UK came out ... What disconcerted them was the Americans, for example, saying to us, well of course you're really just another Voice of America'.[14]

There is no question that the strike – and its extension both to commercial broadcasting and to the World Service – was a key symbolic expression of the profound collective sense of betrayal felt by broadcast journalists throughout the country. The virtual absence of any broadcast news that day underlined to the government in general and the Home Secretary in particular that the BBC could not be intimidated, and that there would be no respite from accusations of outright government censorship until the programme was shown and the BBC's reputation for independent journalism was restored. While BBC senior managers publicly opposed the strikes, they appreciated both the fury that prompted them and their impact on the world at large. And at least one of the Governors was able to communicate to his colleagues the sense of outrage that prompted such an explosion of opposition. Milne described the view of Alwyn Roberts, the only Governor to have formally dissented from the decision to ban the programme, who had canvassed opinion among production staff in Wales: 'they were not in any doubt that the Governors had the right to view programmes or indeed take them off, but they believed fundamentally, deeply and passionately that the Governors had got it wrong, and it was the wrongness of the decision which so infuriated the staff'.[15]

Over the next few weeks, that storm did not abate and was reinforced by some trenchant condemnation in much of the press. With tempers cooled, with the Home Secretary having retreated from battle and with Milne agreeing to an investigation into the breakdown of Governor-Management relations, the first board meeting in September was a less highly charged affair, at the end of which the Governors agreed that 'Real Lives' could be shown in October with a few minor amendments to take account of the new circumstances surrounding its broadcast.

On 16 October 1985, an audience of nearly 5 million watched and probably wondered what the fuss had been about. The BBC's audience research department carried out some post-transmission research, including the question, 'Was it right or wrong of the BBC to have made and transmitted this programme?' In light of the acute sensitivity that had been constructed by the row, and the fact that would-be complainants had been alerted, the results were startling: 10 per cent thought it was wrong, 12 per cent said they didn't know and 78 per cent said it was right – vindication for the editorial judgement of the BBC hierarchy.[16] Milne had no doubt subsequently about the magnitude of the events surrounding the programme nor the importance of the principle that needed to be upheld. He also had no doubt about the terminal impact on his own career at the helm of the BBC: 'It was a major moment of truth for us because that decision had to be reversed. We had to force it through and we never recovered from that really, any of us ... When I engineered that it should go out, they clearly decided that things should change.'[17] Within 18 months, he would be sacked – but only after more journalistic disasters for which he would have to accept some of the blame.

Implications for BBC journalism

In retrospect, the events surrounding 'Real Lives' and its eventual broadcast were a vivid demonstration of the strength of the BBC as an independent journalistic institution – not because it was a spectacular feat of journalism, but because everything was conspiring against it. On the face of it, there could not have been a more inauspicious set of circumstances: a prime minister at the height of her powers with a huge parliamentary majority, instinctively hostile to the BBC and viscerally opposed to any programme that might allow a platform for alleged terrorists; a politically inept Home Secretary intent on carrying her torch; a BBC Chairman appointed by the Prime Minister and the brother of one her cabinet ministers; a powerful and influential Vice-Chairman profoundly out of sympathy with the BBC and who shared most of the Prime Minister's opinions; a Board of Governors in which 10 out of the 11 members had been appointed by the Prime Minister; a Director General who by coincidence was out of the country and not contactable during the critical two days of the crisis; a Deputy General who had just taken over and was not a programme-maker; a predominantly Thatcherite press, happy to play its part in first initiating and then supporting any campaign against the BBC in a febrile and jingoistic atmosphere; a programme that might have breached clear guidelines on interviewing terrorists; and a knowledge vacuum at the top of the BBC where neither the content of the programme nor any suspicion of impending crisis had penetrated top management to prepare them for the fallout. Even the programme's producer, Paul Hamann, later expressed his surprise that the programme was not examined more closely in the light of events in Beirut, and did not offer an outright denial when asked whether the Governors had some justification in pulling the programme.

Despite all these factors, the programme was made and broadcast (albeit two months late) with insignificant changes to an audience at least twice the size of any it would have achieved under normal circumstances. There is no question that the saga weakened Milne's position to the point where it became untenable, although other factors intervened. But, crucially, it did not weaken the BBC, or the resolve of its journalists, or its sense of professional journalistic pride, or its determination to pursue independent and non-partisan journalism even where it became uncomfortable for a powerful government. One of the more thoughtful Governors, Sir John Johnston, who later bitterly regretted his own role in allowing the programme to be banned, reflected on some of his colleagues' misplaced expectation that their decision should have commanded loyalty from the staff, and offered a perspective that could be applicable to any public broadcaster seeking to inculcate journalistic values based on a public service ethos:

> I personally take the view that everyone's loyalty within the BBC has in a sense to be not to the present Board of Governors or even to the present Director General, but to the sort of historical continuum of the BBC, the *idea* of the BBC as it has been running for the last 60 years. And it is to that concept of public service broadcasting, in which Governors come and go, Directors General come and go, but which is one of the most civilising innovations of this century ... to which everyone's loyalty should be directed.[18]

There could be no more elegant appraisal of a journalistic legacy that had started tentatively with Reith, had evolved under Wyndham Goldie and Hugh Greene and consolidated under Trethowan and Milne, and was by now strong enough to withstand even the most concerted political onslaught. An equally bloody confrontation with a similarly powerful government under a Labour prime minister would occur nearly 20 years later, with similarly terminal consequences for top BBC management and for a Labour-appointed chairman. And again, as we shall see, it was to leave the institutional values of BBC journalism intact.

Apart from highlighting the durability of BBC institutional values, the 'Real Lives' episode illustrated a more universal feature of a public broadcaster which Milne was perhaps slow to recognize: the importance of having in place transparent and effective mechanisms of democratic accountability. Decisions that appear to be arbitrary or to conform to no particular code of journalistic conduct, or which may be interpreted as the journalistic whim or prejudice of a particular reporter or producer, are vulnerable to politically motivated attack. Decisions that are clearly rooted in a journalistic tradition of investigation, information, enlightenment or knowledge, and which have clearly followed an agreed code of how such journalism should be practised, can far more easily be protected from partisan attacks by those who would seek to curb it. In the BBC's case, the Board of Governors – and now the BBC Trust – acts as a buffer between those taking uncomfortable editorial decisions and those who would rather see the fruits of those decisions removed from the nation's screens: not just governments and oppositions, but corporations, local authorities, public bodies, private institutions or any individuals whose position of trust and authority may warrant investigation. Those entrusted with this task need to have confidence that proper editorial control is being exercised.

This was manifestly not the case in the BBC of the mid 1980s, and it was not entirely due to a politically motivated board, as Milne himself acknowledged. In their subsequent accounts, several managers and Governors referred to their sadness at the levels of mutual mistrust and resentment that prevailed. The absence of proper referral procedures may have been a technical glitch, but it was not an isolated incident and led directly to senior managers' flat-footedness and their inability to react to the changed political circumstances of the post-Beirut environment and the Home Secretary's ham-fisted intervention. Rees-Mogg, often portrayed as the villain of the piece, was clear that for him the accountability issue was key: 'I didn't in the end mind our showing it because I thought the point had been made. Not that the Governors want to intervene, not that the Governors should intervene on editorial matters, but that unless the editorial systems are properly worked, that in the end the governors will intervene.'[19]

While this might be discounted to some extent as post-hoc rationalization from someone who had so vehemently opposed transmission, there is no question that a Board of Governors with faith in its management's adherence to agreed editorial procedures would have found it much easier to withstand a powerful government, regardless of the board's own political complexion.

Once the internal report into Management-Governor relations had been completed and its conclusions disseminated, Milne himself was shocked by the antagonism being expressed by Governors. A few years later he reflected: 'It was a terrible thing to read. It hadn't been like that three years ago, so I must carry some of the burden of blame for what went wrong.'[20] It was a frank assessment of the constitutional fissures that were opened on his watch, and a warning that can be universally applied to any publicly funded broadcaster. It is, quite simply, what governments do – particularly when they are driven by ideology rather than political pragmatism. Resistance requires both robust mechanisms of accountability to protect independence and a leadership that commands respects.

That lack of respect, combined with another journalistic failure, cost Milne his job. Following Young's death from cancer the following year, the government appointed another Conservative sympathizer, Marmaduke Hussey, not long off the staff of Rupert Murdoch's *Times* newspapers. Shortly before Hussey was due to take over, the BBC was forced to settle an expensive libel claim against two Conservative MPs who has been featured in a 1984 'Panorama' programme investigating links between the right wing of the party and the extreme neo-fascist right. Called 'Maggie's Militant Tendency', it was based on a report by the Young Conservatives, which had amassed considerable evidence and was supported by senior members of the party. But once the case came to court, evidence that had been 'rock solid' at the research stage looked less secure as promised witnesses failed to materialize.[21] It was another disaster which made the BBC look weak and out of control. In January 1987, Milne was sacked by the new Chairman and Milne's deputy, Michael Checkland, was appointed in his place. It heralded a new era of BBC journalism in which John Birt, who had propounded his 'bias against understanding' 12 years earlier, was brought in from LWT as Deputy Director General with a specific brief to sort out the journalism. His institutional influence was to be profound, and would take BBC journalism almost into the next century.

The Story of 'Death on the Rock'

The programme

We saw in the previous chapter how in 1978 ITV replaced 'This Week' with the somewhat more populist 'TV Eye'. In 1985 a new Managing Director at Thames Television, Richard Dunn, suggested that 'This Week' should be brought back to 'restore our status' and reintroduce some heavyweight journalism to the peak-time ITV schedule.[22] The new editor was Roger Bolton, schooled in the BBC journalism of 'Tonight' and 'Panorama' and aware of television's capacity for exaggerating the dramatic. It is hugely ironic that, even as Margaret Thatcher's Conservative government was planning to dismantle the structure that sustained them, both 'This Week' and 'World in Action' continued to conduct difficult journalism in a changing world. Northern Ireland still presented one of the most demanding political and journalistic challenges and commercial television, to its credit, did not retreat from tackling the issue.

In 1988 'This Week' made a programme which – like 'Real Lives' three years earlier – resulted in a brutal confrontation between broadcaster and government, and demonstrated equally universal principles about the need for robust regulatory mechanisms to protect against government intimidation. Titled 'Death on the Rock', this was not a behind-the-scenes documentary but a classic example of investigative journalism that challenged an official version of events, infuriated the Prime Minister and underlined television's ability to hold even the most powerful governments to account. It has been claimed (wrongly) that the programme was responsible for Thames subsequently losing its ITV licence. What is certain is that the programme exemplified the kind of challenging journalism that requires resources, a strong-willed management prepared to go the distance, and a hard-headed regulator acting in the public interest as a buffer between programme-maker and government.

The dramatic events that it covered started on the afternoon of Sunday, 6 March 1988, when three members of the Provisional IRA were shot and killed by security forces in Gibraltar. They were named as Sean Savage, Daniel McCann and Mairéad Farrell whom the IRA quickly claimed as being 'volunteers on active service'. First reports on news bulletins that evening – and in the following day's newspapers – suggested that a car bomb had been found nearby and defused, and that all three IRA members had been armed. They had planned, according to these reports, to blow up the band of the Royal Anglian Regiment, which was due to assemble two days later outside the Governor of Gibraltar's residence. The ITN news that evening spoke of three IRA terrorists being killed 'in a fierce gun battle'. But in the words of journalist Ian Jack, in a forensically detailed report on the events and their fallout, 'this bomb was a fiction. There was not and never had been a bomb in Gibraltar, neither had the crowded streets of Gibraltar witnessed a gun battle'.[23] This corrected version of events was officially confirmed the following day by the Foreign Secretary Sir Geoffrey Howe, who also admitted that those killed 'were subsequently found not to have been carrying arms'. There followed a sequence of violence and revenge that was extreme even by the standards of the Northern Ireland conflict. The funeral of the three IRA activists took place ten days later on Wednesday, 16 March, filmed by a 'This Week' team. The funeral was interrupted by a Loyalist gunman who shot and killed three mourners and injured 68 others. He was chased, caught, beaten unconscious and was only rescued when the police intervened. Three days later, during the funeral procession of one of the victims, two British soldiers were spotted, dragged from their car, beaten and shot dead by some of those attending the funeral.

This was therefore not an auspicious time to be questioning the veracity of events, but Amnesty International had announced by the end of the month its intention to investigate whether the shootings were 'extrajudicial executions'. By then, Roger Bolton had already become concerned by some of the inconsistencies emerging from reports, and decided to pursue the story for 'This Week'. He sent three journalists to Spain, Gibraltar and Belfast to start enquiries, fully aware of the political sensitivity but also certain this was precisely the kind of issue that independent journalism was required to tackle: 'I didn't give a lot of thought to the political repercussions. I knew it would be difficult and possibly controversial but I had decided long ago that I had to judge a story by its importance, not by the political fall-out one might face.'[24]

At the heart of his investigation was the crucial question being posed by Amnesty: were the shootings an example of a 'shoot-to-kill' policy being pursued as a means of dealing with those identified by the security services as IRA terrorists and bypassing all the expense, time and inconvenience of having to amass evidence and go to trial? If so, as Amnesty was suggesting, the UK armed services would be operating outside the rule of law, and the government would be collaborating in a cover-up of what was little more than cold-blooded assassination. His researchers found eyewitnesses to the shootings who denied that warnings had been shouted to the terrorists before shots were fired; reported that the victims had raised their hands in surrender rather than reached for weapons; and claimed that all three may have been shot again after they fell to the ground. While many witnesses found by the research team were reluctant to talk about what they had seen, the two that were gave sworn evidence that was incompatible with the version of events given by the security services and the Foreign Secretary.

The politics

This was clearly going to be an explosive programme, and throughout the preparations the IBA was kept informed of progress. On 29 March it was told informally of a 'sensitive' project under way. On 11 April, transmission date was fixed for Thursday 28 April, and on 25 April it was shown to the Thames legal adviser and left 'largely untouched'. Then, two days before transmission, the government attempted to have it stopped. The Foreign Secretary Geoffrey Howe personally telephoned the Chairman of the IBA, George Thomson and asked him to postpone the programme until after the inquest even though no date for the inquest had been set. By now, the IBA had become more battle-hardened and more confident in its capacity as a protector and facilitator of difficult journalism rather a censor. Thomson recognized the legitimacy of the government's position, but also his own responsibility to resist intimidation. In his own reflection of events later in the year, he wrote that the decision to allow transmission 'was not a difficult one ... Sir Geoffrey Howe did his duty and I did mine, and if you do not like that sort of conflict of duty between Government and broadcaster, then you should not be Chairman of an Independent Broadcasting Authority'.[25]

In a world where governments, corporations and other sources of elite power spend billions on trying to manipulate journalism to their advantage, this remains a fundamentally important acknowledgement of the role that a powerful regulatory body can play. No government – particularly with Margaret Thatcher at the height of her powers – would simply stand by as their determined attempts to eradicate terrorist atrocities were (as they saw it) being systematically undermined by irresponsible troublemakers with access to a mass audience. In such cases, the existence of a protective buffer rooted in a vision of journalistic independence and freedom of speech rather than political pragmatism acts as a guarantor, or as a facilitator, of such independence. It does, of course, require the individual protagonists to play their part and Bolton in his subsequent book acknowledged Thomson's crucial role: 'We owed that brave man a great deal.'

After Howe's intervention, the political pressure intensified. The IBA previewed the programme and asked for three minor changes. On the day of transmission the IBA's Director of Television David Glencross phoned Howe's office to say the IBA had approved transmission 'at the highest level'. Howe phoned back, asked again for postponement and leaked these conversations to the press while the Northern Ireland Secretary told Parliament that the programme amounted to 'trial by television'. When asked the day before transmission by a group of Japanese journalists if she was 'furious' about the programme, Margaret Thatcher said that her reaction 'went deeper than that'.[26] The programme went out as scheduled on 28 April, and its uncompromising opening lines demonstrated why the government had found it so unpalatable: 'Did the SAS men have the law on their side, when they shot dead Danny McCann, Sean Savage and Mairéad Farrell who were unarmed at the time? Were the soldiers acting in self-defence or were they operating what has become known as a "shoot-to-kill policy", simply eliminating a group of known terrorists outside the due process of law without arrest, trial or verdict?'[27]

Intriguingly, the minister responsible for broadcasting, Douglas Hurd, did not share his colleagues' inclination to interfere and had said as much to the Thames Chairman a week before transmission. But because it was Gibraltar, this was a matter on which the Foreign Office took the lead and Hurd remained silent. According to Glencross, interviewed about the events some 15 years later, 'Tory ministers were terrified of Thatcher. Howe came into the attack as Thatcher's poodle. Hurd knew about the programme and never attempted to stand up for the broadcasters.'[28] Luckily, and probably to its eventual cost, the regulatory authority was prepared to do what the minister responsible was not. It was an excellent illustration of how the absence of such institutional safeguards inevitably makes such controversial journalism more vulnerable to the vagaries of political life and political ambition.

The aftermath

While the precise circumstances surrounding the shooting will never be known, there is no question that the programme itself was a triumph of journalistic investigation in a very unforgiving environment. After transmission, the government and its supporters were determined to make life as difficult as possible for those they identified as participating in an act of treachery. The programme-makers were vilified in the right-wing press, while the *Sunday Times* in particular ran an ugly and vicious campaign to discredit the witnesses. The *Sun* attacked the programme as 'a piece of IRA propaganda'. Both papers were now owned by Rupert Murdoch whose unswerving support for Thatcher had not gone unnoticed or unappreciated. It may have been no coincidence that the following month was to see an announcement by Murdoch of his own television ambitions in the United Kingdom, which were to receive a very significant helping hand by the Prime Minister in forthcoming legislation – and within 20 years would, as British Sky Broadcasting, become by far the most profitable commercial television enterprise in the UK.

During the inquest into the shootings, the coroner urged the jury to avoid the ambiguity of an open verdict and to choose between 'justifiable, reasonable homicide' and 'unlawful homicide'.[29] After nearly eight hours of deliberation, on 30 September, the jury returned with a nine to two majority verdict of lawful homicide. Despite their manifest ambivalence, the verdict was greeted as a vindication of the government's position and a serious blow to the programme's credibility. With the spotlight and political pressure now focused firmly on Thames, its Chairman decided to launch an independent enquiry into the programme to discover whether it had been 'responsible' and whether it 'performed a public service by contributing information and insight on a controversial matter of public concern'. It was conducted by Lord Windlesham who, while a Conservative peer and friend of the Foreign Secretary Geoffrey Howe, had himself been a current affairs producer and had written about the importance of Public Service Broadcasting.

Windlesham's report, a detailed examination of the programme published the following January, was a complete vindication. In a fascinating postscript to these tumultuous events, Bolton describes a conversation shortly afterwards with one of his most 'outspoken critics', a man clearly well acquainted with the facts, who gave some explanation as to why the establishment had tried to crush the programme: 'you and I come from different cultures. Mine is the army and politics ... Of course there was a shoot-to-kill policy in Gibraltar just as we had in the Far East and in Aden ... But it's none of your business. There are certain areas of the British national interest that you shouldn't get involved in. *Death on the Rock* just wasn't necessary.'[30] This incomprehension of a vision of journalism committed to exposing premeditated violations of basic tenets of democracy – in this case, the apparent extrajudicial execution of suspected terrorists to avoid a properly conducted trial – underlines why investigative journalism that takes on the established might of the State requires institutionalized support. This is profoundly important for a medium that easily defaults to less expensive, less serious, less rigorous, less controversial forms of journalism when under competitive pressure to avoid unnecessary cost or aggravation. The implications for a healthy democracy are profound. In a resounding echo of Edmund Burke's famous dictum that, 'All that is necessary for the triumph of evil is that good men do nothing.' Lord Windlesham subsequently told the Royal Television Society:

> If the price of harmony is to leave sensitive subjects alone; to ask no awkward questions; to take no risks incurring official displeasure on issues of high public importance; then it is a price set too high. Far from being a symptom that something is wrong in the body politic, I regard periodic rows between governments of whatever colour and broadcasters as genuine marks – stigmata may be the better word – of a free society.[31]

While a fitting finale to this particular row, the programme marked the last time that an independent regulator with real teeth would be able to exert any authority to defend journalistic integrity. By this time, the Peacock Committee had delivered its free-market recommendations for the wholesale deregulation of commercial television. Writing about the events at the time, former ITN editor Nigel Ryan said: 'If the government has its way, *Death on the Rock* may go into history as not so much a programme title, more an epitaph on the ITV system … at risk is the future of the IBA, which sanctioned it, as well as the free operation of public service journalism.'[32] Within five years both the IBA and Thames would be gone, both victims of the Thatcherite revolution that was to culminate in the 1990 Broadcasting Act. Also on the way out would be a system that had nurtured, fostered and protected a consistent level of high-quality, in-depth television reporting on commercial television. Governments acting beyond the limits of democratic values and accountability were able to sleep a little easier as a result.

In the official history of commercial television, Paul Bonner describes the notion of a direct link between that single programme and the demise of the IBA as a myth, which is almost certainly an accurate assessment.[33] Just as 'Real Lives' did not result in Alasdair Milne's sacking but represented an institutional problem with BBC journalism in an era of growing political and democratic accountability, so 'Death on the Rock' did not instigate the end of the IBA but simply offered further evidence to government supporters that there was no advantage in sustaining a bureaucratic institution that interfered with the operation of the free market. It may have hardened Thatcher's resolve to do away with it, but the IBA for her government was already an anachronism in a policy framework that emerged seamlessly out of an ideological commitment to liberal economic theory and deregulation. The Broadcasting White Paper, *Competition, Choice and Quality* (the last word was alleged to have been added at the last minute), was published in October 1988 in the immediate aftermath of 'Death on the Rock', but it owed a much bigger debt to the Peacock Report, and to right-wing think-tanks like the Adam Smith Institute and the Centre for Policy Studies than to a single example of investigative journalism.

Conclusion

It is always dangerous to hold up individual programmes or incidents as microcosms of a wider truth, and these were just two particularly contentious examples of 1980s television journalism that covered a far wider canvass of issues and approaches. 'Real Lives' was a living example of straightforward documentary journalism designed simply to shed some light on an incomprehensible mindset within a barely intelligible conflict. It was an excellent example of using a powerful, populist medium to promote informational journalism. 'Death on the Rock' was a living example of investigative journalism designed to hold to account a powerful political elite through a meticulous interrogation of the official version of events. Both were examples of the kinds of highly professional journalism that were not uncommon on mainstream British television at the time.

What makes them stand out, beyond the monumental controversy that each created within three years of each other, were the institutional and regulatory arrangements that allowed programme-makers the confidence to pursue their ideas through to completion, not only contrary to the well-signposted wishes of a strong-willed government and prime minister, but also in the face of a barrage of press hostility fuelled by blind loyalty to an incumbent government with a huge parliamentary majority. It is no coincidence that in both cases *The Sunday Times*, owned by Murdoch and edited by his then loyal lieutenant Andrew Neil, instigated the most ferocious attacks on the organizations responsible and were supported by other newspapers from the News International stable. These attacks both legitimized the position of the government and placed under intense public scrutiny the accuracy and professionalism of the programme-makers. It is rarely acknowledged that in both cases the quality, accuracy and integrity of the journalism involved in making the two programmes emerged unscathed – which is more than could be said for much of the journalism being practised by the hounding press pack at the time. In the BBC's case, it was the institutional conventions designed to ensure proper sensitivity to the political world outside that were found wanting rather than the programme itself, which was (however objectionable the participants) a model of detached observation. In ITV's case, the regulatory structures proved robust enough to allow for the funding, scheduling and defence of an exemplary piece of investigative journalism.

In that sense, both programmes were illustrative of a wider truth then and now: that the confidence, competence and resources that television journalism requires to be conducted effectively and independently need a robust set of clearly delineated institutional arrangements that will guarantee protection from attempted State interference. Contrary to assumptions by some scholars, this applies to both publicly funded and commercial enterprises; just as a publicly funded broadcaster can operate in the journalistic field independently of the State without surrendering to government interests, so a commercially funded broadcaster can operate similarly without surrendering to the populist dictates of the market. Once those institutional safeguards are removed, that journalistic confidence evaporates. That was precisely the effect of the Conservative government's policy initiatives of the late 1980s, which transformed British television and its journalism.

5   The Propaganda Model and the 1990 Broadcasting Act

The propaganda model and British television journalism

Before looking at the major institutional changes that 'Real Lives' and 'Death on the Rock' presaged – which would set the pattern for the next 25 years of television journalism – I want to consider the news values and news output of that era in the context of a profoundly influential theoretical framework that was published at the time in the United States. In 1988, the same year as 'Death on the Rock' was provoking its cataclysmic reactions amongst the British establishment, Herman and Chomsky published their comprehensive critique of American news values in *Manufacturing Consent*. Their thesis, now universally known as the 'propaganda model', was that news was subject to five structural news filters that severely constrained journalistic practice and ensured a mainstream news culture that did nothing to threaten the dominant political ideology.

These news filters were defined firstly as 'ownership': news organizations were part of large profit-oriented corporations that had nothing to gain by rattling the cage of an established political consensus. Second, 'advertising': news organizations could not alienate their sponsors who demanded safe, uncontentious programming as an appropriate selling environment. Third, 'sources': it was only the well-funded and powerful organizations – particularly government departments or agencies – that could afford the necessary in-house resources to influence, or even create, the news agenda. Fourth, 'government flak': news organizations dare not risk reprisals from official agencies by challenging elite truths (thereby risking, for example, removal of licences to broadcast). And fifth, a pervasive culture of 'anti-communism' – described as 'a national religion and control mechanism' – in which anything that might remotely be cast as representing socialistic values was vilified as unworthy and unpatriotic. The end result of these news filters, said the authors, was a compliant, submissive press that was incapable of offering enlightenment about what was going on in the world outside a narrow range of acceptable, elite views.[1]

The authors themselves acknowledged that their analysis was rooted geographically in the United States, and the eminent British scholar Colin Sparks has more recently attempted to extend the thesis to make it more globally relevant and more contemporary.[2] It nevertheless provides a useful template for examining the news culture that prevailed before the radical structural changes of the late 1980s were implemented, and to challenge on empirical grounds the applicability of Herman and Chomsky's model to the UK environment at the time it was published. For on each of their proposed news filters, it is possible to argue that the traditions and structures of British broadcasting allowed the two main broadcasters to pursue an independent news agenda which was framed by their own traditions of professional journalistic norms rather than impeded by external constraints on news values.

1   **Ownership**. The ITV franchises were owned and operated by companies that, albeit reluctantly at first, had come to accept well-funded journalism as part of their public service responsibility – including the obligation to stand up for their editors when stories provoked seriously uncomfortable confrontations. The BBC, by definition, was publicly owned and accountable to its licence-fee payers and to Parliament. Although vulnerable to political pressure through political appointees, the well-established conventions of journalistic independence were by now sufficiently robust and embedded to see off politically motivated attacks.

2   **Advertising**. The monopoly of advertising revenue enjoyed by ITV – continued even after Channel 4's introduction – insulated it from commercial pressures. While ratings were important to revenue and profits, companies were much less vulnerable to the fluctuations that resulted from a less populist schedule. Advertisers wishing to use the television medium had nowhere else to go, and could therefore exert very little influence on the programme environment for their commercials. The BBC, of course, took no money from commercial sponsorship.

3   **Sources**. A healthy investment in factual programming and original newsgathering, again part of the public service compact for ITV and an integral part of the BBC mission – indeed part of the BBC's DNA – meant that neither organization was reduced to a dependence on using the information provided by third parties. They had the institutional resources to produce their own information and the institutional strength to resist the tempting subsidies being offered by others.

4 **Flak**. Each of these programmes demonstrated that the respective broadcasters had both the means and the will to resist government pressure. This was not necessarily always the case, but in response to the most serious attempts at government interference both broadcasters were able to demonstrate their independence and their ability to resist concerted government pressure – in the case of ITV through the protective shield of a regulator which was prepared to absorb the flak on the broadcaster's behalf.

5 **Anti-communism**. While anti-communist ideology was less relevant in the UK context, there was certainly the same visceral hatred for Irish terrorist organizations, and particularly for the IRA – personified in a Prime Minister who had herself been attacked and had seen one of her closest friends assassinated. Her intolerance of dispassionate treatment of IRA history or background was enthusiastically taken up by cabinet acolytes and was reinforced by an increasingly nationalistic right-wing press, led in particular by the Murdoch-owned *Sun*, *News of the World* and *Times* newspapers.

Despite such deeply ingrained government antagonism to the journalism of detachment on Northern Ireland, all broadcasters – and this applied equally to Channel 4, whose smaller audiences provoked less concern from official sources – remained for the most part committed to their core journalistic responsibilities and confident of their ability to resist the prevailing atmosphere of narrow-minded bigotry. The result was more than just a journalism of enlightenment or even a journalism of accountability. It was a journalism that, in at least two cases, resulted in gross miscarriages of justices being overturned. In the early 1980s, the 'World in Action' editor Ray Fitzwalter had been approached by families of the six Irishmen who had been convicted of the 1974 Birmingham bomb, claiming their innocence. It was not an auspicious time to be taking on a cause that would have little popular appeal and would alienate the Prime Minister, but with the persistence of journalist Chris Mullin (later to become a Labour MP and minister), Fitzwalter was prepared to invest time and resources in investigating the evidence. In his own words: 'After five difficult months we were finally satisfied that there was tangible new evidence worth presenting. No subject could have been more unpopular. It was 11 years old and would suggest that six convicted IRA bombers had been improperly imprisoned, questioning the evidence and decisions of numerous policemen, lawyers and judges.'[3]

The programme was finally broadcast in 1985 and began a chain of events that eventually led to a second 'World in Action' five years later, in which one of the real bombers, heavily disguised, confessed. The case was referred to the Court of

Appeal and in March 1991, following a new investigation by a different police force, the six men were released after 17 years of false imprisonment. Other convictions, in particular those involving the West Midlands Serious Crime Squad whose evidence had led to the conviction of the Birmingham Six, were also quashed and eventually investigations of alleged miscarriages of justice were removed from the Home Office to a new independent commission. This was a classic example of investigative journalism at its very best, resulting not just in the liberation of six wrongly incarcerated men but in a fundamental change to the judicial system. As Fitzwalter says, 'none of these programmes ... would appear on commercial television today'.[4]

The propaganda model and the transformation of British television

There are a number of reasons why Fitzwalter is right, but the greatest responsibility for initiating the change – and for removing many of the barriers that had rendered Herman and Chomsky's thesis virtually irrelevant to British television journalism – lay with the changes being proposed by the government White Paper in 1988. There were essentially four key engines of change being mooted, which were to transform the landscape of British television and, in its wake, the nature of television journalism.

First, ITV franchises were no longer to be decided on the basis of Public Service Broadcasting commitments, but simply auctioned to the highest bidder; the winning licensee would have minimum programming obligations and would focus simply on recouping its auction bid and maximizing its revenues. After substantial lobbying from the industry, an important amendment ensured that bidders would have to pass a quality threshold before proceeding, but the auction principle survived. Inevitably, money would be removed from programme-making to fund the new levy, and the most vulnerable programmes were those requiring major investment without a guaranteed return. Expensive, research intensive (and especially foreign-based) current affairs journalism was in the frontline.

Second, the historic link between ITV and Channel 4 was to be ended, forcing Channel 4 to stand alone as an independent commercial entity and earn its own revenues in competition with ITV. The free-market philosophy that had prevailed in virtually every other area of British industry under Margaret Thatcher was to be applied to broadcasting, much to the satisfaction of the advertisers who had lobbied for several years to end ITV's monopoly of television airtime. Their gain was to be the programme-makers' loss. It meant that for the first time in British television, the agenda of commercial broadcasters would be dictated by the requirement of advertisers to maximize ratings and minimize less familiar or less popular programmes.

Third, an independent production quota of 25 per cent was to be imposed on both the BBC and ITV in order to widen the market for programme-makers. On the one hand, this initiative would certainly help to expand the market for new entrants and therefore add to the diversity of available talent. But there was a significant downside: the 25 per cent to be handed over to the independents would involve losing the same production capacity from inside existing broadcasters. This principle of vertical integration had helped to foster within broadcasters proper training opportunities, career progression and programme teams with a sense of coherence. All were valuable preconditions for the operation of a strong and successful branding in current affairs.

Finally, the Independent Broadcasting Authority, which had developed a strong sense of its own role in fostering quality and diversity, was to give way to a 'light touch' Independent Television Commission (ITC). Crucially, the new body would not be the responsible 'publisher' and would therefore no longer operate as a buffer between commercial television and government (or any other powerful vested interest). This was to be a 'hands off' regulator, with post hoc powers only and no role in protecting an ITV company that dared to confront vested interests with challenging journalism.

There was a fifth critical element in the new legislation, not so much a change to the existing regime but a very significant loophole in new rules restricting simultaneous ownership of a commercial broadcasting licence and a national newspaper. To date, such restrictions had been at the discretion of the IBA, which had developed an established policy of disbarring newspaper proprietors from ownership or control of an ITV licence (and had as a result prevented Rupert Murdoch from taking a controlling stake in London Weekend Television in 1967). With the IBA's powers curtailed, these limitations were to be formally written into the new legislation to prevent simultaneous ownership of television licences and newspapers. But there was to be one significant legislative loophole to these cross-ownership rules: the new restrictions would not apply to satellite channels transmitted from 'non-domestic satellites', i.e. those not originating in the United Kingdom.

Within one month of the transmission of 'Death on the Rock', Murdoch announced that he would be launching four Sky channels aimed at the United Kingdom from the Astra satellite system based in Luxembourg. Margaret Thatcher had no intention of excluding her favourite – and supremely loyal – media magnate from the television table and the 'Murdoch loophole' ensured that despite owning (at the time) over one-third of the national press by circulation, he would not be disqualified from owning a piece of the television landscape, too. He would have to persuade consumers to buy satellite receiver dishes, and he would be in competition (briefly) with Britain's attempt to launch its own domestic satellite operation, British Satellite Broadcasting (BSB). But he would at last have a seat at the television table, and within two years of his launch in February 1989 he would swallow up BSB to form British Sky Broadcasting (BSkyB) as the only television satellite operation targeted at the UK.

It was, ironically, Thatcher's parting gift to her favoured son. On the very day that the 1990 Broadcasting Act received Royal Assent her Foreign Secretary, Sir Geoffrey Howe, told her that he was resigning because he could no longer support her isolationist stand on Europe. Twelve days later, he delivered one of the most devastating resignation speeches ever heard in the Commons. It provoked a leadership contest from which Margaret Thatcher was eventually forced to withdraw after failing to secure sufficient support from her own party. By the end of November 1990, she had been replaced as leader and Prime Minister by the more emollient John Major. Thatcher herself was gone, but her legacy was about to have a very profound impact on broadcasting in general and television journalism in particular.

BBC journalism in the post-Thatcher era

Meanwhile, the BBC was undergoing its own journalistic transformation. It may have escaped the strictures of the Peacock Committee, but Milne's departure and John Birt's arrival as Deputy Director General heralded an organizational upheaval that resulted in a more austere and more institutionalized vision of journalism. His arrival in the wake of a number of journalistic confrontations with the government and a seriously alienated Board of Governors signalled a long overdue need for change – not only to ensure that controversies were better handled, but also to underscore the centrality of journalism to the BBC's purpose. At least two of those institutional changes demonstrated how shifts in organization, philosophy and resource allocation within a public broadcaster can make a dramatic difference to the practice and quality of television journalism.

The first key change was to resolve a structural problem between two key branches of BBC journalism: current affairs and news. Current affairs had evolved a spirit and identity of its own in the sprawling corridors of Lime Grove, a long walk from the BBC's headquarters at Television Centre; BBC news had evolved out of radio and was run separately. Milne decided to preserve that editorial diversity rather than risk subjecting a creative and innovative journalism culture to the potentially homogenizing straitjacket of BBC news values. The downside of such separation was that there were three separate baronies – radio news and current affairs, television news and television current affairs – with little mutual respect for each others' working practices: the news journalists felt that their current affairs colleagues were insufficiently serious or rigorous, while the current affairs team thought their news colleagues were unimaginative and not very bright. More importantly within an organization that was also a cultural leader in drama, entertainment and comedy, this fragmentation meant that journalism was afforded less priority internally than its democratic contribution and its political impact deserved.

In March 1987, therefore, Milne's successor Michael Checkland announced not only John Birt's appointment as Deputy Director General but also his brief to oversee a powerful and newly unified News and Current Affairs Directorate with its own substantial budget, and editorial control over all news and current affairs and journalism training. Given the entrenched divisions and diverse journalistic traditions, it was a hugely difficult and ambitious task, as the Director General himself acknowledged.[5] But Birt compounded the difficulty by appearing to condemn most of what the BBC had been doing as 'soft, woolly journalism' and making it clear that his benchmark of good journalism was the theoretical blueprint outlined in his 'mission to explain'. There were no concessions to the more chaotic forms of television journalism, either the investigative tradition or the documentary tradition that had its roots in film-making rather than in journalism; and there was some anxiety even amongst his supporters that this rigid philosophy could stifle creativity and produce a more conservative and compliant approach.[6]

Despite the protests, Lime Grove, with its more inchoate approach to journalism, was closed. More specialist correspondents were recruited, and four specialist units were established covering politics, economics and industry, social affairs and foreign affairs, each with a weekly programme devoted to its specialism. It was, in effect, an organizational revolution designed to recognize and rationalize one of the most important – some argued *the* most important – area of BBC activity. Although the Birt vision for television journalism was somewhat dry and ascetic – signalling to some extent a return to the purist days of Tahu Hole – there is no question that BBC journalism was enhanced in a way that reached well beyond Birt's particular philosophy. The legacy of that revolution continues today in what remains the biggest broadcast journalism operation in the world.

A second much-needed change, which has also survived, was the appointment of an individual to oversee and promote editorial standards. As 'Real Lives' had shown, there was no adequate early warning system for dealing with particularly provocative programmes in a way which would both alert senior executives to a forthcoming row, and would underscore a commitment to independent as well as high-quality journalism. This was partly an issue driven by the nature of the medium. By the 1980s, television had reached a point of maturity where, whatever the party of government, it was seen as a decisive weapon in the battle for electoral hearts and minds. Because it was not open to the same partisan approach as the press, it was implicitly trusted by voters. Politicians of all colours were therefore becoming more sensitive to its output and more intent on trying to influence it to their advantage. At the same time, BBC reporters were continuing to initiate difficult, challenging and politically uncomfortable programmes, which inevitably resulted in political flak being directed at channel controllers and senior editors. For the BBC credibly and robustly to defend its journalistic independence required a senior editorial figure who could alert senior management about upcoming controversies and reassure them that all appropriate editorial steps had been taken.

Birt therefore created a new position of Controller of Editorial Policy with a wide-ranging brief to develop a set of guidelines for journalistic standards, to offer advice early in the editorial process and to troubleshoot in areas of potential danger. This brief extended to documentaries and even drama, an important institutional acknowledgement that definitions of journalism – particularly when covering difficult issues such as Northern Ireland – should not be confined to simple reporting. A well-constructed drama documentary – as Granada successfully demonstrated in 1990 when it dramatized the wrong conviction and false imprisonment of the Birmingham Six – could be as contentious and enlightening as any current affairs programme. As programme-makers increasingly began to experiment with new and creative ways of exploiting the television medium to address areas of public controversy, the importance of an experienced editorial adviser with a wide brief took on an even greater significance. In today's BBC, the Controller, Editorial Policy remains a pivotal element of the journalistic machinery and a permanent reminder of how publicly funded broadcasters, even in the digital age, must be sensitive to the perceived power of the television medium and have adequate defence mechanisms against any political attacks on their editorial independence.

Compromised journalism or sensible precaution?

Such mechanisms, however, can prove to be a double-edged sword, and prompt inevitable accusations that, rather than facilitating robust watchdog journalism, they promote an overly cautious and servile approach. Thus, Birt's structural changes, combined with his personal determination to impose a new journalistic rigour, raised questions over the next few years about the BBC's continued commitment to challenging the government without pulling its punches. The evidence, however, was very mixed. Soon after taking over, for example, he intervened in a 'Panorama' programme, being prepared by reporter John Ware, involving the MI5 officer Peter Wright, whose book *Spycatcher* had made allegations about a plot to topple the Labour government of the 1960s. Margaret Thatcher had been incensed both about the allegations and the disloyalty of a member of the security services, and attempted to have the book banned in the United Kingdom. Birt insisted on having a detailed script before any filming or interviews took place, and only gave approval after he himself had met a former colleague of Wright. Ware later described Birt's involvement as, 'motivated by a desire to get control of a potentially highly controversial project at the start of his BBC career, not because he had been "nobbled" by the Establishment'.[7] And it was easy to understand why Birt was determined to impose disciplined control on contentious programmes given the journalistic environment he had inherited. In his own memoirs, he describes the fallout from the new Chairman's investigation into 'Maggie's Militant Tendency', as a result of which: 'Hussey [Chairman of the Board of Governors] had concluded that the BBC was out of control editorially, and that It had poor processes for handling legally sensitive programmes. Nor was he impressed with the overall quality of the BBC's journalism. He observed in his first meeting alone with me that no one had told the BBC's journalists that they were not doing well. All the candidates for the director-generalship had agreed on that.'[8]

Perhaps Birt was prepared to accept Marmaduke Hussey's analysis of BBC journalism too uncritically, or perhaps he found in it a convenient excuse for imposing his own analytical vision on BBC journalism. But it was certainly true that a more reliable system of editorial accountability was needed to deflect accusations of journalistic incompetence, however politically motivated they might have been. As Birt himself said 15 years later: 'The BBC had come close to having a nervous breakdown in the mid-eighties ... [It] had been through this horrendous experience, there were a lot people gunning for the BBC; I was determined to get it right; I wanted to do difficult things, but I wanted to get it right.'[9]

Even for Birt's supporters, however, the process of 'getting it right' involved examples of journalistic caution which did suggest an overly deferential attitude to power. In the aftermath of 'Death on the Rock', one 'Panorama' edition about accountability of the security forces in Northern Ireland was timed to coincide with the verdict of the inquest into the Gibraltar shootings. Birt insisted on minor changes, delaying transmission by two weeks and thereby coincidentally avoiding transmission just before the Conservative Party conference. Was it a sensible precaution, a display of journalistic cowardice, or a flexing of managerial muscles to demonstrate that he was 'in charge'? All were possible explanations, but the fact that the programme was made at all was perhaps a tribute to the determination of

BBC journalists to demonstrate that they would not be intimidated by a government that had already vented its fury on ITV and Thames.

Other examples of journalistic compromise were more difficult to explain away. In January 1991, 'Panorama' was due to tell the story of British machine-tool manufacturers exporting equipment to Iraq – in defiance of official government guidelines – which had been used by Saddam Hussein to build a 'supergun' capable of inflicting serious damage on neighbouring countries. The programme was described by David Jordan, then Deputy Editor, as 'an absolutely outstanding piece of journalism ... literally not a millimetre out – down to the size of the thing, the size of the barrel, the size of the parts that were moved, the direction it was pointing, where it was located, the grid references on the map.'[10] It was timed for transmission just days before the land offensive against Iraq was to be launched. Birt unilaterally pulled the programme not because he had any problem with the integrity or accuracy of the journalism but because, in his own words, 'I was extremely concerned that the BBC should maintain the trust of the British people at a time of war.'[11] To the fury of BBC journalists involved, the story ended up on ITV as the main source took his story to 'This Week', while Birt stood accused of saving the government from embarrassment. Those who suspected surrender to government pressure would not have been reassured by Birt's own reflection on that particular time, which fails even to mention the 'Supergun' episode:

> Conservative backbenchers, who had queued up in the 1980s to deliver ferocious broadsides against the BBC, began to mellow as our commitment to good intelligent journalism and to high editorial standards became clear. When the Iraqis invaded Kuwait in August [1990] ... I worked hard with [the Controller, Editorial Policy] to define the special considerations that attach to journalism at time of war, mindful of the hostile criticism the BBC had faced during the Falklands.[12]

Being 'mindful' of government reaction at times of military action is not a wholly unworthy approach (and is certainly not confined to public broadcasters, as the widely criticized coverage of Iraq by the big American networks has since demonstrated). But in this case it was self-evidently more about saving government face than British soldiers' lives, and suggests that institutional (and perhaps self-) preservation was the greater priority. Even less excusable was a clear failure of nerve in the run-up to the 1992 general election, which happened to coincide with a period of review for the BBC itself in advance of the expiry of its Charter in 1996. This time, 'Panorama' had prepared a forensic analysis of the economic problems besetting the country (which was just emerging from recession), ironically written and presented by Birt's former co-author Peter Jay and due for transmission on the eve of the election campaign. The programme, called 'Sliding into Slump', essentially blamed aspects of Conservative economic policy for the current economic malaise. Three days before transmission, the editor of weekly programmes, Samir Shah, decided that it was insufficiently balanced and pulled it – supposedly without any consultation with his superiors.

The decision was greeted with derision. Roger Bolton, having himself suffered from the fallout of 'Death on the Rock' at ITV, wrote in the *Evening Standard*: 'The intimidation from all the political parties has worked. Ironically, as far as I am aware, none of the political parties had complained about this programme. Perhaps they no longer need to do so. Self-censorship will suffice. The instinct for institutional survival has overcome the obligations of broadcast journalism.'[13] The programme was finally shown late on a Monday night after the general election was over and the Conservatives had won. Even those BBC journalists who had vigorously defended Birt's approach to editorial rigour as essential to renewing confidence and coherence in BBC journalism could see evidence of a dangerously subservient attitude to government at certain delicate times. It may have been realpolitik, but it was not unalloyed independence.

These, however, remained the exceptions. Most of the time, challenging, independent programmes were being made and broadcast, albeit according to tighter editorial codes than ten years earlier. Thatcher's replacement as Prime Minister by John Major at the end of 1990 heralded a more emollient tone towards the BBC and a more sympathetic hearing in Downing Street, which was particularly important when it came to negotiating the new BBC Charter. By the early 1990s, the BBC had withstood the Thatcher onslaught and its journalism was arguably better resourced and more internally robust than it ever had been under Milne. Even as new satellite channels were expanding and audiences were beginning to fragment, the BBC had survived as a publicly funded, mass-audience broadcaster with a reinvigorated and reorganized journalistic force. It was probably the only broadcaster in the world that was not being forced by recessionary pressures to make significant cuts in its news operation, and even in the face of powerful, ideologically motivated opposition had secured the longevity as well as quality of an internationally acclaimed broadcast journalism operation. By contrast, its UK commercial competitors were preparing for the fallout from the 1990 Broadcasting Act, and television journalism was in the frontline.

6 Competition and Commercialism into the Twenty-first Century

Deregulation and television current affairs: ITV after the 1990 Broadcasting Act

An almost immediate consequence of the 1990 Broadcasting Act – demonstrating eloquently the direct impact that government legislation can have on television output – was that three ITV companies lost their franchise. By far the biggest casualty was Thames, the broadcaster responsible for 'This Week', whose bid of £33 million was £10 million less than Carlton Communications. In effect, a new business had won the franchise by committing £10 million more to the Treasury that would not go into programmes. More importantly, the power of the old IBA to influence decision-making in the public interest had been emasculated.

Even before the new ITV franchises had started broadcasting on 1 January 1993, it was becoming clear how the new business and market philosophy would impact on commercial television's commitment to investigative journalism. It did not take long for the new masters of ITV to air some deeply antagonistic views about the place for this sort of journalism in a peak-time ITV schedule. Paul Jackson, the new director of programmes at Carlton, insisted that the only guarantor of peak-time current affairs programmes was consistently high ratings. In an interview with the *Daily Telegraph* in May 1992 he said with specific reference to the Granada programmes on the Birmingham bombers: 'If *World in Action* were in 1993 to uncover three more serious miscarriages of justice while delivering an audience of three, four or five million, I would cut it. It isn't part of the ITV system to get people out of prison.'[1]

Jackson expanded on this argument a few months later at the Edinburgh Television Festival, stating that no programme with a regular audience of less than 6 million deserved a place in the peak-time schedules: 'You may not like it but under the new licences ITV is mandated to be a popular channel that gets an audience, earns revenue and sustains a business … those who argue for current affairs to stay in peak time are not accepting things as they are.'[2] Precisely the same point was being made by Central TV's director of programme planning Dawn Airey in the trade magazine *Broadcast*. She cited both 'World in Action' and 'This Week' as having a disastrous effect on peak-time ratings, condemning the latter in particular as the reason why ITV was doing poorly on Thursday nights: 'The ratings rot sets in at 20.30 with *This Week* and we have a devil's own job getting our audience back.'[3]

In other words, attitudes to current affairs in British commercial television had been transformed. It was no longer part of the public service mix – a contribution to democratic welfare that ITV had embraced for 35 years – but a scheduling weakness whose potential damage to the bottom line had to be mitigated. It was certainly true that, in the art of building a television schedule whose only objective was to maximize and retain audiences, a current affairs programme tackling a different subject each week was a potential liability. This was partly because it is more difficult to attract audiences to the unknown, and partly because 'serious' programmes rate less well in a medium better suited to entertainment. Audiences were healthy enough: an average of 5 or 6 million was still more than double the combined circulation of every broadsheet national newspaper at the time. But compared to a movie or popular drama that might earn twice that, this was now regarded as a failure. Added to which, a thoroughly researched current affairs programme – particularly when tackling foreign stories – was more expensive to make than the average light-entertainment programme.

Thus, within three years the spotlight had switched to a current affairs agenda dominated by issues that were most likely to generate the biggest audiences. This was not difficult to discern. In the first six months of 1992, I conducted an analysis of how subject matter impacted on the audience performance of 'This Week' and 'World in Action', and the results demonstrated unequivocally the ratings power of certain 'big ticket' issues. The highest 'World in Action' audience of 10.8 million was achieved by a fly-on-the-wall exposé of the Los Angeles police force, closely followed by a two-part programme using hidden camera photography in which a reporter played a homeless vagrant and recorded the reactions of passers-by (10.6 and 9.7 million respectively). Over 8 million watched programmes on the problem of noisy neighbours and on Los Angeles gangs, temptingly called 'Girls, Guns and Gangs'. This compared with the 'poor' ratings for programmes covering death squads operating in South Africa on instructions from the security forces (5.2 million); the crisis in intensive care in the United Kingdom (5.3 million); and an exposé on financial support behind some of Britain's MPs (5.9 million).

A similar pattern emerged on 'This Week', whose biggest audience of over 8 million went to two programmes featuring the New York mafia boss John Gotti, compared to 4.3 million for an investigation of Pentagon's Star Wars programme in the United States and 4.9 million for a Middle East story of two 25-year-olds, one

Palestinian and one Israeli, separated by conflict. Given the disparity in ratings, any ITV current affairs executive motivated entirely by audience size could only move in one direction. Any programme that featured crime, money, housing or mortgages, or soft human interest stories featuring the aristocracy or royalty could be fairly certain of upwards of 8 million viewers. Subject areas to avoid would include anything happening outside the UK and anything vaguely political. As we shall see, these disparities also persuaded programme executives of the value of market research. Increasingly, programme concepts were road-tested amongst focus groups and the results turned over to programme-makers. As the current affairs agenda became more research-driven, the scope for unpredictability or launching investigations with uncertain results progressively shrank. The overriding issue for cost-conscious programme commissioners became: why spend limited resources on proving allegations of abuse or corruption in some far-flung country when you can guarantee a decent return on investment with revelations about the sex lives of celebrities?

Democratization or emasculation?

There is an argument, sometimes described as a 'postmodern' anti-elitist critique, that these reforms promoted a long-overdue recognition of the demands of audiences rather than the journalistic obsessions of those running or regulating television. According to this school of thought, the legacy of programmes like 'World in Action' was a journalism that was high-minded, male-dominated, pedagogic, dull and more interested in industry or peer recognition than understanding and catering for the audiences they are supposed to be serving.[4] A more market-led system, went the argument, encouraged greater empathy with and responsiveness to audience needs. While it is certainly true that some programmes in the days before CCTV, computer graphics and instant satellite pictures were drier and less sympathetic to audience needs than they might have been, there are two key reasons why the gradual dismemberment of intelligent, peak-time television journalism on commercial television was profoundly regrettable. One is rooted in notions of journalism's contribution to democratic accountability; the second is, ironically, rooted in notions of consumer choice.

The democratic arguments are familiar and flow from the role of the press in operating as an effective fourth estate. It does not require the validation of a huge peak-time audience to justify the production of programmes that provide information on matters of national or international importance; or that offer background explanations, context or analysis of contemporary issues; or that expose corruption, wrongdoing, hypocrisy or greed inside a nation's boardrooms or public institutions.

The importance of watchdog, or accountability, journalism is particularly important in a complex world where public officials or private shareholders in positions of trust and responsibility need to be scrutinized.

From the beginning of commercial television in Britain, the public service compact determined that space would be made available for this kind of journalism in return for lucrative licences to broadcast. This never meant that such programmes had to be dull, inaccessible, male-dominated or high-minded, and we have seen the internal debates that ensured that, by the late 1980s, ITV's current affairs programmes could not be accused of Reithian paternalism. It is, anyway, an intrinsic part of the journalistic ethic to make such stories accessible to viewers through personalization or other narrative techniques, and this was precisely what ITV had succeeded in doing: combining populism and impact with journalistic rigour. To accept the removal of these spaces, or to accept the shift away from important national and international issues as some kind of democratization (or feminization) of television journalism is both to misunderstand the journalism being forsaken and seriously to underestimate the potential for high-quality television journalism to contribute to an informed democracy.

The consumer choice arguments are less familiar but equally powerful. There is a common assumption in analyses of audience behaviour – themselves rooted in market liberal theories of economics – that the higher a programme's rating, the greater the popular justification for its inclusion in the schedules. While this is true for individual programmes, it manifestly does not apply across a whole schedule: an evening's television dominated by, say, soaps, comedy and sport may generate large audiences but this discriminates against those who enjoy original drama, current affairs, documentaries, arts programmes and so on – which turns out to be the vast majority of viewers. Some very illuminating analysis of audience viewing behaviour in the 1980s demonstrated that the vast majority of viewers like to watch a mix of programmes; and that the reason why some programmes rate significantly higher is that nearly everyone chooses to watch them while also choosing to watch a varied mix of other lower rated programmes.[5] Thus, although the economics of commercial television dictate that high-rating programmes dominate the schedule, analysis of consumer preferences suggests that this is to the detriment of the majority who want a variety of programmes to be available. These arguments are even more relevant in the interactive world of the twenty-first century where a variety of recording devices, catch-up TV and downloadable schedules allow viewers to watch programmes at their convenience. The less space that is made available for the kinds of resource-heavy television journalism that once featured prominently in the regulated environment of commercial television, the less choice is available to those viewers who would like to watch them.

There was therefore no postmodern 'silver lining' in the demise of 'This Week' in December 1992 as Thames wound down in preparation for Carlton to take over the London franchise; nor in its partial replacement by a foot-in-the-door consumer rights programme. Important as it is to have the villains who prey on vulnerable consumers exposed for their con tricks, it is no substitute for a programme whose definition of accountability journalism stretched much wider than miscreant hustlers. And while 'This Week' simply disappeared off the nation's screens as a direct consequence of the 1990 Act, 'World in Action' was the victim of a slower but equally inevitable death, with a replacement that also spoke volumes about the new priorities of ITV.

The end of 'World in Action'

In his revealing history of the rise and fall of ITV, Ray Fitzwalter describes a defining moment in 1991 shortly after the appointment of Gerry Robinson as Chief Executive of the Granada Group, when he met Granada television executives: 'He had no time for claims that broadcasting was different from ordinary business ... There was no place in the new Granada for anyone who did not put profit first, second and third.'[6] Thus, when David Plowright, one of the great creative forces behind Granada's success, was sacked at the beginning of 1992, there was very little the new 'light touch' ITC could do. Equally, there was little it could do as the more powerful ITV companies – Granada and Carlton in particular – took advantage of the gradual relaxation of ownership rules to consolidate the number of companies in the federation and reduce investment in local and regional news as well as current affairs. The *volume* of regional journalism remained the same, because it was one of the few remaining obligations left by the 1990 Act, but there was no stipulation about budgets.

By 1995, the former journalist turned MP Chris Mullin was sufficiently concerned to introduce a Media Diversity Bill. Its aim, he told Parliament, was 'to protect our culture and democracy from the barbarism of the unregulated market.' He continued:

> What I fear most is not political bias, but the steady growth of junk journalism – the trivialisation and demeaning of everything that is important in our lives and its consequent effect on our culture; a flat refusal to address what is going on in the world in favour of an endless diet of crime, game shows and soap operas and the unadulterated hate that is already a feature of our most loathsome tabloid newspapers.[7]

There was plenty of parliamentary support for Mullin, but by this time the inexorable logic of the marketplace was taking its toll. There was less stomach for putting journalistic resources into issues that might result in legal action, and two programmes in rapid succession resulted in expensive legal battles that were lost.[8] Combined with the pressure to deliver peak-time ratings and greater profitability, it was only a matter of time before a programme that had produced some of the most compelling journalism on British television was axed. By the middle of 1998, the network had decided on a replacement that would be modelled on America's '60 Minutes' – a magazine programme with a melange of the light and the more serious, fronted by a well-known and marketable personality. The result was to recruit Britain's best-known and well-liked news presenter, Trevor McDonald from ITN's 'News at Ten', to front a new programme called 'Tonight with Trevor McDonald'.

After 35 years, the last edition of 'World in Action' went out in December 1998 and was greeted on the day by an eloquent valediction from one of the most distinguished television journalists of his generation, Martin Bell. Bell, who had temporarily discarded his profession to become an independent MP on a platform of bringing integrity and honesty into politics, understood the significance of the moment for television journalism in Britain: 'We are mourning the death of *World in Action*. For 35 years it exposed wrongdoers, shook politicians, made the unholy tremble – and on occasions even changed the law of the land. It told truths governments did not want told. It withstood corrupt politicians ... With its passing, it is time to write the obituary of factual prime time programmes on independent television.'[9]

An equally trenchant obituary had come a week earlier from a less predictable journalistic source, but another who understood the significance not only of the programme but of the value of the regulatory structure that had sustained it. Andrew Neil, former editor of the *Sunday Times* and scourge of 'This Week' ten years earlier, had written in the *Daily Telegraph*: 'The change marks the end of ITV's pretensions to still be a public service broadcaster and calls into question whether the regulator still has any purpose. World in Action and This Week were quality programmes with a serious purpose, and are now replaced by a tabloid agenda with an emphasis on consumer concerns and stunts.'[10]

How impotent the regulator had become was illustrated by the criticisms of its Director of Programmes, Sarah Thane, when interviewed by Fitzwalter nearly eight years later. She described the new ITV as, 'bland, safe and predictable. I remember the kind of conversations about Tonight with Trevor McDonald – it was light-weight and celebrity driven. It couldn't have got much fluffier.'[11] The ITC's Annual Report of 2000 was critical in particular of the programme's coverage of major foreign stories, but by this time its regulatory powers had long been eclipsed by the driving force of the market.[12] In any case, Tony Blair's Labour government had already started its thinking about the new regulatory future for communications in an era that would be dominated by convergence, digitalization and interactivity. Its political ideology, though more ambivalent about deregulation than the Tory Thatcherites, was careful to emphasize the importance of the marketplace, and the government started to put together a brand new regulatory structure for communications that would embody that ambivalence. By the time the converged regulator Ofcom took over regulation of television from the ITC, all that was left of ITV's current affairs legacy was a pale imitation of '60 Minutes', itself regarded in the United States as a betrayal of the tradition handed down by Ed Murrow. And at the same time as ITV's new barons were imposing market disciplines that were slowly strangling intelligent, in-depth current affairs, they had finally succeeded in convincing the weakened ITC that it should be allowed to move one of the longest standing fixtures of the ITV schedule – its news bulletin at 10 p.m.

Deregulation and commercial television news in the 1990s

While the 1990 Broadcasting Act had more or less abandoned current affairs to the free market, it had been much more interventionist when it came to news on commercial television. This dichotomy was a fascinating symptom of the ambivalence felt within Conservative circles about letting the market loose, and demonstrated that the government was well aware of the power of legislation to influence television output. It also provided an illuminating empirical case study of the consequences for television journalism on a commercial station of both removing and preserving statutory safeguards. In two very significant ways, key statutory changes were made in an attempt to secure the continuing stability of ITN and mandating a properly resourced news output on ITV.

First, ITV companies were forced to sell their majority stake in ITN. This deliberate intervention in the free market arose from concern within ITN that its ITV owners lacked the appetite or ambition to expand the news provider into a bigger, more ambitious operation. ITN's hierarchy argued that new investors would inject more money and new ideas, while also (ironically!) insulating the news company from any adverse consequences of an entertainment-led ITV. It was supported by the IBA, which continued its tradition of protecting the news company from programme companies. According to its then finance director Peter Rogers: 'I didn't think the companies had it in them to make a success of ITN in a wholly competitive world. In practical terms, because of their own protected existence within a monopoly, they didn't have the capacity to go out and develop ITN.'[13] Perhaps more importantly, it offered some protection for the legacy of a high-quality news culture insulated from an entertainment-driven parent company. While there was some sort of logic in the argument that an ambitious, free-standing news company would be a more exciting prospect than a contractor owned by its major client, the corollary was that there was little prospect of decent profits from such a cost-heavy operation. By international standards, it was a rather bizarre rule that prevented the nation's premier commercial channel from owning its own news provider. Not surprisingly, the anticipated rush of investors never materialized and, in the absence of any persuasive economic reasons for retaining it, the restriction was abolished in 2003.

Second, a requirement was inserted into the 1990 Act mandating ITV to transmit news, 'of high quality dealing with national and international matters,' broadcast regularly, and 'in particular … at peak viewing times'.[14] This was to counteract any risk that ITV companies might marginalize, reduce or eliminate news altogether and was included after the Prime Minister – who instinctively opposed any restriction on the free market – had been warned that there would only be one beneficiary if ITV were allowed to reduce significantly their investment in a high-quality news service: the BBC. Thatcher's deep distrust of the BBC trumped her devotion to the market. Moreover, the quality requirement was further reinforced by ensuring that ITV was only permitted to take its news from a 'nominated news provider' approved by the new regulatory body, the ITC. This ensured that a purely profit-driven enterprise would not be allowed to contract its news from any fly-by-night news operation that might offer generous discounts and a discounted journalism to match. The regulator's Chief Executive made it abundantly clear that, in the first instance at least, ITN would be the only nominated provider. Here was concrete proof that even those politicians most wedded to market liberalism understood the potential impact on television journalism of the consequences of removing regulation. In stark contrast to current affairs, it meant that news plurality and a high-quality competitor to the BBC were guaranteed by a statutory safety net.

In the end, however, that safety net was only partially successful in resisting the determined march of a market-led ITV, now beginning to face competition from the incremental growth of cable and satellite channels, and from the imminent launch of a new commercial terrestrial channel, Channel 5. There followed a series of skirmishes between regulator and broadcaster, which were reminiscent of the early battles of the 1950s: the former trying to assert its authority over a cornerstone of public service philosophy, the latter complaining bitterly and kicking against the boundaries to reduce costs and raise profit margins for its shareholders.

Even the arguments were unoriginal. In their bids, the ITV licensees had promised £64 million per annum on news but began to backtrack even before the new franchises became operational in January 1993. When one ITV director asked bluntly in June 1992 why ITN could not reduce significantly its foreign newsgathering operation and replace it with agency material, the ITC responded that it 'would not consider the quality of international news to be adequate if it relied exclusively or significantly on news agency pictures, reports and voice-overs'. In other words, it flexed its regulatory muscle with the backing of the new statutory wording. The following month, the newly appointed Chief Executive of ITV tried a different line: extending the definition of peak-time to 11 p.m. so that 'News at Ten' could be pushed back half an hour. Once again, the regulator stepped in. In a letter to *The Times*, the Chief Executive emphasized the contractual commitment that ITV companies had made and underlined the regulator's determination to stand by it. He wrote: 'The commercial success of ITV will not be jeopardised by high quality news programmes in peak-time.'[15]

In ITV's eyes, this mandated point in its schedule – which had now been a television fixture for 25 years – was a serious commercial inhibition for three reasons. First, as with current affairs programmes, news ratings were lower than might be achieved by a popular drama or quiz show in the same slot – in economic terms, there was an 'opportunity cost' to the channel. Second, it interrupted the flow of the evening schedule and limited the channel's flexibility to start, say, a movie or two-hour drama special at the 9 p.m. junction.[16] Third, there was the BBC. All broadcasters expect a ratings boost when a big story breaks, and this was especially true in the days before 24-hour news channels and the internet. But because viewers have historically turned instinctively to the BBC as the voice of authority in times of crisis, ITV never reaped the full ratings benefit of breaking news. Moreover, ITV had the further disadvantage of transmitting an hour later than the BBC's main 9 p.m. bulletin.[17]

Despite these competitive disadvantages, at the very moment ITV executives were stepping up their pressure on the regulator in August 1992, their two evening news bulletins at 6 p.m. and 10 p.m. were performing precisely the kind of democratic and informational role envisaged by Parliament (the ratings performance of the later bulletin even bettering that of the BBC, averaging 6.8 million versus 6.5 million). Not only were audiences substantial, but plurality was assured by having two strong and well-funded news providers competing with each other for quality, scoops, stories, original angles and alternative perspectives on the national and international issues of the moment. The audience interest was being served, with a consistent average of around a quarter of the adult population watching a high-quality and well-resourced evening bulletin on one of the two main channels.[18] But ITV was convinced that its commercial interests were not being served, and as soon as the new licensees were operational in January 1993 they initiated a furious lobbying campaign to reschedule the later bulletin. The first time, the regulator stood firm. The second time, it crumbled. By 1999, ITV's flagship late evening programme had disappeared in a haze of commercial self-interest that had little to do with serving the audience and nothing at all to do with serving democracy.

The two battles for 'News at Ten'

Given the political background to the new commercialism of ITV, it was particularly ironic to watch Britain's political classes become involved in the battle to 'save' what was often described as a national institution. It was a credit to the original regulatory system and of course to ITN itself to have forged over 25 years such a massive reputation for a single news bulletin that could not only spearhead commercial television's challenge to BBC journalism, but could command enormous popular as well as elite appeal. By the spring of 1993, the two biggest ITV companies, Carlton and Granada, had taken over ownership of ITN and made it clear that they intended to move 'News at Ten'. At this point, astonishingly, both main political leaders became involved. The Labour Party's opposition leader John Smith sent a protest letter to the Chairman of the ITC, saying: 'Were this plan to go ahead, it would be a major blow to the coverage of news and current affairs on British television.'[19] Not to be outdone, the Prime Minister John Major followed with another letter to the ITC, writing that, 'I am concerned that one of the strengths of the independent television network may be seriously impaired if the main evening news is not a central part of the schedule.'[20]

Interviewed ten years later Carlton's Chairman Michael Green expressed his continuing amazement that Britain's political leaders should have become involved: 'the fact that the prime minister of the day came out with a statement as to when the news should be ... That definitely floored me! And the fact that our regulator listened when that happened floored me again!'[21] It may seem extraordinary – particularly given the prevalent political philosophy of laissez-faire and the fact that multichannel television was already on the rise – but in fact such intervention was squarely in the tradition of British television history. Green's fury at having, in his view, a perfectly legitimate commercial decision vetoed by a regulator represented a fundamental cultural clash between two different visions of how television should be run. For the regulator, it was a simple matter of upholding the public service remit specifically laid down by Parliament and holding licensees to the explicit commitments written into their licence bids. For politicians, too, there was a sense of preserving an important public (as well as personal) space for television news and the fostering of a better informed electorate. For ITN, it was a victory for the continuing role of its television journalism at the heart of Britain's only mass audience commercial channel. For ITV, however, it was an unwarranted hindrance that impacted directly on its bottom line. And while its senior executives accepted for the moment that they had underestimated the level of regulatory and political determination, this tussle marked an important transitional moment between an era of real regulatory authority and one of regulatory impotence. In the words of Richard Lindley: 'At ITN it was regarded as a famous victory. Their greedy new Philistine owners had been seen off in no uncertain terms. Television professionals, politicians and, yes, even ordinary viewers had united to repel this new breed of rapacious businessmen. This was natural but unwise; it was also premature.'[22]

During the rest of the 1990s, the number of multichannel households grew as cable and satellite – and in particular BSkyB on the back of its exclusive sporting contracts – began to establish themselves. Channel 5 started broadcasting in March 1997 with even fewer public service obligations than ITV (though it, too, was obliged to show news in peak-time). Worried about an imminent slide in audience share and convinced that their peak-time schedule would be immeasurably stronger without an obligatory news bulletin, ITV executives mounted a determined campaign to persuade the regulator that an early peak-time bulletin of 6.30 should allow them to move their late night news to 11.00 p.m. This time, however, the market-place imperative was more urgent and the ITC felt less able (or less willing) to flex its muscles again: in November 1998, it voted by seven votes to three to allow the proposal through providing there was 'no diminution in the funding, or in the range and quality of national and international news'. There was to be a review after 12 months, making it effectively a year's trial. The last 'News at Ten' – at least for the time being – went out on 5 March 1999. Michael Brunson, ITN's hugely respected political editor who had been instrumental in mobilizing political support for the programme five years earlier, subsequently wrote: 'After thirty-two years it was all over. Straight commercial pressure, unrestrained by the official regulatory body, the ITC, had killed off Britain's favourite and most successful news programme.'[23]

In theory, it should have been possible to shift the centre of ITV's news gravity to 6.30 p.m. In practice, it was never likely to work because 'News at Ten' had both symbolic and real news value. Its symbolic value was a signal – to advertisers as well as audiences – that ITV aimed higher than the fluff and trivia of entertainment, and was genuinely committed to a high-quality news and information service as an alternative to the more po-faced offerings of the BBC. The real news value lay in the programme itself – as opposed to a generic news bulletin from ITV – which had become a national institution, rooted in a public service that recognized the significance of plural sources of high-quality journalism on television. There were very good editorial reasons why 'News at Ten' could not be replicated at an earlier time: there are stories of a certain complexity (such as movements in share prices or foreign diplomacy initiatives) as well as stories featuring war or bloodshed that are simply not suitable for the early evening, and a 6.30 bulletin has very different editorial priorities from a later bulletin. It may not have been realistic in the modern world of competition, deregulation, audience fragmentation and channel proliferation to expect a regulator to stand firm, or to expect a commercial television operator to listen, but ITV surrendered a news presence that was engraved on the public consciousness and that for many viewers helped to define the channel.

As ITV leaders later acknowledged, it turned out to be a poor commercial decision as well as a regulatory mess. After a year, the ITC were confronted with evidence of a 14 per cent decline in ITV's news audiences and, once again under political pressure to act, brokered a confusing deal that saw a shorter 20-minute 'News at Ten' reinstated four times a week, reduced to three when special events such as a football match demanded. By that time, as we shall see, a sharp-eyed BBC had stolen the 10 p.m. slot, but more importantly ITV were now breaking one of the fundamental rules of television news in a competitive schedule: the need for a fixed, inviolable point in the schedule on which audiences can rely. In February 2004, faced with a continuing audience slide, ITV relaunched its late evening schedule once more with a fixed half-hour news slot at 10.30 p.m. Four years after that, in January 2008, ITV voluntarily reinstated 'News at Ten'. It had taken ten years of chaotic scheduling, ceding a valuable spot to the BBC, and a severely emasculated reputation for one of the most recognized and authoritative sources of television journalism, for ITV to realize that its own commercial interests – as well as the public interest – lay in its original starting point in 1998. Michael Grade, then ITV Chairman, admitted as much to a House of Lords committee when he said in 2007:

> It makes good business sense for us. We think if you are going to do news in the second half of peak time, you should do it at a time which is the most relevant – parliamentary votes at 10 o'clock, quite often important moments in the political life of the nation – and what is the point of running news half an hour, immediately after BBC1 has done a very extensive and highly professional and high-quality news provision at 10 o'clock?[24]

Paying for news on commercial television – ITN's funding crisis

While fighting to increase profitability through releasing its peak-time schedule, ITV was involved in another battle to reduce its financial commitment to journalism that was reminiscent of the 1950s. This time, the commercial channel could take advantage of changes in the 1990 Act without risk of intervention from the regulator. According to the Act, once a news consortium had satisfied the regulator of its ability to offer a high-quality news service and therefore became a 'nominated news provider', it would be free to compete for the ITV contract on pure market terms. The ITV news contract was due for renewal in 2001, and in May of that year a new consortium – 'Channel 3 News' led by Murdoch's Sky Television – sought and obtained the requisite status from the ITC.[25] Whether or not ITV was serious about taking its news from its most threatening commercial competitor – and whether or not the political climate would have allowed Rupert Murdoch yet another foothold in the British media landscape – the new consortium fulfilled a very useful purpose in driving down the cost of the contract. By the time negotiations were complete and ITN had secured the new contract, the annual cost had been slashed from £46 million to £35 million or around half what the ITC had been expecting from ITV when licences were first awarded. ITN could not afford to lose a contract that represented around 60 per cent of the company's revenue. And while some savings were possible through efficiencies, new technology and multi-skilling, there was no question that a 25 per cent budget cut impacted on the range and quality of television journalism it was capable of delivering.

ITN was, from the very beginning, a creation which depended for survival on a strong regulator to be able to fulfil its (and Parliament's) objective of a truly high-quality journalistic competitor for the BBC on commercial television. This was underlined by one of its most long-standing and highly regarded editors, Richard Tait (subsequently a BBC trustee), reflecting on the gradual decline of ITN as a journalistic institution:

> I'm not sure that the public service aspects of what ITN was doing have been sufficiently recognized by the regulator or anyone else. Only if public service broadcasters like ITV are held to their obligations can you have a company like ITN that aims at excellence. That has been ITN's aim all its life. Successive governments and regulators have said that news is special and can't be left to the market to decide its fate. But only if the regulator insists on high quality will ITN survive in recognizable shape.[26]

With rapacious businessmen determined to satisfy the City in a multichannel, competitive environment, it was becoming clear that the deregulatory philosophy behind the Broadcasting Act was, albeit belatedly, making an impact on ITV's capacity to deliver decent television journalism in both news and current affairs. The serious competition, which in the 1950s had forced the BBC to raise its journalistic game, was beginning to look decidedly ragged – especially when compared to a

BBC news operation that was now better funded and more tightly run than ever before.

Public service approaches to journalism: BBC television in the 1990s

With the BBC's journalism elevated and restructured under John Birt, and with a significantly less hostile government in place under John Major, the BBC of the 1990s faced a rather different challenge that was to become familiar territory for all public broadcasters looking to justify their existence in the multichannel digital age: how to reconcile its conflicting responsibilities of not replicating the marketplace while maintaining its status as a mass-audience broadcaster at the heart of national democratic and cultural life. As new channels came on stream through cable and satellite technology, as its competitors were becoming more commercial, and with Channel 5 added to the competitive mix from 1997, the BBC faced growing opposition on two fronts: from specialist channels arguing that the BBC should not be competing in their area; and from the consequences of a slow but inexorable decline in audiences, which started to raise questions both about the BBC's relevance and accessibility to people's everyday lives. Hostile newspaper groups (which included the great majority of Britain's national newspapers) would gleefully trumpet any new 'low' in BBC ratings as evidence of the BBC being 'out of touch' with modern audiences, while any initiative designed to maximize its reach invariably provoked accusations about interference with the market. It has been a defining feature of the post-Reithian BBC – probably since the 1960s – that it vacillates between 'distinctive' and 'populist' philosophies of public service, and its journalism had invariably been enmeshed in those internal strategic debates. The pendulum swung noticeably during the 1990s, with a direct impact on the nature and practice of its journalism.

At the beginning of John Birt's tenure as Director General in 1993, emphasis was being placed on reaching out for the 'Himalayan heights' of distinctive programming, a philosophy which fitted well with the Director General's own rather ascetic view of the BBC's role and the substantial investment made in news and current affairs. In news terms, it also left him vulnerable to further accusations of kowtowing to political pressure. A classic example occurred in October 1995 when then opposition leader Tony Blair gave the traditional leader's speech at the Labour Party conference. This was an important political occasion which would normally lead the early evening news, but on this occasion coincided precisely with the lead-up to the hugely anticipated verdict of the O.J. Simpson murder trial in Los Angeles. Anticipating the clash, Blair's Press Secretary, Alastair Campbell, faxed letters to both the BBC and ITN expressing concern that the leader's speech might not lead their bulletins and ending: 'I would implore you not to lose sight of the news value and of the importance to the country of Mr Blair's speech'.[27] While ITN led its early evening bulletin on O.J. Simpson to an audience of over 10 million, the BBC led with Blair's speech (to a still respectable audience of 6.6 million). There were widespread accusations that the BBC was surrendering to political pressure from Campbell (a familiar charge after Blair became Prime Minister), but in fact the decision had already been made by editors: it was consistent with an editorial philosophy which explicitly prioritized the BBC's 'public interest' approach to news over gratifying the public's interest.

However, this austere view of journalism started to come under pressure when publication of ratings figures in the middle of 1994 showed BBC1 at an eight-year low. An internal programme review was swiftly commissioned to understand this decline, and concluded that the BBC served the more upmarket audiences well but, 'there is sense from our research that we perhaps look after them too well ... we need to talk to the whole audience and address them all in different parts of the schedule'.[28] Internally, BBC executives spoke of 'superserving the ABC1s' and began to ask questions about whether it had become – both institutionally and journalistically – too elitist for the postmodern age. 'Panorama' became a living example of how those strategic tensions applied to current affairs.

In the spring of 1992 a new editor of 'Panorama' was appointed: Glenwyn Benson, formerly a deputy editor of 'Weekend World' under Birt and regarded as someone likely to follow the 'Birtist' line with dry, analytical programmes on difficult issues. She did not help her own cause when she was quoted as saying: 'It wouldn't matter if only five people watched, it's a symbol to the country that the BBC considers the subject we're covering is important.'[29] Several months later, however, mindful of the ratings impact on the BBC's Monday night peak-time schedule of consistently low-rating programmes, she sent a memo to the BBC1 Controller that acknowledged that the programme should be able to 'mix and synthesise' different approaches and different issues – whether original domestic stories, long investigations or responses to big news stories.[30] Thus, the agenda of 'Panorama' gradually shifted to include a number of high-profile investigations into issues such as police corruption, England football manager Terry Venables' financial affairs, rape sentencing and vigilantes. Audiences rose from under 2.5 million to between 4 and 5 million, and the programme was reinvigorated. It was a classic result of creative tension between public service purists and public service populists, which demonstrated that peak-time television journalism within a non-commercial environment could be both serious and responsive to audiences.

That responsiveness was embodied in 1998 through a comprehensive strategic examination of news output, based on what the BBC described as 'the biggest research project into news consumption ever undertaken'.[31] The Programme Strategy Review (PSR) of news output was prompted partly by continuing concern about falling audiences in a multichannel world, and partly by recognition that news itself was diversifying and proliferating. Sky had launched the UK's first 24-hour news channel in 1989 and the BBC started its own 24-hour service in 1997 as part of its digital strategy (both covered in more detail in Chapter 10). The government had announced in 1994 its intention to maximize use of the airwaves by switching broadcasting from analogue to the much more efficient digital transmission technology, and the 1996 Broadcasting Act laid the framework for a gradual expansion and eventual reconfiguration of television channels. However, the broad public service framework remained intact, and the BBC was in the vanguard of digital expansion. Its news channel was one of a suite of new channels and radio stations designed to kick-start the 'digital revolution'. Within this impending digital upheaval and further inevitable audience fragmentation, viewer attitudes to television news, as an integral part of the public service mission, needed to be better understood.

From the PSR emerged – not wholly to the surprise of some editors who disliked the centralized, analytical, Birtist approach to news – a sense of significant alienation amongst some sections of the viewing population and a conclusion that news needed to be more 'accessible'. As the next chapter explains, such terminology represents for many commentators the Trojan horse of tabloidization, and the published results led to some ritual denunciations of the BBC dumbing down its news bulletins.[32] Internally, however, it provoked a serious examination not simply of whether individual news bulletins and collective editorial practices should be more flexible, but whether particular social groups – in particular, ethnic minorities, the less educated, the less affluent – were being systematically alienated. In her penetrating study of the BBC of the 1990s, Georgina Born relates the frustration of a female News and Current Affairs executive at the autocratic nature of determining news values under Birt:

> Centralisation has reinforced a normative, macho editorial agenda focused on 'hard' news values: public service is being used to defend a white, male, middle-class agenda. 'Hard' means 'kings and queens'-type reporting, power politics, world events given a macro analysis. 'Soft' stories are dismissed as 'human interest', too easy – they don't involve flak jackets. But 'soft' stories are what people tend to relate to and remember ... public service is used to fend off the 'soft' stories the audience might actually want.[33]

In part recognition of these frustrations, the PSR resulted in a number of concessions to the 'consumer-friendly' lobby, which were applied in particular to a revamped and more domestically oriented 'Six O'clock News' (including more emphasis on regional stories and 'personally useful news'). By contrast, the later bulletin was to be restyled to increase its foreign content to 50 per cent. The impact of this deliberate differentiation – and of changes to commercial television's bulletins – is examined in the next chapter. But it reignited a debate both inside and outside the BBC on issues of editorial prioritization, which apply to all public service broadcasters whose approach is not dictated simply by advertisers, ratings or the bottom line but are matters of institutional discretion and philosophy. In this case, the issue for the BBC was how its editorial values could accommodate audience responsiveness and multiculturalism, and the dangers of confusing high-minded public service news aspirations with elitism, paternalism and an unhealthy uniformity of editorial approach. That particular – and very complex – debate became caught up in the next major institutional change as the austere regime of John Birt gave way to the very different modus operandi of a new Director General who was widely revered (and in some quarters maligned) as a talented populist.

Greg Dyke, who succeeded Birt as Director General at the end of 1999, had made his name 16 years earlier by rescuing the fortunes of the Breakfast News TV station TV-am with a puppet named Roland Rat. It was not exactly path-breaking journalism, but it had proved a commercial triumph. Within a year of his arrival at the BBC, he demonstrated his determination to maintain the BBC1's competitive position in the ratings (and fuelled the fears of his critics) by shifting both the evening news bulletin and 'Panorama'. Dyke's competitive instinct compelled him to grasp the opportunity left by ITV's abdication of the 10 p.m. news slot, thereby liberating BBC1's mid-evening schedule to compete more aggressively with the burgeoning number of commercial channels. In October 2000 the BBC's main evening bulletin, which from September 1970 had been the 'Nine O'clock News', gave way to the 'Ten O'clock News'. This revamp also entailed shifting 'Panorama' from its long-standing post-news Monday night slot of 9.30 p.m., and, to the fury of the public service traditionalists and 'Panorama' journalists, the programme was rescheduled for 10.15 p.m. on Sundays. It was scarcely surprising that over the next three years, as the popular-distinctive pendulum swung back to greater emphasis on ratings and research, the BBC was to be more often accused of dumbing down than of losing touch.

7 Tabloidization

t is one of the perennial questions asked within – and about – journalism: has there been an inexorable tendency towards tabloidization or 'dumbing down'? The charge is frequently heard and hotly contested, but is particularly directed at the medium that thrives on pictures and entertainment values. Has the content and approach of television journalism become progressively more frivolous and insubstantial, less meaningful and instructive than it was? This chapter examines this charge by looking at some of the empirical evidence for television news and current affairs, in particular from two studies I conducted at Westminster University. It starts by examining the definitional issues implicit in any attempt to answer this question, particularly in respect of a medium that does not naturally lend itself to serious analysis. Having considered the evidence, I offer at the end of the chapter a new definition which attempts to address some of the difficult theoretical and operational questions that might inform further empirical work in this area.

Definitional issues

Any serious argument about 'dumbing down' has to acknowledge two potential weaknesses of this critique. First, it often fails to allow for a definition of news simply as 'interesting' information or stories, usually about other people. As Andrew Marr puts it, 'the impulse to tell stories is hard-wired and fundamental to being human. Journalism is the industrialization of gossip.'[1] While a somewhat one-dimensional interpretation of news, it does illustrate a vital element of everyday life: that when an opening gambit in conversation is 'You'll never guess what happened today ...', the much anticipated follow-up is unlikely to be along the lines of 'The Bank of England raised interest rates by half a per cent' or 'The President announced a new programme of peace talks for the Middle East.' That is not because these issues are unimportant, but because for most people they have no immediate or intrinsic interest.

Second, it is one of the most long-standing journalistic axioms that even serious issues of great national and international weight are best told through a human angle. This was the key to success for Britain's first popular newspaper, the *Daily Mail*, launched in 1896 by Alfred Harmsworth with a very different approach from the sober broadsheets of his era, and which redefined the nature of journalism for the twentieth century. Following the failure of previous attempts to launch a popular newspaper, Harmsworth, in the words of Matthew Engel, 'lined up the three bells on the fruit machine ... The content was right; the price was right; the technique was right.'[2]

While price has not so far been an issue for television news, both content and technique are susceptible to wide variations of editorial approach, which can help to offer a measurable definition of how journalistic content changes over time. Engel's emphasis on content and style was echoed in a somewhat more scholarly approach by Colin Sparks who attempted the following definition: '*Tabloidisation is, first of all, a process in which the amount and prominence of material concerned with public economic and political affairs is reduced within the media. It is, secondly, a process by which the conventions of reporting and debate make immediate individual experience the prime source of evidence and value*' (italics in original).[3] At the heart of this definition is an assumption, explicitly acknowledged by Sparks, that an informed and participatory electorate requires access to accurate information about 'economic and political affairs', and that the accusation of elitism levelled at those who despair at the apparent decline of such information is nothing but 'a baseless populist jibe, the actual effect of which is to deny "the people" the resources they need to run their own affairs effectively'.[4]

The second part of this definition is problematic for television because it does not allow for the evocative nature of the television medium. As Peter Dahlgren has written, 'television is exceptional in its ability to mobilize affective involvement and convey the amorphous entity called implicit social knowledge ... And I would emphatically underscore that this quality is by no means entirely detrimental to its role in the public sphere.'[5] In fact, we can go further: affective involvement, properly employed, can be one of the most powerful manifestations of great television journalism, whether it is revealing the misery of single parenthood, the futility of life in an inner-city slum, the agony of a victim of back-street abortion or the unconfined joy of pregnancy for a woman undergoing IVF treatment. There are many ways of conveying the unfamiliar, and for television to exploit the personal and the emotional does not of itself mean a descent into tabloid values.

Elizabeth Bird makes a similar point in relation to American news and the memorability of stories: 'Showing the personal side of public events may be the most effective way to make people understand the impact of those events. Personal narratives, with a clear structure, moral point, and vivid imagery, are memorable'.[6] It is, therefore, legitimate to shock, entertain or personalize – indeed, it may be an essential journalistic tool in the television medium – if the end result is an audience that is better informed or more engaged or galvanized into greater learning or participation. This is, therefore, no more than the televisual manifestation of an honourable journalistic tradition, and we should not confuse the inherent demands – perhaps even virtues – of the medium with messages that are potentially every bit as citizen-enhancing as a thoughtful leader in a broadsheet newspaper.

Later in the chapter, I attempt to reformulate Sparks' definition to take account of the specific journalistic issues raised by television. The first part of his definition, however, still holds as a test of the tabloidization thesis: whether more emphasis is being placed on entertainment, show business, scandal and prurience *at the expense* of more serious and challenging material on matters of public policy – particularly within the high-rating news and current affairs programmes on mainstream news channels. This question of displacement is an essential starting-point for any empirical observation and that, in turn, presupposes a quantitative approach in which stories are classified.

The problem of classification – what is a 'tabloid' news story?

This process of categorizing stories as 'serious' or 'light' lies at the heart of any attempt to test the tabloidization thesis. Some stories are easily classified: the traumas of various royal family relationships, the sexual antics of film stars and politicians, the highs and lows of pop music personalities, and the lurid details of particularly gruesome murders or sex crimes might all be fairly categorized as unnecessary to the functioning of democratic and political life. Equally, details of major policy announcements, analysis of the latest economic trends or coverage of a major parliamentary debate can all be safely allocated to the 'serious' column.

The problem for news editors, as well as scholars, is the growing number of stories that are less easily categorized. Foremost amongst them are consumer-based issues that are directly relevant to people's lives (and therefore sometimes dismissed contemptuously as 'news you can use') but also an integral part of economic life in the twenty-first century. Stories about energy prices, health and safety, tourism, transport, even the environment are frequently couched in terms that combine individual impact (how will the fall in house prices affect *you*?) with a wider societal context (the role of mortgage-lending and debt in fuelling the global economic crisis). Television journalism, in particular, arguably has to work harder to make the serious popular given the heterogeneous nature of its audiences and the entertainment demands of the medium.

This problem of categorization is complicated further when it comes to human disasters or tragedies. No one could remotely question that the Indian Ocean tsunami of December 2004, in which over 200,000 people died, was sufficiently momentous to wipe virtually every other story off every nation's news agenda. But what if the figure had been a hundred rather than hundreds of thousands? Or what if no one had died at all, but there were dramatic pictures of huge tidal waves destroying houses and property? The same argument applies to crime stories. In Britain, the conviction in January 2000 of Harold Shipman after revelations that he had abused his position as a trusted doctor to murder over 200 of his patients raised numerous newsworthy issues beyond the family tragedies of the crimes themselves: about the state of the health service, the rules for prescribing drugs, the process of the Coroners' Court and the adequacy of our punishment system. And the terrible Japanese earthquake of March 2011 in which over 15,000 died raised important global issues beyond the scenes of devastation and tragedy: of the viability of nuclear power as an energy source, of the impact on Japanese businesses and employment overseas, of the future of Japan as a global economic power. How to represent and prioritize these issues are all questions of judgement for news editors and the resultant news output tells us something about the values of the society we live in as well as the journalistic values of a particular news organization. But to come to some meaningful conclusion about whether there has been a progressive move within television journalism towards a less serious news agenda requires some difficult judgements in the process of classification.

Many years ago there was a graphic example within the BBC of how television journalists themselves grapple with these editorial issues. On 25 November 1993, a school minibus crashed on a British motorway killing at least ten teenagers and their teacher. The tragedy occurred on the same day as both the Queen's Speech, which outlined the Conservative government's policy priorities for the coming session of Parliament, and the aftermath of an IRA bomb that had exploded in the northern town of Warrington. While ITN led its main evening bulletin on the motorway crash, the BBC led its equivalent bulletin with the Queen's Speech, followed by the Warrington bomb, and relegated the crash to third. Three days later, the *Independent on Sunday* published a transcript – leaked from inside the BBC – of a fascinating internal debate that had taken place on the BBC's computer system, which revealed some of the profound disagreements surrounding the final running order.[7]

On the one hand, there was a group of BBC journalists who found the editorial decision 'bizarre' and dismissed the argument that, because it was shared by all the next day's broadsheet press, anything else would have been a 'tabloid approach'. One argued that the BBC needed to be sensitive to the news values of the majority because 'we're supposed to be a public-service broadcaster, i.e. accessible to a large part of the population. It's not taking a "tabloid approach", for God's sake, it's just about acknowledging what ordinary people ... want to know about'. This group believed that the news values were so self-evident 'when 10 children die' that any other decision was simply incomprehensible: 'if you'd made that decision in any radio or newspaper newsroom I've ever worked in, you'd have faced the sack'. In other words, for some journalists, this was simply a matter of professional journalistic instinct about the nature of the story.

By contrast, those who supported the running order argued with equal passion that broadsheet news values – which they believed the BBC represented – dictated that evening bulletin's priorities: 'Any day or night editor of a broadsheet who ran the crash as front-page lead ahead of the Queen's Speech would have been hauled up before his superior faster than you could say "tabloid".' Another supporter argued the same point on the basis of longer term repercussions: 'Some of us just happen to think that when the Government sets out what it's going to do – i.e. the myriad number of ways it's going to screw us over – in the next year, it's important enough to lead a news bulletin with.'

This exchange precisely represents the dilemma of both television news editors and scholars assessing the nature of change in our news culture. Human tragedy attracts massive public interest simply because of the sympathy it generates for ordinary people becoming the victims of extraordinary events. Is it a 'tabloid' instinct to follow such stories? If so, we have to define an approach for journalistic endeavour that is predicated on a particularly narrow and elevating role for journalism in society: presumably, as in Sparks' definition above, one based around concepts of citizenship, democracy and knowledge enhancement rather than simply the conveyance of information to audiences about interesting or extraordinary events. This is an approach that is challengeable – as the BBC debate above illustrates – on grounds of elitism, but these difficult debates around the contestable areas of editorial decision-making should not preclude a rigorous attempt to gather evidence on the less ambiguous content of television journalism's output.

While accepting, therefore, that content analysis can be liable to subjective interpretative frameworks and cannot evaluate style or presentation, it can still offer valuable insights into changing trends in television journalism over time. The next section assesses the empirical evidence for tabloidization of news output in the United Kingdom and United States, while the following section looks at evidence for current affairs.

Is TV news dumbing down?

Changing patterns of television news

The first study, which remains the most comprehensive longitudinal content analysis of British television news, was undertaken in 2000 and funded jointly by the BBC and ITC.[8] It analysed over 700 television evening news bulletins spanning nearly a quarter of a century from 1975 to 1999 on the mass audience television channels – starting with the early and late bulletins on BBC1 and ITV in 1975, then adding Channel 4 and Channel 5. A full explanation of the methodology employed is contained in Appendix 1, but the sampling process ensured an even spread of years over the measurement period. The subject matter of each story was classified according to a coding frame that was refined into 31 story categories, and then consolidated into broader categories on two levels.[9] The first level was a simple division into broadsheet, tabloid and foreign. The second was a more finely tuned analysis which grouped categories into five headings and is explained in more detail below.

Findings at the first level

BBC/ITN early evening bulletins

Figures given in the tables are the proportion of the total number of sampled minutes in each year.

7.1   BBC 'Six O'clock News'

	1975	1980	1985	1990	1995	1999
	%	%	%	%	%	%
Broadsheet	59.5	49.8	45.2	59.8	60.7	44.6
Tabloid	18.4	18.8	25.9	6.5	17.0	28.9
Foreign	21.7	31.2	28.9	33.7	21.6	26.5

Monitoring long-term trends helps us to differentiate between fluctuations that can be attributed to external events and those that might be the result of changing institutional or editorial values. Thus, 1990 stands out as the peak of foreign coverage on the BBC 'Six O'clock News' (Table 7.1) partly as a direct result of the major foreign stories of that year: the Gulf War and the continuing collapse of communism in Eastern Europe. After falling slightly in 1995, the volume of foreign news had risen again by 1999.

7.2 ITN 'Early Evening News'

	1975	1980	1985	1990	1995	1999
	%	%	%	%	%	%
Broadsheet	59.5	49.8	44.3	55.8	51.4	43.0
Tabloid	15.4	22.6	32.2	18.7	29.5	33.0
Foreign	24.2	28.5	23.5	25.6	19	25.6

It is more difficult, however, to explain in similar terms the dramatic decline in tabloid news in 1990 to just 6.5 per cent of BBC output, followed by a fourfold rise to an all-time high by 1999. Certainly, there were big domestic stories in 1990 with a gathering recession and the political drama of Margaret Thatcher's forced resignation. Comparison with the figures for ITN (Table 7.2), however, suggests that the dramatic changes in tabloid content are far more likely to be a consequence of deliberate shifts in the BBC's editorial agenda – from John Birt's more austere journalistic regime in 1990 to the deliberate popularisation in 1999 which followed the Programme Strategy Review. By 1999, the volume of tabloid news in the BBC early evening bulletin was double that of the later bulletin (Table 7.3), and this was the first time that the two bulletins contrasted so significantly. This editorial shift to a more popular agenda was not accompanied by a diminution of foreign coverage, which continued at over a quarter of the total content.

As Tables 7.1 and 7.2 show, there was for 25 years an astonishing similarity between the two early evening bulletins. ITN demonstrated throughout its commitment to foreign news, and the only real divergence was the periods of 1990 and 1995 following the BBC's deliberate editorial shift. Perhaps the most significant change for ITN has been the longer term shift over time: a comparison of the first and last years of analysis show that, by 1999, the early evening news had more than doubled its tabloid coverage from 1975, whereas the equivalent BBC increase was just over 50 per cent. Early analysis of data from 2004 and 2009 suggests that this divergence has been consolidated but, contrary to expectations, has not widened further. Broadsheet coverage on the BBC bulletin rose to 52 per cent in 2004 and 55 per cent in 2009, reflecting widespread coverage of the global economic crisis and its implications, while its tabloid coverage shrank to 20 per cent and 23 per cent respectively. ITV's broadsheet coverage increased initially to 47 per cent in 2004, then reverted to 44 per cent in 2009. Its tabloid coverage has not increased, remaining at around one-third for both 2004 and 2009.

BBC/ITN late evening bulletins

7.3   BBC 'Nine O'clock News'

	1975	1980	1985	1990	1995	1999
	%	%	%	%	%	%
Broadsheet	59.7	39.2	44.6	56.0	56.3	43.0
Tabloid	16.2	17.1	22.6	4.9	13.2	13.3
Foreign	24.0	43.6	32.9	39.2	29.7	42.8

7.4   ITN 'News at Ten' (and 'Nightly News')*

	1975	1980	1985	1990	1995	1999
	%	%	%	%	%	%
Broadsheet	55.5	46.9	45.0	53.3	48.3	29.8
Tabloid	14.8	18.9	24.9	10.9	26.1	42.1
Foreign	29.4	34.7	28.9	35.9	25.6	28

Note: *ITV changed the timing of both its bulletins during the course of 1999. The research separately analysed the bulletins before and after the change, but found no significant difference.

After a substantial dip between 1975 and 1980 – almost entirely due to the rise in foreign coverage – broadsheet coverage on the BBC 'Nine O'clock News' rose steadily until 1995, with a significant rise between 1985 and 1990. As with its early bulletin, this reflects the deliberate editorial shift towards a more serious agenda under John Birt. The substantial drop in broadsheet coverage is deceptive, reflecting the impact of the Programme Strategy Review which called for half the late evening news to be devoted to foreign coverage. Thus, by 1999, the level of BBC foreign reporting on its late evening bulletin matched that of 1980 when news was dominated by the American hostage crisis in Iran, US presidential elections and the cold war implications of Russia's invasion of Afghanistan. As well as reflecting the BBC's changing editorial priorities, the 1999 figures would have been inflated by coverage of the war in Kosovo and the ensuing refugee and military problems (which, by contrast, had minimal impact on ITN).

It is the contrasting levels of tabloid news that really distinguished the two bulletins in the 1990s. While ITN has never been far behind the BBC's level of foreign coverage – and in 1975 exceeded it – the last two bulletins of the measurement period saw the first significant divergence in editorial agendas. While the BBC implemented its commitment to a serious-minded agenda for the late evening, ITN appeared to move in the other direction. By 1995, the level of tabloid coverage in 'News at Ten' had exceeded a quarter for the first time, but the most dramatic change was between 1995 and 1999 when there was a rise from 26 per cent to 42 per cent of the total. At this point, the ITN bulletin had over three times as much tabloid news as the BBC 'Nine O'clock News' and substantially more than at any time in the previous 25 years. This was the first point at which it was possible to see the impact of commercialism and deregulation on the nature of television news in the commercial sector – and even then, less than half the bulletin comprised material defined as tabloid. Moreover, early analysis of the 2004 and 2009 data suggests that this trend on ITV has to some extent been reversed, although the most recent data may be attributable to the seriousness of the unfolding economic crisis during 2009. While the BBC's broadsheet coverage increased from 43 per cent in 1999 to 47 per cent in 2009 at the expense of foreign coverage (down to just over one-third), ITV's broadsheet coverage jumped from 32 per cent to 41 per cent and its tabloid coverage declined from 39 to 34 per cent (compared to 19 per cent on the BBC). Thus, although there is now clear water between the main BBC and ITV bulletins, it would be wrong to say there has been a progressive flight downmarket in the news bulletins of the UK's main commercial channel.

Channel 4 and Channel 5 news

7.5 'Channel 4 News' and '5 News'

	Channel 4:	1985	1990	1995	1999	Channel 5:	1999
		%	%	%	%		%
Broadsheet		49.0	54.8	54.8	51.9		30.8
Tabloid		11.1	5.1	4.8	10.6		45.6
Foreign		39.4	40.7	39.3	37.5		23.6

The figures for 'Channel 4 News' are remarkable. They remind us that an established regulatory structure can protect a wholly commercial channel from the early peak-time ratings pressure and enable it to achieve astonishing editorial consistency. Over 20 years the agenda of 'Channel 4 News' has barely moved, with around half its bulletins devoted to domestic broadsheet issues, around 40 per cent to foreign issues and around 10 per cent to tabloid issues. This is confirmed by provisional figures for 2004 and 2009, which show that the bulletin's broadsheet coverage is virtually unchanged (although tabloid coverage appears to have risen from 11 per cent to 18 per cent at the expense of foreign news). The legacy of its original framework and Jeremy Isaacs' interpretation continued into the twenty-first century, demonstrating how strong editorial commitment to serious news values can be imposed on a bulletin and still generate a loyal and significant audience: an average of one million each evening may be small by mass audience standards, but still exceeds the circulation of most British broadsheet newspapers.

Given Channel 5's launch in 1997, there were no longitudinal data but the volume of tabloid coverage was by far the highest of the six bulletins – and to be expected, given the 'brand image' of the channel as youth-oriented, edgy and fun. It appears from the 2009 figures that Channel 5 is determined to reinforce that brand image, with tabloid coverage rising to just over half the bulletin, mostly at the expense of foreign news (down from 24 per cent to 17 per cent). As the more detailed second level tables show (Tables 7.6–7.8), '5 News' in 1999 was particularly strong on sport and crime, a pattern that is likely to be confirmed by the more recent data.

Findings at the second level

A more detailed classification grouped together domestic stories under five particular headings in order to achieve a more granular picture of television news trends over time. The five headings were: political affairs (politics, EU issues, foreign relations); social policy (covering education, health, social affairs, environment, transport, culture); sport; crime; and 'light' stories comprising royalty, human interest, celebrities or quirky humour. This last category was deliberately designed as a 'definitive' classification of tabloid or 'soft' news by excluding any ambiguous stories and in particular the two categories of crime and sport.

Full results for all five categories are given in Appendix 2, but the three tables here demonstrate the trends on each bulletin for political affairs, social policy and 'light' stories. In enlightenment terms, the first two categories constitute the kind of information that potentially empower citizens and enable a more informed democracy. On this basis – and remembering that at least a quarter of these bulletins are devoted to foreign news – the story is largely positive. With the exception of

Channel 5, at least a further quarter of the country's main news bulletins were still dealing with matters of social and political significance by 1999. While political coverage had diminished somewhat from the particularly tempestuous year of 1990, a renewed emphasis on social policy issues is clearly visible in the BBC and Channel 4 bulletins. Perhaps most significant of all, there was virtually no movement in the unequivocally tabloid category of 'light' stories, which even on Channel 5 comprised little more than 10 per cent of the total.[10]

7.6   Political affairs

	1975	1980	1985	1990	1995	1999
	%	%	%	%	%	%
BBC Six p.m.	25.6	15.2	14.1	32.6	20.8	14.6
BBC Nine p.m.	31.6	22.1	19.0	32.8	22.1	15.3
ITN Early Eve	22.2	17.9	16.2	31.3	19.7	17.4
ITN Ten p.m.	30.2	24.7	18.9	30.0	19.9	16.3
C4 News			17.6	33.3	25.4	15.8
C5 News						5.8

7.7   Social policy

	1975	1980	1985	1990	1995	1999
	%	%	%	%	%	%
BBC Six p.m.	5.3	13.8	11.7	7.9	17.2	15.1
BBC Nine p.m.	5.4	12.3	7.2	3.3	10.8	9.9
ITN Early Eve	2.4	9.4	6.7	8.4	10.1	9.7
ITN Ten p.m.	2.1	10.0	8.3	10.6	8.3	7.0
C4 News			11.9	7.8	8.2	15.5
C5 News						13.5

7.8   Light stories

	1975	1980	1985	1990	1995	1999
	%	%	%	%	%	%
BBC Six p.m.	5.2	7.5	7.3	0.8	5.1	4.8
BBC Nine p.m.	3.9	9.7	8.0	0.5	2.9	0.8
ITN Early Eve	3.6	7.1	7.8	3.1	10.9	4.1
ITN Ten p.m.	2.4	7.2	6.4	2.1	8.8	5.3
C4 News			2.5	0.7	0.8	0.5
C5 News						10.0

By the beginning of the new millennium, then, all the evidence suggested that – in terms of *quantity* and *subject matter* – British television news had defied the conventional charge of a commercialized, dumbed down editorial agenda, and had sustained a healthy balance of serious, light and international coverage despite the transition to a far more competitive and fragmented broadcasting environment. Even Channel 5, whose policy was to be unapologetically rooted in entertainment and the lighter touch, produced a bulletin where foreign and broadsheet coverage outweighed tabloid content. Moreover, in one important respect, television news improved over the 25-year period of the study period: compared to 1975 when the four evening news bulletins were almost indistinguishable in the nature of their content, the bulletins of the twenty-first century proved much more diverse – from the more highbrow BBC 'Nine O'clock News' and 'Channel 4 News', to the slightly more populist ITV bulletins and the BBC 'Six O'clock News', and the very populist and youth-oriented '5 News'.

Other evidence

While we need to wait for the detailed results from the updated research, there are two reasons for hypothesizing that TV news content in the United Kingdom will not have deviated significantly in the first decade of the twenty-first century. First, the structural and regulatory building blocks that mandated and sustained television news – and the professional values of those who provide it – have not changed substantially, although we would expect some attempt by ITV's late evening news to differentiate itself from the BBC following its American-style competitive scheduling from January 2008 opposite the BBC's 'Ten O'clock News'. Second, the dominant stories of the 2000s – terrorist attacks, contentious wars in Afghanistan and Iraq, heightened security issues, growing diplomatic tension with Iran and Russia, a coalition government in the United Kingdom and change of leadership in the United States, culminating in the biggest global economic meltdown since the Great Depression with major financial and political consequences for Europe and the future of the euro – are likely to militate against any demonstrable shift downmarket.

Such evidence as exists supports the status quo argument, although there will always be issues of comparability when assessing other research. One study analysed late evening bulletins on the two main UK channels in February 2001, comparing them with data from equivalent bulletins collated by the Glasgow Media Group in 1975. It appeared to demonstrate a quadrupling of crime stories, a significant decline in political news and the virtual disappearance of 'industrial' news, which featured heavily in 1975.[11] Crucially, however, the study was based on data generated during a single week, making results highly susceptible to the problems outlined above of a single story (in this case, possibly, a single crime) dominating the week's bulletins. Moreover, the unit of measurement was the number of stories rather than the time allocated, which would result in a disproportionately higher showing for those issues where stories are comparatively short. As ever, we must be wary of methodological shortcomings that can easily compromise research in this area.

Another study, published by the Independent Television Commission just before it was merged into Ofcom, analysed the content of seven days of news bulletins across a three-week period in May 2002.[12] Although the categories were not exactly comparable, the data suggest that the only significant change between 1999 and 2002 was a decline in political coverage on the ITV early evening bulletin with a concomitant increase in crime coverage (see Table 7.9). The general increase in sports coverage across all channels is attributable to the build-up to the soccer World Cup and again illustrates why a more extensive sampling process is essential to represent output accurately. The authors also carried out an analysis of the top three stories in the ten-week period from May to July 2002 as a means of 'corroborating the priorities of different television news broadcasters'. This essentially confirmed the findings of the more detailed enquiry: at least a quarter of lead stories were international on every channel, rising to 45 per cent for the BBC late bulletin and 52 per cent for 'Channel 4 News'.

In 2007, Ofcom published its first extensive enquiry into television news with the results of its own content analysis during a three-week period in October 2006, which purported to update the ITC's 2002 work. It reported its conclusions in the main discussion document in a fairly cursory two paragraphs, which suggested that, if anything, 'hard' news reporting was on the rise: 'Content analysis of main bulletins on the five PSB channels suggests that output remains of similar high

7.9   ITC research (2002) v Westminster research (1999) (All figures are proportions of sampled output for that bulletin; figures in brackets are from the Westminster study)

	International	Politics	Crime	Sport	Entertainment
	%	%	%	%	%
BBC early	27.4 (26.5)	14.7 (14.6)	10.1 (6.8)	13 (8.7)	8.4 (4.8)
BBC late	35 (42.8)	16.6 (15.3)	7.6 (5.2)	12.9 (3.8)	1.2 (0.8)
ITV early	22.8 (25.6)	8.9 (17.4)	13.1 (4.4)	20.3 (7.5)	5.3 (4.1)
ITV late	24.8 (28)	13 (16.3)	8.4 (8.0)	17.8 (12.8)	11.1 (5.3)
C4 News	48.3 (37.5)	22.2 (15.8)	9.0 (5.5)	5.8 (1.6)	5.0 (0.5)
C5 News	17.6 (23.6)	12.1 (5.8)	11.7 (11.3)	20.2 (13.8)	21.3 (10.0)

quality to that observed in previous studies, and is dominated by hard news. A greater proportion of time was devoted to major political stories in 2006 than in 2002.'[13]

However, a closer reading of the research and evidence base that accompanied the main report suggests a number of problems with this study, which render it unreliable and probably inaccurate.[14] It again demonstrates the need to apply rigorous methodological scrutiny to any study on tabloidization. In measuring the balance between 'hard' and 'soft' stories, Ofcom counted the number of stories in each bulletin during its three-week period rather than the duration. Its data appeared to demonstrate an astonishing preponderance of hard stories: 87 per cent for both BBC bulletins; 84 per cent of the ITV early evening bulletin and 81 per cent of its late bulletin; 90 per cent of 'Channel 4 News'; and 75 per cent of '5 News'. Moreover, the vast majority of non 'hard' stories were sport. Excluding sport, in three weeks of continuous monitoring, Ofcom could find only eight 'soft' stories in each of the ITV bulletins, just six in the BBC's early bulletins and precisely two in its late bulletins! Even Lord Reith would have permitted a little more levity.

There are clues as to how these results became so distorted. In its definition of news categories, Ofcom states that items are classified as soft if 'they have no time related element to them [sic], have a features-type content and treatment; deal with entertainment; or are quirky/humorous'. In a written communication to James Curran, this definition was further clarified by Ofcom as being 'predominantly entertainment or celebrity based' and not including 'human-interest-centred crime stories, or sports reports'.[15] There is no mention of whether these classifications are consistent with the ITC research, which it seeks to use as a benchmark, but such a narrow interpretation of 'soft' news suggests not. This particular study should therefore be treated with some caution.

Poor research techniques notwithstanding, a combination of the ITC and Ofcom research as well as anecdotal evidence suggests that the United Kingdom has maintained a consistent and broadly serious approach to the issues covered by television news.[16] Partly because of the presence of a well-funded public broadcaster and partly because of the regulatory obligations that allowed a strong commercial competitor to flourish, viewers on the mass-audience channels still have access to serious coverage of important domestic and foreign issues alongside a reasonable proportion of lighter, more tabloid issues. Moreover, neither the volume of television news nor its peak-time accessibility has diminished. Both mass-audience channels continue to boast two half-hours of news during the peak hours of 6 and 11 p.m. as well as their breakfast and lunchtime bulletins. At the same time, two other commercial public service channels offer very distinctive, peak-time bulletins at different times aimed at different audiences while maintaining a substantial proportion of serious content.

Presentation and style

Content analysis is limited, by definition, to analysing subject matter rather than approach and tends to ignore the more subjective issues of presentation, language or treatment, which can vary significantly. A small-scale study of one day's evening news output in 1997 highlighted, for example, the distinctively more youthful and entertainment-led approach to news presentation being adopted by '5 News' on Channel 5. Presented by Kirsty Young ('a young glamorous woman dressed in casual, fashionable clothes'), the programme's opening sequence is described as 'like the beginning of a fictional drama series, fast, upbeat and dramatic'.[17] It was, and remains, a self-consciously youth-oriented approach that impacted more on the way in which news was being framed than the selection of stories.

The same report also offers some insights into the fairly desperate presentational techniques occasionally employed on other channels. One was attempted by a short-lived entertainment-based cable station, L!ve TV, which began life in June 1995 with its hourly news bulletins accompanied by a 'News Bunny' offering a verdict on each story by giving a thumbs-up or thumbs-down. Even this paled into dullness compared to presentation of the channel's business news, provided by a young woman taking off one item of clothing for each of her reports from the City. Since this was the channel that gave us 'Topless Darts' and 'Trampolining Dwarfs' perhaps nothing should surprise, although its closure four years later in November 1999 suggested that British audiences were not yet ready for the kind of tabloid approach being promoted by the channel's main moving spirit (and former editor of the *Sun*), Kelvin MacKenzie.[18]

Apart from creating alternative or idiosyncratic presentational environments, approaches to language and storytelling can also differ markedly. One illustration emerged from a major story during one of the evaluation periods in the Westminster study: floods in Mozambique, which caused widespread misery and homelessness. While ITV concentrated on the very human story of a mother giving birth in a tree, others (notably the BBC's late evening bulletin and 'Channel 4 News') took a more political, economic and historical approach to its coverage. Similar comparisons can be seen in approaches to environmental issues and, during 2008–9, to the impact of the global credit crunch and economic crisis. Attempts to explain difficult economic concepts beyond the notion of 'meltdown' and 'crisis' become more important as people look to television news for an explanation of the upheavals that are about to impact on their own lives. The tabloidization thesis would suggest that more simplistic and sensationalist language and imagery is likely to accompany a greater emphasis on more trivial stories, but this requires more systematic investigation. As competition increases still further and news competes for fragmenting television audiences, a more sophisticated analysis is needed of the language, storytelling, presentational and journalistic techniques employed, as well as the impact of dramatic pictures in framing television's news agendas.

US comparisons

No cross-cultural content analysis will be entirely valid given different interpretations and approaches to classification, but it is nevertheless worth comparing the longitudinal trends in the United Kingdom with trends in evening news output in the United States. As we have seen, many American commentators and former journalists despaired at what they saw as the progressive disintegration of serious American television journalism towards the end of the last century, supported empirically by studies such as Harvard University's 'soft news' project cited in the Introduction.[19] Since then, we have had the terrorist attacks of 9/11 and substantial American military involvement abroad, so would expect the agenda to have shifted somewhat. The Project for Excellence in Journalism (PEJ) has been monitoring the nightly network news bulletins since the 1970s and, as the table opposite demonstrates, their findings up to June 2001 echoed the Harvard conclusions: government (that is, political) news had declined to just 5 per cent while crime, celebrity and sports news had risen over the years to nearly a third.[20]

The agenda shifted markedly in the aftermath of September 2001, but the authors of the 2008 report suggested that the agenda is now shifting back. They pointed, in particular, to political news falling back to its lowest levels, although this is compensated to some extent by election campaigning and Iraq policy debates. They also suggest that the rise in 'domestic affairs' includes coverage of health and medicine and wonder whether this is 'particularly attuned to an older audience that watches nightly news, or toward lifestyle stories about diet and other news you can use?' Although that particular question remains unanswered there is concern about a rising number of special reports on health which are consumerist rather than informational or revelatory, and about the increase in accident/disaster stories. Against that, the crime/celebrity/sport combination that accounted for 30 per cent in 2001 only accounted for half that volume by 2007. While overall a lower proportion of evening news is devoted to serious citizenship issues than in the United Kingdom, the difference is not as stark as some critics have portrayed.

Much more significant in terms of international comparisons are the lower *volume* of news and the lack of any *diversity* in either scheduling or content. The PEJ notes in its 2011 report that once commercials and trailers are subtracted from the notional 30-minute programmes, the bulletins actually come in at just over 19 minutes.[21] Although this has been rising gradually from just over 18 minutes in

7.10   Commercial nightly news topics, over time (percentage of all stories)[22]

	1977	1987	1997	Jun 2001	Oct 2001	2002	2003	2004	2007
Government	37	32	18	5	7	5	16	27	5
Foreign Affairs/ Military*	22	20	18	23	39	37	28	15	25
Elections								9	7
Domestic Affairs#	8	7	5	18	34	12	16	21	24
Crime	8	7	13	12	4	12	6	2	6
Business/Economics	6	11	7	14	5	11	12	8	10
Celebrity/Entertain.	2	3	8	5	0	2	2	2	1
Lifestyle/Sports	4	11	14	13	1	17	6	5	8
Science and Technology	4	5	6	4	11	2	2	3	2
Accidents and Disasters	9	5	10	4	0	3	10	4	7
Other+	N/A	N/A	N/A	3	0	N/A	2	4	5

Notes: Totals may not equal 100 due to rounding.
*Foreign Affairs in 2007 includes much of Iraq policy debate, US foreign diplomacy and non-U.S. involved foreign events.
#Domestic Affairs includes topics such as health and immigration that in other charts are broken out separately.
+Other in 2007 includes media.

2003, it is still low when compared to the actual news transmission times of UK bulletins: even with commercials, the ITV bulletins are well over 20 minutes, the commercial-free BBC is close to 30 and the hour-long 'Channel 4 News' would run to at least 50 minutes. Moreover, in terms of their homogeneity of approach to news, the networks are much more akin to the undifferentiated bulletins of ITV and BBC in the 1970s. As Table 7.11 demonstrates, in 2007 there was scarcely any deviation between the three major American networks in the proportion of time allocated to different stories. According to the PEJ, out of 2,303 minutes devoted to the war in Iraq on the three evening news programmes over the course of the year, their total volume of coverage varied by just eight minutes (CBS 771, ABC 769, NBC 763). Following the presidential election of 2008, PEJ analysis produced the same result a year later reporting that 'there was virtually no difference in the news agenda of the three big commercial broadcast networks'.[23]

7.11   Differences among nightly newscasts by topic (percentage) in 2007

	ABC	CBS	NBC
Government	5	5	5
Elections/Politics	8	9	7
Crime	6	6	5
Economics/Business	8	6	7
Environment	2	3	4
Health/Medicine	8	10	8
Science/Technology	2	3	1
Immigration	1	1	2
Other Domestic Affairs*	15	15	15
Disasters/Accidents	7	7	7
Celebrity/Entertainment	1	1	1
Lifestyle/Sports	10	10	8
Miscellaneous & Media	3	3	4
U.S. Foreign Affairs	15	15	16
Foreign (Non-U.S.)	8	7	9
Total Minutes	**4,680**	**4,837**	**4,938**

Notes: Totals may not equal 100 due to rounding.
*Other Domestic Affairs includes such things as development, transportation, education, religion, abortion, gun control, welfare, poverty, social security, labour, aging, court/legal system, race and gender issues, etc.

Thus, the unregulated marketplace of American television seemingly provides no editorial incentive to develop a different agenda or a different approach to news: the fear of losing a fractional per cent of audience share to a fierce competitor drives the networks to a uniformity which offers no new perspectives or different emphases. Unfettered competition, in other words, results in the diametric opposite of genuine consumer choice. This is perhaps not quite the conclusion that most critics of television news would expect, because the traditional charge of tabloidization – of lighter material driving out the more serious – is only somewhat proven in the United States and hardly at all in the United Kingdom. In terms of viewer accessibility, editorial diversity and the sheer volume of available news, however, there is no question that the regulated system of the United Kingdom has managed to sustain a breadth of service on its main free-to-air channels which the United States is unable to match.

Is TV current affairs dumbing down?

If the performance of television news in Britain is generally holding up in terms of its contribution to democratic life, the same cannot be said for current affairs. We have seen how current affairs gradually became marginalized on ITV, while Channel 4 was facing a new commercial reality in competition with ITV and the BBC was struggling to reconcile the need to maintain audiences with its duties as a publicly funded broadcaster. There was also growing awareness that the new digital channels and personal video recorder (PVR) technology were likely to have a profound impact on viewing behaviour. At the end of the 1990s, I carried out a study for the Campaign for Quality Television (CQT) to investigate how this confluence of industrial, political and technological upheaval had impacted on current affairs programming on UK television.[24]

This study had both quantitative and qualitative elements. As with the news study, there was a longitudinal content analysis that examined volume and subject matter of peak-time current affairs in 1977–8, 1987–8 and 1997–8.[25] In addition, a total of 18 interviews were carried out with current affairs programme-makers and commissioning editors, mostly selected at random from industry lists. Although the research is over ten years old, both the trends themselves and the qualitative evidence from current affairs producers help us to understand the underlying and continuing pressures on non-news television journalism, most of which can be generalized to competitive television systems in other countries.

Programme findings

In stark contrast to television news, there was a marked decline in current affairs output over the 20-year period, and a significant shift in editorial agendas away from the 'harder' areas of foreign, political and economic affairs – particularly on commercial television, which effectively evacuated the area completely. Table 7.12 shows how the proportion of peak-time current affairs nearly doubled between 1978–9 and 1988–9 before dropping to its original level ten years later. That decline was entirely due to ITV more than halving its current affairs output from over 17 hours during the sampled period of eight weeks to fewer than 8 hours, while the BBC's output continued to rise in recognition of its public service obligations. Channel 4's contribution also reduced significantly between the 1980s and the 1990s, although that was addressed in the following decade.

7.12   Change in volume of peak-time current affairs output on UK TV (number of hours and proportion of total peak-time hours)

	1977–8	1987–8	1997–8
Total hours (100 per cent)	22.5 hours (2.7 per cent)	55 hours (4.9 per cent)	37.8 hours (2.7 per cent)
BBC	14.8 hours	21.5 hours	23.8 hours
ITV	7.8 hours	17.2 hours	7.3 hours
Channel 4	N/A	16 hours	3.1 hours

More striking than the volume decline of current affairs was the tangible shift in editorial agendas, particularly on commercial television. As Table 7.13 demonstrates, foreign coverage declined from over a quarter of all current affairs content to less than one-fifth (and more detailed analysis showed that it had almost disappeared completely from ITV). Similarly, coverage of the 'hard' current affairs issues of politics, industry and business had declined from 28 per cent to 21 per cent overall and had also virtually disappeared from commercial television. Conversely, there were two significant growth areas over the measurement period: programmes relating to crime and police issues more than doubled from 6 per cent to over 13 per cent (and tripled as a proportion of ITV's coverage); while consumer stories, which had not even featured in the 1977–8 period, comprised 8 per cent of output by 1997–8. There was also a growth in programmes devoted to moral or ethical issues such as abortion and animal rights, as more programmes tackled the politics of the individual.

7.13 Change in editorial content of peak-time current affairs on UK TV (proportion of total peak-time hours)

	1977/8	1987/8	1997/8
	%	%	%
Foreign	28.5	16.7	19
Politics/economics	14.4	12.2	15
Industry/business	14	17.5	6
Home affairs	8.9	3.1	4
Consumer issues	-	0.9	8
Crime/police stories	5.8	3.7	13.4
Ethical/moral issues	-	2.7	6.4

No systematic evidence exists on whether these trends have continued into the 2000s, but anecdotal evidence suggests that there is now more emphasis on the personal, on human interest and on celebrity issues than in the late 1990s. In its final annual report before handing its regulatory duties to Ofcom, the Independent Television Commission was less than enthusiastic in its review of ITV's only remaining current affairs programme, 'Tonight with Trevor McDonald'. It noted the heavy reliance on exclusive interviews with the 'genuinely newsworthy' (such as George Bush) but commented wryly that others such as Maria Carey and Michael J. Fox 'stretched the definition of current affairs to its limit'. Overall, it concluded, there was 'insufficient analysis, coverage of international issues or investigations'.[26] A more recent small-scale analysis of recent editions of 'Panorama' concluded that 'many of its investigations appear to be based on finding popular subjects and presenting the results in ways that put almost as much emphasis on production values as on editorial content'.[27] Just about the only mainstream broadcaster that seems to have escaped the critics' attention is Channel 4, which, as we have seen, has been determined to protect its serious current affairs agenda despite entering a period of enormous financial uncertainty. A more systematic analysis is required, but one might assume that the economic crisis of 2008 onwards prompted a greater emphasis across all channels on issues around banking, regulation and management of the economy.

Interpreting the evidence – has current affairs dumbed down?

As with the changing news agenda, there are two standard defences to charges that current affairs has become more trivialized and less serious. First, that agendas are merely reflecting the concerns and changing priorities of the world outside. Reduced coverage of world affairs, for example, could simply reflect the end of the cold war, the fading spectre of industrial disputes and access to greater personal wealth for the majority, i.e. Francis Fukuyama's 'End of History' thesis, which was enthusiastically embraced by many during the 1990s. In its place, it is argued, there emerged a different societal agenda with more emphasis on the individual and on consumption. An ageing population, for example, raises concerns about health and pensions as well as ethical issues such as euthanasia. If personal security is threatened by anxieties about crime, that too becomes a more relevant area for journalistic scrutiny. While there is some truth in this defence, it will have fallen apart after 9/11, wars in Iraq and Afghanistan, heightened instability in places like Pakistan and Iran; the near collapse of the global economy during 2007–8 and its repercussions; and the 'Arab Spring' uprisings of 2011 in Egypt, Tunisia, Libya and elsewhere in the Middle East. If television current affairs was doing its job, we would expect a significant uplift in the serious and the international during the 2000s; there is little indication that this has happened on either side of the Atlantic.

The second related argument is that current affairs journalism was too paternalistic and elitist, run by journalists according to their own whims with little attention to the concerns of the viewing audience. This argument interprets the shift in the current affairs agenda as a belated symptom of the television industry realigning itself away from producers and towards the audience. Again, there is some truth in this; the more diverse agenda of British current affairs journalism in the 1990s compared to the two earlier decades suggests a culture of production driven less by journalistic diktat and more by the interests of viewers. Arguments about the democratization of journalism, however, can also be used as a convenient excuse for sacrificing the more challenging or serious issues – which happen also to be the most expensive and the lowest rating.

The counter-argument, rehearsed in Chapter 6, is that the exclusion of more difficult programmes is itself undemocratic in two senses. First, as Sparks argues above, it allows television to abdicate any responsibility for making a meaningful contribution to democratic life. British television has historically offered audiences some of the most well-researched and accessible opportunities for understanding their world and their society better, thus helping them to make informed electoral choices as well as informed lifestyle and consumption choices. Depriving citizens of this opportunity results in a shallower, less well-informed citizenry and therefore a poorer democracy.

Second, serious journalism is still enjoyed and actively selected by – in absolute terms – very large numbers of viewers. Just as the overwhelmingly serious agenda of 'Channel 4 News' can routinely attract a million viewers, so serious examinations of foreign affairs or difficult areas of politics and economics can still – even in the multichannel, online era – easily attract audiences of 2 to 3 million. By eliminating these programmes from current affairs television, not only is democracy itself diminished, but the significant minority who choose to watch such programmes are disadvantaged. This 'tyranny of the majority', which slavishly follows the cultural tastes of the largest audiences, is as fundamentally undemocratic as ignoring altogether the wishes of those majorities.

These, however, are conceptual and normative arguments about the 'proper' approach to television current affairs rather than empirical statements about what is actually happening to television journalism and why. Having established that current affairs agendas materially shifted away from the serious by the end of the last century, we can examine the reasons given by practitioners themselves behind these changes. If editorial values had indeed changed in recognition of the changing needs of audiences, the democratization argument might hold. In practice, our interviews revealed that professional journalists were responding far more to structural pressures within a deregulating industry.

Interview findings

A consistent set of themes emerged from practitioners about the pressures that were transforming the nature of their craft. While a few were optimistic about the potential for positive journalistic outcomes, they were heavily outnumbered by those who saw the changes in almost wholly negative terms. Their responses can be analysed under four headings.

A growing obsession with ratings and audience research

A common theme was the replacement of journalistic or editorial instinct with an unhealthy focus on ratings targets and consumer research. This did not just affect the commercial channels. According to one BBC producer: 'Editors whose instincts lie normally with stories we would have covered five or ten years ago are pressing the button automatically and are looking over their shoulder at the sort of ratings that each programme could be expected to deliver.'[28] Another talked about the thinking behind an ill-fated BBC early evening current affairs programme, 'Here and Now', which was designed around the results of audience research: 'We started going to the focus groups and asking them what stories we should do – and that's our job really'.

Inevitably, when audience research is substituted for the judgement of professionals, subjects like Northern Ireland fall off the agenda despite the major diplomatic achievements of the 2000s. While bombs were going off on the British mainland and the Army was embroiled in dangerous peace-keeping missions, it was both a proper subject for enquiry and attracted audiences. Despite the huge investment of political capital and its importance as an integral part of British political history, the Northern Ireland peace process was largely conducted in a state of public ignorance. In the words of one producer, 'we can't do it for television, people can't stand it, and they don't want to know about Northern Ireland'.

On ITV, any shortfall in audience targets was regarded as failure – even if the previous or subsequent week more than exceeded the target. This inevitably made 'doing foreign stories ... or doing Ireland really difficult. You just began to feel that whereas before you could balance it up, you couldn't any more.' Highly competitive advertising-funded television systems – such as the United States or Italy – have been accustomed to decisions being dictated wholly in audience measurement terms. For television journalists working on UK current affairs programmes, the repercussions of this transition to 'painting by numbers' came as something of a shock.

A shift in subject matter from thoughtful to attention-grabbing

Related to the greater emphasis on ratings was the manifest shift to lighter topics, preferably with dramatic or sensational footage. The problem for some current affairs producers was that these editorial priorities were being dictated by television's demands for arresting pictures rather than any intrinsic news value. One who worked on 'Tonight with Trevor McDonald' described it as 'lots of video of people doing bad things, even when there's no story to tell; there's one-sided sentimental interviews; there is an obsession with crime and scary health stories.' Others talked of the pressure to bring pace and 'edge' to every story which inevitably led to techniques such as hidden camera work with an emphasis on the emotional and dramatic rather than the narrative: 'I know people working on [Tonight with Trevor McDonald] and one of the prime drives of the editorial team now is to deliver CCTV video ... of something bad happening. An entire item constructed not because there's any journalistic or public service ... just so long as you can cram as much video of people getting hurt or cars crashing, or whatever. It's an utterly cynical form of journalism.'

This is not, in other words, about presenting serious or provocative issues in a more populist way but about privileging presentation and storytelling above content. The end result is a bankrupt vision of current affairs involving, in the words of another interviewee, 'a sort of manufactured journalism, rather than reporting what's actually happening in our names behind closed doors'. Although the BBC was not immune from censure, the most trenchant criticism was reserved for commercial television and the widespread view that the single-issue programmes of ITV in its heyday had been replaced with 'something that might offer you a little bit of Kosovo, but wrapped around in miracle cures and sick kids and pseudo celebs and lots of video of people kicking off'. The new current affairs was, they said, being driven by the need to titillate audiences without any pretence of making a meaningful contribution on matters of public interest.

Budget cuts, penny pinching and the elimination of risk

Once competition for revenue became an integral feature of the UK's television system, the generosity that had once been a feature of current affairs programming budgets began to evaporate. Producers were clear about how those reductions invariably narrowed the range and vitality of current affairs journalism: 'Every year they keep cutting, and we are constantly being asked for different ways in which we might be able to save money … We feel we've become so budget oriented that we've clipped our own wings – we don't even suggest ideas because we think it will be too expensive.'

Even before the major BBC cuts of the 2000s, diminishing current affairs budgets had become an issue. One long-standing BBC editor said: 'Now every single decision I take in terms of where I send people, who I hire, which newspapers we read, is dictated purely and simply by money and it can be very dispiriting. Sometimes you just can't send someone overseas.' Constraints on foreign stories was a particular theme on commercial channels where it had a tangible impact on programme content: 'We had to think very hard … about travelling anywhere outside the M25, never mind go to Scotland, never mind occasionally go abroad. There was nothing in the budget for us ever to do anything foreign … You can go to Holland, because you can go on Easyjet and it costs the same as going to Manchester on the train. Northern Ireland's expensive, so we don't go.'

Budgetary constraints therefore added to the pressure to maintain an essentially domestic agenda, but they also dictated a cautious approach to subject matter. As with drama or comedy, the more competitive the system and the greater the pressure to secure instant success, the less room there is for investment without a guaranteed return. Failure to deliver a story is not an option:

> All current affairs has to have the ability to fail, to waste, and you have got to
> have in your budget a certain amount of money you know you are going to

take a chance with. Now ... every time you leave the office you have *got* to get stuff that is going to go on air, there is no latitude for 'well, it didn't work, this whole story's gone down the pan'.

This kind of budgetary constraint has particularly corrosive consequences for long-form investigative journalism, which requires patience, checking of sources, often painstaking legwork and several researchers, adding up to a significant investment of resources that may well amount to nothing – or, as we saw with 'Death on the Rock', a huge post-transmission outlay in fighting your corner. The fourth estate often trumpets its responsibility to hold the powerful to account but, especially in an expensive medium like television, tackling corruption in high places requires deep pockets and an appetite for risk-taking that broadcasters are finding increasingly uncomfortable. According to one award-winning investigative television journalist with a dazzling track record of successful independent productions:

> If you're an independent you have to argue every penny of the budget. So if you say, 'I can get the dirt on X' – a policeman on the take or compromising his independence – 'but it will take eight months', they will not give you eight months' money ... So that is why [Channel 4's] *Dispatches* will never reach the heights of a *Panorama* or of an old *World in Action*, because every now and then they will invest significantly, but really they rely on other people funding the very hard work investigation requires.

In other words, why risk public opprobrium and shareholder wrath for a courageous but ultimately fruitless investigation when an 'exposé' of, say, teenage crime in Brixton (accompanied by dramatic CCTV footage) will guarantee a decent audience, low budget, no objections and maybe even a front page splash in the *Daily Mail*? Editors and journalists who are committed to tackling serious issues, or to finding ways of making serious issues more interesting and accessible through some of the popularizing techniques of television, are increasingly being thwarted by institutional caution and financial constraints that naturally militate towards the sensational, the dramatic, the inexpensive and the 'quick fix' – all the direct antithesis of challenging and enlightening journalism.

A transformed working environment and the demise of institutional teamwork

For most television journalists, the key to successful current affairs is an institutional framework that provides not only resources but committed, experienced colleagues who work as a team. Unlike the print media, where highly successful investigative reporters have often worked alone, television requires production and research support to function properly. Structural changes in broadcasting – exacerbated in the United Kingdom by the 1990 Broadcasting Act – have led to increased casualization and shedding of permanent staff, the widespread use of short-term contracts, and the loss of studios and facilities, all of which has worked against the establishment of a permanent team with a body of knowledge and experience. Moreover, well-established programme strands and guaranteed airtime provided vehicles for journalists to use their own judgement and initiative rather than have editorial priorities dictated by commissioning editors or channel controllers. These programmes constructed their own professional ethos rooted in a securely structured environment and congenial working practices: 'World in Action, Panorama, programmes like that had a remarkable esprit de corps – they're quite supportive places in many ways, much more so than other newsrooms. There is less competition for jobs and a much greater sense of the identity of the programme you're working on. There's a real sense of the history that you're part ot.'

There are huge implications here for training, because this institutional culture provided a learning space for a new generation of television journalists. The virtual disappearance of job security in current affairs had two consequences. First, it squandered the talent and expertise that had been fostered over 20 years; second, and much more importantly, it dismantled the training framework and therefore heralded a serious shortage of new talent. The role of assistant producer used to be pivotal to the training of current affairs journalists who would learn the art of filming and editing as well as understanding the legal complexities and compliance issues. Those opportunities are disappearing in the casualized world of today's television.

Apart from the abdication of responsibility for training, there was an overwhelming feeling amongst practitioners that a whole value-system was being carelessly discarded. Programmes were being commissioned as slot-filling product without a great deal of imagination and according to formulae invented by backroom number-crunchers poring over printouts of audience demographics. In the United States, this had been common practice for some time. In the United Kingdom, it was a new phenomenon that flowed directly from increased competition and 'light touch' regulation, and it was profoundly troubling to long-standing journalists whose concerns were not rooted in some misty-eyed golden-ageism but in a clear understanding of how intelligent, well-produced and well-researched current affairs on television can contribute meaningfully to democratic welfare. This was best articulated by one BBC journalist who emphasized the importance of public service journalism outside television news, and what was being lost as we moved closer to the American model:

When you've built a tradition over thirty years of having some hard-hitting, serious, investigative current affairs, analysis, political debate, finance programmes, consumer programmes ... [it] makes all our lives richer and aids democracy. [In the United States] factual television and current affairs ... is all hinged on emotion, and you limit the facts to as few as possible. That is the way we are beginning to go, and it doesn't have to be like that.

Conclusion

Given the limitations of the medium, there is only so much that television journalism can achieve, even when supported by a professional culture and regulatory mechanisms designed to maximize its potential. Nevertheless, for the reasons rehearsed at the beginning of this book, that potential is huge and has in the past largely been fulfilled both by British news and by British current affairs journalism. The evidence presented in the first half of this chapter suggests that, in contrast to the United States, news journalism in the United Kingdom largely continues to offer a serious, non-sensationalized, diverse and high-quality mix of national and international news that has not yet suffered the shift in style or content to what is generally defined as 'tabloid'. The evidence presented in the second half, however, suggests that those tendencies *are* being manifested in British current affairs, primarily because the protective regulatory mechanisms have been progressively reduced and current affairs journalism is now suffering the consequences of exposure to severe competitive pressures.

This is not to take a Reithian view that current affairs programmes should always be devoted to matters of great social or political significance. There must be scope for satisfying our collective appetite for gossip and fun as well as our collective needs as citizens. Moreover, humour – like emotion – can sometimes be an evocative technique for drawing attention to serious issues, and has long been exploited by political satirists to provide insightful commentary on the contemporary political scene. Ultimately, the issue is one of intent: whether programme-makers are being driven by the values of professional journalism or by television's gravitational pull towards the values of escapist entertainment. Where the charge of tabloidization is legitimate is when there is no attempt to engage or inform and no other aim than to maximize audiences through cynical techniques of shock and sensationalism.

This distinction was well illustrated by Myra Macdonald in her analysis of two different editions of 'Panorama', one from 1997 looking at single mothers on benefits, the other in 1998 looking at nuisance neighbours. Both used traditional storytelling devices involving individual families, but the second programme exploited surveillance videos to provide a simple exercise in voyeurism and offered no positive contribution to understanding social life in Britain. The programme was driven by the availability of exciting footage rather than journalism and was a good example of 'how personalization can divert attention from serious issues, by replacing analysis with emotion and substituting voyeuristic thrills for knowledge-enabling engagement'.[29] There are plenty of recognizable parallels from other programmes and news bulletins, both in style and content: the celebrity interview, the sex lives of the rich and famous, dramatic images of police chases, cute videos of performing animals or CCTV footage of supermarket raids: news items largely devoid of any serious meaning, but capable of generating large audiences for relatively little outlay.

In terms of the argument around tabloidization, the question can therefore be posed in terms of both displacement and presentation. First, is the trivial, the sensational and the need for dramatic pictures driving out material of cultural and civic value? And second, is the selection and treatment of issues increasingly being dictated by reference to maximizing audiences with little thought for how content might have to be distorted or debased to increase its attraction? We can therefore rewrite a definition for tabloidization in television journalism as follows:

> Tabloidization is the progressive displacement of citizen-enhancing material with material which has *no other purpose* than to shock, provoke, entertain or retain viewers; and the progressive erosion of professional journalistic values in favour of televisual techniques involving sensationalism, distortion, misrepresentation and dramatization of the trivial.

As ever in journalism, there will be grey areas between honest popularization and cynical populism, and definitional issues around what constitutes 'citizen-enhancing' material. However, I believe that the responses from those current affairs journalists recorded above – who were serious about their trade and concerned about its direction – demonstrate that it is possible to differentiate between serious journalistic intent and commercially driven populism. Some years ago, the distinguished BBC journalist Martin Bell wrote about the values and principles of dedicated journalists and how professional attachment to those values could be summarized in one word: integrity.[30] The question is how to sustain the integrity that is the lifeblood of enlightened (and enlightening) journalism. The answer is partly through professional training reinforced by professional codes of conduct. But even the most ethical, well trained and high-minded practitioners cannot be impervious to institutional pressures and need a sympathetic framework to support their aspirations. Ultimately, that must come down to a regulatory system which protects the integrity of citizen-enhancing television journalism. As we move towards an even more deregulated and competitive future, we have to fear for the survival of that integrity.[31]

8 The BBC and the Aftermath of Hutton

Popularization, BBC 'bias' and Greg Dyke's appointment as Director General

Given Greg Dyke's reputation as an inveterate ratings chaser, his arrival at the BBC at the very time that accusations of tabloidization were being levelled at all areas of television journalism did little to reassure his critics. In fact – although he did engineer the rescheduling of the late evening news from 9 p.m. to 10 p.m. to fill the slot left vacant by ITV – his spirit was felt more through his management style than in any major shift towards entertainment values. John Birt had overseen a massive reorganization of and investment in BBC journalism, neither of which was compromised by the new regime. But he had also introduced an ascetic managerialism that left many BBC producers and editors feeling hampered by a sense of institutional caution, which stifled innovation and creativity.

Dyke, true to his own extrovert and entrepreneurial style, was to encourage a more adventurous and innovative environment of risk-taking – embodied in his rallying cry to BBC staff of 'Cut the crap and make it happen.'[1] It was a refreshing change and a boost to staff morale, but it came at a price. The problem with a philosophy of liberating producers – and journalists – from the burden of managerial oversight was that it risked another failure in the BBC's mechanisms of accountability and the kinds of confrontation with government that had engulfed the BBC in the 1980s. In 2003, that was precisely what happened with unprecedented consequences for both the Director General and the Chairman.

There was another reason why Dyke's appointment as Director General had been hugely controversial: he had previously donated £50,000 to the Labour Party, which in 1997 had won a crushing election victory for the first time in 18 years. While his appointment drew predictable objections from the opposition Conservative benches, senior BBC executives were also profoundly concerned that someone with known party affiliations should be appointed to the job that constitutionally oversaw all BBC journalism. Will Wyatt, one of the most respected and long-serving members of BBC senior management, was adamant that the appointment of a known political sympathizer (on either side of the political spectrum) would compromise the BBC and, during the selection process, had written to the then BBC Chairman, Sir Christopher Bland:

> There has never to my knowledge been a director-general of the BBC, whose political views were overt and publicly known. This has been crucial to the independence of the corporation and to the integrity, real and perceived, of the decisions that the director-general and lieutenants have to make. I believe that it is essential to the long term independence of the BBC that this position is continued ... in the event of [Greg Dyke]'s selection the cloud of political suitability would henceforth hang over the office.[2]

Antagonism to Dyke was somewhat tempered not only by a fairly universal acclaim for his abilities, but also because the appointment fell to a BBC Chairman who was himself a recognized Conservative supporter and had been appointed by the Conservative Prime Minister John Major in 1996. When Dyke took over from Birt in April 2000, there was therefore a notional political balance at the top of the BBC hierarchy to counter the fears of Wyatt and others about perceptions of bias.

That position changed dramatically in 2001 when Bland unexpectedly stood down to become Chairman of British Telecom and the Labour government appointed the Deputy Chairman, Gavyn Davies, as his successor. Davies had been co-author of a government-appointed study on the future of BBC funding in 1999 and was therefore highly knowledgeable about the BBC as well as being a highly respected businessman and merchant banker. But he also had close links to the Labour government: his partner Sue Nye ran the office of the Chancellor of the Exchequer and future Prime Minister, Gordon Brown. There was now a clear imbalance at the top, with Davies as Chairman and a known Labour sympathizer as Director General. It was to prove a combustible combination as the duo strived to demonstrate their resistance to any suggestion of government pressure.

Prelude to war: government, the BBC and the 'threat' from Iraq

The events that precipitated one of the gravest crises in BBC history have been told many times and need not be described in detail here.[3] They are, however, essential to understanding some of the core institutional characteristics of BBC journalism, to correcting some of the misunderstandings about the relationship between the State and the BBC, and to appreciate the mostly benign repercussions for BBC journalism in the twenty-first century. They therefore require a brief outline.

In the aftermath of the 9/11 terrorist attack on the twin towers of the World Trade Center and the US occupation of Afghanistan, it became clear that President George W. Bush was intent on pursuing a war with Iraq, and that the British Prime Minister Tony Blair was determined to support the President. However, popular support would be contingent on persuading Parliament and the people that Saddam Hussein was not only a vicious dictator but a threat to the West. The crucial issue therefore became whether Saddam was still concealing the weapons of mass destruction (WMD), which threatened mass slaughter well beyond the arena of the Middle East. On 24 September 2002, the British government published an intelligence dossier entitled *Iraq's Weapons of Mass Destruction: the assessment of the British government*, which appeared to provide unequivocal evidence that Saddam Hussein not only had WMD, but also chemical weapons that could be launched at 45 minutes notice. With considerable press support on the back of these revelations,[4] Tony Blair and his cabinet colleagues launched a passionate campaign throughout the country and in Parliament to convince a sceptical nation that the existence of WMD made Saddam's Iraq a real and present danger that required military intervention.

In this febrile political atmosphere the BBC worked hard to convey both sides of the argument. But as with Suez, the Falklands and Northern Ireland, it faced a concerted and systematic campaign of complaints from a government communications machine that was both better resourced and more sophisticated than it had been under Eden, Wilson or Thatcher. This culminated on 19 March 2003 with a letter by the Prime Minister himself to the Director General complaining that, 'you have not got the balance right between support and dissent; between news and comment; between the voices of the Iraqi regime and the voices of Iraqi dissidents'.[5] Dyke repudiated the accusation and made it clear he would 'fight back'. Reflecting on this confrontation a year later, he recognized that the BBC should accept the legitimacy of sustained government attack while having the determination to protect its independence against such an onslaught. In a clear echo of the words of IBA Chairman George Thomson ('he did his job and I did mine'), Dyke quoted Grace Wyndham Goldie: 'Nowhere more than in broadcasting is the price of freedom eternal vigilance; resistance to political pressures has to be constant and continuous. But it must be realized that such pressures are inevitable, for the aims of the political parties and those of broadcasting organizations are not the same.'[6]

By 1 May 2003, the military operation and allied occupation of Iraq was complete. No WMD were found in Iraq, and the head of a US government commission subsequently told a US Senate committee that, 'I don't think they existed.'[7] Six months later, a British inquiry into intelligence failure concluded charitably that 'judgements in the [September] dossier went to (although not beyond) the outer limits of the intelligence available'; but that the Prime Minister's description of the intelligence information to Parliament may have reinforced the impression that the intelligence was fuller and firmer than it actually was.[8] It also described the intelligence that Iraq had recently produced biological agents as 'seriously flawed' and concluded that the 45-minute claim should not have been included without proper clarification.[9] There was, in other words, very good reason for sceptical and inquisitive journalists to question the basis on which Britain went to war once the military campaign was over.

Aftermath of war: how the BBC raised questions about government intelligence

One such journalist was Andrew Gilligan, defence correspondent of the BBC's 'Today' programme on Radio 4.[10] His appointment and the editorial latitude he was allowed are both arguably traced back to Dyke, casting an intriguing light on how the institutional practices of journalism can be significantly influenced through a change in management personnel and ethos. There were two significant factors here. First, Gilligan had come from the less journalistically rigorous print media, having been the *Sunday Telegraph*'s defence correspondent before being recruited in 1999 by the then editor of the 'Today' programme, Rod Liddle. Liddle was concerned that too much of the BBC's defence reporting relied on official government briefings, and both he and Dyke shared a desire to prioritize original, headlining journalism for the BBC. Part of Gilligan's brief on one of the BBC's flagship journalism programmes was to challenge the government.

Second, Dyke was determined to loosen a perceived managerial stranglehold over editorial decision-making. At the beginning of 2000, he removed a layer of 'super editors' who had been imposed under the Birt regime to act as buffers between editors and the Board of Management, and who had become synonymous with suffocating journalistic initiative. Roger Mosey, the new head of Television News, described the new philosophy: 'I want people to take imaginative decisions, enforced by BBC values … I don't want to suffocate editors under a bureaucratic structure where they feel unable to take decisions. Editors edit. That's the whole point of it. I want editors to feel free to innovate.'[11] This sense of institutional liberation invigorated the 'Today' programme both of Liddle and, when he left in 2002, his successor Kevin Marsh. But it reached across all news departments, and was as relevant to BBC journalism practice in television and online as it was to radio.

A key contact of Gilligan's was David Kelly, a weapons inspector and leading expert on Iraqi WMD. Kelly's view was that the interpretation of fairly ambivalent intelligence material had been strengthened after interventions from Downing Street, and that the intelligence community was unhappy with the way its conventionally dry material had been repackaged for public consumption. Intriguingly, two other BBC journalists, both working for BBC television news programmes, independently found Kelly as a key source. It was Gilligan, however, who turned Kelly's information into the story that plunged the BBC into its deepest crisis since 1986, with long-term implications for the institution and its journalism.

At 6.07 in the morning on 29 May 2003, Gilligan introduced his story on the 'Today' programme for the first time:

> What we've been told by one of the senior officials in charge of drawing up that [intelligence] dossier was that, actually the government probably knew that that 45-minute figure was wrong, even before it decided to put it in ... Downing Street, our source says, ordered a week before publication, ordered it to be sexed up, to be made more exciting and ordered more facts to be er, to be discovered.[12]

This was a serious allegation that, effectively, the government had deliberately lied. It was, at best, unproven and Gilligan subsequently admitted to the Hutton Inquiry that it was 'the kind of slip of the tongue that does happen often during live broadcasts'. In subsequent reports, Gilligan said only that the 45-minute claim was 'questionable', and his television colleagues who themselves had made contact with Kelly were similarly circumspect. On that evening's BBC 'Ten O'clock News', Gavin Hewitt said that, according to his sources, 'spin from Number 10 did come into play'. And on BBC's 'Newsnight', science correspondent Susan Watts reported her source talking about 'the government seizing on anything useful to the case, including the possible existence of weapons being ready within 45 minutes'. All three had used Kelly, but it was Gilligan's more adventurous spirit that had set the agenda and rightly pinpointed disquiet within the intelligence service at political intervention.

The matter escalated when Gilligan wrote an article in the *Mail on Sunday* three days later naming Alastair Campbell, the government's communications strategy director and Blair's most influential adviser, as the culprit behind the transformation of the original intelligence material. Campbell accused the BBC of lying and demanded an apology while Richard Sambrook, the BBC's Director of News, determinedly stood by the story. Meanwhile, Kelly informed his superiors that he had met with Gilligan and, through some judicious briefing by the Ministry of Defence, his name was published in three newspapers on 10 July. Appearing in front of the Foreign Affairs Select Committee in Parliament five days later, Kelly vigorously denied that he was the source for either Gilligan or Susan Watts' reports. Watts, however, had recorded her interview with Kelly. Two days later, on 17 July, he took his own life. The Prime Minister immediately ordered an independent judicial inquiry, headed by Lord Hutton, into the circumstances surrounding Kelly's death.

The Hutton Report, its aftermath and BBC accountability

Hutton's report, published on 28 January 2004, was catastrophic for the BBC. It concluded that Gilligan's allegation of 'sexing up' was unfounded; that the BBC's editorial system was 'defective'; that BBC management failed to investigate properly the government's complaints about the 6.07 a.m. broadcast; and that BBC Governors failed to investigate fully whether Gilligan's allegations could be supported. Moreover, it concluded that the Governors failed to recognize fully that such scrutiny was not incompatible with their duty to protect the independence of the BBC. The BBC Chairman Gavyn Davies resigned immediately. Dyke reluctantly offered his resignation at the emergency Governors' meeting the following day, fully expecting it to be turned down. It was accepted. A few days later, Gilligan resigned.

Here, on the face of it, was the biggest capitulation of independent BBC journalism in the corporation's history. Faced with a furious onslaught by government, the Chairman, the Director General and the journalist responsible for some very uncomfortable revelations had fallen on their swords. The government was triumphant, and this time – unlike the crisis with 'Real Lives' – there was no act of redemption. All, however, was not quite as it seemed. It is possible to argue that out of this immediate catastrophe emerged a significantly more benign outcome for BBC journalism, and for the BBC as an institution, than was apparent at the time. There were two short-term reasons, and two with repercussions that will continue well into the 2010s.

First, Hutton's conclusions were met with widespread disbelief as well as condemnation. Some commentators accused him of a deliberate government whitewash, although a closer inspection of the report suggested that his tightly defined legalistic approach was simply naive about the normal conduct of journalism: in one passage, he suggested that a single source would always be insufficient for a story, however trusted and authoritative it might be.[13] As a result, even the most triumphalist government supporters found it difficult to support the report or the anti-BBC sentiments it espoused. If anything, Hutton succeeded in enhancing the journalistic reputation of the BBC. According to one commentator, 'The print media and the public have rallied round the BBC … The almost complete absence of schadenfreude in the rest of the media is partly down to the esteem we all hold for the BBC, and partly to a feeling that Lord Hutton's failure to understand the journalistic process could have implications for us all.'[14]

Moreover, journalists within the BBC demonstrated – as they did so effectively during the 'Real Lives' affair – that they would not be cowed and would jealously defend their deep-rooted reputation for journalistic independence. In a remarkable display of solidarity, 10,000 BBC staff each paid £5 towards a full-page newspaper advertisement expressing their dismay at Dyke's departure. It read in part: 'Greg Dyke stood for brave, independent and rigorous journalism that was fearless in its search for the truth. We are resolute that the BBC should not step back from its determination to investigate the facts in pursuit of the truth.'[15] Within four months, 'Panorama' was ignoring bitter criticism from the Home Secretary to run a hard-hitting programme about the lack of readiness within London's emergency services for a major terrorist attack on the capital. Given the public backlash, Hutton's one-sided conclusions militated against any overt display of government aggression towards critical BBC journalism.

Second, although the credit took longer to emerge, there is no question that the BBC had single-handedly tackled and broken a story of enormous public significance. There can be no more contentious decision than for a government to send its soldiers to war. If the criteria on which those calculations are discussed in the nations' living rooms, as well as in Parliament, are questionable or fallacious then it is a matter of the utmost importance that governments are properly held to account. As many American critics subsequently lamented, the watchdogs of the American press conspicuously failed to bark and there was no serious interrogation of George W. Bush's single-minded determination to invade Iraq.[16] In the United Kingdom, the press was not so servile. But even the predominantly anti-war papers of the Mirror Group and the *Independent* were slow to question the quality of intelligence material.

On television, neither ITN nor Sky News could boast the same contacts, resources or vigour. ITN, as we have seen, was weakened by a series of enforced cuts and redundancies and no longer carries the potent competitive threat of the old duopoly days. And Sky News, whose undoubted quality and professionalism has been recognized several times with industry awards, is ultimately controlled by Rupert Murdoch. It is difficult to see how its journalists could easily have pursued such an explosive story if their main shareholder was fervently pro-war and pro-government. In the end, both the evidence to the Hutton Inquiry and the subsequent Butler report proved unequivocally the validity of the story and the authenticity of Kelly as an international authority on WMD. And the whole episode demonstrated that only one news organization – and a publicly funded one at that

– had the resources, determination, independence and journalistic confidence to carry out the vital democratic function of questioning the evidential justification for going to war.

Beyond these immediate consequences, the Hutton report prompted reflections on the implications of journalism within a publicly funded organization – in particular, that both the professionalism and the accountability mechanisms of the institution itself must be, like Caesar's wife, above suspicion. And on both counts, the BBC had failed. Whatever the quality of his and the BBC's subsequent reporting, Gilligan's initial 6.07 a.m. report was erroneous and should have been corrected – if necessary with a public apology. Many BBC journalists who were committed to the story and to the BBC's democratic duty to pursue it were apprehensive about management's apparent determination to defend that report at all costs. And those who were appointed to scrutinize managerial competence were themselves found wanting. Here, the problem was different to 'Real Lives', when a schism between Governors and management triggered a constitutional crisis. This time the Chairman, perhaps conscious of questions around his own political leanings, was determined to defend the BBC against perceived intimidation. In an email to Governors in advance of their emergency meeting on 29 June 2003, which emerged in evidence to Hutton, Gavyn Davies wrote: 'I remain firmly of the view that, in the big picture sense, it is absolutely critical for the BBC to emerge from this row without being seen to buckle in the face of government pressure ... This, it seems to me, really is a moment for the Governors to stand up and be counted'. A Chairman who felt less compelled to demonstrate his autonomy might have first instituted an internal inquiry and demanded systematic evidence of the robustness of the story. Greg Dyke's determination to liberate BBC journalism perhaps demanded a more rigorous oversight than his Chairman was able to deliver.

In other words, the resignations of the Chairman and Director General were not the successful culmination of a rampaging government bringing an awkward public institution to its compliant knees, but necessary recognition of demonstrative failures at the top of the organization – by the Chief Executive to guarantee the highest standards of journalistic professionalism, and by his Chairman to fulfil his constitutional duty by scrutinizing the efficacy of management decisions. The BBC played a significant part in its own downfall by not appreciating in the highly inflamed atmosphere of the moment that its status, funding and constitution demanded a more considered response. It is perhaps all the more extraordinary that, in the years that followed, neither its survival nor its journalism were compromised.

Longer term impact on BBC journalism: the Neil report and a new regime

In both these respects, it is the longer term consequences that are of more significance. In the immediate aftermath of the Hutton report, the acting Director General Mark Byford commissioned an independent report from Ron Neil, a former Director of News and Current Affairs, to 'examine the editorial issues for the BBC raised by the Hutton inquiry' and 'identify the learning lessons and make appropriate recommendations'. Neil's report, which involved consultation with editors and senior journalists within the BBC as well as a thorough examination of BBC values and editorial controls, reported to the Board of Governors in June 2004.[17] It articulated the editorial principles which now constitute the backbone of BBC journalism throughout its television services, as well as radio, online and World Service.

It is based on five core values: truth and accuracy; serving the public interest; impartiality and diversity of opinion; independence; and accountability. It also offered a glimpse of the huge contribution that the BBC was making to journalism in the first decade of the twenty-first century: over 7,000 personnel working in BBC journalism, with ten times as many journalists in BBC News than on a national newspaper, broadcasting 120 hours of output every day. As the report acknowledged, such a vast scale carries inherent risks, and there is a delicate balance to be struck between imposing an institutional straitjacket and allowing journalistic anarchy. The report made it clear that, 'all programmes operating under the BBC's journalistic banner must work to the same values, professional disciplines, and journalistic culture,' but that programmes should still be allowed to 'develop their own house styles and approach' as long as the BBC's core values were universally observed and practised. In her evidence to the House of Lords select committee inquiry on News in 2007, the BBC Director of News Helen Boaden explained the BBC's approach:

> For every hour of the day there are four and a half hours of news and current affairs. The only way you can possibly run something like that is by what the army calls mission command. You set the strategy, you set the values, you set and regulate quality control and you appoint the right people who you think understand those values inside out, and then you have to let them get on with it.[18]

At the heart of the Neil report was a proposal designed to ensure that this codification of journalistic integrity was understood and implemented throughout the BBC: a new College of Journalism, which would consolidate a previously fragmented approach to training, would be compulsory for all BBC journalists, and would ensure a standardized approach to standards and ethics. While the proposal was met with predictable derision as senior journalists of 30 years standing considered the prospect of 'going back to school', what emerged was a series of online modules covering everything from politics to grammar, law and the Middle East, which even the most cynical of practitioners reluctantly conceded could help them make difficult editorial calls in the ferociously competitive and fast-moving world of 24-hour news. What started as a response to politically motivated accusations of corporate failure became a respected educational source of conducting journalism for the BBC. In December 2009, its website was opened to the public and now constitutes an important learning resource for aspiring reporters as well as a highly visible statement of BBC journalistic standards.

The second long-term consequence was corporate rather than journalistic. With both a chairman and a director general to be replaced, there were widespread fears that the government might use the opportunity to appoint a more compliant chairman. Conscious of the universal outrage that such an overt political move would have provoked, the Labour government instead appointed the former Channel 4 Chief Executive (and former BBC1 Controller) Michael Grade, an experienced and widely respected broadcaster with no history of political affiliation. It was a hugely significant appointment in the run-up to the next BBC Charter because the government understood that Grade was not interested in presiding over a downsized BBC. He would – and did – champion not just the BBC's independence but its continued scale and vitality. The sense of optimism was further enhanced by Grade's appointment of Mark Thompson as Director General: a former 'Panorama' and news editor, he was a journalist by training and had been a successor to Grade as Chief Executive of Channel 4.

Grade was quick to welcome the Neil report and emphasized again the BBC's commitment to independent, serious journalism. In what was interpreted by some as an acknowledgement that the 'news review' of 1999 may have tipped the balance of BBC journalism too far towards populism, he outlined his vision for BBC journalism in the twenty-first century:

> The BBC mission here is becoming increasingly important as the market for news and information changes, and the pressures mount to abandon serious and thoughtful news coverage … One result is that serious news values are coming under increasing strain. The BBC may indeed have unwittingly contributed to this by the emphasis on audience accessibility in news in recent years. This may have created a tension – on the one hand the expectation that editors should deliver the traditional, serious BBC news

agenda; on the other, a perceived pressure on editors to win audiences – with the result that a certain confusion may have taken root about which was the right road to follow.[19]

In essence, he was reaffirming the core 'mission statement' of BBC news for those who feared Dyke's populist approach may have required some reining in: that as well as being impartial, distinctive, rigorous, independent and stimulating it should always be striving to 'make the important interesting'. The problem, as ever for the BBC, was how different news editors serving different audiences at different times on different channels, and competing with different commercial services, interpreted their corporate brief. By this time, less than a year after Lord Hutton's conclusions had provoked a national and international furore about government interference, the BBC narrative had returned reassuringly to its favourite conundrum: establishing the balance between popular versus serious, broadsheet versus tabloid, distinctive versus accessible. These inherent journalistic tensions will continue to be debated within the BBC for as long as it exists and will – as they always have done – concentrate the minds of BBC editors considerably more than concerns about independence from political pressure.

As if to underline that autonomy, at the very moment that the government was bringing forward its initial proposals for renewal of the BBC Charter (due to expire at the end of 2006), 'Panorama' broadcast a programme alleging that Sir Richard Dearlove, head of MI6, had told Tony Blair in July 2002 that war with Iraq was inevitable and that US intelligence was being 'fixed' round the Bush administration's policy of aggression. It was not quite an allegation of lying to the country, but it was not far from Gilligan's core narrative. There was barely a murmur of dissent from government offices.

BBC independence, journalism and the future

When the Labour government's proposals for the future of the BBC were published in March 2005, it was abundantly clear that there was no appetite for dismantling or restructuring the BBC.[20] Based on extensive opinion research, they arrived at three key decisions which cemented the BBC's journalistic role: that its survival and its independence would be guaranteed to 2016 with another ten-year Royal Charter starting on 1 January 2007; that it would continue to be funded through a compulsory licence fee (with a funding review around 2012); and that it would continue as a broadcaster 'of scale and scope', including the development of new technologies and platforms where appropriate.[21] In fact, as an essentially social democratic project the BBC has generally found more political favour on the centre-left than the centre-right and, in spite of the furore created by the intelligence row and Hutton, there remained an instinctive sympathy within Labour government circles for a publicly funded BBC of real cultural significance. A greater threat to the BBC's future emanated from two sources: the growing likelihood of a Conservative government, which was instinctively more ideologically hostile to publicly funded bodies; and growing opposition from the burgeoning number of commercial competitors who were insisting that the BBC should be required to scale back its activities.[22]

It was in response to these latter pressures that the most fundamental constitutional change was in BBC governance. From January 2007 the Board of Governors – which had existed since 1927 – was abolished to make way for a new BBC Trust. The rationale for a new administrative system emerged ostensibly out of the Hutton report and its trenchant criticisms of the dual role played by the Governors: simultaneously protecting the BBC's independence from government and scrutinising the performance of management. In fact, the new structure did little to reduce a tension which is inherent in a publicly funded broadcaster that is independent from government but must remain accountable to the paying public. In announcing the changes, the Culture Secretary Tessa Jowell called the Trust the 'eyes and ears of the licence fee payer', focused on the public interest, committed to transparent decision-making and a guarantor of independence from government interference.

With the BBC's survival safely negotiated Michael Grade jumped ship to become Chairman of ITV, leaving Mark Thompson as Director General to resolve the final element of the Charter review: negotiations with the government about a funding settlement. Following pressure from the Treasury, the final settlement amounted to a £2 billion shortfall on the BBC's bid to cover the following six years. While it allowed for certainty in budget and programme planning, it heralded a period of cuts that impacted particularly on BBC journalism. In October 2007 the BBC announced the net loss of 400 jobs in journalism, still leaving it as by far the largest employer of journalists in the world.[23] Even with job losses of 400, BBC journalism still emerged in considerably better health than its global competitors, particularly given the scale of enforced job losses in the private media sector following the global recession.

It was that recession, and the massive retrenchment of public expenditure that followed, which created the political context for a further round of enforced negotiation with the new Conservative-led coalition government that was elected in May 2010. The BBC had already received a coded warning that a new administration led by David Cameron was unlikely to break with traditional Conservative mistrust of the BBC's public funding nor its long-standing conviction of entrenched liberal bias. Writing for the *Sun* newspaper as leader of the opposition towards the end of 2008, Cameron said:

> I am a slightly rare creature – a lifelong Conservative who is a fan of the BBC ... [but] the BBC has become oversized and over-reached itself ... The squeezing and crushing of commercial competitors online or in publishing needs to be stopped. We need the BBC, but we also need healthy competition to the BBC to boost choice and drive up quality.[24]

By the time he had become Prime Minister 18 months later, he was committed to a programme of massive public spending cuts in order to cut the national deficit: the BBC was vulnerable to accusations that it was out of touch with the new hair-shirt mood. Faced with a powerful political narrative that it should cut its cloth alongside the rest of the public sector, the BBC accepted in October 2010 a freeze in the licence fee to the end of the Charter period (2016) as well as a number of new spending commitments, which included the World Service (previously funded by the Foreign Office) and universal rollout of broadband. The funding settlement – which was negotiated over a period of a few days with no public consultation – amounted to a real terms cut of 16 per cent in BBC revenue to the end of 2016.

For both BBC critics and supporters, the sudden and brutal imposition of a funding settlement that is certain to result in reduced BBC services was evidence of a BBC which could no longer claim to be independent of political interference. But this analysis fails to understand the distinction between editorial integrity and journalistic independence, and complete corporate separation, which is impossible for a publicly funded organization that must ultimately be responsible to Parliament. As we have seen, the BBC will always be institutionally vulnerable to government attempts at inappropriate pressure, and has repeatedly demonstrated a robust determination to resist. Speaking shortly after the negotiations had been completed, Director General Mark Thompson acknowledged that continued vigilance to protect institutional and financial independence was crucial and that, 'there is an increasing danger that, as governments grapple with other serious policy and financial issues, this foundation of our independence is underplayed or even forgotten'.[25] But he qualified this warning with a legitimate argument that, while financially challenging, the net result of the settlement was to increase the BBC's independence: 'Six years of financial certainty and a guarantee that the Government will place no further duties on the BBC or interfere in that period with the scale and scope of our services are themselves new and welcome supports to independence.' In other words, despite the opposition of commercial competitors and a more sceptical government, the BBC and its journalism will survive as a mass-audience broadcaster with a predictable revenue flow at least until the end of the current Charter in 2016.

In a world of huge economic upheaval, and particularly increasing uncertainty for a media world that has yet to understand the structural impact of advertising revenue moving to online outlets, this financial safeguarding of BBC journalism is hugely significant. But while the political threat of a new government and constrained public funding may have been diverted, it is precisely this stability and income predictability that will continue to rile its commercial competitors. Rival news organizations in the United Kingdom have demonstrated an unhealthy appetite for highlighting stories which might discredit the BBC and therefore undermine the public's trust, and this probably constitutes the greatest threat to BBC journalism over the next ten years. Despite its commitment to a set of journalistic values, which is now explicit, which is being embedded throughout the institution, and to which it is held to account through new and tougher governance structures, its competitors will continue to argue for self-interested commercial reasons that a BBC of such scale and (relatively) generous funding is a danger rather than a net contributor to democratic pluralism. While the United Kingdom will come to depend more heavily on the BBC for its broadcast journalism than ever before, its continuing strength and contribution to democratic life will depend partly on the political climate following an election due in 2015 and partly on the success of its commercial competitors' lobby for further reductions.

9 Television Journalism, the Market and the Future

Protecting television journalism: The 2003 Communications Act and News

As with most advanced democracies over the last 20 years, British media policy in the 2000s was dominated by the rhetoric of deregulation and marketization. The Labour government, however, tempered a market-based approach with a recognition of the cultural and democratic significance of broadcasting. Its 2000 White Paper on Communications, which set the philosophical and operational framework for broadcasting well into the twenty-first century, therefore steered a delicate path between deregulation and protecting the most vulnerable areas of broadcast content. There was, on the one hand, a competition- and efficiency-led objective to 'make the UK home to the most dynamic and competitive communications and media market in the world,' which was clearly dictated by the policy preferences of the Department for Trade and Industry.[1] There was also, however, a chapter on 'Quality', authored by the Department for Culture, Media and Sport, which was probably the most explicit endorsement of Public Service Broadcasting seen in a government document since the 1970s. The fashionable 1980s view that more channels and more platforms would automatically enhance quality and diversity was dismissed with a clearly articulated argument in favour of the 'democratic importance of public service broadcasting [which] is as great as the economic justification'.[2] The long-running tension between the two departments manifested in the White Paper was equally apparent in the 2003 Communications Act (CA03) that followed three years later.

While following the deregulatory line and eliminating many of the programme quotas for commercial public service television, there was one crucial area in which the CA03 fulfilled the 'democracy' rhetoric of the White Paper: news. The Act not only consolidated existing regulation on quality and quantity, but added a resourcing obligation for the main commercial channel. Thus, Ofcom was required to ensure that licensed services include news and current affairs programmes that were 'of high quality and deal with both national and international matters', and also to set annual peak and off-peak quotas for news and current affairs on all the commercial channels. For the mass-audience Channel 3 licences, however – by now mostly owned by ITV plc – it also required that any news provider appointed by Channel 3 must satisfy Ofcom that it was properly resourced and 'able to compete effectively with other television news programmes broadcast nationwide in the United Kingdom'.[3] This was explicit recognition of the importance of *funding* commercial television news adequately, and a vital safeguard in light of two other statutory changes: first, the abolition of restrictions that had prevented ITV companies from owning their own news provider; and second, the abolition of overseas ownership restrictions that had previously debarred any non European (essentially American) takeover of the United Kingdom's most popular commercial television channel.

These changes theoretically allowed ITV's long-standing news provider ITN to be wholly owned by ITV, which in turn could be wholly owned by a global corporation such as Time-Warner or Disney – and thus be transformed into a news division along the same lines as American networks.[4] Given the competitive instinct to cut costs, it was felt that news would need protection from the ravages of corporate accountants closely monitoring the bottom line. No such resourcing obligations were imposed on Channel 5, on the basis that its average 5–6 per cent share of viewing did not warrant statutory protection.[5] In light of Channel 4's public ownership, there was no statutory news provision beyond the channel's continuing remit to be innovative, distinctive and culturally diverse. Nevertheless, Ofcom was given a role in determining and monitoring Channel 4's news output, and of being consulted by the BBC Trust should the BBC ever wish to reduce its output from the 2002 benchmark levels. In addition to national and international news, both the BBC and ITV were required to carry regional news bulletins.

Much of the detailed implementation was therefore left to Ofcom, who followed the inherited patterns of news in the schedule by setting the weekly quotas shown in Table 9.1 opposite.[6]

Current affairs quotas were also set for all the public service channels, again differentiated by peak time and by day.[7] Each year, as part of its annual Public Service Broadcasting Annual Report, Ofcom reports on the news and current affairs output for each channel, and in particular on any shortfall; in the first six years of reporting, to 2010, no shortfall was recorded – in fact, following ITV's reinstatement of its 10 p.m. bulletin, its peak-time national news output from 2009 was twice the required minimum.[8]

Television news and current affairs, therefore, retained its place as the focus of regulatory attention, with enhanced mechanisms for ensuring that it did not slip

9.1   Ofcom weekly quotas for news

	National News (total)	National News in peak (6–10.30 p.m.)	Regional News (total)	Regional News in peak (6–10.30 p.m.)
BBC1	26h 28m	5h 16m	4h 25m	2h 16m
ITV1	7h 00m	2h 24m	5h 30m	2h 30m
Channel 4	4h 00m	4h 00m		
Channel 5	7h 50m	1h 55m		

Note: There was an additional requirement for GMTV, the breakfast franchise for Channel 3, to provide 5 hours of national and 15 minutes of regional news.

down either the commercial or the BBC agenda. This raises two key questions: for how long in a multichannel digital world can such regulatory oversight be realistically maintained? And what would be the consequences of removing it?

New problems, new solutions: regional TV journalism and the market

All of these questions concentrated the minds of both broadcasters and politicians in anticipation of the UK's switch from analogue to digital transmission, due for completion by the end of 2012. We have seen how both of the commercial free-to-air broadcasters, ITV and Channel 5, have traditionally accepted public service obligations in return for privileged access to the scarce analogue broadcasting spectrum. As more and more households adopted multichannel digital television, it was clear that this long-standing 'analogue compact' could not survive the switchover process. Following detailed analysis of these fundamental changes to UK television in their second Public Service Broadcasting review in 2008–9, Ofcom concluded: 'public service broadcasting in the UK is at a crossroads. Audiences value an alternative to the BBC, but commercial broadcasters are finding it increasingly difficult to sustain their output of public service obligations and the costs of being a public service broadcaster will soon outweigh the benefits for some licensees.'[9]

This raised serious questions about ITV's continuing commitment to non-profitable programming areas; as a last resort, if the company felt that the regulatory burdens were too great, it could opt simply to surrender its digital terrestrial licence and move itself on to cable and satellite as one of the plethora of channels with no obligations beyond returning a profit (albeit without guaranteed universal access). Under those circumstances it could either ditch news altogether or, more likely, maintain a news presence without any requirements on scheduling, quality, volume or investment. News would become no more than a branding ingredient in an entirely market-oriented commercial channel. Ofcom's research established that plural provision – that is, programming in addition to the BBC's – was valued by viewers in most areas 'with news and current affairs the top priorities'.[10] A delicate balance therefore had to be struck between the market realities of the television business and the demands both of audiences and democracy: it is at least a tribute to the legacy of public interest regulation in the United Kingdom that the debate about television news remained very much alive even as the country moved towards the digital multichannel era.

With the economic crisis heaping even greater pressure on ITV, its Chairman Michael Grade made clear that its statutory commitment to regional news might not survive: 'Beyond [national news], we intend to sustain regional output for as long as possible, but given the economic realities, there can be no bankable guarantees as there were in the past'.[11] At the beginning of 2009, with Ofcom's approval, 17 regional newsrooms were consolidated into 9 in order to save £40 million. With 430 jobs lost, and 'regional' newsrooms now serving areas at least 200 miles away, the definition of regional was being stretched to its very limit. Even with 17 newsrooms, ITV had struggled to offer a genuinely local service that could meet the information needs of local communities about their hospitals, schools, employers, local councils, MPs, football teams or planning decisions. It was now becoming virtually impossible to sustain in journalistic terms one of the original rationales for a federal network of locally based ITV franchises: that they should reflect the variety of cultures, histories and characteristics of the British regions.

During 2009–10, intriguingly, the whole issue of local and regional television journalism became a significant area of policy-thinking and contestation between regulators, broadcasters and politicians. Conscious of the need to assist struggling competitors where public interest objectives were at risk, the BBC offered to pool video coverage and share studios and technical facilities.[12] Ofcom itself pursued an alternative model as part of its PSB review, proposing that ITV's regional slots could be opened up to Independently Funded News Consortia (IFNCs), essentially third parties who would compete for franchises. It would, however, require some mechanism of public funding, at a time of severe fiscal constraints on the Treasury.

The idea was enthusiastically pursued by the incumbent Labour government whose 'interim' policy statement in January 2009 acknowledged the high value placed by viewers on television news in the nations and regions and, interestingly, added that, 'the Government sees it as central to the ITV companies' identities as public service broadcasters'.[13] This was a timely reminder of the political significance of regional news in a constituency-based model of parliamentary democracy: when audiences themselves have voiced strong opinions about preserving regional news plurality, and MPs envisage the prospect of a reduced number of local opportunities for advancing their own political messages on television, there is a powerful alliance of the popular and political, which can drive policy initiatives.

In the government's final policy document of June 2009, over eight pages were devoted to 'The importance of news and local journalism for democracy'.[14] It endorsed IFNCs as a means of resolving not only the funding crisis for ITV, but also the much wider crisis throughout local journalism, which was seeing newspapers closing and journalists being made redundant. IFNCs were therefore described as, 'a joining of interested parties who will provide a more ambitious cross-media proposition and enhanced localness compared with current commercial television regional news,' and proposals were advanced for the relaxation of local cross-ownership restrictions to permit cross-platform operations. Consortia were to be chosen against public criteria, and would be funded – controversially – by top-slicing the BBC licence. The process of inviting bids and selecting winners was, however, interrupted by the 2010 general election and change of government to a Conservative-led coalition.

Perhaps for the first time in modern political history, competing policy approaches to local and regional journalism featured in all three main party manifestoes. While Labour promised to complete its programme of IFNC initiatives, the Conservative Party stuck to its traditional free-market approach, which eschewed public money and embraced deregulation. Its stated objective was to strengthen local democracy: 'Our plans to decentralise power will only work properly if there is a strong, independent and vibrant local media to hold local authorities to account. We will sweep away the rules that stop local newspapers owning other local media platforms and create a new network of local television stations.'[15] Once in power, the new Culture Secretary Jeremy Hunt pursued his vision of a new network of local television stations operating in tandem with other local media, despite widespread disbelief that his vision could ever be achieved. He even ensured that a measure of capital funding would be made available by securing £25 million from the BBC licence fee.

Despite this new (if fairly meagre) source of funds, there are three reasons why traditional local television in the United Kingdom is unlikely to become a serious journalistic force. The first is economic: for historical reasons, Britain's national media have always been stronger than its local media despite significant cultural and linguistic variations across regions. It is possible that the rapid evisceration of local print media – badly affected by the migration of classified advertising revenue to the internet – may reinvigorate other local media forms, but any such displaced revenue is more likely to find its way to online. Second, even in an era of sophisticated technology and multi-skilling, television still requires significant levels of coordination and investment in resources to bring quality journalism to the screen. Third, partly because of the greater investment required to maintain levels of quality to which audiences are accustomed, local television has traditionally generated insignificant (and commercially unsustainable) audiences. It is possible that very local television through IPTV (internet protocol television, using broadband distribution) will become technically feasible in the longer term, but a more efficient online distribution mechanism is no guarantee of quality journalistic content. Local television, as with local and community radio, is more likely to be a participative refuge for those wishing to involve themselves in the local community rather than a new source of high-quality, widely accessed journalism.

National news and the market: commercial television and editorial influence

Given the dire prognosis for local journalism in UK television, what is the future for news on national commercial channels and how far can any conclusions be generalized to other countries? For the main commercial terrestrial channel in Britain, ITV, its then Chairman Michael Grade made it clear to a parliamentary inquiry in 2007 that news bulletins remained integral to ITV's future as a mass commercial broadcaster:

> It is one of the few milestone points in your schedule every day of every week of every month of every year. Having a quality, distinctive, impartial news service is one of the things that helps you to distinguish your network from other networks. So it is a very high priority for us. It also gives your audience a clear signal that your network is relevant to their daily lives in a way that I think is crucial.[16]

Two market-related reasons, therefore, suggest that national and international news should be less problematic for any mass-audience commercial broadcaster: first, reinforcement of channel branding through a 'halo effect', which is increasingly important in a world of proliferating digital channels; and second, a rootedness in everyday audience experience. Neither is related to the primary consideration for statutory provision, to sustain a plurality of properly resourced information sources, which in turn fuels a well-informed and vibrant democracy. This mismatch between market imperatives and democratic imperatives raises interesting questions about editorial values and the influence of the marketplace. For while it is possible to legislate for the volume, scheduling and even resourcing of news and current affairs on commercial television, there is little that regulatory intervention can – or ought – to do about the subtle influences of market and corporate values on the journalism itself.

As we have seen, there is some evidence of a gradual polarization of news agendas on British television, a clear demonstration of institutional forces at work beyond a journalism driven by autonomous professional values. Theoretically, if the newsrooms of ITN were operating independently of their respective clients – at ITV and Channel 4 – its journalism would be impervious to any change of ownership or editorial direction from ITV. However, the reality is much more ambiguous. When asked in 2007 by the same parliamentary committee whether a new owner of ITV – such as Disney – could exert editorial influence, the Chief Executive of ITN, Mark Wood, responded with a categorical denial but then continued:

> We provide a service to [broadcasters] around their requirements and we agree with them in quite intense coordination of what kind of news service they want. We produce three major programmes for ITV during the day – lunch time news, early evening news and evening news – each of those is different in that it is calibrated for a different target audience, a different demographic. That is all agreed with ITV … However, there is then a very clear dividing line, on the other side of which is editorial control. Editorial control is with the editorial management with ITN and is, if you like, sacrosanct. Customers never try to cross that line; they are very aware of it.[17]

ITN's Deputy Editor of ITV news agreed that lead stories, running order, choice of interviewees and all the other details of individual bulletins are not divulged to ITV who 'never ask [and] we would not tell them if they did ask'. A subtle distinction therefore emerged between, on the one hand, 'intense coordination' on overall editorial strategy, which was centred around channel requirements and the demographics of particular bulletins, and, on the other hand, a mutual recognition of journalistic autonomy in approaches to content. Michael Grade referred in his evidence to 'regular meetings with ITN to review their performance, how we think the programme is going,' but emphasized also that, 'on a day-to-day news basis we delegate entirely to the very talented team of editorial experts of ITN'. Such delegation and non-interference extended to any news items that might reflect poorly on ITV itself. Moreover, although this was not explicitly covered in evidence, journalists would certainly expect it to extend to any attempted influence by advertisers seeking to minimize coverage of negative stories about themselves.

This evidence about the delicate process of negotiated editorial influence provides some insight into how television news on the UK's main commercial channel is mediated by a mixture of historical, cultural, professional and regulatory forces – all of which can be expected to mitigate against the most deleterious consequences of a purely market-driven approach. Thus, ITN's approach is partly a legacy of its institutional history, rooted in the public service ethos of British broadcasting. We have seen how its values evolved as a serious but more populist competitor to the BBC, and its journalism has generally sought to eschew the most blatant tabloid approaches of, for example, the British red-top press.

In addition, an integral part of the cultural tradition in British television news has been long-standing reticence amongst advertisers to exert any commercial pressure on editorial content. By contrast, in the United States, for example, a 2001 survey of 118 news directors from American local TV stations found that, '53 per cent reported that advertisers pressure them to kill negative stories or run positive ones'.[18] As the battle for television advertising becomes more intense – and corporate cultures become more globalized – we might expect the editorial pressures from advertisers to increase. How commercial broadcasters respond to those pressures will partly depend on national cultural, historical and regulatory traditions, but also on the attitudes and values which channel owners bring to their journalism.

Commercial television and the impact of ownership

In a revealing exchange during the parliamentary hearings, Michael Grade was asked whether it might be possible for an iconoclastic new owner 'to completely degrade and change the news agenda' of ITV. He responded:

> Should some less scrupulous owner of ITV decide that they wish to turn the news to their own commercial advantage or whatever, they would first have to find some decent journalists who were prepared to do that. That would be the first thing. Let us assume they could, then they would run foul immediately of the regulatory and statutory rules, and I think they would have the devil's own job to do it.[19]

Grade, therefore, placed his faith in the determination of professionals to stand up for their journalistic independence, with regulatory protection as a backstop. However, on both counts, in the competitive multichannel environment of the future, his confidence is likely to be misplaced.

Whilst it is certainly true that professional journalistic values have traditionally been upheld in the broadcast environment, these have not been properly tested in Britain by an iconoclastic and determined owner – such as a Silvio Berlusconi, perhaps or, so far, a Rupert Murdoch. And while the limits of interference are better defined in British and much European broadcasting through a continuing regime of statutory impartiality (covered in more detail in Chapter 11), this offers little protection in vast swathes of television journalism's agenda, which can be susceptible to executive interference. For example, decisions about the trade-off between national and international news, or the balance between serious and light coverage, or the level of investment in groundbreaking investigative reporting, or whether more emphasis should be placed on crime or immigration issues at the expense of politics or the economy, can all be dictated by an aggressively interventionist owner. Equally, the regulatory framework cannot protect against subtle pressure from shareholders to 'go easy' on a negative story about a major advertiser. Given the struggle to retain major advertisers in a high-spend medium like television, a new owner or major shareholder of ITV may not wish to see hard-won advertising business from, for instance, a big oil company endangered by a major story on environmental damage.

Indeed, this raises the very tricky question of how any regulator should interpret a legislative requirement for 'high quality' news, and the efficacy of this safeguard from the 2003 Communications Act. Let us suppose that ITV's putative new owners avail themselves of minute-by-minute audience data showing thousands of viewers deserting the station in droves at the very mention of Afghanistan, but hanging on for every word of a Britney Spears story; and then insist to their news provider that more Britney stories are expected. Even if the regulator comes to hear of such interventions, does it substitute its own normative judgement of 'quality' and demand a rebalancing? It would be a courageous and perhaps foolhardy regulator that intervenes without systematic and blatant examples of falling quality or falling investment, which would have to be well-defined and empirically verifiable to be defensible. In an era when regulation is still – even in the wake of an unprecedented banking crisis – regarded as intrinsically undesirable, such interference in the operation of a news service might easily be condemned as 'Nanny Statism' and a compromise of free speech. There are plenty who would agree with one British media commentator that, 'The declining standard of ITV news, which 20 years ago used to rival BBC news, is close to being a national tragedy,' but to demonstrate such deterioration beyond doubt, and to substitute its own journalistic criteria for those of the news provider – especially given the contested definitions of 'broadsheet' discussed in Chapter 7 – is well beyond the scope of any modern-day regulator.[20]

The Unites States again provides ample evidence of the potentially corrosive influence of corporate power on television's editorial agenda. One well-documented example, which subsequently became the subject of the Hollywood movie *The Insider* (1999), was an explosive CBS '60 Minutes' story in 1995 that was to feature allegations against the Brown and Williamson Tobacco Company, a subsidiary of British American Tobacco. Evidence from Dr Jeffrey Wigand, a former Vice President for research and development, suggested that Brown and Williamson had suppressed research on 'safer' cigarettes and had lied to Congress about the addictive qualities of tobacco. CBS was in merger negotiations with Westinghouse Electric and decided to kill the programme rather than risk the threat of a multibillion dollar lawsuit from a wealthy tobacco corporation which might have scuppered the deal.[21]

Another example occurred in 1998 within ABC, following its takeover by Disney Corporation. An ABC investigative reporter had obtained substantial evidence that convicted paedophiles were being employed at the Disney World theme park in Florida, the worst possible story for a child-oriented brand such as Disney. The project was approved by President of ABC News, David Westin. In September, however, Westin pulled the programme claiming that, 'the script did not meet ABC News editorial standards'. A few days earlier Disney Chairman Michael Eisner, speaking on National Public Radio, had said, 'I would prefer ABC not to cover Disney ... I think it's inappropriate for Disney to be covered by Disney'.[22] Two years later, a profile of Westin in the *New Yorker* magazine cited other examples from the ABC newsroom (such as a feature about the film *Chicken Run* being dropped because it provided free publicity to Disney's movie-business rival, Dreamworks) and referred to an 'atmosphere of self-censorship and timidity'.[23]

These are the examples that have emerged into the public domain, but veteran American journalists who have spent years working for the networks suggest that the corrupting effect is deeper and wider than the few examples that have surfaced. One long-standing CBS correspondent, Tom Fenton, spent more than 25 years in the CBS London bureau and painted a bleak vision of corporate influence on American news based on his own experience and interviews with a number of leading American television journalists:

> Parent corporations, advertisers, and commercial interests operate invisible levers over the news a great deal of the time, but for obvious reasons the public rarely hears about such influence ... Several journalists who, on condition of anonymity, described instances where documentaries or investigative segments were pulled or softened, ultimately refused to participate in this book, for fear of being identified and blacklisted.[24]

Despite the American experience – and, indeed, the Italian experience where Berlusconi has ruthlessly used his own TV channels to further his prime-ministerial ambitions – the legacy of over 50 years of television journalism rooted in professional independence and public service values has perhaps created a certain naivety about the potential impact of market censorship. Even more worryingly, Grade's assumptions about the potent combination of journalistic autonomy and regulatory protection seemed to be shared by Britain's competition regulator when it was assessing whether BSkyB – the satellite TV operation then majority-owned by Rupert Murdoch – could hang on to the 17.9 per cent of ITV, which it had suddenly acquired in November 2006.[25] When the Competition Commission (CC) published its findings just over a year later, it declared itself unconcerned about Murdoch's News Corporation's potential influence on ITV news because, 'the regulatory mechanisms, combined with a strong culture of editorial independence within television news production, are likely to be effective in preventing any prejudice to the independence of ITV news'.[26] By contrast, Ofcom's own evidence to the CC reflected a better understanding of the realities of everyday life in a television newsroom when it argued that, 'a person seeking to exert influence could readily exploit informal communications by expressing a strong point of view which could affect [editorial] decisions'.[27]

This particular case was decided (against BSkyB) on competition rather than journalistic grounds (in contrast to a subsequent bitter controversy about the potential impact of ownership on television journalism – this time involving Sky News and covered in the next chapter – which focused on the pluralism issue). It therefore leaves unresolved the potential threat to ITN's journalism from either new ownership of ITV or from the battle to retain viewers in a multichannel world. Although regulatory mechanisms and market forces are likely to guarantee news and current affairs a place in the ITV schedule – and while a culture of professionalism and independence will provide some protection for blatant intrusions into television journalism practice – the news output of Britain's main commercial channel during the 2010s and beyond is more likely to be shaped by ownership and competition factors than at any point during its first 55 years of gradual evolution.

A different commercial model – news and Channel 5[28]

We have seen that, as the youngest of Britain's commercial terrestrial channels, Channel 5 deliberately pursued a news strategy that would distinguish it from its rivals – younger, pacier, iconoclastic, less constrained by traditional television conventions such as newsreaders sitting behind desks, and with a youth-oriented agenda focusing more on lifestyle and celebrity issues. From its inception in 1997, ITN had been Channel 5's chosen news supplier. From the beginning of 2005, however, it switched its £8 million news budget from ITN to Sky News which – as we will see in the next chapter – had established itself as an authoritative and award-winning news channel. Apart from being competitive on price, Sky did not supply any other terrestrial channel and could therefore offer Channel 5 unique access to their pictures, their journalism and their infrastructure.

As with ITV, Channel 5 places great emphasis on the branding benefits of a peak-time news service. Its then head of news and current affairs, Chris Shaw, told the parliamentary committee in 2007 that, despite news being unprofitable, it still represented a vital ingredient in the channel's construction of its own identity and in preserving its reputation in a world of multiple digital channels:

> [News] is part of the personality and ... the brand of your whole channel. Who your newsreaders are, the face of your news, the type of news you do, says a lot about you as a channel; so I think it would be really unlikely that we would stop doing it. I cannot talk for our shareholders in five or six years' time, but it is a very important part of our personality as a channel. We will continue to do news.[29]

The reference to future shareholders became especially pertinent in July 2010 when the channel was sold by its owners, the Luxembourg-based group RTL, to Richard Desmond, owner of the *Express* and *Star* newspapers as well as the celebrity magazine *OK!* and a number of pornographic satellite television channels. As with most proprietors, Desmond had demonstrated his willingness to influence the editorial output of his newspapers and lost little time in earmarking news as part of the rebranding of his new TV channel.[30] Within a few months of his takeover, Chris Shaw had departed and the *Guardian* reported that Desmond wanted 'greater personal control over the Channel 5 News bulletins' and that the new look bulletin was expected 'to shift downmarket with a heavy emphasis on celebrity stories'. In order to achieve a news revamp, he was attempting to terminate early the contract with Sky News and was in negotiations with other potential news suppliers.[31]

Here, therefore, we have a potentially fascinating case study of how a single proprietor with a different approach to the marketing and branding potential of his TV station could exploit television journalism to 'market' the channel. This returns us to the antagonistic dilemma posed above between – to put it crudely – market-driven journalism on the one hand and democracy-driven journalism on the other. Even if we wish to make normative judgements about the kinds of television journalism that are conducive to an informed and participative democracy – itself a dangerous undertaking – it is very difficult to see how even the most enlightened regulator equipped with full statutory support could guarantee the breadth and depth of journalism that would fulfil those democratic functions. In practice, given that Channel 5 is bound only by news scheduling obligations, it is highly likely that news resources will be cut at the same time as news output moves closer to the celebrity and sensationalism models more associated with the United States.

A different approach to the market: the future of journalism on Channel 4

Channel 4, meanwhile, remains a fascinating example of a commercially funded organization, insulated from direct market pressure both by its status as a publicly owned body and by its continuing statutory responsibility to be different. The 2003 Communications Act reinforced the channel's original remit and obliged it to demonstrate 'innovation, experiment and creativity', to appeal to 'the tastes and interests of culturally diverse society' and generally to exhibit 'a distinctive character'.[32] We have seen how, despite initial reservations, Channel 4's first Chief Executive, Jeremy Isaacs, was persuaded to hand over its news supply contract to ITN. And we have seen how, despite the importance of a peak-time hour to a commercial channel, 'Channel 4 News' has maintained Isaacs' editorial vision. A new £20 million annual deal with ITN in April 2006 included provision for the opening of a new bureau in Beijing, the recruitment of extra journalists across Africa, the Middle and the Far East, and a new Foreign Affairs specialist, thus underlining the channel's commitment to international coverage.

Through its contractual relationship with ITN, Channel 4 ensures that its editorial priorities are properly reflected in its on-screen journalism. In her evidence to the 2007 parliamentary committee, Channel 4's Head of News and Current Affairs, Dorothy Byrne, gave an illuminating insight into how the process works:

> There is a very detailed editorial specification for each programme which lays down contractually what that programme's aims are. For example, one of the aims of Channel 4 News is that it should have its own independent agenda and should not follow slavishly the agenda of other news programmes. That is its point of difference. The format of the programme is all laid down but on a day-to-day basis the decision on the news running order has to lie with the people who are making the news programme.[33]

Byrne made it clear that ITN's editor of Channel 4 news understood the channel's priorities and that, 'instinctively we both know what our important Channel 4 News stories are' through daily conversations and a weekly forward-planning meeting. This osmotic relationship therefore helps to guarantee the continuing seriousness of Channel 4's news agenda, despite its commercial funding. While Channel 4's status as a public service broadcaster was confirmed by the 2010 Digital Economy Act, two difficult questions still remain for its journalism over the next ten years: the future of ITN as a standalone news supplier; and the financial viability of Channel 4 itself.

It is a somewhat eccentric legacy of the UK's public service system that Channel 4 relies for its news on a supplier that in turn relies for 40 per cent of its revenue (and effectively its survival) on a continuing deal with a bigger commercial rival, ITV.[34] This raises some crucial questions for Channel 4 about the sustainability of the ITN model, and what happens if ITV takes complete control of ITN or if ITN itself changes ownership? Channel 4 would find it difficult to turn to Sky in a television news market where Sky News already provides a 24-hour news channel and supplies the news to Channel 5. It does not have the resources to run its own news operation, and its options would be limited either to using news agencies (which have little experience in television journalism) or starting its own independent operation on limited funds. None are likely to offer the depth, breadth and infrastructure of global news coverage that remains the channel's hallmark.

The second is a more serious institutional problem about the survival of Channel 4 itself and to what extent it can continue to subsidize its non-profitable programmes through the rest of its schedule. Throughout its existence, 'Channel 4 News' has lost money. An internal report in 2000 established that the flagship 7.00 p.m. bulletin earned about half its costs in advertising revenue and acknowledged that, while commercial imperatives might dictate a move to 7.30, such a move would be potentially 'extremely damaging' to the channel's reputation.[35] This was reinforced in the select committee hearings when Byrne told the committee, to some astonishment, 'I am proud to say that *Channel 4 News* loses more money for Channel 4 than any other programme that we make'. She confirmed that costs of around £20 million were met by revenues of around £10 million, leaving a funding gap of £10 million. Despite this, she remained adamant about the role of Channel 4 news, not – as for ITV and Channel 5 – simply as a marketing or branding tool but in terms of its democratic contribution:

> If we continue, as we must, with our one-hour, serious news programme in which 40–50 per cent of its content is foreign, that programme is not going to make money. But we should not cut back on its seriousness, its quality or its length – I am absolutely sure of that … not just for Channel 4 but also for British democracy. I think the existence of *Channel 4 News* is vital as a very serious competitor to the BBC.[36]

In fact, as the Chairman of Channel 4 was later at pains to point out in his evidence, this calculation underestimated the true deficit because it did not allow for the *opportunity cost* of scheduling a serious news bulletin at peak-time instead of a high-rating show. As he put it, 'if we scheduled *Ugly Betty* or *Desperate Housewives* or ... an overtly commercial broadcast, then potentially we would be making more money out of the advertising because of the higher audiences'.[37] During the course of Ofcom's 2008–9 Public Service Broadcasting review, it became increasingly clear that this was not just an academic debate about which programming areas were being subsidized, but about how Channel 4 would survive: in other words, the problem was institutional rather than genre-based. Ofcom concluded that audiences wanted a public service alternative to the BBC and that 'a second institution with clear public purpose goals and a sustainable economic model will help to ensure wide availability of public service content'.[38]

When the government subsequently extended the remit of Channel 4 in the 2010 Digital Economy Act as a means of delivering longer term 'public policy objectives' of pluralism, quality and distinctiveness, it omitted one crucial ingredient from its wish-list: underpinning the organization's financial independence.[39] Channel 4 remains an anomaly in the world's television ecology: a free-standing public body, funded entirely from advertising, and committed to editorial priorities in journalism that it has championed since 1982. Moreover, it now has a brief to extend that vision beyond television to mobile, interactive and digital platforms. For the moment, that vision remains intact. It is yet to be seen how long the institution itself or its journalism can survive the harsh realities of competitive funding in a multichannel world.

The counterfactual: television news in a free market

This continuing emphasis on institutional, regulatory and legislative approaches to Public Service Broadcasting – and specifically to the importance of broadcast news – is a somewhat puzzling cultural phenomenon to those free-market liberals who traditionally condemn any interference in the dissemination of news as a potential distortion of free speech. This antagonism to intervention in the market is particularly strong in the United States, which allows an insight into what economists like to call the counterfactual: that is, what happens to institutional and professional approaches to television journalism in the *absence* of any regulatory obligations? We saw in Chapter 7 how the homogeneity of content and scheduling in the United States contrasted with the diversity of television news in the United Kingdom. This cannot be explained through any lack of professional integrity or training in the United States, where journalism schools have been an integral part of the educational landscape for decades, with a much longer tradition of debating the ethics and principles of journalism than in Europe. Why, then, the massive divergence in on-screen manifestations of professional journalism?

There are essentially three answers: ratings; revenue; and lack of regulatory oversight.

For his book, cited earlier, the CBS foreign correspondent Tom Fenton interviewed a number of his fellow senior professionals about the nature of their industry and the pressures faced in particular by foreign news. Dan Rather, anchor of CBS News for 24 years from 1981 to 2005, described to Fenton the futility of attempting to win any argument about the news agenda on the basis of the company's public responsibility: 'It's gone out of fashion. It's gone. To talk in those terms is the equivalent of wearing spats to the office.'[40] Andy Rooney, another CBS correspondent, told him that, 'Money has taken over news. It was always a factor, but never what it is now.' In an environment where a fraction of 1 per cent of a rating point is equivalent to hundreds of thousands of dollars, every item of television content is scrutinized for its ratings implications. It only requires a small minority to switch channels during, for instance, an item on Afghanistan for the great majority – some of whom may have a keen interest in life outside the United States – to be deprived of something slightly more serious.

Much the same point is made by the television journalists interviewed by Leonard Downie Jr. Tom Brokaw, anchor of NBC's 'Nightly News' from the early 1980s until December 2004, told Downie that every item on a broadcast carries the weight of the entire programme: 'One false step and you've lost a viewer, or a million of them.'[41] While American networks have always been driven by the needs of shareholders and profit, Downie argues that it was only from the 1980s that news divisions were subjected to the same corporate and marketplace disciplines. It became a conventional wisdom that the highest ratings were achieved by concentrating on entertainment, health and stories which, in the words of ABC's Peter Jennings, 'focus on the comedy and tragedy of life'.[42] For many network news executives, it was the live drama of the O.J. Simpson trial in 1995 that finally tipped the balance of network news towards the entertainment values that dominate today. Paul Friedman of CBS called this 'a pivotal moment' for American news coverage when a single explicitly tabloid story covered in intricate detail was rewarded by uniformly high ratings across the networks.[43]

The financial realism that was imposed by the new corporate owners of American networks – and the inadequacy of federal regulation – was encapsulated by the journalist Zoë Heller in her vivid account of what happened to former *Sunday Times* editor Andrew Neil, tasked by Rupert Murdoch to launch a current affairs programme on his Fox Network. 'On Assignment' (later changed to 'Full Disclosure') was originally planned as a serious but iconoclastic response to what Murdoch and Neil saw as the 'political correctness' of current affairs on other networks. As the pilots came and went, pressure grew to inject softer or more 'fun' items to leaven the mix, which was perceived as too sober. In a telling interview with Heller, Neil's co-executive producer David Corvo told her:

> Look, we're all a bunch of whores in the end. There is pressure. When I started out at NBC years ago, the news division lost a hundred million dollars a year, but RCA owned us and they saw a news service as their civic responsibility. They took the loss as the cost of a Federal Communications Commission licence. It was the same attitude over at CBS and ABC. But news has to make money now, and inevitably journalism has suffered.[44]

It is this third element of the trilogy mentioned above – the progressive removal of effective regulatory intervention – which is perhaps at the heart of the gradual evisceration of serious television journalism in the United States. It was abundantly clear from the evidence given by American civil society groups to the visiting parliamentary committee in 2007 that the legacy of 1980s Reaganite deregulation (outlined in Chapter 3) was the complete absence of any content obligations on American television beyond those associated with taste and decency; and that, moreover, any such intervention would be regarded with enormous suspicion given First Amendment priorities.

Bill Buzenberg, of the Center for Public Integrity, argued that the government had rejected regulation and that the Federal Communications Commission (FCC) 'is serving financial interests but not the interests of consumers and citizens'.[45] This was echoed by the Consumers Union and by the Project for Excellence in Journalism (PEJ) who said they believed that the FCC had 'decided to get out of the content business'.[46] It is equally clear, however, that even a more benign FCC oriented towards promoting the public interest would find it difficult to overcome the natural inclination of American courts to avoid what would be characterized by the media companies themselves as regulatory interference with freedom of expression. This was confirmed by the Senior Counsel to the Senate Committee on Commerce, Science and Transportation (which oversees the FCC) who acknowledged public concern about the quality of journalism but believed that legislators were virtually powerless to intervene: 'the First Amendment makes it very hard for public policy to directly address content'.[47]

But can regulation still work?

This hands-off approach, derived from the United States' constitutional and cultural history, contrasts starkly with the legislative, regulatory and cultural legacy in the United Kingdom and most other European countries. It also, however, highlights the problematic nature of the British interventionist approach when it collides with the realities of the market. There is no question, as this chapter has shown, of Parliament's willingness to intervene to protect diversity and quality, nor of the regulator's willingness to interpret and implement the statutory obligations laid down by Parliament. While fundamentally deregulatory in many of its activities, Ofcom has demonstrated a continuing concern for sustaining a healthy culture of television journalism on-screen. It has not yet, however, really grappled with the definitional or interpretational issues of 'quality' as laid down in the Communications Act, nor offered an approach to quantification of investment in journalism. And while it struggles at the beginning of the 2010s to meet the challenges of audience fragmentation, financial meltdown, channel proliferation and market demand for 'light-touch' regulation, it becomes ever more difficult for even the most well-intentioned regulator to find the practical regulatory solutions to protect journalistic content. While the United States' problem, in other words, is embedded in its constitution and its wholehearted embrace of the market as guardian of unfettered free speech, Britain's problem (shared by most other European countries) is a pragmatic dilemma of finding solutions to identified structural issues – while still, of course, acknowledging and protecting the right of private media corporations to pursue their commercial interests.

In that sense, the FCC reservations are probably right: it is indeed highly problematic to justify regulatory intervention beyond merely quantitative measures, because to do so involves inevitably subjective judgements about 'quality' journalism. Britain has benefited from pursuing a policy for over 50 years of empowering institutional structures which – through regulatory fiat and imaginative funding regimes – have fostered public service definitions of television journalism to thrive even in relatively difficult commercial environments. On-screen judgements have therefore not been ordained by some bean-counter with a ruler divorced from the reality of front-line journalism, but have emerged from institutional philosophies about what journalism should be doing, whom it should be serving, according to what principles and with what ends.

With those public service institutional arrangements coming under the severest economic and technological pressure they have ever witnessed, it is difficult to see the shape of new interventions that could successfully ameliorate the problems inflicted by the market and by technology. ITN will struggle to survive and may eventually be emasculated completely, Channel 5's owner is unlikely to champion the cause of serious, well-resourced journalism, and Channel 4's resources will continue to be stretched. It may be that, despite Ofcom's insistence that pluralism must be preserved, the BBC will eventually prove to be the only healthy survivor in British broadcast journalism. Some regard that outcome as disastrous for a medium that is still remarkably powerful as an instrument of democracy. Others, however, believe that the real future for television journalism – indeed, for democracy itself – lies in exploiting the very technologies and opportunities that have made the *ancien régime* so vulnerable.

10 24-hour News Channels and the 'New' Television Journalism

As the news credits roll, two sombre-looking newscasters sitting behind their standard-issue television newsdesk take it in turns to read lines from the top story from their autocue: 'Athens tonight where a 59-year-old woman has been taken to hospital with a number of symptoms. It's thought that the disease could cause millions of deaths worldwide if enough people caught it. Our illness correspondent Ben Green has been looking at what we might know so far ...' At the bottom of the screen, the words 'Tomato Flu' are flashed up in bright red to identify the nature and the gravity of the story. The picture switches to an earnest young man standing next to a map of the world superimposed on rows of tomatoes. He continues the story: 'The existence of Tomato Flu was first suspected back in 2004 when a worker on a tomato farm in the Philippines complained of feeling unwell before being taken to a hospital and pronounced dead. Ever since then, scientists have been trying to find a link between tomatoes on that particular farm and anything that might cause death. In other words, the so-called smoking tomato.' The bulletin continues at breathtaking speed for the next 30 minutes, with repeated updates 'live' from an Athens hospital as our intrepid reporter waits for information about an expected announcement that there might soon be further information about an announcement of a possible press conference.

Thus began the opening sequence of 'Broken News', the BBC's 2007 pastiche of life and death on a 24-hour news channels, an uncomfortable caricature that contained more than a few grains of truth. 24-hour news channels are where the conventions of television journalism collide with the dramatic imperatives of the television medium. Television news demands that something should be 'happening' even when the news itself is not inherently dramatic, and 24-hour news channels compensate for periods of inaction through a number of dramatic conventions: opinionated commentary, a 'breaking news' ticker at the bottom of the screen, a manufactured confrontation between protagonists holding mildly different views, or the 'live two-way' where the very element of liveness is designed to inject immediacy in a story where, in truth, very little is happening.

In theory, 24-hour news channels could be the vehicle for a detached, analytical, unhurried approach to contemporary issues, which harnesses the power of the visual medium and combines it with resources, vision and a more reflective form of narrative journalism. Very occasionally, that is what some 24-hour channels deliver. Far more often, however, they are shoestring operations with too few reporters to move beyond mainstream stories or countries, preferring to contrive drama rather than break new stories or expand the horizons of existing ones. They provide an immediate point of reference for those really dramatic, unfolding events where audiences have come to expect instant news gratification: an earthquake, a plane crash, a bombing, a raging bush fire. The successful rescue of 33 Chilean miners in October 2010, beamed as it happened into hundreds of millions of households around the world, was a textbook happy ending human drama made for 24-hour news channels. But for the most part, these channels have come to rely (particularly in the United States, where impartiality is not an issue) on controversial pundits and talk-show hosts to maintain their profile and relieve the daily tedium. As one British documentary-maker has written:

> The limitations of continuous coverage are easy to discern. In between rare peaks of drama come vast deserts of boredom. Blandness is a result of 'palm tree journalism' – reporters never straying from their satellite link, gesturing towards rooftop air-conditioning plants … Will these new channels enhance our experience of the world – or will they merely supply the same diet of hastily edited stories punctuated by instant, often misleading commentary?[1]

In a content analysis of UK news channels, Lewis, Cushion and Thomas suggested that they ideally served three main purposes for audiences: immediacy, or watching events as they unfolded; convenience, or watching news whenever the viewers wished; and engagement, or providing more context and analysis.[2] Their analysis suggested that it was convenience that 'most clearly informs the way 24-hour news is structured'. Despite the reputation – and the promotional rhetoric – of news channels, they found that liveness is more illusional than real, thus confirming the satirical approach of 'Broken News': 'The only live action on view, most of the time, is that provided by the reporters themselves, who we see speaking in front of an appropriate location, generally in conversation with an anchor.' Moreover, the strapline of 'breaking news', which so effectively adds to the sense of immediacy and urgency was 'as much a matter of branding as any more well-defined or intrinsic quality', an artifice sometimes even applied to routine and predictable diary events.

More surprisingly, and counter-intuitively, the study found that fewer than 20 per cent of stories contained any analysis or contextual explanation compared to over

40 per cent of stories from the BBC 'Ten O'clock News' covering the same period. The authors conclude, depressingly, that news channels actually deliver 'rolling bulletins', which in consumerist terms offer a convenient 'news when you want it' service but would leave viewers with less information and less understanding than an evening bulletin on a mainstream channel.

The pioneer – CNN

This was probably not what Ted Turner had in mind on 21 May 1979 when he announced to the convention of the National Cable Television Association in Las Vegas that he was going to launch the world's first round-the-clock television news service the following June. It needed a wealthy iconoclast to break the mould of the big network news divisions, and Turner fitted the bill: a university dropout with a reputation for drinking and partying who had launched the Turner Broadcasting System in 1970, bought the Atlanta Braves baseball team in 1974 and won the America's Cup yacht race in 1977, thus earning himself the nickname of 'Captain Outrageous'. Turner's vision for the mould-breaking Cable News Network was a service that 'would resemble a working newsroom, avoiding the appearance of being packaged into polished program segments. Anchors would appear alongside producers, directors, editors, and even technicians'.[3] It was an untried, hugely risky proposition, requiring an initial $100 million investment, 300 staff and news bureaux around the country; but at 6.00 p.m. on 1 June 1980, just 374 days after Turner's announcement, CNN opened its doors with a lead story on the shooting of civil rights leader Vernon Jordan. The landmark programme was only available in 1.7 million of the United States' 16 million cabled homes.[4]

Disparaged by the US networks as the Chicken Noodle Network, CNN's early days were characterized by what one observer has called 'a maverick opportunism and a great deal of luck'.[5] It was assisted by launching within a television economy that had three vital characteristics: a population at least four times the size of any other developed country; large numbers of households with a high disposable income; and a tradition of paying for television packages, which was still nascent in most other countries and non-existent in the United Kingdom. By 1985, on the back of revenues from advertising and subscription, Turner had transformed an outrageous idea into a net annual profit of $20 million, albeit after a total investment of nearly $80 million. More importantly, he had pioneered a concept of television news whose emphasis on immediacy, liveness and rawness overturned the traditional narratives of mass-audience television news programmes and their packaged, carefully scripted approach. It elevated the importance of the here and now and, according to one analysis, 'redefined news from something that *has* happened to something that *is* happening'.[6] It is precisely this redefinition of news as manufactured drama that has attracted the most trenchant criticism of the genre.

Over the course of two to three years at the end of the 1980s, however, history was on CNN's side and offered a series of real-life, uncontrived dramas that earned it worldwide recognition. In May 1989, the network had five correspondents and a news crew in Beijing covering a Sino-Soviet summit when the student protests in Tiananmen Square erupted. The evocative image of a lone protestor in a white shirt standing defiantly in front of a procession of tanks, then climbing on to its turret to speak to the soldiers inside, is still hailed as one of the great iconic moments of live television. On air throughout the protests, the CNN anchor Bernard Shaw tried to convey to American audiences what was then a revolutionary technical marvel:

> If you're wondering how CNN has been able to bring you this extraordinary story ... we brought in our own flyaway gear, about eighteen oversized suitcases with our satellite gear ... So whatever you've seen in the way of pictures and, indeed, in the way of words, came from our microwave units at Tiananmen Square bounced right here to the hotel, through the control room on one of the upper floors ... back down through cables, up on the CNN satellite dish, up on the satellite, and to you across the world.[7]

While the Chinese authorities soon crushed the dissident protests – and prevented further live coverage of events – the unravelling of communist regimes in Eastern Europe gathered speed. More iconic images followed in November 1989 as East and West Germans combined to begin dismantling the Berlin Wall, so long the symbol of communist supremacy in the East. And on 17 January 1991, CNN and 24-hour news came of age as Peter Arnett provided the live commentary to graphic images of the first missile attack of the Gulf War on Baghdad. Those images, even more than Tiananmen Square, guaranteed the place of 24-hour news channels in television's ecology as well as validating Turner's original gamble. In his biography of Rupert Murdoch, William Shawcross wrote that, 'The [Gulf] war established CNN as the most influential network in the world. More than any other station, it had helped to create the reality of the "global village", in which the manor house was the United States ... Throughout the world, diplomats, politicians and statesmen would watch CNN to know what was happening everywhere else. Bush, Saddam and Gorbachev were all known to watch it.'[8]

The 'CNN effect'

In the years following this very first 'television war', a number of politicians and officials began to talk in vague terms about the 'CNN effect': the impact of live television coverage of world events on the policymaking process. Two British Foreign Secretaries, Douglas Hurd and David Owen, referred to the influence of 24-hour television news coverage on foreign policy, while former US Secretary of State James Baker III wrote: 'In Iraq, Bosnia, Somalia, Rwanda, and Chechnya, among others, the real-time coverage of conflict by the electronic media has served to create a powerful new imperative for prompt action that was not present in less frenetic [times]'.[9] Their anxieties about the damaging impact of 24-hour media scrutiny on delicate diplomatic negotiations have been reinforced by some disturbing 'what if ...?' reflections by those at the centre of two global political confrontations before the era of instant journalism. Both crises were resolved peacefully but – according to those involved – would have ended catastrophically in the twenty-first century television environment.

The first was the American hostage crisis of 1979–80. When 66 US hostages were seized in 1979 at the American embassy in Tehran – and 52 subsequently held for over a year – the pressure on the then US President Jimmy Carter to take immediate remedial action was intense and sustained. According to the US State Department spokesman at the time, the situation would have been unsustainable in today's media environment: 'In the current media world, I don't think we could have bought as much time as we bought. Faced with the drumbeat of war, the political side of the House would have pushed for meaningful military action pronto'. The result, he was certain, would have been the death of the hostages.[10]

The second, even more alarmingly, was the Cuban missile crisis of 1962. According to Ted Sorensen – special counsel to President John F. Kennedy and present throughout the unfolding crisis – when American surveillance planes discovered Soviet-built offensive missile sites in Cuba, which clearly threatened the United States, the instinctive military and political response was a 'surgical strike' to bomb the missile sites. Instead, they deliberated for a week, recognized that the probable consequence would be nuclear war, and embarked on a delicate and protracted period of diplomacy that resulted – after nearly two weeks – in a carefully managed Soviet climbdown. But Sorensen believes the media environment of the twenty-first century would not have allowed time for contemplation:

> In all likelihood, today's media pressure would have made it impossible for the Kennedy team to keep confidential for one week the fact that we knew Soviet missiles were in Cuba ... [The public panic] would have meant our selecting everyone's initial first choice, an air strike against the missiles and

related targets which, in all likelihood, would have required, according to the Pentagon, a follow-up invasion and occupation of Cuba.[11]

At that point, given that Soviet troops stationed in Cuba were equipped with and authorized to use tactical nuclear missiles against an American attack, 'in all likelihood ... the result would have been a nuclear war and the destruction of the world'.

It is an apocalyptic vision of an old world transplanted into a new media age, which perhaps does not properly acknowledge the adaptation of today's politicians and diplomats to the speed of the twenty-first century news cycle. Over the years, a more nuanced and sophisticated approach to analysing the nature, direction and context of any 'CNN effect' has emerged, which argues that – insofar as it really does constitute a new media phenomenon – it only manifests itself in the absence of real political leadership.[12] An even more diluted version of the argument holds that, although the term itself derives from the beginnings of round-the-clock news coverage, it is merely the continuation of a pre-CNN and even pre-television phenomenon that saw foreign policy decisions frequently laid at the door of the mass media. One military historian talks of a press, in 1889, 'obsessed with the threat to Britain and the Empire of foreign spies,' which partly accounted for the Official Secrets Act of that year, and similar press agitation resulting in an even more draconian successor Act in 1911.[13] This is perhaps a good example of the assumed power of an innovative media form that in many respects is simply the refashioning of a well-established theory of old media power.

It therefore remains unproven that foreign policymaking in the age of 24-hour television news is any more susceptible to pressure from those channels than from mass-circulation newspapers. But even if the end result may not have been Sorensen's worldwide conflagration, it is almost inevitable that the conduct of diplomacy in the real-time glare of television's headlights allows less time for calibrating the consequences of political action. This is perhaps a twenty-first-century version of the 'CNN effect': that while political action has for decades been subject to – and sometimes determined by – the public gaze, that process is now accelerated and distorted to fit the television narrative of drama and immediacy.

The UK pioneer – Sky News

Just as it took one maverick entrepreneur with deep pockets to start 24-hour television news in the United States, so too in the United Kingdom. When on 5 February 1989, Rupert Murdoch pre-empted Britain's domestic satellite television operation British Satellite Broadcasting (BSB) with four channels beamed in from

Luxembourg's Astra satellite, one of the four was Sky News. Its audiences were tiny as Murdoch set out to persuade a reluctant British public to nail receiving dishes to their walls, but the scale of the operation and investment was not dissimilar to Turner's nearly ten years earlier: £40 million set-up costs with a starting annual budget of £30 million and a staff of 260.[14] However, the business model was very different, with virtually no prospect of early returns for two reasons: first, there was very little appetite for subscription television in the United Kingdom, where over-the-air reception was excellent and most viewers were satisfied with their existing free-to-air channels. Second, Sky's tiny audiences were of very little interest to advertisers.

There was, inevitably, speculation and anxiety about Murdoch's intentions. During the 1980s, his (then) five national newspapers had championed Margaret Thatcher's Conservative government with an unswerving loyalty, and there was some concern (and not just from the left) that this might be the beginning of a long-term assault on the long-standing tradition of impartiality in British broadcasting. In fact, Sky News never became a vehicle for deliberate bias. Staffed by television journalists who were steeped in the BBC and ITN traditions of broadcast news, there was neither professional inclination nor – importantly – managerial diktat to pursue anything other than conventional norms of television news. So why bother with a demonstrably loss-making enterprise that had little chance of returning a profit in the foreseeable future? There were essentially two reasons. The first positioned Sky News as a vital ingredient in the branding and promotional package, elevating the image of Sky. In the words of William Shawcross: 'The money, effort and time put into Sky News reflected its importance in deflecting the criticism that the more populist output of Sky's other channels attracted'.[15]

The second reason was a more important strategic imperative: the leverage which a respected news channel could offer in political circles, especially when it came to asking for regulatory favours. A more critical Murdoch biographer, Bruce Page, records a hugely significant moment towards the end of 1990 when Murdoch's Sky channels and rival satellite broadcaster BSB had concluded that their satellite TV businesses could not survive as competitive rivals.[16] Murdoch had engineered a deal, effectively a takeover of BSB by Sky to form BSkyB, but the resulting monopoly would almost certainly face regulatory hurdles. He had faced similar situations with airline and telecoms businesses in Australia, both of which had been neatly finessed through astute political manoeuvring. He needed to cut a similar deal to secure his satellite TV takeover in Britain. On 29 October Murdoch went to see the Prime Minister Margaret Thatcher to explain the situation. Page continues:

She was showing out a foreign visitor, and said to him, 'Here is Mr Murdoch, who gives us Sky News, the only unbiased news in the UK'. Murdoch said, 'Well you know it is costing us a lot, and we are going to have to do a merger.' The Prime Minister nodded. And as with the airline and telecom deals in Australia, it was basically that simple.[17]

It was a lesson which was not lost on Murdoch or the News Corporation PR machine. Over the following 20 years, in debates on Public Service Broadcasting, the future of the BBC, the size of the licence fee or the need for regulatory oversight, there have been frequent references by ardent critics of public sector involvement to Sky News as a shining example of the 'public service' content that the private sector can deliver. In evidence to a House of Commons select committee inquiry into Public Service Content in 2007–8, Ofcom Chief Executive Ed Richards said that, 'Sky News is in many ways meeting many of the purposes and characteristics that we would associate with public service broadcasting.'[18] There is no question that it has maintained over its 20-year history a standard of television journalism whose commitment to professionalism and impartiality is at least the equal of its competitors, frequently winning the coveted Royal Television Society award for News Channel of the Year. But it also serves as a useful PR weapon in Murdoch's long-standing insistence that there is far too much superfluous public intervention in British broadcasting.

Despite its political status and professional recognition, Murdoch himself has indicated that he is less enamoured of Sky News and would prefer something closer to his American news channel, Fox News. When asked by the *New York Times* in 2003 whether Sky News had begun imitating Fox, Murdoch's reported response was: 'I wish. I think that Sky News is very popular and they are doing well, but they don't have the entertaining talk shows – it is just a rolling half-hour of hard news all the time.' He thought its presentation was staid and that it had a liberal bias.[19] He reiterated these views in 2007, telling a visiting delegation from the House of Lords Communications Committee that, 'Sky News would be more popular if it were more like the Fox News Channel,' and then raised several eyebrows when, asked by the committee about his lack of editorial intervention, responded that 'nobody at Sky listens to me!'[20] It suggested that only Sky's independent directors, appointed by its other shareholders, had prevented him from imposing his personal stamp on Sky News and pushing it towards the more populist and provocative presentational style of Fox News.

Murdoch's somewhat insouciant response to the committee's questions took on much greater import at the end of 2010 when News Corporation initiated a bid in the United Kingdom to take over the 61 per cent of BSkyB that it did not already own (a legacy of the original merger of Sky and BSB in 1990), immediately sparking a furious debate in UK media and political circles about pluralism and media power in a democracy.[21] There followed some frantic bargaining, which focused almost entirely on Sky News and how its independence from proprietorial interference might be secured. The resultant compromise would have involved the news service being hived off into a separate company for ten years, and the creation of an independent editorial committee to oversee journalistic appointments. Critics of the deal argued vigorously that similar 'independent' committees – at *The Times* newspapers and the *Wall Street Journal* – had proved completely ineffectual in resisting Murdoch's interference, and that Sky News would inevitably suffer a similar fate. In the event, the political fallout from the Murdoch-owned *News of the World* phone-hacking scandal in July 2011 culminated in an unprecedented all-party vote in the House of Commons calling on Rupert Murdoch to abandon his full takeover bid, thus making it impossible for him to continue. Although it is very unlikely that the bid will be reinstated, News Corporation's 39 per cent still gives it effective control of BSkyB and therefore Sky News. While theoretically, therefore, there could still be some proprietorial meddling there are two reasons why any interference may be more restrained than elsewhere.

First, there would almost certainly be professional resistance to any major strategic shift in editorial policy from broadcast journalists whose background – for the most part derived from the BBC or ITN – would be out of kilter with the more tabloid, dramatized approach of Fox News. Unlike print journalism, where tabloid instincts have been honed and perfected in the United Kingdom at least since 1896, the conventions of UK television journalism have helped to prevent the kinds of sensationalism and gratuitous melodrama that characterizes much of the tabloid press. Intriguingly, the reverse is true of the United States where print journalists have been imbued with a long-standing commitment to a more discerning journalistic ethic while American television, as we have seen, imposes its entertainment narrative framework on even the most serious-minded journalist. This deep-seated differentiation between television journalism cultures either side of the Atlantic would make a wholesale transformation of Sky News difficult to achieve, although a more subtle shift of emphasis and editorial approach may well become apparent.

Second, on the basis that Sky News is more political plaything than valuable profit-centre, Murdoch may be prepared to accept continued financial losses in return for continuing political capital (and, indeed, the absence of any objections to continuing losses from the independent BSkyB directors is an indication of where corporate control really lies). Although figures have never been published, it is well established that Sky News has never been profitable. One reliable report in the middle of 2006 put the annual budget at £35 million, subsequently subjected to cuts as the recession hits BSkyB's revenue, which its small advertising revenue would barely dent.[22] In fact, had Sky News been allowed to keep its unique status as the only UK 24-hour news channel in the multichannel market, it might have started to return a small profit after seven to eight years of operation – particularly since it had established itself as a respected and reliable operator in the best traditions of British television journalism. Its inability to make money – and the virtual certainty that there is no long-term prospect of profitability – is almost entirely down to the existence of the BBC's 24-hour news channel, launched some eight years after Sky News.

The UK's latecomer – BBC News

BBC News 24 launched on 9 November 1997 as part of its plan for extending television and radio services into the digital age. Given the BBC's domestic and worldwide reputation for broadcast journalism, it is perhaps surprising that it was so late into the field but it had both to satisfy government that the additional channels were justifiable and face down resistance from commercial competitors. BSkyB was particularly hostile, attempting to use European Union competition rules on State aid to prevent the channel's launch – an interesting position for an organization controlled by someone renowned for his opposition to Europe and his enthusiastic devotion to the principles of competition.[23]

Despite the BBC brand name and institutional resources, however, News 24 struggled to overcome the eight-year start it had ceded to Sky, and was unfavourably compared to its rival. In 2002, an independent report commissioned by the government on News 24 came to some fairly damning conclusions. It was particularly critical of the channel's performance on breaking news:

> It is a fair bet that anyone who walks around a newspaper office where televisions are turned on the whole time will find them tuned to Sky News rather than to News 24 … This may be because Sky has been around longer, or it may be a legacy of News 24's bad start in life. But Sky has a strong record of being first with the news, especially when it comes to domestic politics. The fact that its style is rather snappier and a bit less discursive than News 24's probably also helps.[24]

Somewhat controversially, it went on to recommend that, 'An absolute determination to be the first to break accurate news must be at the heart of everything the channel does.' While an uncompromising statement of traditional journalistic values, this privileging of immediacy was an inversion of traditional BBC values: for those running BBC journalism, if not all the journalists themselves, the institutional imperative of journalistic integrity trumped the professional imperative of journalistic immediacy. These institutional priorities were recognized and internalized under the new BBC governance arrangements introduced in 2007 whereby the BBC Trust establishes and monitors specific remits for every BBC service. The new 'service licence' for the news channel, introduced in April 2008 to coincide with the rebranding from BBC News 24 to BBC News, states unequivocally that: 'The channel should aim to deliver breaking news first and, wherever possible, immediately but not to the detriment of accuracy.'[25] The Trust also set the annual budget at £46 million, around 25 per cent greater than that of Sky News.

In 2006, News 24 finally wrested control of the News Channel of the Year award from Sky News (repeating the trick in 2009) having seen its audience share inch ahead of Sky's for the first time: while audiences remain very small by mainstream channel standards, the fact that News 24 took a 0.6 per cent share of viewing compared to Sky's 0.5 per cent at the end of 2005 was regarded as a major milestone by the rival channels, and finally established the BBC as the UK's leading 24-hour news channel.[26] Given the BBC's continuing commitment to news and journalism, and its reputational advantage, this position is unlikely to be threatened even by the cuts that will follow the 2010 licence fee settlement. It is quite possible, however, given its clearly articulated journalistic values of accuracy, impartiality and reliability, that the BBC News channel will be vulnerable to a competitor less constrained by traditional imperatives of journalism and more determined to prioritize drama, immediacy and controversy – should Sky News follow its owner's stated preference and move it closer to the Fox model.

A new approach – Fox News

While Sky was finally conceding its front-runner status to the BBC in Britain, another Murdoch incursion into television news was demonstrating brilliantly on the other side of the Atlantic how to exploit the absence of impartiality requirements by offering conviction news. On 7 October 1996, Murdoch's Fox News Channel (FNC) launched to around 10 million households in the United States. To run the channel, Murdoch had recruited the former hard-hitting Republican political strategist Roger Ailes, advisor to both the Nixon and Reagan presidential campaigns before he masterminded Bush senior's successful presidential campaign in 1988. Under the tutelage of Murdoch and Ailes, the narrative style of Fox News combined splenetic talk radio, dramatic current affairs television, sensationalizing tabloid newspapers and the patriotic fervour of the American right to create a channel that within five years had overtaken CNN in the ratings and redefined the definition of 'balance'.

There were four potent ingredients to the Fox success story. First, a heavy emphasis on attention-grabbing visual presentation: dramatic pictures, creative use of graphics and bullet points to illustrate the headline issues. The pace was fast, with liberal use of 'Fox Alerts' for breaking news stories, which were frequently new angles on old stories or, more likely, not very newsworthy at all. Because the essence of the channel was drama, liveness was elevated above traditional values of journalism. Second, content was skewed towards the traditional tabloid agenda of crime, celebrities, gossip and scandal rather than politics or economics. Third, evenings were dominated by opinion and interview shows, which thrived on confrontation and controversy, rather than straight news reporting. These were, ostensibly, occasions for serious discussion about current issues; in practice, as on many American talk radio stations, they were opportunities for programme hosts to indulge in angry denunciation or ritual humiliation of any poor wretches from the left of centre who agreed to be interviewed. It was the entertainment of the Colosseum rather than the journalism of engagement.

Fourth, most potently of all, the station cleaved to a coherent approach to American politics – driven from the top by Murdoch and Ailes – which was patriotic, overtly Conservative and openly supportive of the Republican Party. From the start, any political bias was vehemently denied by the channel whose trademark slogans were 'Fair and Balanced' and 'We report, you decide'. They told the visiting House of Lords delegation in 2007 that, 'Fox News was launched because Roger Ailes and Rupert Murdoch believed that there was space in the market for "fair and balanced" news', that 'most news reporting has a left of centre bias' and that 'the channel has no particular political agenda and an effort is made to balance the stories they produce, although ... on some days the channel acts as a balance to the rest of the media'.[27] Over the years, however, that argument has become increasingly unsustainable. In the lead-up to the Iraq War and during Iraq's occupation, the channel was particularly enthusiastic in supporting White House claims that Saddam Hussein was not only concealing weapons of mass destruction but had links to 9/11. In 2002, a former Fox producer who had just completed six years at the channel published a letter alleging that the newsroom was 'under the constant control and vigilance of management'. Fox was, he said, 'a news network run by one of the most high-profile political operatives of recent times. Everyone there understands that [Fox] is, to a large extent, "Roger's Revenge" against what he considers a liberal, pro-Democrat media establishment that has shunned him for decades.'[28]

A year later, the writer and comedian (since turned politician) Al Franken wrote a trenchant critique of Fox, its content and its journalistic modus operandi with the unambiguous title, *Lies and the Lying Liars who Tell Them: A Fair and*

Balanced Look at the Right. Having detailed numerous instances of alleged distortions and inaccuracies in pursuit of its political objectives, he concluded that Fox's entertainment value came from 'their willingness to lie and distort'.[29] In an astonishing sequel, Fox News demonstrated its determination to be taken seriously by suing Franken and attempting to stop publication of the book because of its use of their trademarked slogan 'Fair and Balanced'. By the time the trial judge had dismissed the case as being 'wholly without merit, both factually and legally', Franken's book had become a bestseller and Fox's reputation as a fearless champion of free speech had self-destructed.[30]

Further evidence of the conservative, pro-Republican bias of Fox News came in 2004 from a documentary film by director Robert Greenwald, which included as evidence a number of leaked internal memos from editorial Vice President John Moody to news personnel. These memos featured a number of 'lines' that news anchors and pundits were expected to take during discussion of the day's events. In one memo in April 2004, for example, to ensure that references to American soldiers in Iraq were positive, he instructed presenters to 'refer to the U.S. marines we see in the foreground as 'sharpshooters' not snipers, which carries a negative connotation'.[31] On the military assault on Fallujah, he wrote: 'Do not fall into the easy trap of mourning the loss of U.S. lives and asking why are we there? The U.S. is in Iraq to help a country brutalized for thirty years protect the gains made by Operation Iraqi Freedom and set it on the path to democracy.'[32]

Similar examples have been unearthed more recently by the liberal monitoring group Media Matters following the election of Barack Obama in 2008. It published an email sent by Fox News' Washington managing editor Bill Sammon at the height of the debate on Obama's proposed health care reforms in 2009, which directed Fox journalists to use the phrase 'government option' rather than 'public option' when describing the proposals, following a recommendation from a Republican pollster that the first option carried negative connotations that were more likely to deter voters.[33] Obama's election provoked some astonishing outbursts of vitriol from, in particular, Fox's ultra Conservative pundit Glenn Beck who called him a racist with 'a deep-seated hatred for white people'. Fox's relentlessly hostile rhetoric became a particular focus for debate following the shooting in Tucson, Arizona, in January 2011 when six people were killed by a lone gunman at an open meeting being held by the Democrat member of Congress, Gabrielle Giffords. Giffords herself survived despite being shot in the head at point-blank range in an assassination attempt that some commentators linked to splenetic right-wing shock-jocks in general, and the toxic influence of Fox News in particular. Writing on his *New Yorker* blog, George Packer described the desensitizing effect of such partisan rhetoric on mainstream political discourse:

For the past two years, many conservative leaders, activists, and media figures have made a habit of trying to delegitimize their political opponents. Not just arguing against their opponents, but doing everything possible to turn them into enemies of the country and cast them out beyond the pale … We've all grown so used to it over the past couple of years that it took the shock of an assassination attempt to show us the ugliness to which our politics has sunk.[34]

By using the catch-line 'fair and balanced' for an all-news channel on a medium that, traditionally, had been associated with an impartial approach to journalism, Fox News cleverly and successfully exploited a gap in the television market. But in the process, it breached all the tenets of conventional television journalism: overt partisanship instead of objectivity; angry denunciation instead of dispassionate reporting; humiliation of politically unwelcome guests instead of proper interrogation. In doing so, it significantly influenced other players with more serious intent. In the words of one observer, Fox 'has almost rewritten the rules of US television news coverage … with its penchant for presenting politics as a gladiatorial sport, all sound, fury and popular entertainment, in which fact and reasoned analysis are ditched in favour of outrage, anger and patriotic pride'.[35] Partly because it was so close to the Republican Party during the eight years of George W. Bush's presidency from 2000 to 2008, and partly because it mastered the art of a fast-paced presentational style that satisfied the entertainment imperatives of the television medium, Fox News was taken seriously by its viewers, its competitors and by the political classes. It has now established itself as the voice of right-wing America, but in truth its 'news' is almost stripped bare of professional journalism.

Costs and profitability

There was, and remains, another reason to take the Fox channel seriously, despite professional disdain for its techniques: its unquestionable success in both ratings and revenue. Its brashness appealed to viewers brought up on a Hollywood approach to television and its politics struck a nerve with large swathes of the United States in the so-called 'flyover' zone – instinctive conservatives who felt disenfranchised by much of the mainstream media. While in the United Kingdom it took the BBC – with its established brand name, authority and cross-channel promotion – eight years to overhaul Sky News in the ratings, in United States it took the unknown upstart Fox News just six years to overtake CNN. After five years of losses and a total investment of $900 million, it started to earn its keep around 2000–2001.[36] By 2009, its earnings had overtaken CNN with annual revenues of nearly $1.3 billion returning profits of nearly $640 million. Equivalent figures for CNN were annual revenues of just under $1.2 billion returning profits of $525 million, while even the relative minnow of the cable news trilogy, MSNBC, returned a healthy profit of $160 million on revenues of $357 million.[37]

The financial health of American 24-hour news channels – in stark contrast to the vast majority of such channels in other countries – is down to two factors: a population of around 115 million TV households with 290 million viewers (aged two or over); and the relatively high proportion of US homes, around 60 per cent, which are cabled and thus have access to pay-TV. News channels can therefore command two income streams, advertising and subscription, which allow some protection in difficult economic times when advertising revenue (as in 2008–9) goes into steep decline.[38]

As a result, the economic power of these news channels is enormous: according to the Project for Excellence in Journalism, their combined investment in television journalism was around $1.6 billion in 2010 – well over ten times the combined resources of the UK's news channels.[39] In Europe, the reliance of operators on advertising revenue – and the comparatively small audiences attracted to news channels – makes it virtually impossible to construct a workable business model for a commercially viable 24-hour news channel. According to Ofcom figures in 2008, news is the second most expensive genre of programming for specialist multichannel operators at just under £1,900 per hour – second only to sport at just over £7,000 per hour. In return, however, sport generated revenues of over £11,000 per hour compared to just £2,000 for news. This represented a 4.3 per cent return on investment, by far the lowest of all the specialist programme genres.[40]

This partly explains why in Europe and most other countries around the world, news channels are largely funded by the State or by generous benefactors – usually with very specific cultural or political objectives. One notable exception is India where the 130 million television households eclipses the United States and over 80 million of those were connected to cable or satellite by 2010. According to Daya Thussu, one of the leading international scholars on Indian media, the number of dedicated news channels had grown within ten years from one in 1998 to nearly 40 by 2008, of which most were profitable, benefiting from the multiplicity of languages, regions and cultures in India and from the 'popularity and diversity of debate in a complex political scene and the "argumentative" nature of Indians'.[41]

Dewesternizing news – the rise of Al Jazeera

Without doubt, the news channel that has made the most international impact – and has helped to crystallize some fundamental debates about westernized values embedded in most of the developed world's television journalism – is Al Jazeera. During the invasion of Afghanistan and subsequent Iraq War, it became the target of American vitriol as most observers in the West were encouraged to believe that any channel emanating from the Arab world (wrongly assumed to be a homogenous political entity) would be nothing more than a propaganda tool. In fact, the channel was established in 1996 in Doha by the Emir of Qatar – a tiny country with Iraq, Iran and Saudi Arabia amongst its neighbours – as a means of counteracting the power of the Saudis and establishing an independent identity and stature in a notoriously unstable part of the world.

With initial funding of $150 million from the Emir's personal wealth, Al Jazeera drew its professional ethos (and much of its staff) from a BBC World Service Arabic language channel that had been closed down. According to one history of the channel: 'There were no red lines that could not be crossed. Al Jazeera liked to compare itself to the BBC, funded indirectly by the state but free to say whatever it wanted.'[42] Though a somewhat idealized vision of the channel – it has never, for example, overtly criticized the Emir of Qatar – there is no question that it began with a journalistic approach that was neither State propaganda nor dominated by Western cultural perspectives.[43] It was a recipe that, ironically, ensured vilification both from Arab neighbours unused to journalistic scrutiny from within, and from Western countries unused to an agenda that was not framed by the military and policy perspectives of the West.

Al Jazeera first established itself in 1998 during Operation Desert Fox, a four-day US and UK bombing campaign of Iraqi targets, when it was the only international news operation on the ground. It was also instrumental in ensuring that Israeli missile-strikes on Gaza reached an international audience in the intifada of 2000. Following the 2001 terrorist attacks of 9/11, and the allied invasion of Afghanistan, the channel became a target of venomous attacks in both the United States and the United Kingdom when its unique access to pictures on the ground – including bombed hospitals and villages razed to the ground – drew accusations that it was acting as a propaganda mouthpiece for Osama bin Laden. Shortly afterwards, the Al Jazeera bureau in Kabul was flattened by an American bomb, which the Pentagon unconvincingly denied was a premeditated attack.

By the end of 2002, the world was schizophrenic about Al Jazeera because each competing interest saw it through its own cultural lens: 'It was popularly held in the Arab world that Al Jazeera was a pawn of the CIA, the American press regularly decried the station as a mouthpiece for terror, the Israelis complained about its alleged pro-Palestinian bias, while the Kuwaitis had shut Al Jazeera's bureau for supporting Saddam Hussein.'[44] This confusion was the product of three factors: a journalism that, because it aspired to fairness and seriousness, could not be dismissed as worthless propaganda; access to pictures in places such as Kabul and Gaza, where Western news organizations either chose not to or were unable to go; and the resources to mount a 24-hour news operation that could exploit the lightweight news technology of the twenty-first century (such as laptop editing of footage on the ground) as well as the new satellite and cable technologies of transmission. It did not take long for other countries to understand the significance of this confluence of technology and television's agenda-setting ability. Among the new channel initiatives in the lead-up to the Iraq war was Al Arabiya, launched in February 2003 with a $200 million start-up fund, based in Dubai and sponsored by a conglomerate of Saudi, Lebanese and Kuwaiti businessmen: rather more conservative regimes that had no intention of letting the tiny State of Qatar set the Arab agenda.

Once the bombing of Iraq started, these internal schisms diminished and unity about the illegitimacy of the war within the Arab channels mirrored its virtually unchallenged justification within the American press. Whilst reporters in the West referred unanimously to 'coalition forces', the Arab news channels soon followed Al Jazeera's uncompromising description of 'invasion forces'. Al Jazeera's coverage of the war not only showed the bombing of Baghdad – including graphic images of mutilated bodies – but the widespread protests around the Middle East that followed.

Hardline Western critics cast the channel as a pro-Arab propaganda machine, but in truth the fundamental change was that they no longer had television's agenda-setting field (and potential propaganda advantage) to themselves.[45] Nor did the simple British/American narrative – that this was the liberation of a long-suffering people from a tyrannical regime – go unchallenged. Both in terms of factual coverage on the ground, and the context within which the conflict was reported and explained, there was now a different approach to television journalism: one which aspired to traditional journalistic tenets of accuracy and fairness but emanated from a different cultural perspective. In the words of Hugh Miles, Al Jazeera 'had broken the hegemony of the Western networks and, for the first time in hundreds of years, reversed the flow of information, historically from West to East'.[46]

Moreover, it exposed traditionally closed and authoritarian societies in the East to the kind of democratic interrogation previously associated with the developed nations, and which – by general consensus – had been missing from much of the American coverage. The former BBC journalist Rageh Omaar, who covered the Iraq War for the BBC, defended his decision to join the English-language version of Al Jazeera by writing of the transformative moment when he realized that Arab nations were being exposed for the first time to a clash of opinion: 'I will never forget seeing Israeli politicians and spokesmen being interviewed, arguing Israel's case, some of them speaking Arabic as they did so. It was a shocking and breathtaking sight. The truth is that Al Jazeera has completely transformed the Arab world, which was accustomed to muzzled state broadcasters.'[47]

The English-language version, Al Jazeera English (AJE), was launched on 15 November 2006 featuring, in the first week and amidst much fanfare, the veteran journalist David Frost interviewing the then Prime Minister Tony Blair. It underlined its internationalized news agenda by announcing that it would 'follow the sun' during its 24-hour news cycle, with four broadcasting centres based in Doha, London, Washington, DC, and Kuala Lumpur. According to a spokeswoman, it was available by 2009 to 130 million homes in over 100 countries.[48] Audience figures, however, are less easy to come by. While it is now unquestionably one of the 'big three' global English-language news channels along with BBC World and CNN International, its global impact has been constrained partly by the long-standing reluctance of American cable networks to offer distribution deals and partly by its determination not to go down the route of committed, propaganda journalism. A number of staff defections from AJE in March 2008 were attributed, amongst other things, to a sense that the channel 'does not have the swash-buckling reputation of its Arabic sister [Al Jazeera Arabic] … It is more like a sensible, good, reliable, slightly impersonal channel running on a mountain of liquid gas dollars.'[49] Both this somewhat unflattering description and the difficulty in breaking into the US market might be transformed by the astonishing scenes in Egypt in early 2011, when a huge popular uprising succeeded in dislodging President Mubarak. Its outstanding wall-to-wall coverage in an area notoriously fraught with tension and with huge implications for both democracy and diplomacy in the Middle East made Al Jazeera compulsory viewing for many world leaders including, it was reported, the US President Barack Obama and Secretary of State Hillary Clinton. The Egyptian crisis was widely reported to be Al Jazeera's 'CNN moment', giving it the worldwide must-watch momentum which the first Gulf War afforded CNN.[50]

The 24-hour TV news club expands

Al Jazeera's pioneering approach to television journalism rooted in a different cultural perspective (and thereby internationalising the news agenda) has spawned a number of initiatives from other countries equally keen to exploit the cheaper technologies, wider reach and cultural mission of 24-hour news channels. Russia Today (also known as RT), started its State-funded English language operation in December 2005 with an annual budget of $60 million and 100 journalists. The *Washington Post* was not alone in interpreting RT as part of an international charm offensive designed to propagate a post-Soviet, cuddlier image of the host nation:

'At first glance it looks a lot like CNN, but it can be a breathless cheerleader for the Kremlin'.[51]

A year later, in December 2006, it was France's turn to pump money into a 24-hour English-speaking news service: a joint venture between the State-owned France Televisions and the commercial broadcaster TF1, with 270 journalists and an annual budget of £60 million. France 24 (pronounced *vingt-quatre*, even in the English version) has an avowed purpose of covering international news from a French perspective, which its Chief Executive Alain de Pouzilhac defined in terms of diversity, culture and debate. When told by Richard Sambrook, Director of BBC Global News, that the BBC never set out to portray a British view but was 'objective', de Pouzilhac's response was revealing and characteristically Gallic: 'Bullshit. Nobody's objective. In international news you're linked with your religion, with your nation, with your education, with whether you are rich or poor. That means when you are developing an international news channel, you have to be honest, you have to be impartial, you have to be independent, but no one is objective.'[52]

A similar approach was outlined when Iran added its own English-language voice to the proliferating mix. Press TV was launched in July 2007 and described by its Vice President Mohammad Sarafraz as offering an 'unbiased' point of view to distinguish it from Western channels on the one hand and Al Jazeera, which 'had supported the Taliban and the regime of Saddam Hussein' on the other.[53]

It is tempting to attempt some kind of taxonomy of news channels in order to impose an element of analytical order on the cacophony of different journalistic voices now available through cable and satellite television. In practice, given the variety of economic, political, cultural, institutional and professional provenances, such analytical neatness is impossible. In pure economic terms, for example, Sky News is comparable to Al Jazeera: both are reliant on advertising models of funding, both are consistently failing to generate enough revenue to sustain a profitable operation, and both are therefore entirely dependent on the continuing goodwill of individual benefactors. Rupert Murdoch may not enjoy comparison with the Emir of Qatar, but their respective channels only survive on their patrons' generosity.

Politically, however, each channel serves a different purpose for their sponsor. Culturally, they have wholly different – sometimes polarized – worldviews, not only on self-evident areas of controversy such as the Middle East but on news agendas, approaches to stories, locations of foreign bureaux and definitions of impartiality. De Pouzilhac's blunt response to Sambrook was essentially correct in that, even allowing for internationalized conventions of journalism ethics (itself a problematic assumption), the journalism of every news channel will ultimately be the bastard product of a particular nation's culture, history, geography, religion and politics.

Thus, Fox News is not just a creature of Rupert Murdoch's political ideology: it is a (very profitable) creature of the United State's innate conservatism, Hollywood tradition, religious conformity, large population and high discretionary expenditure on home entertainment.

The 24-hour problem – 'don't just do something, sit there'

In journalistic terms, whatever their cultural origins or economic orientations, all the 24-hour channels share the same fundamental dilemma: on limited budgets and commanding small audiences amongst a burgeoning number of different channels, how to attract an acceptable number of viewers while still delivering journalism of reasonable quality. It is almost inevitable that, under budgetary and time pressures, the quality of the journalism will suffer. In addition, such channels tend to be driven much more by the journalistic imperative of speed and 'liveness' than by the equally valid – but less appealing – imperative of investigation and analytical rigour. The dramatic artifice so brilliantly captured by 'Broken News' is an integral part of the 24-hour news narrative and, combined with the lack of resources that necessarily inhibits large-scale investment in journalism, results in journalists spending more time talking to camera than in the field gathering stories. It is perhaps unsurprising that newsrooms coined the pejorative term 'dish monkeys' to describe those on-screen figures who are semi-permanently tethered to their portable satellite dishes.

This was the point made by Martin Bell, formerly one of the BBC's most senior foreign correspondents, following the capture of Saddam Hussein in December 2003 and the breathless live reporting of the 24-hour news channels. He reflected on the partial and inauthentic versions of news that these channels conveyed: 'They offer roof-top television [which] consists of correspondents perched on the roofs of hotels and television stations, exchanging guesswork with other correspondents on other roofs, about the crisis of the moment.'[54] Similar concerns have been expressed by other professionals on the 24-hour conveyor-belt who believe that the length of on-screen time is inversely correlated to the quality of their journalism. By being constantly in demand for live two-ways with their studio, they argue, they do not have the time to fulfil the essentials of good journalism: talking to contacts, attending relevant meetings or court hearings or parliaments, collecting information, familiarizing themselves with the local customs, local people and local environments – and therefore becoming better able not just to report relevant facts but accurately to convey ambiance and attitudes. Time, ironically, is an unaffordable luxury for the 24-hour news channel.

Thus, the most corrosive characteristic for some of these channels – in particular, those driven by commercial imperatives rather than tasked with conveying a cultural perspective – is the emphasis on speed. In trying to capture the audience's imagination and sustained attention, the 'breaking news' tagline is a vital weapon in the news channel's armoury, used with an increasingly cavalier attention to accuracy and detail. As Martin Bell pointed out, these are the channels to which we turn at the very moment that they are at their least reliable: 'In times of crisis, of war and terrorism, the rolling-news channels have special responsibilities as the primary source of news for millions of people. They are defined by F-words. They aim to be first and fastest with the news. Their nature, too often, is to be feverish, frenzied, frantic, frail, false and fallible.'[55] In their book on the 24-hour news cycle and what they call 'the menace of media speed', the vastly experienced American journalists Howard Rosenberg and Charles Feldman worry in particular about the inevitable impact on responsible journalism of a fast-moving culture which demands instant response, speculation, comment or interpretation at the expense of proper reflection. They suggest that the new mantra for those caught up in the 24-hour news whirlwind should be 'Don't just do something, sit there'.[56]

Conclusion

In an ideal world, a combination of cheaper, lightweight news technology and new opportunities for distribution and reception of niche television channels might have prompted a revitalized form of television journalism, covering more places with more range, depth and professional insight than ever before. In truth, much of the 24-hour news offering reverts to television's baser characteristics: more drama, glamour, personality and opinion, at the expense of analysis, context and serious reflection. It is certainly true that the English-speaking channels originating from such places as Qatar, Moscow and Paris have expanded the range of cultural perspectives and encouraged a less exclusively Westernized approach to news-agenda priorities. But the drive for audiences and lack of resources have also brought to the screens more contrived drama, more manufactured controversy and more opinionated commentary. Moreover, the proliferation of news channels has led directly to claims that the only way truly to liberate television journalism from the confines of the medium is to encourage a more explicitly biased and opinionated approach – in other words, to remove the traditional restrictions around impartiality that still govern the norms of most European television cultures. This is the argument I address in the penultimate chapter.

11 Television Journalism and Impartiality

A part from the problem of speed, this relatively new panoply of journalistic approaches on 24-hour channels – from the subtle Gallic perspective of France 24 to the blatant opinionizing of Fox News – poses interesting dilemmas for a regulatory regime in the United Kingdom, which still insists (as with most European countries) on impartiality. The UK's statutory framework has been almost unchanged since the BBC's original mission was first imposed by law on commercial television in 1954.[1] Its most recent incarnation, in the 2003 Communications Act, requires that 'news included in television and radio services is presented with due impartiality' and also requires that due impartiality be applied throughout television and radio to 'matters of political or industrial controversy' and to 'matters relating to current public policy'.[2] The BBC is subject to a different regulatory mechanism through its Charter and Agreement but the requirements are almost identical.

Throughout the twentieth century, then, there was an unchallenged expectation that television and radio programmes – once they were allowed to tackle contemporary political affairs – would be subject to a very different journalistic regime from the printed press. Overt expressions of opinion were outlawed and this journalistic imposition – with its roots both in spectrum scarcity and the perceived power of the medium – was internalized by two generations of broadcast journalists. As the new century and new technology introduced new television cultures into the UK, it was inevitable that the conventional wisdom would be challenged by the influx of news channels with different global perspectives. It was perhaps equally inevitable that the first complaint about a breach of impartiality rules should be levelled against the Fox News Channel.

Fox News was available in the United Kingdom via the BSkyB satellite platform and was therefore licensed – like all commercial television stations received in the UK – by the Independent Television Commission. As a licensed channel, it was obliged to abide by the laws on impartiality as set down in statute and interpreted by the ITC's editorial code. In June 2003, in one of its final judgements before being folded into Ofcom, the ITC gave its verdict on the complaints against Fox News:

it found that the channel had not breached impartiality rules on the basis that the channel's cultural origins were elsewhere, that its audiences were tiny and that the phrase 'due impartiality' allowed for a flexible interpretation in such cases. It was a pragmatic decision, but formed part of a more significant intellectual shift amongst elites and policymakers who started to question whether such rules were relevant, enforceable or, indeed, potentially damaging for democratic pluralism.

Questioning the impartiality regime: news and political engagement[3]

Even before its verdict on Fox News, the ITC itself introduced a more critical approach to impartiality in a study of television news commissioned from academics at Cardiff University in 2002. Although a comprehensive examination of consumption, content and policy, the study was explicitly contextualized in terms of 'a perceived crisis in journalism ... which is blamed for the decline in levels of political engagement and voter participation in advanced democracies'.[4] Its rationale for questioning impartiality therefore rested on anxiety over what was seen as a crisis in democratic engagement where particular demographic groups – in particular, ethnic minorities and young people – were deserting political news and eschewing political participation. The evidence for this 'crisis' was problematic, relying on a narrow definition of political engagement; but much more dubious was the arbitrary link between disengagement and a journalistic culture of impartiality in broadcasting. The authors not only made this unsupported correlation, but then linked it explicitly to a policy recommendation:

> There is among Britain's ethnic minorities and indeed other groups, such as the young, a sense that mainstream broadcast news does not represent them or their interests well, fairly or with insight. It may be that a more opinionated style of broadcast news, originated from well outside the UK broadcasting mainstream, is helpful in the overall news mix ... The time has come when a range of experimentation should be encouraged.[5]

Criticism of this intellectual confusion did not prevent Ofcom from revisiting the same arguments five years later in a follow-up to the ITC's study. Strangely, despite lacking any empirical evidence, it again posited a causal link between declining interest in news, disengagement with politics and the impartiality regime in television journalism. A chapter headed 'Disengagement, trust and impartiality' was devoted to 'the public policy questions arising from increased disengagement from news; and whether due impartiality is still relevant as a core value in television news' – thereby connecting two entirely separate issues.[6] Despite this fairly cavalier approach to the basic tenets of social science enquiry, the regulator felt justified in raising two policy-related questions about the continuing relevance of applying an impartiality regime to all broadcasters: 'For channels other than the main PSBs, is impartiality still important, or is it a barrier to diversity in an era with a wide range of services available to viewers? Subject to changes in legislation, should other channels be allowed to offer partial news in the same way that newspapers and some websites do at present?'[7]

In theory, these might be legitimate questions if there was indeed evidence of widespread disillusionment with the political process *and* if such disillusionment could be directly linked to television's requirement for balance. It might even be argued that democracy itself could be enhanced by the removal of such rules. In practice, there is little empirical evidence to justify such conclusions. Rising membership in campaigning, political and civil society groups suggests that informal engagement in the political process is healthy and dynamic, even if formal political parties may be suffering from declining memberships. As one independent report has concluded, it is undue emphasis on 'highly visible formal democratic institutions of elections and political parties' that has contributed to a myth of widespread political apathy.[8]

Moreover, there is no evidence at all that a highly partisan and committed media will foster greater political engagement. As we have seen, the United States' impartiality restrictions were lifted in the mid 1980s, and yet concerns about the health of participatory democracy there have scarcely abated. In the absence of any clear indication to the contrary, it is difficult to find any reliable proof that the removal of impartiality rules will make the slightest difference to citizen involvement in the political sphere. By contrast, as I argue below, there is a very good case that a continuing commitment to impartiality within the television medium makes a significant and still highly relevant contribution to democracy and public life.

Questioning the impartiality regime: diversity and relevance

While policymakers sought to establish a highly tenuous connection between impartiality and political disengagement, a few senior journalists began to raise objections on editorial grounds. Television agendas, they argued, had become almost indistinguishable, with a homogeneity of issues, approaches and reportage that suffocated any potential for editorial diversity. Chris Shaw, then Head of News and Current Affairs at Channel 5, expressed his frustration in 2002: 'What annoys me is how same-ish all this news is. We're all covering the same stories in pretty much the same way.'[9] His concern was echoed the following year by Roger Mosey, then head of BBC television news, who argued that beyond clearly designated services with an obligation for truth and impartiality, 'the rest should have the freedom to take any view within the law of the land … [Fox News Channel] is feisty, provocative and engaging: a stone chucked into the pool of the broadcasting consensus.'[10] Other journalism professionals worry about the uniform narrative forms of television news and an apparent lack of creative ambition in presentation and editorial approach.

As we saw in Chapter 7, it is certainly true that television bulletins tend to show little variation: some deviations in running orders, perhaps some different footage, but usually covering a broad similarity of issues. There are good cultural and structural reasons for such homogeneity rooted, as we have seen, in the nature of the medium as well as in professional and audience expectations of what constitutes newsworthiness. To believe that, if broadcasters were relieved of their obligation to provide balance, editorial agendas would suddenly be transformed and new creative talents would be liberated is simply absurd. It is anyway contradicted by 20 years of evidence from the United States where, as we have seen, market imperatives have ensured an even more marked homogeneity of output than in the United Kingdom. And it is further contradicted by broadcast news, which adheres to tenets of impartiality but which emanates from different cultural perspectives or is specifically designed to reach particular demographic groups. Al Jazeera does not require a licence to be partisan in order to prioritize a different set of economic, political or cultural issues that usually follow a rather different editorial agenda to Western-based broadcast news. Similarly, the news output from BBC3 – aimed at young people – or from the BBC's Asian Network radio station deliberately pursues a news agenda that fits its audience profile without compromising its institutional or statutory commitment to impartial reporting.

In fact, it is at least arguable that British television of the last 25–30 years can boast a number of variations in form and content across different channels and different bulletins. We have seen how the main broadcasters have deliberately shifted the editorial agendas of their early and late evening bulletins to suit the changing demographics, while Channel 4 has provided more serious, analytical depth and Channel 5 has offered a more dynamic and younger approach. These variations have been enabled rather than encumbered by a regulatory framework that mandates both space and investment for television news, and is scarcely going to be invigorated by an opinionated free-for-all stripped of traditional editorial values of accuracy and fairness.

A related argument links the routinization and lack of diversity in news agendas to a sense of alienation from mainstream news amongst certain audience groups, in particular the young and ethnic minorities. Ofcom's qualitative research amongst

Asian, Afro-Caribbean and Muslim groups in 2007 suggested that many found television news unengaging and unfulfilling, with little relevance to their own lives. There are shades here of the dominant framework thesis that characterized critical approaches to television news in the 1970s and 1980s and what Golding and Elliott called 'the development of news as a service to elite groups'.[11] Critiques of television news grounded in theories of hegemony and the 'unconscious' bias inherent in the organizational structures of news have become less popular over the last 20 years, but anyway bear little relationship to contemporary arguments about whether and why particular population groups may feel marginalized by today's news agendas. These arguments are more narrowly focused on a vague conviction – unsupported by any empirical evidence – that a more partisan approach would somehow reconnect minority groups to television journalism. In fact, it is more likely that those groups that feel inadequately served by television will take refuge in other forms of online or social media.

Questioning the impartiality regime: convergence and new technologies

Probably the most commonly held objection to sustaining impartiality – and the most difficult to rebut – is centred on enforceability. The problem is both the sheer number of television channels now available, and the converging of distribution platforms that might eventually render the notion of a television 'channel' redundant. It was the proliferation of channels that might require monitoring which most concerned Ofcom's senior executive in charge of regulating content in 2007: 'With some 750 or so channels broadcasting under an Ofcom licence, the regulator's ability to monitor output, even if it wished to, would be severely limited. Furthermore, that output includes a large number of channels ... targeting either non-UK audiences or specific linguistic and ethnic communities within the UK.'[12]

As a reason for abandoning impartiality altogether, this argument is unsustainable. In 1999 Ofcom's predecessor, the ITC, was content to revoke the licence of Med TV, a channel aimed at Kurdish viewers, for persistent breaches of its impartiality code following complaints from viewers who were unsympathetic to the Kurdish cause. Since Ofcom responds to complaints on a post-hoc basis rather than relying on 24-hour monitoring, there is no technological barrier to scrutinizing complaints that relate to impartiality in a similar way.

There is no question that web-based transmission mechanisms will pose a more formidable challenge, as unrestricted online sites become more easily receivable through the television. In theory, the notion of the 'licensing' of television channels could eventually become redundant, and therefore any regulatory oversight beyond breaches of the criminal law could become unworkable. As I argue in the Conclusion, however, television is and will remain different from the computer for many years, in terms of its audience reach, impact and visibility. As long as television journalism can be properly distinguished from web-based journalism, there is no reason why medium-specific codes cannot continue to be applied. Nor is there any reason why Ofcom could not continue to apply the flexibility of interpretation that its Broadcasting Code allows in adjudicating on complaints about 'due' impartiality: '"Due" means adequate or appropriate to the subject and nature of the programme … The approach to due impartiality may vary according to the nature of the subject, the type of programme and channel, the likely expectation of the audience as to content, and the extent to which the content and approach is signalled to the audience.'[13]

It is this flexibility that continues to allow even Fox News to be broadcast in the United Kingdom, although it certainly operates at the very limit of the code's discretion. An interesting initiative that could resolve this continuing ambiguity – and cater for a 'converged' future – has been proposed by the distinguished former BBC journalist Phil Harding, involving a two-tier system of carefully labelled 'News' and 'Comment' channels, with the former having access to regulatory benefits such as priority on electronic programme guides.[14] Should we reach a point where television and online become genuinely indistinguishable, this would be an imaginative and workable compromise; for the moment, however, there is no technological urgency in compromising the long-standing and well-recognized rules of engagement.

Arguments for retaining impartiality rules

While arguments against the retention of impartiality rules are unconvincing, there are at least three good reasons for retaining them. First, they are an important stimulus for investment in the expensive process of newsgathering rather than relying on the much cheaper alternative of talking heads. As one very experienced news editor and BBC Trustee put it:

> In broadcasting, more than any other form of journalism, comment is so much cheaper than first-hand reporting that a relaxation of the impartiality rules could encourage the emergence of a new and unwelcome form of television news consisting of partisan opinion and agency pictures. Far from encouraging diversity, the risk is that cost-cutting will lead to a greater uniformity of content.[15]

In other words, these rules can serve as a safeguard against a growing tendency within all journalism to cut costs (and corners) by relying on PR handouts, second-hand footage and declamatory columnists who barely leave their computers. Almost certainly, a television environment in which there were no restrictions on opinionated journalism would discourage the time-consuming effort involved in uncovering and checking stories, while providing more opportunities for the voluble and the prejudiced to vent their opinions and manufacture confrontation.

Second, viewers trust television and believe impartiality is an integral part of its journalistic role. In a world where the public is increasingly sceptical of journalists, television still stands out as a beacon of dependability. In the UK, ever since the BBC's self-imposed mission was embedded by law into the commercial sector, television has been understood to be different and that sense of confidence in the essential truthfulness of the medium has survived well into the twenty-first century. Ofcom research in 2009 found that 72 per cent of the public cited television as the source that they 'trust the most to present fair and unbiased news coverage' of world events, while 69 per cent gave the same answer for national events. Moreover, 93 per cent of the public believed it was important that television news reporting was impartial, a huge vote of confidence in a regime which applies to the medium rather than individual channels.[16] To voluntarily surrender it for what would be – despite protestations to the contrary – little more than commercial pragmatism would inevitably undermine that confidence and run counter to the wishes of the vast majority.

Third, there is a mistaken assumption that liberation from the straitjacket of impartiality would somehow allow 'a thousand flowers to bloom', giving voice to a panoply of competing views and opinions on contentious issues. This is an idealized vision of libertarian consumer choice theory that bears little relationship to the reality of where media power really lies. In truth, there would be little to stop a few individuals seeking power and influence by bankrolling their own television stations in order to propagate their own world vision. In her 2002 Reith Lectures, the philosopher and academic Onora O'Neill underlined the point in reference to John Stuart Mill and the role of the press in facilitating a clash of ideas:

Like Mill we may be passionate about individual freedom of expression, and so about the freedom of the press to represent individuals' opinions and views. But freedom of expression is for individuals, not for institutions. We have good reasons for allowing individuals to express opinions even if they are invented, false, silly, irrelevant or plain crazy, but not for allowing powerful institutions to do so. Yet we are perilously close to a world in which media conglomerates act as if they too had unrestricted rights of free expression.[17]

A similar warning about the overweening power of well-funded voices to distort the range of available opinions came from Lord David Puttnam, who in 2003 chaired an all-party review of the Broadcasting Bill before it became enacted. In response to those then seeking relaxation of the regulatory regime, he wrote: 'The idea that loosening regulation would enhance diversity is … a fool's bargain. In practice, it's likely that one very well-funded partisan voice, probably a deviant version of Sky News, would drown out most of the others.'[18] This certainly represented a majority view in Parliament as well as amongst the public – a unity of purpose between the political classes and the electorate that has so far ensured that impartiality rules remain intact. It is the best response to those who continue to insist that regulatory intervention by the State distorts the sensitivity of the free market to the unrefracted wishes of news 'consumers'. Apart from being a wholly unworkable application of liberal economic theory to broadcasting, such an approach ignores the unquantifiable damage that might be inflicted on civic life by transforming a news medium that commands widespread trust into one that privileges the opinionated commentary of those who can afford to pay.

Impartiality and the BBC

In contrast to the growing debate about impartiality on commercial television, there is no debate about whether the BBC should continue to be subject to impartiality requirements. Given a reputation forged over 80 years of broadcasting history, and given its status as an independent and publicly funded institution, the BBC's commitment to impartial journalism is axiomatic. We have seen how reporting of current affairs was first excluded altogether and then heavily circumscribed before gradually evolving into a self-imposed journalistic framework that carefully mirrored the bipolar nature of Westminster politics. With post-war Parliaments in Britain dominated by the Labour and Conservative parties, the institutional assumption was that equal time given to each party on matters of policy would satisfy in most people's minds the BBC's impartiality requirements.

There were, of course, periodic and predictable spats with individual politicians and prime ministers, punctuated by more wide-ranging debates with the minor political parties such as the Liberals, the Ulster Unionists and the nascent Social Democratic Party in the 1980s. There was also a serious intellectual debate within the academy about both the practical and theoretical limits of a 'value-free' approach to news, a recognition that news was necessarily a social and professional construct, and a widespread belief that the BBC's particular construction was part of an established social order. According to one radio reporter interviewed at the time for Philip Schlesinger's seminal study, 'The Corporation's view is middle-class liberalism. Strikes, Communists, Black Power, Fascists are all bad. Social Democrats and Tories are good.'[19] This notion of the BBC sustaining an essentially conservative consensus was also a key theme of the Glasgow Media Group studies of the 1970s. Notwithstanding those political and theoretical debates, the principle of a BBC dedicated to an editorial code which *aspired* to impartiality as a journalistic ideal was never seriously questioned. By the turn of the century, however, the *practical* implications of that aspiration were becoming recognized as increasingly difficult.

It was this practical issue of impartiality in a changing world (and, by implication, a world whose priorities had been transformed by the terrorist attacks of 9/11 and its aftermath) that was broached by the then BBC Chairman Michael Grade in May 2005:

> Social attitudes have changed. Many new groups have entered British society, bringing with them their own cultures, and religions, and value systems – all of them legitimate expressions of belief. Now, when legitimate value systems compete, the BBC must act impartially. That applies to areas of cultural controversy, just as much as to the traditional areas of political and industrial debate as defined in the impartiality regulations.[20]

Grade's speech presaged a new period of serious examination by the BBC into both specific areas of its coverage and to more general definitional arguments which addressed issues of relevance and audience engagement in a more complex, fragmented and multicultural world. It was developed the following year by the BBC's Head of News, Peter Horrocks, who emphasized the need to keep the BBC editorially attuned to the distinctive tastes of its different audiences and to 'look again at what we mean by impartiality and transform editorially to re-find our lost audiences'. He described the new purpose of BBC journalism as: 'to provide the widest range of information and views … so that the bulk of the population sees its own perspective reflected honestly and regularly. We must also provide the opportunity for people to regularly come across alternative information and perspectives that provide a wider viewpoint.'[21]

Impartiality was therefore being explicitly reworked to accommodate those very concerns about wider perspectives and diversity of opinion that so concerned some of its critics. In particular, Horrocks emphasized the importance of widening the range of views being transmitted, even including those which many might find 'abhorrent'. He labelled this a 'radical impartiality' in which interviews with members of the Taliban and the far-right British National Party would sit alongside those speaking out against Europe or against immigration. This wider embrace would, in his view, restore some lost credibility amongst those who felt that their views had been neither represented nor respected. It would not fall victim to 'commercial' approaches to television journalism that were concerned solely with maximizing audiences (and particularly audiences with high disposable income). But it would appeal to broader constituencies by acknowledging that there was no longer a shared vision of the world. This newly articulated reinterpretation of a long-standing set of practices was then subjected to a much more detailed interrogation, as BBC Governors and Management jointly commissioned a study to examine the implications for the BBC of the cultural and technological changes articulated by Grade. Its aim was to deliver 'a set of principles underlying impartiality in the twenty-first century' and their implications for the BBC.[22]

From Seesaw to Wagon Wheel

This groundbreaking report was inherited by the new BBC Trust when it succeeded the BBC Governors in January 2007. It was preceded by a seminar called 'Impartiality: Fact or Fiction?' in September 2006, attended by most of the BBC's senior editorial figures as well as a number of external observers. The report's title, *From Seesaw to Wagon Wheel*, was designed to convey the new complexities of the contemporary political world: where once it was conceived as a simple bipolar division of political opinion, 'in today's multi-polar Britain, with its range of cultures, beliefs and identities, impartiality involves many more than two sides to an argument'.[23] It argued that the old two-dimensional seesaw should be replaced by the wagon wheel borrowed from television's diagrammatic coverage of a batsman's innings in cricket, 'where the wheel is not circular and has a shifting centre with spokes that go in all directions'.

This somewhat clumsy symbolism was arguably a belated recognition of those arguments from the 1970s and 1980s, outlined above, that significant voices – and in particular those detached from the mainstream for ethnic, economic, regional or political reasons – had been systematically marginalized in television's representation of reality. It was, however, a welcome articulation of aspirational principle and practice within an institution dedicated to the pursuit of rigorous, accurate and independent journalism. At the heart of the report were 12 'guiding principles' designed to complement the internal Editorial Guidelines on impartiality:

1   Impartiality should be a 'source of pride' rather than a legal or institutional requirement. It had been conceived and developed culturally rather than legalistically, and must remain an evolutionary process to meet the needs of a more diverse society. Particularly in a world where opinions and ideas are

colliding in a maelstrom of online opportunities, impartiality should be valued as an immutable element of the core BBC identity.

2 The audience should be an integral part of determining impartiality, and the growth of user-generated content should be welcomed as an additional resource (subject to checks on authenticity). Qualitative research suggested that free debate, unmoderated by the BBC, was welcomed by audiences as contributing to the ideal of impartiality.

3 Impartiality should be applied beyond political and industrial controversy to embrace a broader range of opinions, appreciating that contemporary political activity and expression had moved outside the confines of Parliament and Westminster. In particular, it should be aware of the extra-parliamentary voices that may not have formal institutional representation but should still be acknowledged and reported: 'Parliament can no longer expect to define the parameters of national debate.'

4 Reporting from the centre ground is 'often the wrong place to be' and impartiality can be breached by omission. There should be space for rational or honest opinion, however contentious or out of the mainstream. For example, 'a historian who denies or downplays the Holocaust may cause distress to many ... but Holocaust-denial is not a crime in Britain, and it is legitimate every now and then to challenge a maverick in person'. Similarly, the notion of man-made climate change still has 'intelligent and articulate opponents' who deserve to be heard even if they are not granted equal time.

5 There should be room for controversy, passion and polemic; impartiality need not be a recipe for bland or insipid programming, as long as authorship is clear and a balance is provided over time. On the other hand, the integrity of BBC journalism requires that its reporters do not compromise their own authority by voicing their own opinions.[24] Thus, the rule which forbids BBC staff journalists and presenters from writing columns which deal with political or industrial controversy 'should be applied with greater consistency'.

6 Impartiality applies beyond journalism to the whole spectrum of BBC output, including drama, comedy and entertainment. Plot lines of soap operas can be as imbued with one-sided meaning as the most partisan political coverage, and the BBC needed to stay alert to implicit bias. Even sport presents its own unique challenges of balancing the BBC's position as

national champion and cheerleader with an open mind on issues of whether, for example, the London Olympics represent a sensible investment.

7 Campaigns should be treated with particular care when they appear to be uncontroversial but may have a political subtext. This care must be balanced with the BBC's involvement with major national events that capture the imagination. The report quoted the 2005 humanitarian campaign Make Poverty History as an example of an event whose purpose, while apparently uncontroversial, in fact had 'contentious political goals' such as cancelling third world debt and doubling international aid.[25]

8 Individual journalistic dilemmas will always be hotly contested. There is no 'template of wisdom' but the BBC's journalistic experience is an invaluable resource. Potential editorial dilemmas debated at the September seminar, such as whether an interview offered by Osama bin Laden in a mountain village in Pakistan should be accepted, produced some fascinating divisions of opinion between cautious BBC editorial figures and their commercial counterparts. The instinct of any good journalist is to jump at the opportunity but the institutional position of the BBC renders such an instinctive reaction more problematic.

9 Programme-makers, editors and producers should constantly be challenging their own positions and guard against 'shared assumptions'. While dismissing the notion of any conspiracy theory, the report suggested there was 'wider support for the idea that some sort of liberal consensus existed' and that it might not be unexpected within a large organization to find programme-makers inhabiting 'a shared space, a comfort zone, which if unacknowledged may cause problems for impartiality'.

10 The BBC must examine its own 'institutional values' and be aware that its corporate behaviour may unconsciously convey a message to the audience which affects judgements of impartiality. There is an assumed knowledge of Christianity, for example, as being part of the cultural mainstream in the United Kingdom, or of democracy being appropriate to all continents and cultures. There are clear institutional guidelines within the BBC which support equal rights for women and gay people, but how might this affect programmes which address inequalities in other countries? The BBC needs to remain aware and self-critical of its own institutional (and essentially western, democratic) perspective.

11 Transparency is fundamental to the process, and any breaches of impartiality should be acknowledged openly and quickly, to secure audience confidence in the BBC decision-making process. Moreover, the BBC should be open about the nature of its own in-house debates and institutional soul-searching, to demonstrate that impartiality is a dynamic process rather than some pre-determined pillars of wisdom to be handed down to audiences.

12 It is incumbent on every individual from junior researcher to Director General to apply the principles of impartiality at every stage of the programme-making process, across platforms and from the earliest stage of idea creation. Thus, the BBC's Editorial Policy unit should not be viewed as an institutional censor, ready to pounce at any transgression of the golden rules, but rather an integral part of the creative process 'helping producers to achieve their goals by ensuring the content is editorially and ethically secure'.

On the face of it, this report stands as a welcome antidote to two opposed but commonly articulated theoretical arguments against impartiality: that either it is a futile ambition whose lack of achievability in the real world of implicitly subjective journalism means it is not worth the struggle; or that it is such a self-evident set of professional practices that it barely needs elaboration. By acknowledging the complexity of twenty-first century political and cultural life, and by recognizing the many voices which have arguably felt excluded from the cultural mainstream of BBC journalism, this report cements the BBC's position as holder of the impartiality flame as well as offering a self-referential template for any institution seeking to turn ideal-type theory into professional reality. On that level, it can be applauded as an important contribution to the debate not just on television journalism but on the conduct of serious, professional journalism more generally.

A hidden agenda?

There is, however, a less well-meaning and rather more old-fashioned subtext, which was grasped immediately – and wildly exaggerated – by press coverage of the report. While many of the heavyweight accusations of institutional bias levelled at the BBC during the 1970s had emanated from the left, an increasingly concerted effort had emerged since the 1980s and into the new century from the right (and in particular the right-wing press) to establish that the BBC has an ingrained leftwards or liberal bias. This refrain was embraced at the 2006 'Impartiality: Fact or Fiction?' seminar by two speakers with a right-of-centre perspective, Janet Daley of the

Daily Mail and Jeff Randall of the *Daily Telegraph*, representing newspapers with a long tradition of alleging deep-seated political bias within the BBC. Participants were treated to a few entertaining anecdotes as evidence of such bias without any properly adduced empirical evidence, and the effect was magnified by an unfortunate summing up that appeared to suggest that a 'consensus' had emerged that a liberal bias did indeed exist.[26]

When the *From Seesaw to Wagon Wheel* report was published some nine months later, many of these perspectives seemed to be embedded – subtly but unmistakeably – within its narrative. There were no fewer than 11 references to 'political correctness' and subtle implications that the BBC might be trying too hard to privilege ethnic minorities. The report quite properly raised the question of whether a true spectrum of opinions were being adequately represented, but gave as a specific example the UK Independence Party's policy of withdrawal from the EU. UKIP's support, said the report, took the BBC by surprise but there was no mention of the Green Party's similarly unheralded support at previous elections.

Moreover, two examples of ideas that had travelled from the outlandish to the mainstream – and therefore served as a warning that the prevailing consensus should always be properly interrogated – were monetarism and Euroscepticism, both policies generally associated with the right and supported by right-wing newspapers. In a section on contentious programmes, the report cited a BBC2 series, 'The Power of Nightmares', as a 'challenge to American foreign policy [which] had no effective counterblast', but dismissed an excellent documentary series which was precisely that because it was 'forensic rather than polemical'.[27] Both the Make Poverty History and Live 8 campaigns, which came in for a particularly close and critical examination, were causes embraced by the left.

Perhaps the clearest indication of an underlying agenda was the space given to some particularly vituperative comments about the BBC from the *Daily Mail* editor Paul Dacre. Invited to give the prestigious annual Hugh Cudlipp lecture a few months earlier Dacre had launched an extraordinary assault on the BBC, accusing it of imposing its own worldview and of being 'hostile to Britain's past and British values, America, Ulster Unionism, Euroscepticism, capitalism and big business, the countryside, Christianity, and family values. Conversely it is sympathetic to Labour, European federalism, the state and state spending, mass immigration, minority rights, multiculturalism, alternative lifestyles, abortion and progressiveness in the education and the justice systems.'[28]

This outburst was a familiar, if slightly manic, refrain from someone representing traditional right-of-centre values and renowned as a long-term scourge of the BBC. Having quoted Dacre, the report went on to quote contributions to the September debate as evidence of 'wider support for the idea that some sort of liberal consensus existed', with passing mentions for the failure to empathize with or give airtime to supporters of the Democratic Unionist Party in Northern Ireland, capital punishment and the anti-abortion movement. It was therefore hardly surprising that the report was gleefully seized upon by press commentators whose animus towards the BBC was fuelled (as with Dacre) by a deep-rooted ideological hostility.[29] In the end, the report itself and the somewhat hysterical press coverage prompted an ironic conclusion: that a well-intentioned study designed to demonstrate the multidimensional nature of modern political culture was itself so implicitly one-sided as to demonstrate the complete antithesis: that in many areas of political life, the bipolar left-right axis is still highly pertinent.

Whatever the complexity of twenty-first century postmodern, post-communist, post-9/11 political and cultural debates, those cleaving to a right-of-centre perspective will continue – even in the absence of empirical evidence – to be convinced that the BBC is institutionally opposed to their worldview. A similar conviction has for many years permeated American debates, as organized religious and conservative groups made concerted efforts to shift the media balance of opinion to the right by repeating the mantra of a persistent 'liberal' bias in the mainstream media. As former *Independent on Sunday* and *New Statesman* editor Peter Wilby put it, three months after *Wagon Wheel* was published, 'the British right hopes to emulate the success of the US right in convincing the public that the main organs of news and opinion are gripped by a leftwing conspiracy ... [their aim] is to alter the definition of the "middle ground" in British life, moving it to the right of any government of the past 30 years'.[30]

Conclusion

Perhaps the main achievement of the BBC's report was to move beyond definitions of impartiality to the basic issue of professional and institutional values and notions of intent: what are the prime purposes of the programme editors, on-screen journalists, off-screen producers and researchers who are responsible for creating today's television journalism? What are the normative expectations of the institutions for which they work? If their prime purpose is to maximize ratings, pursue a single-minded ideological vision, create publicity or elevate an on-screen personality, then journalistic rigour will most likely be compromised or sacrificed entirely.

Perhaps the fundamental issue might be characterized less as impartiality than as 'integrity': a state of mind which requires decision-makers to interrogate themselves about their purpose. Writing about the myriad pressures on television journalists even before the twenty-first century, former BBC journalist Martin Bell wrote:

It does no harm for all journalists … to ask ourselves a simple question: What do we believe in? If it is only making money, then we are clearly in the wrong business because money can deflect, if not corrupt, us. But if we have standards and values and principles, then we should stand by them because they are what we believe in and what sustains us. There is actually a word for it. The word is *integrity*.[31]

This is, perhaps, the most helpful way in which both to interpret the BBC Trust's report and to understand the vital importance of maintaining statutory safeguards on impartiality. While the report itself may have been hijacked by those seeking to wrench the political debate towards their own perception of the 'centre ground', its longer term impact can be seen as a sophisticated instrument for institutionalizing integrity not only in the BBC but in the practice of all television journalism. Bell argued that, 'Most TV news in Britain is responsible and honest and, within the limits of the medium, truthful,' while wary of the financial and self-aggrandisement pressures that were driving it in the opposite direction. Those pressures have intensified markedly since he wrote, and the statutory requirement to maintain balance provides the kind of professional bulwark for all practitioners of television journalism which the BBC requires institutionally in its own. Impartiality is therefore a powerful and effective safeguard of the public interest for a medium which still commands – even in the digital era of fragmented audiences – easily the highest levels of credibility in the provision of local, national and international news.

Conclusions: What is Television? What is Journalism? And Why does it Matter?

Given some of the hype about convergence, the rise of new technologies, the role of social media and the 'new' journalism of user generated content (UGC or 'citizen journalism'), a book on television journalism might for some be analogous to a book about the Middle Ages: a mildly interesting historical diversion, but with little relevance or resonance for the second decade of the twenty-first century. There are two strands to this argument, and it is important to disentangle them in order to understand the empirical reality: that television journalism will have an enduring significance in Britain, in the United States and in most countries around the world.

Television's future

We have seen throughout this book how television in the UK (and, by extension, in most other developed countries with a strong tradition of Public Service Broadcasting) has evolved gradually from monopoly through a restricted number of channels to the panoply of cable, satellite and online channels that exist today. Audiences have become fragmented, publicly funded broadcasting is under political threat, and commercial channel revenues are endangered both by the explosion of channels and the rise of new online advertising opportunities. And now it is being widely predicted that the whole future of traditional, linear, real-time television itself is being threatened by new technologies that allow online, mobile, timeshift, catch-up and on-demand consumption. A widespread and ill-informed assumption is growing that television is a legacy medium in terminal decline and, perhaps like the printed press, will shortly be confined to the technological dustbin.

If true, this could have particularly serious consequences for time-sensitive programmes that do not lend themselves to timeshifting or catch-up, in particular news and current affairs journalism. So far, however, evidence from the UK suggests that, whatever may be technologically feasible, real-life behaviour has changed surprisingly little: rather than being displaced by online activities, total TV viewing is actually rising, and the vast majority of that viewing time is the traditional live and linear model of consumption.

Official industry figures show that average daily viewing in Britain, which had hovered around 3 hours 45 minutes for most of the 2000s, rose to just over 4 hours in 2010.[1] Moreover, according to recent data for 2011, even in those 'converged' homes with a full range of cable and satellite channels as well as recording hard drives and broadband access, live TV viewing on television sets still accounts for 80 per cent of viewing time. Of the remainder, about 10 per cent is timeshifted viewing via PVRs (personal video recorders) and a further 8–9 per cent is catch-up TV which is available on platforms such as Sky and Virgin. Only 1–2 per cent of television viewing is true video on demand, where material is being watched live or as downloads on a computer.[2]

Both these findings – the rise in overall TV viewing and the very high proportion of it that continues to be live – are counter-intuitive but provide clues as to why trends are unlikely to change fundamentally. First, television remains an easy, inexpensive and universally available form of relaxation. Second, widescreen TVs and high definition have considerably enhanced the quality of, in particular, the main living-room viewing experience. Third, there has always been and is likely to remain a clear distinction between what consultants like to call a 'lean-back' versus a 'lean-forward' experience, the latter referring to the greater interaction and concentration involved in computer use. While faster broadband and convergence on main living room screens may produce gradual shifts in viewing behaviour over time, there is no reason to believe that the basic ethnography of television and its role in people's lives is likely to undergo a fundamental shift.

This has important consequences, in particular, for television news audiences, which have been in apparently steady decline as channels have proliferated. In the UK, Ofcom figures show that national news viewing fell by 15 per cent from 108.5 hours in 1994 to 90.8 hours in 2006.[3] More recent ratings figures for individual bulletins suggest that this gradual slide has continued: in the third quarter of 1993, the BBC and ITV late evening bulletins were each attracting over 6 million viewers; by the equivalent period of 2010, the BBC's late bulletin was down to 4.5 million while ITV's – now in direct competition with the BBC at 10 p.m. – was struggling around the 2.5 million mark. Early evening news ratings were similarly down from just under 6 million to 4.5 million for the BBC and 4.5 million to just over 3 million for ITV.[4] Much the same story applies to the United States, where the Pew Research Center reports that evening news networks have lost over half their audience in the last 30 years, declining from over 50 million viewers in 1980 to just under 22 million in 2009.[5]

These downward trends, however, must be seen in the context both of audience fragmentation across all traditional mass media, and the vast numbers which these figures still represent in absolute terms. As the Pew report itself said, 'Network evening news is … still an extraordinarily powerful source of information in America. Some 21.6 million people on average watched one of the three programs each night. That is roughly four times the combined number watching each cable news channel's highest-rated program.'

Similarly, in Britain the combined early evening news audience on the mainstream terrestrial channels is well over 7 million, and the combined audiences for all peak-time television news is around 16 million viewers or a third of the total adult audience. Even allowing for some viewer overlap (those who watch more than one bulletin), that still makes terrestrial news bulletins a dominant force in news dissemination, dwarfing the impact of 24-hour news channels and putting each individual bulletin on a par with the readership of a national popular newspaper. While these bulletins may not carry the same agenda-setting or opinion-forming weight as mass circulation print media, they remain a vital conduit for news and information in twenty-first-century democracies.

Despite the rhetoric of imminent decline, then, it is reasonable to conclude that the combination of technological, ethnographic, economic and sociological reasons that first accounted for television's emergence as a hugely powerful means of mass communication will ensure its continuing survival at the heart of people's domestic lives. No doubt delivery platforms will continue to evolve and both on-demand and online viewing will gradually increase. But for the next 20 years at least, we can be confident that for all its weaknesses as a reliable tool of communicating journalism, the medium itself will remain as central to the lives of citizens as ever.

Journalism's future

Can the same be said for journalism? In her seminal work about news and the academy, Barbie Zelizer wrote in 2004 of the 'existential angst [that] continues to permeate conversations about journalism's viability' and cites four articles by major scholars in the previous decade titled or subtitled 'The end of journalism'.[6] In the second half of the 2000s this trickle of pessimism became a waterfall. The reasons have been well documented elsewhere as well as earlier in this book: a 'perfect storm' of recession-led falls in advertising revenues, a structural and irreversible shift of press advertising to the internet, and smaller television audiences earning less money for commercial broadcasters, while public broadcasting is simultaneously threatened by free-marketeers seeking public sector retrenchment and self-interested competitors seeking commercial advantage. Zelizer's existential angst turned quickly to desperation amongst scholars and practitioners alike about the impending 'crisis' in journalism.

This pessimism has been tempered, however, by the faith placed by some observers in what has become widely known as 'citizen journalism' or user generated content. While not itself a new concept – Walter Lippman warned against relying on 'untrained accidental witnesses' over 90 years ago – the concept has been revived by a combination of new technologies and the failing business models of traditional journalism. The technology advances are twofold: a distribution network via the internet that obviates the need for hard-copy print-runs or expensive transmission networks over the air; and a digital revolution in mobile phones and camcorders that enable on-the-spot witness reports to be relayed by whoever happens to have a half-decent camera phone. The first decade of the twenty-first century saw a rapid rise in grainy and jerky pictures from ordinary civilians caught up in, for example, the Asian tsunami of 2004, the 7/7 terrorist attacks in London in 2005, the Mumbai bombings in 2008, the Arab spring demonstrations of 2010 and the Japanese earthquake of 2011. As technology improves, so the sounds and images become clearer even if no less amateur.

Beyond those dramatic moments of live photography, the new journalism also provides an online environment for bloggers who either have no wish to or have failed to penetrate the distributors of traditional journalism. In the (slightly exaggerated) words of one author: 'The media's gatekeeper function was increasingly obsolete in a world where there suddenly were no fences.'[7] The subject matter can range from the emotional outpourings of those who want to vent their feelings, such as relatives of the victims of 9/11, to those who want to provide – sometimes under the cloak of anonymity – insights into their private or professional lives.

Citizen journalism certainly offers great potential for broadening the scope both of who can participate in 'journalism' and in bringing to wider audiences the immediacy of dramatic or unheralded events as they unfold. It can help to democratize journalism, offering greater diversity of input and interpretation. It can challenge the professional norms and routine practices of journalists, and contribute not just information that might be inaccessible or unavailable to professional reporters but new or different perspectives. And it can provide an outlet for the suppressed voices of those who are being silenced by authoritarian regimes determined to stamp out dissent. Clay Shirky, perhaps the most articulate and forceful apologist for citizen journalism, told the story of a Thai woman who defied news censorship during the 2006 military coup to post photos on her website of what was really happening.[8] At its best, citizen journalism can offer a new, exciting dimension to the public information and enlightenment roles of journalism.

There are, however, major weaknesses which its adherents are sometimes slow to acknowledge. First is the problem of authenticity. To what extent are the moving images that have been uploaded or sent to a news agency, or the blogger who posts heart-rending personal testimony on the web, really what the authors say they are? A classic example emerged in June 2011 when the widely read blog 'Gay Girl in Damascus', supposedly written by a lesbian in Syria to reveal the repression being faced by homosexuals, turned out to be the fictional creation of Tom MacMaster, a 40-year-old American PhD student from Edinburgh. Trained journalists have both the means and the professional imperative to verify the accuracy and provenance of sources. Without such authentication, the unchecked journalism of the web could be little more than a collection of wildly inventive fairy tales.

The second weakness is that citizen journalism is no substitute for what Richard Sambrook, the BBC's former Director of Global News, has called 'bearing witness': a firsthand engagement with events – especially in foreign countries – which can first be verified and then explained and contextualized for domestic audiences. For more than 50 years the BBC radio programme "From Our Own Correspondent" has been providing the journalistic background to stories originating in other countries to provide a richness and colour that can only come from someone immersed in the relevant culture. This problem is likely to accelerate for foreign news given, as we have seen, the progressive closure of foreign bureaux. Even on the domestic front, specialist correspondents with expert knowledge, contacts and experience of a particular field can add background, texture and explanation to stories which the 'amateur' reporter is rarely able to do.

Third, citizen journalists cannot perform one of the most vital journalistic functions: holding power and authority to account. This 'watchdog' function is widely accepted to be one of the pillars of a well-functioning democracy, in which properly resourced investigative reporters are engaged in rooting out corruption or wrongdoing within public or corporate bodies. In this book we have seen early examples on both ITV and BBC of first-rate investigative journalism. More recently, the most glaring examples within Britain have tended to come from newspapers: the *Daily Telegraph*'s revelations about MPs abusing their expense allowance; the *News of the World*'s exposure of match-fixing by Pakistani cricketers; and, of course, the *Guardian*'s dogged (and frequently lonely) efforts to demonstrate a culture of journalistic criminality within the *News of the World*, which appeared to extend into the higher echelons of the newspaper's publisher, Rupert Murdoch's News International. This kind of 'heavy lifting' in journalism requires dedicated resources and strong support systems to protect journalists from threats or intimidation by the targets of their investigation. It cannot be carried out by untrained amateurs.

In fact, much the same argument applies even to online journalism enterprises, whether or not they are staffed by professionals. The economic advantages of online newsrooms are clear, and in theory the massive savings in distribution costs could be reinvested in the process of journalism. In fact, such operations are more usually shoestring operations dependent on secondary sources such as press releases, news agencies and other online sources. This is a fairly universal problem, as one trenchant critique recently observed: 'Various large scale research projects covering many countries in Europe and beyond report similar findings and can be summarized as follows ... online newsrooms are understaffed, journalists' working time is overwhelmingly concerned with editing news items delivered by other sources ... own investigations by online journalists are rare and fall prey to speed and immediacy, the social status and reputation of online journalists within the media company is low.'[9] Online journalism rarely (with the possible exception of one or two political blogs with insider knowledge) breaks stories.

Finally, much of the citizen journalism found on the blogosphere is subjective, opinionated and skewed towards the personal prejudices of the author. There is nothing at all wrong with adding to the cacophony of voices available on the web, whether they be angry, emotional, frustrated, politically motivated or determined to prove some outlandish outer-space conspiracy. But none of this is journalism, conducted according to a set of professional standards that demands accuracy, balance and respect for the truth. These are little more than the online incarnations of the fist-waving shock-jocks and anti-establishment protesters which, in the United States, flood the airwaves and, in Europe, can be seen in street demonstrations – raw, colourful and absolutely essential for a vibrant democracy that promotes debate and dissent, but not, by any definition, a journalism that deserves trust or holds to account. As Bill Keller, executive editor of the *New York Times*, said in a lecture in 2007: 'I am a convert to blogs, those live, ad-libbed, interactive monologues that have proliferated by the millions, with an average audience consisting of the blogger and his immediate family ... But most of the blog world does not even attempt to report. It recycles. It riffs on the news. That's not bad. It's just not enough. Not nearly enough.'[10]

Protecting television journalism

So television matters because it remains central to people's lives and television journalism matters, partly because it still commands proper resources and mass audiences, and partly because it upholds the central tenets of professional practice: truth-telling and holding power to account. One of the best expositions of its value and contribution to British public life has been expressed by Georgina Born:

Britain's television journalism has certainly tried to animate something approaching the public sphere ideal; providing information to nurture a responsible citizenry, staging rational debate with the input of specialist expertise, exercising a critical oversight of the state and other powerful institutions, and encouraging participation in collective debates about common concerns and the public good. However imperfectly, it has achieved this in a pluralistic way not only institutionally, but through the deployment of a range of journalistic tones from 'heavy' to 'light', the intellectual and investigative to the familiar and domestic.[11]

Born's observations are important because she moves beyond the BBC to television's contribution more generally. This raises the question that has been at the heart of this book: what institutional structures, statutory interventions and regulatory frameworks are required – if any – to sustain this 'public sphere ideal'? It should now be clear, having seen the trajectories in television journalism either side of the Atlantic outlined in this book, that an unrestrained, unregulated free market in television journalism would be catastrophic. That, remarkably, was also the view of long-time conservative Robert Lichter, president of the Washington-based Center for Media and Public Affairs and a paid consultant to Fox, who said in 2003 in relation to cable television's battle for viewers: 'I've never been able to figure out how competition makes cars better and television news worse … In other industries, competition creates new and different products. In television, it makes all the products look the same. That's weird.'[12]

Weird, perhaps, but, as we have seen, a very accurate analysis: television companies subjected to the relentless drive for profit maximization are forced – almost always against the better judgement of senior journalism executives – to make sacrifices in the quality, volume, professionalism and breadth of their coverage. While in some industries, this unbridled competition benefits the end user, in others it can demonstrably have damaging consequences. In this respect, broadcasting is not alone. In a fascinating analysis of some of the pressures of modern capitalism (which he labels 'Supercapitalism'), Robert Reich – the former Secretary of State for Labor under President Bill Clinton, now Professor of Public Policy at Berkeley – describes how an old-style, fairly benign form of capitalism that served citizens, consumers and employees has become transformed into something altogether less desirable. He argues that technology, globalization and deregulation have conspired to allow consumers and investors to shift their allegiances more quickly than ever before, forcing corporations to concentrate almost exclusively on the bottom line for all their decisions. The consequences are good for us as consumers but not as citizens: 'Markets have become hugely efficient at responding to individual desires for better deals but are quite bad at responding to goals we would like to achieve together. As companies are pressured to show profits, tougher measures are needed to guard public health, safety, the environment, and human rights against the possibility that executives may feel compelled to cut corners.'[13]

Reich does not mention the media generally, nor television specifically. But his central thesis about the need to protect social and democratic principles is directly applicable. This position contrasts starkly with endemic suspicion of regulatory oversight in American corporate life, a suspicion almost as great as that which greets the notion of investing in publicly funded broadcasting. Hence, the well-established, hands-off position of the FCC and the stark contrast with the UK and most other European countries where the benefits of positive regulatory obligations and public investment have been longer and better protected.

That, however, as this book has tried to demonstrate, is changing. The narrative of Reich's Supercapitalism is extending rapidly to the United Kingdom and Europe, exacerbated by continuing economic instability in the Eurozone and louder political calls for reducing investment in the public sector. We have seen how the incoming coalition government rapidly imposed long-term cuts of 16 per cent on the BBC – which would, without doubt, have been considerably more had the Conservative Party won an overall majority. That will undoubtedly have consequences for the breadth and scope of BBC journalism in the years leading up to the review of its Royal Charter in 2016. And in May 2011, the Culture Secretary Jeremy Hunt kick-started the process for a new Communications Act in 2015 with an 'open letter' setting out the government's guiding principles. The rhetoric was familiar: an emphasis on competition with an explicit commitment to removing regulation – 'a deregulatory approach … is the aim'.[14] This is hugely ironic at the very moment when Britain's unrestrained, unfettered press has been exposed, through the *News of the World* phone-hacking scandal, as incapable of policing ethical standards in its own industry.

That is certainly not to argue for statutory regulation of the press. But it should help us to understand that a sensible and independent regulatory framework – supported by strong institutional cultures, as has operated in Britain for years – can not only protect but actually promote the kind of intelligent, information-rich, analytical and watchdog journalism which most professionals crave and on which democracy thrives. The scandal which left Britain's press and political classes reeling in the summer of 2011 was in large part down to the unrestrained commercial and corporate forces which drove journalism remorselessly in an unsavoury direction, to the disgust of the vast majority of practising reporters. That broadcast journalists were not remotely implicated in these practices – which almost certainly extended beyond the *News of the World* to other tabloid newspapers in Britain – demonstrates how a positive and beneficial journalistic environment is achievable through a thoughtful approach to independent regulation.[15] As media enterprises increasingly strive to exploit their investment in journalism across platforms – and therefore the notion of television-specific journalism becomes more diluted – this principle of independent regulation, rooted in ideals of democracy and the public interest, ought to become more rather than less important.

It will not be sufficient to rely on the professional journalistic values of practitioners. In his *The Sociology of News*, the eminent scholar Michael Schudson is – rightly – keen to emphasize the cultural and professional influences on journalism as well as the political and economic. He reminds us that Jürgen Habermas' critique of the negative impact of commercialization on the media in the nineteenth century omitted a second equally crucial historical development: that journalism became professionalized at the same time as it became commercialised, and that journalists (especially in the western tradition) have internalised values which help them to remain autonomous. He explains the so-called dumbing-down phenomenon as follows: 'Can the trend towards soft news be seen not as a submission to market forces but as an expansion of an overly narrow, rigid definition of news to encompass a wider range of important topics?'[16]

As I believe this history has shown, at least within the television medium, that now appears to be an overly optimistic assessment of the power of autonomous professional values to resist exogenous forces. Within a regulated, professionalized environment, British television journalism has for most of its life adapted to changing audience and cultural needs while at the same time remaining faithful to those ideal professional values identified by Schudson. That it has not so far followed American journalism down the tabloid route is due primarily to the structural frameworks that protect it. Social scientists will recognize here the classic sociological dichotomy of structure versus agency and the empirical evidence suggests that, in the absence of those carefully framed regulatory and institutional structures, there is overwhelming corporate pressure on journalists, which frequently defines their work and overrides their own professional instincts.

The demise of hard-hitting, well-resourced current affairs journalism on British commercial television is testimony to what happens when those protective mechanisms are progressively removed. With both regulatory philosophy and public institutions under threat, the risk extends beyond a slide in professional standards to issues of national self-identity and a healthy democracy. Emily Bell, a very experienced British journalist now immersed in the American academy, has reflected on the implications of the United States' paucity of broadcast journalism: 'America lacks a central voice in terms of both reporting itself to the world and the world to its diverse citizens. This puts the country at a disadvantage. The quality of its democracy suffers, as does its global image.'[17]

Thus, at the beginning of the second decade of the twenty-first century, television journalism in Britain helps to establish the country's place in the world as well as offering an important counterpoint to the inherent weaknesses (and strengths) of the national press. It is not declamatory, not prone to fits of moral outrage, not suffused by a commentariat which feels it has to shout louder, sink lower, witch-hunt more aggressively or express more extreme opinions simply to be heard amongst the clamour of competing media voices. It is perhaps less colourful as a result, but that is balanced (with interest) by a raucous press. It is a journalism that invests in newsgathering rather than commentary, in reporting, explaining, contextualising, investigating and holding to account. We might call it an explanatariat rather than a commentariat. Murrow's legacy is still visible in Britain but it is being progressively eroded by the forces of competition, deregulation and institutional dismemberment. We should heed the warnings from the United States before it is too late.

Appendix 1　Methodology for News Study

Sampling

The sampling method was a sophisticated process designed to cover an even spread of years over the period, to avoid election years (which would have distorted the level of political news) and to ensure a representative sample of bulletins within each year. The study therefore analysed bulletins every five years starting in 1975 until 1999, and within each year selected five periods of five weeks to cover the months of February, April, June, September and November. One of the weaknesses of many news content analyses is that results are distorted by a major story that dominates the sampling period. In order to avoid that, one weekday was randomly selected within each five-week period, thus ensuring that each day of the week was selected once only.

Our final selection therefore consisted of a random 25 days of analysis in each year, offering a genuinely representative picture of a year's news output. The bulletins that were included in the analysis were all the evening bulletins on terrestrial television: the BBC 'Six O'clock News' and 'Nine O'clock News'; ITN's 'Early Evening News' and 'News at Ten' (subsequently 'The Early Evening News' and 'The Nightly News'); 'Channel 4 News'; and '5 News'. A more ambitious project would include breakfast news, lunchtime bulletins and a selection of news output on the 24-hour news channels to get a more complete picture of TV news availability and long-term trends, but the evening bulletins are – in audience and impact terms – unquestionably the ones that matter. Even at the end of the first decade of the twenty-first century, with fragmented audiences and the proliferation of online news sources, it is the evening bulletins that still command the highest audiences and the largest TV news budgets.

Coding

Each story was coded for content and format, with a coding frame which was refined into 31 discrete story categories. It is this process that defines the social scientific nature of content analysis and makes it most vulnerable to criticism:

the classification of a story involves an element of subjective judgement, which itself can say more about the nature of news than the quantified data that results (sociologists will recognize here the long-standing tension between positivism and phenomenology as an approach to understanding social reality). Although there are always plenty of opportunities for differential interpretation in a content analysis, consistency can be ensured by minimizing coder variations. In this case, coding was undertaken by a single individual and grey areas were discussed with project directors so that all coding decisions were consistent. It is the longitudinal nature of this kind of content analysis that gives it its intellectual rigour, and we were therefore confident that the changes recorded over time were real.

For reporting and analysis purposes, the 31 categories were then consolidated into a simple division of broadsheet, tabloid and foreign, a fairly simplistic approach and necessarily a blunt instrument for assessing trends. Once again, however, it is change over time that most concerns us, and these consolidated terms are useful descriptors for analysing longitudinal shifts in news output. The categories were allocated according to Table A1.1. A separate category for foreign news was used out of recognition that most foreign stories were neither obviously 'broadsheet' nor 'tabloid' in tone or content, and also presented a useful indicator of whether television news bulletins were becoming more insular and less international in flavour.

A1.1   News study categories

Broadsheet	Tabloid
Politics/economic policy	Crime
Business/industry/finance	Consumer
Social affairs	Tragedy
Legal	Weather (general)
Foreign relations/diplomacy	Sport
European Union issues	Royalty
Unrest/civil disturbance	Showbiz/entertainment
War	Human interest/animal stories
Northern Ireland	Humour/quirky stories
Health	Expeditions/adventure

Broadsheet	Tabloid
Education	Other
Employment/industrial relations	
Environment/ecology/planning	
Natural disasters	
Science/technology	
Transport	
Religion	
Culture/media/arts	
Moral/ethical issues	
Military/national security	

Appendix 2   Detailed Breakdown of Story Types on UK News Bulletins 1975–99

(Figures in the following tables are the proportion of total sampled minutes devoted to each category.)

A2.1   Political affairs

	1975	1980	1985	1990	1995	1999
	%	%	%	%	%	%
BBC Six p.m.	25.6	15.2	14.1	32.6	20.8	14.6
BBC Nine p.m.	31.6	22.1	19.0	32.8	22.1	15.3
ITN Early Eve	22.2	17.9	16.2	31.3	19.7	17.4
ITN Ten p.m.	30.2	24.7	18.9	30.0	19.9	16.3
C4 News			17.6	33.3	25.4	15.8
C5 News						5.8

A2.2   Social policy

	1975	1980	1985	1990	1995	1999
	%	%	%	%	%	%
BBC Six p.m.	5.3	13.8	11.7	7.9	17.2	15.1
BBC Nine p.m.	5.4	12.3	7.2	3.3	10.8	9.9
ITN Early Eve	2.4	9.4	6.7	8.4	10.1	9.7
ITN Ten p.m.	2.1	10.0	8.3	10.6	8.3	7.0
C4 News			11.9	7.8	8.2	15.5
C5 News						13.5

A2.3   Sport

	1975	1980	1985	1990	1995	1999
	%	%	%	%	%	%
BBC Six p.m.	3.9	7.7	4.7	3.0	3.3	8.7
BBC Nine p.m.	5.9	9.5	3.9	1.9	3.0	3.8
ITN Early Eve	4.3	9.9	7.9	5.0	4.6	7.5
ITN Ten p.m.	7.5	9.2	7.1	4.2	5.0	12.8
C4 News			2.4	0.3	0.6	1.6
C5 News						13.8

A2.4   Crime

	1975	1980	1985	1990	1995	1999
	%	%	%	%	%	%
BBC Six p.m.	6.3	6.5	5.6	2.1	6.0	6.8
BBC Nine p.m.	3.9	6.2	5.4	1.2	3.6	5.2
ITN Early Eve	7.1	6.9	7.4	6.4	10.0	4.4
ITN Ten p.m.	6.6	6.8	5.3	3.2	7.8	8.0
C4 News			2.6	3.2	2.0	5.5
C5 News						11.3

A2.5   Light stories

	1975	1980	1985	1990	1995	1999
	%	%	%	%	%	%
BBC Six p.m.	5.2	7.5	7.3	0.8	5.1	4.8
BBC Nine p.m.	3.9	9.7	8.0	0.5	2.9	0.8
ITN Early Eve	3.6	7.1	7.8	3.1	10.9	4.1
ITN Ten p.m.	2.4	7.2	6.4	2.1	8.8	5.3
C4 News			2.5	0.7	0.8	0.5
C5 News						10.0

Notes

Introduction

1 Speech to the Radio-Television News Directors Association (RTNDA) convention, Chicago, 15 October 1958.

2 Mort Rosenblum, *Who Stole the News?* (New York, NY: John Wiley and Sons, 1993), p. 15.

3 Thomas E. Patterson, *Doing Well and Doing Good: How Soft News and Critical Journalism Are Shrinking the News Audience and Weakening Democracy – And What News Outlets Can Do About It* (Cambridge, MA: Joan Shorenstein Center, John F. Kennedy School of Government, Harvard University, 2000), p. 3.

4 Mark Thompson, 'The Future Begins Here', text of a speech delivered in July 2007 (London: BBC Press Office), p. 6, http://www.bbc.co.uk/pressoffice/speeches/stories/thompson_summit.shtml [accessed 26 July 2011].

5 Those who missed it can relive the moment on http://uk.youtube.com/watch?v=6VdNcCcweL0 [accessed 26 July 2011].

6 Neil Postman, *Amusing Ourselves to Death* (London: Methuen, 1985), p. 81.

7 Pierre Bourdieu, *On Television and Journalism* (London: Pluto Press, 1998), p. 19.

8 John Whale, *The Half-Shut Eye* (London: Macmillan, 1969).

9 Andrew Marr, *My Trade: A Short History of British Journalism* (London: Pan Books, 2005), p. 269.

10 Peter Fincham, The James Mactaggart Memorial Lecture, 22 August 2008.

11 Leonard Downie Jr and Robert G. Kaiser, *The News about the News: American Journalism in Peril* (New York, NY: Vintage, 2003), pp. 64 and 125.

12 Marr, *My Trade*, p. 281.

13 However, even television's trust figures have declined significantly since 2003 in the wake of various 'fakery' scandals on UK television. See Steven Barnett, 'On the road to self-destruction', *British Journalism Review* (vol. 19, no. 2, 2008), pp. 5–13.

14 Nicholas Lemann, 'The Murrow doctrine: Why the life and times of the broadcast pioneer still matter', *New Yorker* (23 January 2006).

15 Rupert Murdoch, 'Freedom in Broadcasting', The James MacTaggart Lecture 1989, in Bob Franklin (ed.), *Television Policy: The MacTaggart Lectures* (Edinburgh: Edinburgh University Press, 2005), pp. 137–8.

16 Robert G. Picard, *Journalism, Value Creation and the Future of News Organizations* (Cambridge, MA: Joan Shorenstein Center, John F. Kennedy School of Government, Harvard University, 2006), p. 5.

17 Patterson, *Doing Well and Doing Good*, p. 15.

18 Michael Dimock and Samuel Popkin, 'Political knowledge in comparative perspective', in S. Iyengar and R. Reeves (eds), *Do the Media Govern?* (Thousand Oaks, CA: Sage, 1997), p. 219.

19 James Curran, Shanto Iyengar, Anker Brink Lund and Inka Salovaara-Moring, 'Media systems, public knowledge and democracy: A comparative study', *European Journal of Communication* (vol. 24, no. 1, 2009), pp. 5–27.

20 Program on International Policy Attitudes/Knowledge Networks, 'Misperceptions, the media and the Iraq War' (College Park, MD: University of Maryland, October 2003).

21 Jeremy Paxman, 'Never mind the scandals: What's it all for?', The James MacTaggart Memorial Lecture, 24 August 2007.

22 Peter Dahlgren, 'Introduction', in Jan Wieten, Graham Murdock and Peter Dahlgren (eds), *Television Across Europe* (London: Sage, 2000), p. 3.

23 Karol Jakubowicz, 'PSB 3.0: Reinventing European PSB', in Petros Iosifidis (ed.), *Reinventing Public Service Communication* (London: Palgrave Macmillan, 2010), p. 9.

24 Daniel Hallin and Paolo Mancini, *Comparing Media Systems. Three Models of Media and Politics* (Cambridge, New York, NY: Cambridge University Press, 2004).

25 Peter Humphreys, 'A political scientist's contribution to the comparative study of media systems in Europe: A response to Hallin and Mancini', in Natascha Just and Manuel Puppis (eds), *Trends in Communication Policy Research: New Theories, Methods and Subjects* (Bristol: Intellect, 2011).

1   Laying the Foundations: Policies, Practices and a Public Monopoly

1 Grace Wyndham Goldie, *Facing the Nation: Television and Politics 1936–76* (London: Bodley Head, 1977), p. 19.

2 Wyndham Goldie, *Facing the Nation*, p. 20.

3 Sir Frederick Sykes, *Report of the Broadcasting Committee* (London: HMSO, 1923), p. 6.

4 Sykes, *Report of the Broadcasting Committee*, p. 24.

5 Sykes, *Report of the Broadcasting Committee*, p. 31.

6 Earl of Crawford, *Report of the Broadcasting Committee* (London: HMSO, 1926), p. 6.

7 Crawford, *Report of the Broadcasting Committee*, p. 13.

8 Asa Briggs, *The History of Broadcasting in the United Kingdom, Vol. I: The Birth of Broadcasting 1896–1927* (Oxford: Oxford University Press, 1961), p. 361.

9 Ian McIntyre, *The Expense of Glory: A Life of John Reith* (London: HarperCollins, 1993), p. 142.

10 Another account goes further, suggesting that there was 'a large number of totally inaccurate reports of returns to work', and that, more worryingly, immediate corrections sent over to the BBC by the relevant unions were never given air-time. Christopher Farman, *The General Strike: May 1926* (London: Panther, 1974), p. 184.

11 Briggs, *The History of Broadcasting in the United Kingdom, Vol. I*, p. 378.

12 Asa Briggs, *The History of Broadcasting in the United Kingdom, Vol. II: The Golden Age of Wireless 1927–1939* (Oxford: Oxford University Press, 1995), p. 120.

13 Quoted in James Curran and Jean Seaton, *Power without Responsibility* (5th edition, London: Routledge, 1997).

14 Briggs reports only one occasion in the early 1930s when the Postmaster General, Kingsley Wood, threatened a ban, involving a proposed talk by an ex-German U-boat Commander. In the event, and under huge government pressure, 'the decision to cancel was taken by the Board of Governors, with Reith dissenting'. Thirty years later, when Reith asked Wood whether he would have used the ban, the answer was, 'not on your life. I would never have done it'. Briggs, *The History of Broadcasting in the United Kingdom, Vol. II*, p. 121. We shall come across this political reluctance to use express powers to intervene in the BBC's editorial

discretion again – and the BBC's own institutional ambivalence about how to respond to severe government pressure.

15 Curran and Seaton, *Power without Responsibility*, p. 123.

16 Lord Ullswater, *Report of the Broadcasting Committee* (London: HMSO, 1936), s. 85.

17 McIntyre, *The Expense of Glory*, p. 186.

18 Paddy Scannell and David Cardiff, *A Social History of British Broadcasting* (Oxford: Blackwell, 1991), p. 106.

19 Scannell and Cardiff, *A Social History of British Broadcasting*, p. 113.

20 Jonathan Dimbleby, *Richard Dimbleby* (London: Hodder and Stoughton, 1975), p. 64.

21 Scannell and Cardiff, *A Social History of British Broadcasting*, p. 133.

22 Stewart Purvis, 'News International Lectures on the Broadcast Media', Lecture 1, Oxford University, January 2005. The critics were Henry Wickham Steed, a former editor of *The Times*, and A.J. Cummings of the *News Chronicle*. The newsreel had been shown in 100 cinemas by the time the Foreign Office had been alerted and had 'met with considerable applause'. The Foreign Office approached the American Ambassador to London, Joseph. P. Kennedy, who in turn passed on the government's reservations to Paramount.

23 Purvis dates this report (undated in the BBC Written Archives) as from the month after Munich, but Scannell and Cardiff describe it as 'compiled some years later', Scannell and Cardiff, *A Social History of British Broadcasting*, p. 87.

24 Quoted in Scannell and Cardiff, *A Social History of British Broadcasting*, pp. 88–9.

25 Scannell and Cardiff, *A Social History of British Broadcasting*, p. 101.

26 Asa Briggs, *The History of Broadcasting in the United Kingdom, Vol. III: The War of Words 1939–45* (Oxford: Oxford University Press, 1970), p. 34.

27 Reported in *World's Press News*, as quoted in Briggs, *The History of Broadcasting in the United Kingdom, Vol. III*, p. 35. Three years earlier, someone had written 'The defeat of journalism by the BBC continues.'

28 Briggs, *The History of Broadcasting in the United Kingdom, Vol. III*, pp. 58–9.

29 Quoted in Wyndham Goldie, *Facing the Nation*, p. 41.

30 Wyndham Goldie, *Facing the Nation*, p. 43.

31 Wyndham Goldie, *Facing the Nation*, p. 58.

32 Greg Philo, *Seeing and Believing: The Influence of Television* (London: Routledge, 1990), p. 148.

33 Daniel J. Boorstin, 'The image', in Howard Tumber (ed.), *News: A Reader* (Oxford: Oxford University Press, 1999), p. 16.

34 Asa Briggs, *The History of Broadcasting in the United Kingdom, Vol. IV: Sound and Vision 1945–55* (Oxford: Oxford University Press, 1979), p. 528.

35 Paddy Scannell, 'The Social Eye of Television 1946–1955', *Media Culture and Society* (vol. 1, 1979), pp. 97–106. The following analysis is derived substantially from this excellent article.

36 Scannell, 'The Social Eye of Television', p. 103.

37 These programmes were presented by high-profile figures such as Ed Murrow who were strong personalities as well as highly regarded journalists. Such a personality-led form of television journalism would have been anathema to the likes of Hole and Haley.

38 Wyndham Goldie, Facing the Nation, p. 193.

39 The full story is given in Wyndham Goldie, *Facing the Nation*, p. 124ff; and Briggs, *The History of Broadcasting in the United Kingdom, Vol. IV*, p. 554ff.

40 Quoted in Briggs, *The History of Broadcasting in the United Kingdom, Vol. IV*, pp. 554–5. Subsequent Speakers of the House would have great sympathy. More than one government minister had to be warned during the ten years of Tony Blair's government about not pre-empting policy announcements to Parliament by first informing the nation via judicious leaks or exclusives.

41 The BBC gained strength from publication of the Beveridge Report early in 1951, which had come to the unanimous conclusion that the 14-day rule should be 'reconsidered'.

42 Barry Turner, *Suez 1956* (London: Hodder, 2006), p. 348.

43 Wyndham Goldie, *Facing the Nation*, p. 184.

44 Quoted in Turner, *Suez 1956*, p. 351.

45 Dimbleby, *Richard Dimbleby*, p. 204.

2   Competition and Commercialism: The Early Days

1 Lord Beveridge, *Report of the Broadcasting Committee 1949* (London: HMSO, 1951), para. 265.

2 Beveridge, *Report of the Broadcasting Committee*, para. 314.

3 Wyndham Goldie, *Facing the Nation*, p. 105.

4 Quoted in Bernard Sendall, *Independent Television in Britain, Vol. 1 Origin and Foundation, 1946–62* (Basingstoke: Macmillan, 1982), p. 44.

5 Quoted in Richard Lindley, *And Finally …? The News from ITN* (London: Politicos, 2005), p. 9.

6 The ITA's first Director General, Sir Robert Fraser, was an Australian born, highly respected senior civil servant. Its first Chairman, with impeccable cultural credentials, was Chairman of the Arts Council and former Director of the National Gallery Sir Kenneth Clark (later to become one of the most distinguished communicators of the arts on commercial television).

7 Lindley, *And Finally …?*, p. 35.

8 Sendall, *Independent Television in Britain*, p. 141.

9 Quoted in Lindley, *And Finally …?*, p. 35.

10 Quoted in Sendall, *Independent Television in Britain*, p. 143.

11 Geoffrey Cox, *Pioneering Television News* (London: John Libbey, 1995), p. 48.

12 Robin Day, *Day by Day: A Dose of My Own Hemlock* (London: Kimber, 1975), pp. 178–82.

13 Sendall, *Independent Television in Britain*, p. 148.

14 Cox, *Pioneering Television News*, p. 45.

15 Quoted in Lindley, *And Finally …?*, p. 22.

16 Cox, *Pioneering Television News*, p. 92.

17 Cox, *Pioneering Television News*, p. 61.

18 Cox, *Pioneering Television News*, p. 77.

19 Sendall, *Independent Television in Britain*, p. 283.

20 Wyndham Goldie, *Facing the Nation*, p. 197.

21 Quoted in Sendall, *Independent Television in Britain*, p. 365.

22 Sir Henry Pilkington, *Report on the Committee on Broadcasting, 1960* (London: HMSO, 1962), paras 308–22.

23 Cox, *Pioneering Television News*, p. 130.

24 Quoted in Sendall, *Independent Television in Britain*, p. 328.

25 Quoted in Patricia Holland, *The Angry Buzz: This Week and Current Affairs Television* (London: I.B. Tauris, 2006), p. 5.

26 Holland, *The Angry Buzz*, p. 21.

27 Holland, *The Angry Buzz*, p. 33.

28 Raymond Fitzwalter, *The Dream that Died: The Rise and Fall of ITV* (Leicester: Matador, 2008), p. 2.

29 Sendall, *Independent Television in Britain*, p. 354.

30 Quoted in Marr, *My Trade*, p. 279.

31 Wyndham Goldie, *Facing the Nation*, p. 191.

32 Quoted in Dimbleby, *Richard Dimbleby*, p. 267.

33 Dimbleby, *Richard Dimbleby*, p. 272.

34 Wyndham Goldie, *Facing the Nation*, p. 215.

35 Cox, *Pioneering Television News*, p. 167.

36 Marr, *My Trade*, p. 273.

37 Steve M. Barkin, *American Television News: The Media Marketplace and the Public Interest* (Armonk, NY: M.E. Sharpo, 2003), p. 20.

38 Cox, *Pioneering Television News*, p. 9.

39 Cox, *Pioneering Television News*, p. 11.

40 Barkin, *American Television News*, p. 28.

41 Helen Thomas, *Watchdogs of Democracy* (New York, NY: Scribner, 2006), p. 181.

42 Quoted in Barkin, *American Television News*, p. 26.

43 Tom Fenton, *Bad News: The Decline of Reporting, the Business of News, and the Danger to Us All* (New York, NY: Regan, 2005), p. 55. Jack Benny was one of the foremost comedy acts of the era, whose shows generated huge ratings and therefore healthy revenues for CBS.

44 Cox, *Pioneering Television News*, p. 29.

45 Barkin, *American Television News*, pp. 30–31.

46 Barkin, *American Television News*, p. 34.

3   Competition, Commercialism and the 'Golden Age'

1 Holland, *The Angry Buzz*, p. 52.

2 Holland, *The Angry Buzz*, p. 58.

3 Cox, *Pioneering Television News*, p. 185.

4 Quoted in Lindley, *And Finally …?*, p. 87.

5 Cox, *Pioneering Television News*, p. 189.

6 Cox, *Pioneering Television News*, p. 185.

7 Holland, *The Angry Buzz*, p. 58.

8 The ITA had become disillusioned with Associated-Rediffusion's dogged insistence on continuing with quiz shows such as 'Double Your Money' and 'Take Your Pick' even in the face of a more sober post-Pilkington mood. The ITA Chairman, Lord Hill, was determined to pursue the public service aims of the Television Act, and was not enamoured of Rediffusion's unconcealed commercial ambitions. Rediffusion was forced to merge with ABC to form Thames as a new contractor for London's weekday franchise. The full story is told in Brian Sendall, *Independent Television in Britain, Vol 2: Expansion and Change 1958–68* (Basingstoke: Macmillan, 1982), pp. 343–7.

9 Holland, *The Angry Buzz*, p. 62.

10 Catholic claims that the British army shootings were unprovoked were wholly vindicated by a fresh inquiry set up in 1998 under Lord Saville which was finally published on 15 June 2010.

11 Philip Schlesinger, Graham Murdock, Philip Ross Courtney Elliott, *Televising Terrorism* (London: Comedia, 1983).

12 The first programming casualty was a 'World in Action' programme due for transmission in November 1971, which saw ITA Chairman Lord Aylestone summoned to the Home Office and informed of official fears that it might be too critical of the Army. The programme was pulled. Jeremy Potter, *Independent Television in Britain, Vol. 4: Companies and Programmes 1968–80* (Basingstoke: Macmillan, 1990), p. 209.

13 Jonathan Dimbleby, *News Statesman* (31 December 1971), quoted in Holland, *The Angry Buzz*, p. 125.

14 Fitzwalter, *The Dream that Died*, p. 21.

15 The regulator's establishment credentials had been confirmed in 1970 when the educationist and former headmaster of Charterhouse Brian Young took over the ITA's leadership, and remained in charge through its transition to the IBA.

16 Quoted in Potter, *Independent Television in Britain*, p. 210.

17 Holland, *The Angry Buzz*, p. 163.

18 Fitzwalter, *The Dream that Died*, p. 23.

19 Holland, *The Angry Buzz*, p. 103.

20 Fitzwalter, *The Dream that Died*, p. 11.

21 Birt had made a name for himself in 1967 as a 22-year-old researcher on 'World in Action': two members of the Rolling Stones had been imprisoned for drugs offences, and Birt had brought together their iconic leader, Mick Jagger, and the editor of *The Times*, William Rees-Mogg (an unlikely supporter of the Stones' cause) to discuss the issues.

22 According to one of those involved, 'we were developing Birtian television journalism on the hoof, and there were people who understood it and people who didn't … it was like Trotskyists and Stalinists'. This and subsequent quotes are taken from interviews conducted for my earlier book on the BBC: Steven Barnett and Andrew Curry, *The Battle for the BBC* (London: Aurum Press, 1994).

23 John Birt, 'Broadcasting's journalistic bias is not a matter of politics but of presentation', *The Times* (28 February 1975), p. 14.

24 John Birt, 'The radical changes needed to remedy TV's bias against understanding', *The Times*, 1 October 1975, p. 14.

25 He did find an immediate fan in the then BBC Chairman Sir Michael Swann, who endorsed the thesis at a university seminar in March 1975 and added that 'the need for greater public understanding of the intractable problems which beset us is so pressing that no effort is too great'. Barnett and Curry, *The Battle for the BBC*, p. 79.

26 1990 Broadcasting Act, s. 25(1). The 2003 Communications Act updated this to demonstrating 'innovation, experiment and creativity in the form and content of programmes', appealing to 'the tastes and interests of a culturally diverse society' and exhibiting 'a distinctive character'. See also Peter Goodwin, *Television Under the Tories* (London: British Film Institute, 1998), p. 28.

27 Jeremy Isaacs, *Storm Over 4: A Personal Account* (London: Weidenfeld and Nicolson, 1989), p. 126.

28 Isaacs, *Storm Over 4*, p. 127.

29 Support for ITN also came from the IBA, from ITN's own editor David Nicholas and from Home Secretary William Whitelaw himself who in 1979 had praised ITN's 'admirable record' – an intriguing reflection on how ITN had established itself as an attractive option to a Conservative Party, which was even more convinced than Labour that the BBC was innately biased against it. Lindley, *And Finally …?*, p. 261.

30 Maggie Brown, *A Licence to Be Different: The Story of Channel 4* (London: British Film Institute, 2007), p. 24.

31 Lindley, *And Finally …?*, p. 269.

32 Holland, *The Angry Buzz*, p. 184.

33 One of its more famous and more trivial items featuring a skateboarding duck is still talked about in the news corridors of Broadcasting House – though it is not widely known that the duck in question was in fact glued to the skateboard.

34 He said later: 'I thought the producer regime at the BBC at that time was moving away from the traditional standard of the BBC in respect of impartiality, was showing a kind of assertion of arrogance towards the rest of the community which in the end was not going to be acceptable.' See Barnett and Curry, *The Battle for the BBC*, p. 19.

35 Newton N. Minow, 'Television and the Public Interest', speech to the National Association of Broadcasters delivered 9 May 1961, http://www.americanrhetoric.com/speeches/newtonminow.htm [accessed 15 June 2010].

36 Daniel Hallin, *We Keep America on Top of the World* (London: Routledge, 1994), p. 98.

37 Downie Jr and Kaiser, *The News about the News*, p. 132.

38 Downie Jr and Kaiser, *The News about the News*, p. 142.

39 Quoted in Barkin, *American Television News*, p. 173.

40 Fenton, *Bad News*, pp. 72–3.

41 William Shawcross, *Rupert Murdoch: Ringmaster of the Information Circus* (London: Chatto & Windus, 1992), p. 429.

42 Shawcross, *Rupert Murdoch*, p. 430.

4 **'Real Lives' v 'Death on the Rock': Journalism, Terrorism and Accountability**

1 This and, where indicated, subsequent quotes from those involved are taken from transcripts of interviews conducted by Frank Gillard in the immediate aftermath of the 'Real Lives' episode as part of 'The Oral History of the BBC'. All interviews were embargoed for five or, in some cases, ten years. This is the first time they have been made public. Paul Hamann interview, 25 November 1985.

2 *Radio Times* (3–9 August 1985), p. 76.

3 Or, perhaps, had the connection made for him. Writing in his memoirs, Head of Documentaries, Will Wyatt says that 'I am pretty certain with hindsight that the newspaper was tipped off by a member of the production team, intent on stirring up some eye-catching controversy.' Will Wyatt, *The Fun Factory: A Life in the BBC* (London: Aurum Press, 2003), p. 130. If even remotely true, it must rate as one of the most spectacularly backfiring PR stunts ever.

4 '"Real Lives", The Oral History of the BBC' interview with Alan Protheroe, 18 December 1985.

5 The last time the principle had been breached was 14 years previously when an equally contentious programme about the outgoing Labour government's cabinet, 'Yesterday's Men', had grievously upset the former Prime Minister Harold Wilson and the prior viewing of the programme by governors had only fuelled the confrontation.

6 '"Real Lives", The Oral History of the BBC' interview with Stuart Young, 4 November 1986.

7 According to the BBC Secretary, who traditionally acted as intermediary between Government department and the BBC and was in close touch with Home Office officials, 'Officials did draft

letters for him. He rejected all the drafts, and he rejected all the advice and he wrote his own letter in his own room in his own hand … The work of the Home Secretary was not the work of the Home Office but the work of the man himself.' '"Real Lives", The Oral History of the BBC' interview with David Holmes, 22 January 1986.

8 A fuller text of the letter can be found in Michael Leapman's well-informed account of this affair, published in 1987. Michael Leapman, *The Last Days of the Beeb* (London: Coronet, 1987), p. 304.

9 '"Real Lives", The Oral History of the BBC' interview with Leon Brittan, 17 March 1986.

10 '"Real Lives", The Oral History of the BBC' interview with Brian Wenham, 3 December 1985.

11 '"Real Lives", The Oral History of the BBC' interview with William Rees-Mogg, 24 January 1986.

12 This near unanimity owed more to Young's insistence on collective cabinet responsibility – had a vote been taken, he himself and at least one other governor would almost certainly have voted for transmission.

13 James Hawthorne, 'Real Lives: At the Edge of the Union', written commentary attached to the '"Real Lives", The Oral History of the BBC' archive.

14 '"Real Lives", The Oral History of the BBC' interview with Alan Protheroe, 15 January 1986.

15 '"Real Lives", The Oral History of the BBC' interview with Alasdair Milne, undated, January/ February 1986.

16 '"Real Lives", The Oral History of the BBC' interview with Will Wyatt, 25 November 1985. See also Wyatt, *The Fun Factory*, p. 137. Wyatt also records the volume of letters that had been received up to the date of the board meeting which reversed the decision: '614 letters against showing the programme, 473 in favour and 560 in appreciation of the music that had replaced programmes on the strike day.'

17 Alasdair Milne, personal interview, 2 June 1993.

18 '"Real Lives", The Oral History of the BBC' interview with Sir John Johnston, 18 December 1985.

19 '"Real Lives", The Oral History of the BBC' interview with Sir William Rees-Mogg.

20 Alasdair Milne, personal interview. See also Milne's own memoirs where he describes himself as 'shocked at the depth of the Governors' antagonism and for that I must take the heavy share of blame'. Alasdair Milne, *The Memoirs of a British Broadcaster* (London: Coronet Books, 1989), p. 198.

21 This was not just bad luck: the very same dossier of evidence had been sent to 'World in Action' first and rejected because the Young Conservatives 'were heavily dependent on Conservative politicians as witnesses, who were likely to melt away at the first sound of gunfire'. Fitzwalter, *The Dream that Died*, p. 37.

22 Holland, *The Angry Buzz*, p. 190.

23 Ian Jack, 'Gibraltar', in Ian jack (ed.), *The Granta Book of Reportage* (London: Granta, 2006), p. 174.

24 Roger Bolton, *Death on the Rock and Other Stories* (London: W.H. Allen, 1990), p. 192.

25 George Thomson, *Daily Telegraph* (28 December 1988), quoted in Bolton, *Death on the Rock*, p. 232.

26 Jack, 'Gibraltar', p. 191.

27 Holland, *The Angry Buzz*, p. 199.

28 Fitzwalter, *The Dream that Died*, p. 61.

29 Jack, 'Gibraltar', p. 235.

30 Quoted in Bolton, *Death on the Rock*, p. 305.

31 Quoted in Bolton, *Death on the Rock*, pp. 305–6.

32 Quoted in Bolton, *Death on the Rock*, p. 271.

33 Paul Bonner with Lesley Aston, *ITV in Britain, Vol. 5: The Old Relationship Changes 1981–92* (Basingstoke: Macmillan, 1998).

5   The Propaganda Model and the 1990 Broadcasting Act

1 Edward S. Herman and Noam Chomsky, *Manufacturing Consent: the Political Economy of the Mass Media* (New York, NY: Pantheon, 1988), pp. 1–35.

2 Colin Sparks, 'Extending and Refining the Propaganda Model', in *Westminster Papers in Communication and Culture* (vol. 4, no. 2, 2007), pp. 68–84.

3 Fitzwalter, *The Dream that Died*, p. 29.

4 Fitzwalter, *The Dream that Died*, pp. 85–6.

5 When Sir Michael Checkland was interviewed for *The Battle for the BBC*, he said that he told Birt: 'You're going to have immense problems in light of the established reporters who aren't going to like some of the things that we're suggesting but you've got to have the courage to do it. And I used the word courage deliberately because I think it was a very difficult job for anyone, to come in and create the fusion of radio and television news and current affairs.' Personal interview, 23 March 1994. Barnett and Curry, *The Battle for the BBC*, p. 84.

6 This is covered in more detail in Barnett and Curry, *The Battle for the BBC*, pp. 85–8.

7 Quoted in Richard Lindley, *Panorama: Fifty Years of Pride and Paranoia* (London: Politicos, 2002), p. 329.

8 John Birt, *The Harder Path* (London: Time Warner, 2002), pp 252–3.

9 Quoted in Lindley, *Panorama*, p. 333.

10 Quoted in Barnett and Curry, *The Battle for the BBC*, pp. 162–3.

11 Quoted in Lindley, *Panorama*, p. 347.

12 Birt, *The Harder Path*, p. 300.

13 Quoted in Lindley, *Panorama*, p. 353.

6   Competition and Commercialism into the Twenty-first Century

1 Quoted in Steven Barnett, 'Ducking the Issues', *Impact* (August 1992), pp. 14–17.

2 Quoted in Holland, *The Angry Buzz*, p. 213.

3 *Broadcast* (19 June 1992), p. 12.

4 These arguments are well laid out in Brian McNair, *News and Journalism in the UK* (London: Routledge, 1999), pp. 46–50.

5 Patrick Barwise and Andrew Ehrenberg, *Television and its Audience* (London: Sage, 1988).

6 Fitzwalter, *The Dream that Died*, p. 121.

7 Hansard, quoted in Fitzwalter, *The Dream that Died*, p. 166.

8 One involved a programme claiming that Marks and Spencer was selling clothes manufactured abroad under sweatshop conditions (the facts were true, but the goods were supplied by a third party and the company denied any knowledge); another followed a programme about a prisoner who had died in a police cell and involved a damages payment to three policemen. Fitzwalter, *The Dream that Died*, p. 195.

9 Martin Bell, 'The end of the road for a TV institution', *Daily Mail* (7 December 1998), p. 17.

10 Andrew Neil, *Daily Telegraph* (1 December 1998), p. 15.

11 Fitzwalter, *The Dream that Died*, p. 199.

12 Independent Television Commission, *Annual Report and Accounts 2000* (London: ITC, 2000), p. 75.

13 Quoted in Lindley, *And Finally ...?*, p. 293.

14 1990 Broadcasting Act, s. 31(1) and s. 31(2).

15 Steven Barnett, 'News at ... when?', *British Journalism Review* (vol. 3, no. 3, 1992), p. 72.

16 Ironically, the public interest function of news on a mass commercial channel was significantly enhanced by ITV's practice of surrounding 'News at Ten' with blockbuster movies, thereby sometimes producing some spectacular ratings as the news benefited from this 'hammocking' effect. For example, on 31 January 1990, the programme had registered a massive 13.8 million viewers, courtesy of the James Bond movie *View to a Kill*, which preceded and followed it.

17 In the four weeks after Iraq's invasion of Kuwait in August 1990, the BBC's main bulletin audience rose from just over 7 million to 8.5 million, while ITN's remained static at 7 million. For the dramatic resignation of Geoffrey Howe, which precipitated the downfall of Margaret Thatcher, the BBC news audience was more than double that of its commercial rival – 11.1 million compared 5.4 million. On the day she resigned, equivalent figures were 8.5 and 4.9 million. Steven Barnett, 'Art versus reality: One up to art', *British Journalism Review* (vol. 2, no. 2, 1990), pp. 72–4.

18 Barnett, 'News at ... when?', p.73.

19 Michael Brunson, *A Ringside Seat* (London: Hodder and Stoughton, 2000), p. 317.

20 Lindley, *And Finally ...?*, p. 332.

21 Lindley, *And Finally ...?*, p. 333.

22 Lindley, *And Finally ...?*, p. 333.

23 Brunson, *A Ringside Seat*, pp. 332–3.

24 Oral evidence, House of Lords Select Committee on Communications, *1st Report of Session 2007–08, Vol. 2: Evidence*, HL Paper 122-II (London: The Stationery Office, 2008), Q997.

25 As we shall see in Chapter 10, Sky News, although effectively controlled by Rupert Murdoch's news corporation, had established an authoritative reputation as an impartial 24-hour news channel.

26 Quoted in Lindley, *And Finally ...?*, p. 391.

27 Philip Johnston, 'Blair aide pleaded with BBC not to lead news on OJ', *Daily Telegraph* (5 October 1995), p. 2.

28 Barnett and Curry, *The Battle for the BBC*, p. 210.

29 Quoted in Richard Lindley, *Panorama*, p. 359.

30 Lindley, *Panorama*, pp. 360–1.

31 *BBC News: The Future – Public Service News in the Digital Age* (London: BBC, 1998).

32 For a particularly intemperate example, see Ronald Stevens, 'For "dumbing down" read "accessible"', *British Journalism Review* (vol. 9, no. 4, 1998), pp. 32–5. See also Jane Robins, 'Here is the BBC news, and this is audience research dictating it', *Independent* (7 October 1998), p. 3. Also *Guardian* (7 October 1998), p. 8; *Daily Telegraph* (7 October 1998), p. 4.

33 Georgina Born, *Uncertain Vision* (London: Secker and Warburg, 2004), p. 391.

7 Tabloidization

1 Marr, *My Trade*, p. 57.

2 Matthew Engel, *Tickle the Public: One Hundred Years of the Popular Press* (London: Victor Gollancz, 1996), p. 59.

3 Colin Sparks, 'Introduction', 'Tabloidisation and the media' issue, *Javnost* (vol. V, no. 3, 1998), p. 7.

4 Sparks, 'Introduction', p. 10.

5 Peter Dahlgren, *Television and the Public Sphere* (London: Sage, 1995), p. 59.

6 S. Elizabeth Bird, 'Audience demands in a murderous market', in Colin Sparks and John Tulloch, *Tabloid Tales: Global Debates over Media Standards* (Lanham, MD: Rowman and Littlefield, 2000), p. 217.

7 'How bad is the Nine o'clock News?', *Independent on Sunday* (28 November 1993), p. 4.

8 Steven Barnett, Emily Seymour and Ivor Gaber, *From Callaghan to Kosovo: Changing Trends in British Television News 1975–1999* (London: University of Westminster, 2000). A further analysis of the years 2004 and 2009 has been funded by the Leverhulme Trust and will be published in full in 2012. Early headline data are reported here.

9 These categories were not dissimilar to the 50 categories (33 domestic and 17 international) established by Harrison in an earlier study in the mid 1990s. Jackie Harrison, *Terrestrial TV News in Britain* (Manchester: Manchester University Press, 2000), pp. 216–31. Again, a full list of the 31 categories is provided in Appendix 1.

10 As the table in Appendix 2 shows there was also no movement in the crime category, which is often used as a barometer of tabloidization because of the compelling combination of human tragedy and dramatic pictures.

11 Brian Winston, 'Towards tabloidization? Glasgow revisited 1975–2001', *Journalism Studies* (vol. 3, no. 1, 2002), pp. 5–20.

12 Ian Hargreaves and James Thomas, *New News, Old News* (London: Independent Television Commission, 2002).

13 Ofcom, *New News, Future News: The Challenges for Television News after Digital Switchover* (London: Ofcom, July 2007), p. 20.

14 Ofcom, *New News*, pp. 93–102.

15 James Curran, 'Media diversity and democracy', in Tim Gardam and David A.L. Levy (eds), Tim Gardam and David A.L. Levy (eds), *The Price of Plurality: Choice, Diversity and Broadcasting Institutions in the Digital Age* (London: Ofcom with the Reuters Institute for the Study of Journalism, 2008), p. 109, note 5.

16 Further corroboration comes from an unpublished study that tracked coverage of general election campaign news from 1979 to 2005 on ITV and BBC. Using similar categories to the Westminster study, Ramsay found that 'tabloid' coverage never accounted for more than 9 per cent of the BBC's late evening bulletin, and no evidence that this was increasing over time. ITV's equivalent bulletin showed a gradual rise in tabloid coverage over time, but in 2005 this still accounted for less than 20 per cent of the total. Gordon Ramsay, 'The evolution of election coverage on British television news, 1979–2005' (unpublished PhD thesis, Glasgow: University of Glasgow, 2011).

17 Shelley McLachlan, 'Who's afraid of the news bunny?: The changing face of the television evening news broadcast', Working Paper 3 (Loughborough: Information and Democracy Research Project, Loughborough University, 1998), p. 19.

18 The full story can be read in Chris Horrie and Adam Nathan, *LIVE TV: Tellybrats and Topless Darts* (London: Simon and Schuster, 1999).

19 Patterson, *Doing Well and Doing Good*, p. 3.

20 Pew Research Center Project for Excellence in Journalism, 'The State of the News Media 2008: An Annual Report on American Journalism', *The State of the News Media*, http://www.stateofthenewsmedia.com/2008 [accessed 27 July 2011].

21 Pew Research Center Project for Excellence in Journalism, 'The State of the News Media 2011: An Annual Report on American Journalism', *The State of the News Media*, http://www.stateofthenewsmedia.com/2011 [accessed 27 July 2011].

22 This is potentially subject to criticism, as above, that measurement of number of stories is less valid than measurement of time allocated. In this case, however, the consistency of approach over a long period of time renders the data much more reliable as an indicator of trends in TV news output.

23 Pew Research Center Project for Excellence in Journalism, 'The State of the News Media 2009: An Annual Report on American Journalism', *The State of the News Media*, http://www.stateofthenewsmedia.com/2009 [accessed 27 July 2011].

24 Steven Barnett and Emily Seymour, 'A shrinking iceberg travelling south ...' Changing Trends in British Television: A Case Study of Drama and Current Affairs (London: University of Westminster, 1999). The study was funded by the Esmee Fairbairn Foundation and examined trends in both current affairs and original drama on British television.

25 For each of the three sampled years, two sampling periods were selected of four weeks each, amounting to a random 15 per cent of peak-time programming. After piloting, a 22-point coding frame was agreed. As with the news study there were grey areas, but the overriding purpose was to categorize on the basis of a programme's core purpose. (Thus, a programme looking at failings in the NHS through personal stories was classified as health rather than human interest.) A detailed description of the methodology and coding process can be found in Barnett and Seymour, 'A shrinking iceberg', pp. 74–6, with the full coding frame on pp. 80–2.

26 Independent Television Commission, *Annual Report and Accounts for 2002* (London: ITC, 2003), p. 34.

27 Ivor Gaber, 'The myth about Panorama', *British Journalism Review* (vol. 19, no. 1, March 2008), pp. 10–14.

28 All quotes in the 'Interview findings' section are from Barnett and Seymour, 'A shrinking iceberg', pp. 20–42.

29 Myra Macdonald, 'Rethinking personalization in current affairs journalism', in Sparks and Tulloch, *Tabloid Tales*, p. 260.

30 Martin Bell, 'The truth is our currency', *Harvard International Journal of Press/Politics* (vol. 3, no. 1, 1998), pp. 102–9.

31 I examined this argument, and Bell's analysis, in more detail some years ago. See Steven Barnett, 'Dumbing down or reaching out: Is it tabloidisation wot done it?' in Jean Seaton (ed.), *Politics and the Media: Harlots and Prerogatives at the Turn of the Millennium* (Oxford: Blackwell, 1998), p. 89.

8   The BBC and the Aftermath of Hutton

1 At one point early in 2002, Dyke announced a football-style initiative in which yellow cards inscribed with this phrase could be brandished at meetings by any member of staff who felt they were being obstructed by unnecessary bureaucracy.

2 Wyatt, *The Fun Factory*, pp. 20–1.

3 I have covered the events around the Hutton Report in some detail in Steven Barnett, 'Opportunity or threat? The BBC, investigative journalism and the Hutton Report', in Stuart Allen (ed.), *Journalism: Critical Issues* (Milton Keynes: Open University Press, 2005), pp. 328–41. See also, Simon Rogers (ed.), *The Hutton Inquiry and Its Impact* (London: Politicos, 2004), pp. 309–22; Born, *Uncertain Vision*, pp. 453ff.

4 Support included the headlines '45 minutes to attack', *Evening Standard* (24 September 2002), and 'He's got 'em ... let's get him', *Sun* (25 September 2002).

5 Greg Dyke, *Inside Story* (London: Harper Perennial, 2005), p. 254. The letter was sent the day after 139 Labour MPs voted against its own leadership, the largest ever parliamentary rebellion against a sitting government.

6 Dyke, *Inside Story*, p. 255.

7 The Iraq Survey Group, headed by Dr David Kay, had been detailed by President Bush to comb the country to find evidence of WMD. Kay resigned on 23 January 2004, a week before his evidence to the Senate, saying that there had been a systemic intelligence failure. Jonathan Freedland, 'Tugging back the veil', in Rogers, *The Hutton Inquiry*, p. 353.

8 Lord Butler of Brockwell, *Review of Intelligence on Weapons of Mass Destruction*, HC898, (London: The Stationery Office, 2004), p. 82.

9 Butler, *Review of Intelligence*, pp. 101 and 126.

10 The 'Today' programme runs every morning between 6.00 and 9.00 a.m., attracting between 6 and 7 million listeners. It is the BBC's flagship radio news programme and is closely followed by politicians and opinion leaders, so its output (and any issues arising) will often have repercussions for all BBC journalism.

11 Maggie Brown, 'All hell is set to break loose', *Guardian*, Media section (17 January 2000), p. 2.

12 Matt Wells, 'The story of the story', in Rogers, *The Hutton Inquiry*, p. 36.

13 One particular recommendation would have crippled most tabloid print journalism whose standards were considerably less rigorous than those of the BBC: 'Where a reporter is intending to broadcast or publish information impugning the integrity of others the management of his broadcasting company or newspaper should ensure that a system is in place whereby his editor or editors give careful consideration to the wording of the report and to whether it is right in all the circumstances to broadcast or publish it.' Lord Hutton, *Report of the Inquiry into the Circumstances Surrounding the Death of Dr David Kelly C.M.G.*, HC 247, (London: The Stationery Office, January 2004), para. 291 (2).

14 Peter Cole, 'It's beyond reasonable doubt: Reporters must not be cowed by the BBC's defeat', *Independent* (1 February 2004).

15 Matt Wells, '"Bring Back Greg"', in Rogers, *The Hutton Inquiry*, p. 333.

16 See for example Thomas, *Watchdogs of Democracy*.

17 Ronald Neil, *The BBC's Journalism after Hutton, The Report of the Neil Review Team* (London: BBC, June 2004).

18 House of Lords Select Committee on Communications, *The Ownership of the News, Vol. II: Evidence*, HL Paper 122-II (London: The Stationery Office 2008), Q370.

19 Michael Grade, 'Making the important interesting: BBC journalism in the 21st Century', The Cudlipp Lecture, London College of Communications, 24 January 2005.

20 Even the Conservative opposition was unwilling to consider any radical alternative. A report commissioned by the Conservative Party, which recommended turning the BBC over to subscription funding, was never seriously considered by Conservative shadow ministers: Broadcasting Policy Group, *Beyond the Charter: The BBC after 2006* (London: Premium Publishing, 2004). Similar radical proposals had a year earlier even been proposed by one of the government's own advisers and were also ignored: Barry Cox, *Free for All? Public Service Television in the Digital Age* (London: Demos, 2004).

21 Department for Culture, media and Sport, *Review of the BBC Royal Charter: A Strong BBC, Independent of Government*, Green Paper (London: DCMS, March 2005).

22 For a more detailed argument along these lines, see Steven Barnett, 'Can the public service broadcaster survive? A case study of renewal and compromise in the new BBC charter', in Jo Bardoel and Gregory Lowe (eds), *From Public Service Broadcasting to Public Service Media* (Gothenburg: Nordicom, 2008), pp. 87–104.

23 BBC evidence suggested that by the end of 2007, 7,200 journalists were employed by the BBC itself compared to estimates of 5,700 at NBC News, 4,000 at CNN, 3,500 at ABC News, 3,250 at Agence France-Presse, 3,000 at Associated Press, 2,400 at Reuters, 1,250 at Fox News and 1,100 at Voice of America. House of Lords Select Committee on Communications, *The Ownership of the News*, p. 75.

24 David Cameron, 'Bloated BBC out of touch with the viewers', *Sun*, 3 November 2008, p. 4.

25 Mark Thompson, 'The BBC and the new settlement', speech to the Voice of the Listener and Viewer conference, 24 November 2010.

9   Television Journalism, the Market and the Future

1 Department of Trade and Industry and Department of Culture, Media and Sport, *A New Future for Communications*, White Paper, Cm 5010 (London: The Stationery Office, December 2000), para. 1.2.1.

2 Department of Trade and Industry and Department of Culture, Media and Sport, *A New Future for Communications*, para. 5.3.9.

3 *Communications Act 2003* (London: The Stationery Office, 2003), s. 279 and s. 280.

4 The only statutory ownership restrictions that remained, after a fierce parliamentary battle was effectively won by the government, was to prevent any organization with more than 20 per cent of the national newspaper market from owning Channel 3 licences – aimed explicitly at Rupert Murdoch's News Corporation.

5 A backstop power was included for the Secretary of State to make an order for an appointed news provider if Channel 5's audience share reached that of Channel 3.

6 Figures taken from Ofcom, *New News*, p. 16. In response to pressure from ITV, Ofcom reduced the regional news requirement to four hours per week from the beginning of 2009.

7 The quota for current affairs (hours per year) is 365 for BBC1 and BBC2 combined; 78 for ITV; 208 for Channel 4; and 130 for Channel 5. Peak-time figures are, respectively, 105, 35, 80 and 10. Figures for quotas from Ofcom, *The UK Communications Market 2008* (London: Ofcom, 2008), p. 201.

8 These and more detailed figures on trends in television news and current affairs expenditure can be found in Ofcom, *Public Service Broadcasting Review 2010, C: Output and Spend* (London: Ofcom, 2010), pp. 34–42. While expenditure figures overall have decreased from 2005–2009, in line with the reduction in overall programme spend, peak-time expenditure has remained remarkably stable.

9 Ofcom, *Ofcom's Second Public Service Broadcasting Review: Putting Viewers First* (London: Ofcom, 2009), p. 16.

10 Ofcom, *Ofcom's Second Public Service Broadcasting Review*, p. 7.

11 Speech at the Royal Television Society Patron's Breakfast, 8 October 2008.

12 A detailed description of the proposal and Ofcom's reservations are given in Ofcom, *Ofcom's Second Public Service Broadcasting Review*, Final Statement and Recommendations, pp. 85–99.

13 Department for Business, Enterprise and Regulatory Reform and Department for Culture, Media and Sport, *Digital Britain: The Interim Report*, Cm 7548 (London: The Stationery Office, 2009), p. 47.

14 Department for Business, Enterprise and Regulatory Reform and Department for Culture, Media and Sport, *Digital Britain: Final Report*, Cm 7650 (London: The Stationery Office, 2009), pp. 149–57.

15 Conservative Party, *Invitation to Join the Government of Britain* (manifesto for the 2010 general election) (London: Conservative Party, 2010), p. 76. The Liberal Democrats expressed similar

sentiments: 'We will help to maintain independent local sources of news and information by enabling partnerships between TV, radio and newspaper companies to reduce costs.' Liberal Democratic Party, *Liberal Democrat Manifesto 2010* (London: Liberal Democratic Party, 2010), p. 46.

16 House of Lords Select Committee on Communications, *The Ownership of the News*, Q991.

17 House of Lords Select Committee on Communications, *The Ownership of the News*, Q12.

18 Marion Just, Rosalind Levine and Kathleen Regan, 'News for sale: Half of stations report sponsor pressure on news decisions', *Columbia Journalism Review* (special supplement, November–December 2001).

19 House of Lords Select Committee on Communications, *The Ownership of the News*, Q 1033.

20 Stephen Glover, 'What's happening to The Daily Telegraph is a national tragedy', *Independent* (22 December 2008), p. 43.

21 For the full story on which the film was based, see Marie Brenner, 'The man who knew too much', *Vanity Fair* (May 1996).

22 Elizabeth Lesly Stevens, 'mouse.ke.fear', *Brill's Content* (December 1998/January 1999), pp. 95–103. I cover this and other examples in more detail in Steven Barnett, 'Impartiality redefined: Protecting news on commercial television in Britain', in Damian Tambini and Jamie Cowling (eds), *New News? Impartial Broadcasting in the Digital Age* (London: IPPR, 2002), pp. 51–64.

23 Jane Meyer, 'Bad News', *New Yorker* (14 August 2000), p. 30.

24 Fenton, *Bad News*, p. 97.

25 For the full story of this attempted coup by Murdoch, the regulatory dilemmas it posed and how it was resolved, see Steven Barnett, 'Media ownership policy in a recession: Redefining the public interest', *Interactions: Studies in Communication and Culture* (vol. 1, no. 2, Autumn 2010), pp. 217–32.

26 Competition Commission, 'Acquisition by British Sky Broadcasting Group PLC of 17.9 per cent of the shares in ITV PLC', Report sent to Secretary of State (Department of Business, Enterprise and Regulatory Reform) (14 December 2007), para. 5.75.

27 Competition Commission, 'Acquisition by British Sky Broadcasting', para. 5.65, note 195. This difference of opinion was reiterated in evidence to the House of Lords inquiry by Ofcom's Chief Executive Ed Richards who professed himself 'a little surprised' at his fellow regulator's conclusion: House of Lords Select Committee on Communications, *The Ownership of the News*, Q900. Interestingly, on appeal, the Competition Appeals Tribunal (CAT) sided with Ofcom: Competition Appeals Tribunal, 'Judgement on BSkyB v Competition Commission and Virgin v Competition Commission' (29 September 2008), para. 263.

28 Between 2002 and 2010, Channel 5 rebranded itself as 'Five' before returning to its original name. To avoid confusion, I refer to it as 'Channel 5' throughout.

29 House of Lords Select Committee on Communications, *The Ownership of the News*, Q125.

30 For examples, and for more on the Desmond takeover, see Steven Barnett, 'Dangermen: Over to you Mr Cable', *British Journalism Review* (vol. 21, no. 4, 2010), pp. 13–18.

31 Tara Conlan, 'Channel 5 plans revamp of news programmes', *Guardian* (23 November 2010).

32 *Communications Act 2003*, s. 265(3).

33 House of Lords Select Committee on Communications, *The Ownership of the News*, Q85.

34 In April 2007, ITV signed a deal with ITN to supply its news until the end of 2012 for £42 million per year. Even with ITN's ambitious attempts to expand its areas of core expertise into archive sales, multimedia and radio news, the essence of its business is still television news, with the ITV contract at its core. Figures quoted by ITN Chief Executive Mark Wood in

evidence to House of Lords Select Committee on Communications, *The Ownership of the News*, Q11.

35 Brown, *A Licence to Be Different*, p. 225.

36 House of Lords Select Committee on Communications, *The Ownership of the News*, Q73.

37 House of Lords Select Committee on Communications, *The Ownership of the News*, Q2227.

38 Ofcom, *Ofcom's Second Public Service Broadcasting Review*, p. 63. Ofcom's approach stemmed directly from their statutory requirement under s. 264(3) of the 2003 Communications Act to carry out a five yearly review, 'with a view to maintaining and strengthening the quality of public service broadcasting in the United Kingdom'. This single paragraph is an excellent example of the potentially far-reaching and benign impact of some communications legislation. *Communications Act 2003*, s. 264(3).

39 For how the government saw the contribution of Channel 4 in public policy terms, see Department for Business, Enterprise and Regulatory Reform and Department for Culture, Media and Sport, *Digital Britain: The Interim Report*, p. 51; and Department for Business, Enterprise and Regulatory Reform and Department for Culture, Media and Sport, *Digital Britain: Final Report*, p. 148.

40 Fenton, *Bad News*, p. 150.

41 Downie Jr and Kaiser, *The News about the News*, p. 118.

42 Downie Jr and Kaiser, *The News about the News*, p. 139.

43 As recorded by a minute of the House of Lords select committee visit to the United States: House of Lords Select Committee on Communications, *The Ownership of the News*, Appendix 4, para. 22.

44 Quoted in Zoë Heller, 'Full Disclosure', *Granta 53: News* (London: Granta Publications/ Penguin, 1996), p. 90.

45 Recorded in House of Lords Select Committee on Communications, *The Ownership of the News*, Appendix 4, para. 96.

46 Personal notes of meetings with the Consumers Union and PEJ 19 September 2007. In its meeting with the Lords committee, the FCC stated that it deliberately avoids judgements about the quality of news because this is 'fraught with constitutional issues'. Recorded in House of Lords Select Committee on Communications, *The Ownership of the News*, Appendix 4, para. 85.

47 House of Lords Select Committee on Communications, *The Ownership of the News*, Appendix 4, para. 90.

10 24-hour News Channels and the 'New' Television Journalism

1 Nick Fraser, 'Turning up the volume', *Financial Times*, magazine section (16 July 2005), p. 10.

2 Justin Lewis, Stephen Cushion and James Thomas, 'Immediacy, convenience or engagement? An analysis of 24-hour news channels in the UK', *Journalism Studies* (vol. 6, no. 4, 2005), pp. 461–77.

3 Barkin, *American Television News*, p. 108.

4 We should remember that many 24-hour news channels, including CNN, are still not universally available today. Despite their impact, audiences for 24-hour news channels are still in most countries a fraction of those for news bulletins on mainstream channels.

5 Lucy Küng-Shankleman, *Inside the BBC and CNN* (London: Routledge, 2000), p. 80.

6 Küng-Shankleman, *Inside the BBC and CNN*, p. 79.

7 Quoted in Barkin, *American Television News*, p. 110.

8 William Shawcross, *Rupert Murdoch*, pp. 519–20.

9 Quoted in Eytan Gilboa, 'The CNN effect: The search for a communication theory of international relations', *Political Communication* (vol. 22, 2005) pp. 27–44.

10 Howard Rosenberg and Charles S. Feldman, *No Time to Think: The Menace of Media Speed and the 24-hour News Cycle* (New York, NY: Continuum, 2008), pp. 184–6.

11 Rosenberg and Feldman, *No Time to Think*, pp. 186–8.

12 See, for example, Piers Robinson, *The CNN Effect: The Myth of News, Foreign Policy and Intervention* (London: Routledge, 2002); and Steven Livingston, 'Beyond the "CNN effect": The media-foreign policy dynamic', in Pippa Norris (ed.), *Politics and the Press: The News Media and Their Influences* (London: Lynne Rienner, 1997), pp. 291–318.

13 Nick Wilkinson, 'Spookmania and the media', *British Journalism Review* (vol. 20, no. 1, March 2009). This Act, which included the notorious and later discredited Section 2, was passed in a single day in Parliament with no opposition, considerably assisted by the manufactured hysteria of the press.

14 Shawcross, *Rupert Murdoch*, p. 452.

15 Shawcross, *Rupert Murdoch*, p. 452.

16 BSB's launch had been disastrous; it was burdened by debt and excessive technical obligations, and was carrying huge staff numbers. It had been conceived and capitalized on the basis of having a monopoly of direct to home satellite broadcasting in the United Kingdom, a position that was scuppered by Thatcher allowing Sky to broadcast on the Astra satellite despite Murdoch's control of over a third of the national press. For the full story of the 'merger' see Peter Chippindale and Suzanne Franks, *Dished! Rise and Fall of British Satellite Broadcasting* (London: Simon and Schuster 1992); and Shawcross, *Rupert Murdoch*, pp. 508–12.

17 Bruce Page, *The Murdoch Archipelago* (London: Simon and Schuster, 2003), p. 419. The origin of the story was Murdoch's interview by Matthew Horsman for his book: Matthew Horsman, *Sky High* (London: Orion Business, 1998).

18 House of Commons Select Committee on Culture, Media and Sport, *Public Service Content, First Report of Session 2007–8*, HC36-1 (London: The Stationery Office, 2007), para. 89.

19 David D. Kirkpatrick, 'Mr Murdoch's war', *New York Times*, Section C (7 April 2003), p. 1.

20 Minute of the House of Lords select committee visit to the United States: House of Lords Select Committee on Communications, *The Ownership of the News*, Appendix 4, para. 47. As a participant in that meeting, I was keen to establish whether Murdoch saw impartiality regulation as a hindrance to Sky becoming, in his view, more like Fox. His response that this was not an issue came as a surprise, but may have been more measured given that he was speaking to a parliamentary committee.

21 The bid was first referred by the government on public interest grounds to the regulator Ofcom, which in December 2010 found that the proposed merger might operate against the public interest and recommended that it should be referred for a more thorough investigation to the Competition Commission. However, News Corporation was entitled to offer 'Undertakings in Lieu' of a formal referral, which the Secretary of State was bound to consider and would almost certainly have formed the basis of an agreement had the phone hacking scandal not intervened and forced Murdoch to retract his takeover bid.

22 James Silver, 'Adam Adamant', *Independent*, Media section (24 April 2006), p. 4. The £35 million figure is also mentioned in Richard Lambert, *Independent Review of BBC News 24* ('The Lambert Review') (London: Department for Culture, Media and Sport, December 2002), p. 16.

23 In December 1999, over two years after the complaint was lodged, the European Commission decreed that the State aid was both proportionate and justified under the 'Amsterdam Protocol', which devolved to Member States the ability to define the remit of any public service intervention. European Commission, 'BBC News 24 (State aid), financing of a 24-hour advertising-free news channel out of the licence fee by the BBC', Case NN 88/98, Decision of 14 December 1999.

24 Lambert, *Independent Review*.

25 BBC Trust, 'BBC News service licence' (21 April 2008), p. 2.

26 Sky's figures suffered from an expensive relaunch in October 2005 when it tried to introduce two current affairs-type flagship programmes between 7 and 9 p.m. The 7 p.m. 'Sky Report' was designed as a news magazine programme, while the 8 p.m. 'World News Report' brought in – at some cost – Bill Clinton's former US State Department spokesman James Rubin to add real political weight.

27 Minute of the House of Lords select committee visit to the United States: House of Lords Select Committee on Communications, *The Ownership of the News*, Appendix 4, para. 25.

28 Anonymous, 'The leader of the Fox pack', *Business* (21 August 2005), p. 13.

29 Al Franken, *Lies and the Lying Liars who Tell Them: A Fair and Balanced Look at the Right* (Harmondsworth: Penguin, 2004), p. 362.

30 Franken's account of the trial and its fall-out are well worth reading: Franken, *Lies and the Lying Liars*, pp 365–72.

31 Alexandra Kitty, *Outfoxed: Rupert Murdoch's War on Journalism* (New York: Disinformation, 2005), p. 97. Kitty's book was based on Greenwald's documentary film which was distributed on DVD by MoveOn.org.

32 Kitty, *Outfoxed*, p. 76.

33 Ben Dimiero, 'Leaked email: Fox boss caught slanting news reporting', *Media Matters* (9 December 2010). The pollster, Frank Luntz, had argued that, 'if you call it a "public option", the American people are split [but] if you call it the "government option", the public is overwhelmingly against it'.

34 George Packer, 'It doesn't matter why he did it', *New Yorker* (9 January 2011), http://www.newyorker.com/online/blogs/georgepacker/2011/01/judging-from-his-internet-postings.html [accessed 28 July 2011].

35 Andrew Gumbel, 'All sound, fury, and popular entertainment one decade on, Fox is top dog in the ratings', *Independent* (7 October 2006), p. 38.

36 Figures from Fox News evidence to House of Lords Select Committee on Communications, *The Ownership of the News*, Appendix 4, para. 29.

37 All figures from Pew Research Center Project for Excellence in Journalism, 'The State of the News Media 2011'.

38 CNN's revenues are weighted more heavily towards subscription while those of Fox are more dependent on advertising.

39 Pew Research Center Project for Excellence in Journalism, 'The State of the News Media 2011'.

40 Ofcom, *The UK Communications Market 2008*, pp. 182–3.

41 At least six of these channels were English-speaking, with NDTV, 24x7, Star News and DD News available in the United Kingdom through the BSkyB digital satellite platform. Daya Kishan Thussu, *News as Entertainment: The Rise of Global Infotainment* (London: Sage, 2007), p. 98.

42 Hugh Miles, *Al Jazeera: How Arab TV News Challenged the World* (London: Abacus, 2005), p. 59.

43 This reputation was somewhat dented during 2010 by the emergence of American embassy cables – through the Wikileaks disclosures – that revealed that the channel was being used by Qatar as a bargaining tool in foreign-policy negotiations with its Arab neighbours.

Nevertheless, senior editors past and present have insisted that there has never been any interference in editorial direction from above.

44 Miles, *Al Jazeera*, p. 219.

45 For example, Al Jazeera exposed widespread reports in the British and American media of a Shiite uprising in Basra as entirely false, thus holding to account those Western media outlets that colluded in trying to pass off government PR offensives as journalism.

46 Miles, *Al Jazeera*, p. 279.

47 Rageh Omaar, 'This is the new voice of Arabia', *Sunday Times*, News Review section (12 February 2006), p. 3.

48 Noam Cohen, 'Al Jazeera provides an inside look at Gaza conflict', *International Herald Tribune* (1 January 2009), http://www.iht.com/articles/2009/01/11/technology/jazeera.php [accessed 28 July 2011].

49 Ben Dowell, 'Disillusioned of Doha', *Guardian*, Media section (31 March 2008), p. 1.

50 'Is this a revolution in world news?' in Media Guardian, 7 February 2011.

51 That the editor in chief of Russia Today refused the *Washington Post* an interview unless granted right of approval over her quotes suggests that the channel's commitment to journalistic scrutiny may have some way to go. Peter Finn, 'Russia pumps tens of millions into burnishing image abroad', *Washington Post* (6 March 2008).

52 Ciar Byrne, 'A Gallic view of the world', *Independent*, Media section (15 October 2007), p. 10.

53 'Iran launches English TV channel', *BBC News* website (2 July 2007), http://news.bbc.co.uk/1/hi/world/middle_east/6260716.stm [accessed 28 July 2011].

54 Martin Bell, 'Say no to news on tap', *Independent* (16 December 2003), p. 17.

55 Bell, 'Say no to news on tap'.

56 Rosenberg and Feldman, *No Time to Think*, p. 193.

11   Television Journalism and Impartiality

1 Section 3 of the 1954 Television Act placed a duty on the new regulatory body, the Independent Television Authority, to ensure that 'programmes maintain a proper balance in their subject matter'; that 'any news given in the programmes (in whatever form) is presented with due accuracy and impartiality'; and that due impartiality must be preserved on 'matters of political or industrial controversy or relating to current public policy'.

2 *Communications Act 2003*, s. 319(2)(c) and s. 320(2).

3 I have covered the following arguments (which oppose retention of impartiality rules) in more detail elsewhere. See Steven Barnett, 'Imposition or empowerment? Freedom of speech, broadcasting and impartiality', in J. Harrison, L. Woods and M. Amos (eds), *Freedom of Expression and the Media* (The Hague: Martinus Nijhoff, 2011); Steven Barnett, 'Broadcast journalism and impartiality in the digital age: Six fallacies and a counter-factual', in Gregory Ferrell Lowe and Jeanette Steemers (eds), *Regaining the Initiative for Public Service Media* (Gothenburg: Nordicom, 2011).

4 Hargreaves and Thomas, *New News*, p. 9.

5 Hargreaves and Thomas, *New News*, p. 105.

6 Ofcom, *New News*, p. 59.

7 Ofcom, *New News*, p. 71.

8 Power Inquiry, *Power to the People. The Report of Power: An Independent Inquiry into Britain's Democracy* (York: Joseph Rowntree Charitable Trust, 2006). A BBC study in 2002 also suggested that there was a 'disconnection' between the public and the formal political institutions represented by Westminster and Whitehall, but did not assume that this extended

to disengagement from other forms of political participation: BBC, 'Beyond the Soundbite': BBC Research into Public Disillusion with Politics (London: BBC, 2002).

9 Hargreaves and Thomas, *New News*, p. 98. Shaw reiterated his views a year later: 'I feel very strongly that this is the way forward for television news. It upsets me that we have genuine diversity in the printed press and very little diversity in the TV news world.' Matt Wells and John Cassy, 'Ungag us', *Guardian*, Media section (14 April 2003), p. 2.

10 Wells and Cassy, 'Ungag us', p. 3.

11 Peter Golding and Philip Elliott, *Making the News* (London: Longman, 1979), p. 209.

12 Tim Suter, 'Impartiality – the case for change', in Tim Gardam and David A.L. Levy (eds), *The Price of Plurality: Choice, Diversity and Broadcasting Institutions in the Digital Age* (London: Ofcom with the Reuters Institute for the Study of Journalism, 2008), p. 117.

13 Ofcom, *Broadcasting Code, Section 5: Due Impartiality and Due Accuracy and Undue Prominence of Views and Opinions* (London: Ofcom, December 2010), http://stakeholders. ofcom.org.uk/broadcasting/broadcast-codes/broadcast-code-december-2010/impartiality [accessed 30 July 2011].

14 'Only those channels prepared to be fully regulated for impartiality would be allowed to call themselves News Channels on programme guides.' Phil Harding, 'News and comment: separate stables?', *British Journalism Review* (vol. 22, no. 2, June 2011), pp. 32–8.

15 Richard Tait, 'Impartiality – why it must stay', in Tim Gardam and David A.L. Levy (eds), *The Price of Plurality: Choice, Diversity and Broadcasting Institutions in the Digital Age* (London: Ofcom with the Reuters Institute for the Study of Journalism, 2008), p. 112.

16 Over two-thirds (68 per cent) regarded it as 'very important'. Ofcom, *Perceptions of, and Attitudes towards, Television: 2010*. Part of PSB Report 2010 – Information Pack H (London: Ofcom, July 2010).

17 Onora O'Neill, *A Question of Trust: The BBC Reith Lectures 2002* (Cambridge: Cambridge University Press, 2002), pp. 93–4.

18 David Puttnam, 'News: You want it quick or good?', *British Journalism Review* (vol. 14, no. 2, 2003), pp. 50–57.

19 Philip Schlesinger, *Putting Reality Together* (London: Routledge, 1992), p. 166.

20 Michael Grade, *Goodman Media Lecture: The Future of Impartiality* (London: Institute of Mechanical Engineers, 11 May 2005).

21 Peter Horrocks, 'Finding TV news' lost audience', lecture delivered at St Anne's College and the Reuters Institute, Oxford (28 November 2006).

22 BBC Impartiality Project Terms of Reference, accessed at http://www.bbcgovernorsarchive. co.uk/docs/reviews/rev_impartiality_termsofreference2.pdf [accessed 30 July 2011]

23 BBC Trust, *From Seesaw to Wagon Wheel: Safeguarding Impartiality in the 21st Century* (London: BBC, 2007), p. 5.

24 The report quoted a typically colourful description from the BBC's former Political Editor Andrew Marr: 'The first thing that happens to you as a BBC journalist is that you're taken down into a dank basement to have your trousers pulled down and your organs of opinion removed with a pair of secateurs by the Director-General and popped in a formaldehyde bottle. You're told you're allowed them back when you leave.'

25 Similar issues were involved when covering the Live 8 concert in July 2005, designed to raise awareness of worldwide poverty and timed deliberately to take place just before a summit meeting of the G8 leaders in Scotland.

26 As one of the invited guests, I subsequently wrote to the seminar organizer enquiring why left of centre commentators such as Nick Cohen (of the *Observer*) or Shami Chakrabarti (of the civil liberties group Liberty) had not been invited. He replied that they had, but were unable to

attend and continued: 'I would dearly like to have had a presentation from that perspective ... and [that sort of critique] would have been a useful extra dimension' (personal email, 25 September 2006). It is therefore perhaps surprising that the subsequent report appeared to echo some of the unsupported allegations heard during the seminar without any contrary perspective.

27 A revealing passage went on to suggest that perhaps the BBC should find room for 'an authored programme about the War on Terror from an uncompromisingly "neo-conservative" position'.

28 Paul Dacre, the Hugh Cudlipp Lecture (22 January 2007).

29 Headlines included 'BBC admits its PC bias has left it out of touch', *Daily Mail* (19 June 2007), 'BBC viewers angered by its "innate liberal bias"', *Daily Telegraph* (19 June 2007) and 'The BBC can't kick its addiction to bias', *Daily Telegraph* (19 June 2007), 'The BBC's admission of bias is no surprise to the licence payers', *Daily Express* (19 June 2007) and 'BBC is beating itself up but nothing will change', *Sun* (19 June 2007).

30 Peter Wilby, 'Why rightwingers are on the warpath', *Guardian*, Media section (24 September 2007), p. 7.

31 Bell, 'The truth is our currency'.

Conclusions: What is Television? What is Journalism? And Why does it Matter?

1 Broadcasters Audience Research Board, *Trends in Television Viewing 2010* (London: BARB 2011), Table 2. It is worth noting, though, that the methodology changed slightly from previous years.

2 Patrick Barwise, 'Waiting for "Vodot": Why "video on demand" won't happen', *Market Leader* (Quarter 2, 2011), pp. 30–33.

3 Ofcom, *New News*, p. 19, figure 3.4.

4 1993 figures from Steven Barnett, 'The Beeb back on form', *British Journalism Review* (vol. 4, no. 4, 1993), p. 74. 2010 figures from Broadcasters Audience Research Board, *Trends in Television Viewing 2010*.

5 Pew Research Center Project for Excellence in Journalism, 'The State of the News Media 2011'.

6 Barbie Zelizer, *Taking Journalism Seriously: News and the Academy* (Thousand Oaks, CA: Sage, 2004), p. 204.

7 John Kelly, *Red Kayaks and Hidden Gold: The Rise, Challenges and Value of Citizen Journalism* (Oxford: Reuters Institute for the Study of Journalism, 2009), p. 8.

8 Clay Shirky, *Here Comes Everybody: How Change Happens when People Come Together* (Harmondsworth: Penguin, 2009).

9 Josef Trappel and Gunn Sara Enli, 'Online media: Changing provision of news', in Josef Trappel, Werner Meier, Leen d'Haenens, Jeanette Steemers and Barbara Thomas (eds), *Media in Europe Today* (Bristol: Intellect, 2011), p. 103.

10 Bill Keller, 'Not dead yet: The newspaper in the days of digital anarchy', The Hugo Young Memorial Lecture, Chatham House, London (29 November 2007).

11 Born, *Uncertain Vision*, p. 378.

12 Neil Hickey, 'Cable Wars', *Columbia Journalism Review* (January–February 2003), pp. 12–17. Very similar sentiments were expressed in a rousing speech by Barry Diller, former Chairman and Chief Executive of the Fox Network, in 2003 when he told the National Association of Broadcasters that, 'The conventional wisdom is wrong – we need more regulation – not less', and talked about the 'historic public interest responsibilities' implicit in the word 'broadcaster'.

Barry Diller, Keynote speech to the National Association of Broadcasters, Las Vegas, 7 April 2003.

13 Robert Reich, *Supercapitalism: The Transformation of Business, Democracy, and Everyday Life* (New York, NY: Alfred A. Knopf, 2007), p. 126.

14 Jeremy Hunt, 'A communications review for the digital age' (London: Department for Culture, Media and Sport, 16 May 2011).

15 To what extent phone hacking was more widespread may emerge through the judicial inquiry under Lord Justice Leveson, which was established in the wake of the scandal. However, we already have ample evidence of illegal activity in other newspapers: in two reports published in 2006, the Information Commissioner revealed that illegal trading in confidential information was systematic within the press. The most frequent transgressors in its published list of over 6,000 transactions involving newspapers were the *Daily Mail* and the *Sunday People*. The *News of the World* came fifth. Information Commissioner's Office, *What Price Privacy?* (London: The Stationery Office, HC1056, May 2006); and Information Commissioner's Office, *What Price Privacy Now?* (London: The Stationery Office, HC36, December 2006).

16 Michael Schudson, *The Sociology of News* (New York, NY: W.W Norton and Co, 2003), p. 91.

17 Emily Bell, 'Signal and noise', *Columbia Journalism Review* (July–August 2011), pp. 26–9.

Index